WESTMINSTER COMMENTARIES
EDITED BY WALTER LOCK D.D.
SOMETIME LADY MARGARET PROFESSOR OF
DIVINITY IN THE UNIVERSITY OF OXFORD
AND D. C. SIMPSON D.D.
ORIEL PROFESSOR OF THE INTERPRETATION
OF HOLY SCRIPTURE IN THE UNIVERSITY OF
OXFORD, CANON OF ROCHESTER

# THE BOOK OF
# PROVERBS

# THE BOOK OF
# PROVERBS

WITH INTRODUCTION
AND NOTES

BY

W. O. E. OESTERLEY, D.D.

PROFESSOR OF HEBREW AND OLD TESTAMENT EXEGESIS
KING'S COLLEGE, UNIVERSITY OF LONDON

METHUEN & CO. LTD.
36 ESSEX STREET W.C.
LONDON

*First Published in 1929*

PRINTED IN GREAT BRITAIN

# PREFATORY NOTE BY THE GENERAL EDITORS

THE primary object of these Commentaries is to be exegetical, to interpret the meaning of each book of the Bible in the light of modern knowledge to English readers. The Editors will not deal, except subordinately, with questions of textual criticism or philology; but taking the English text in the Revised Version as their basis, they will aim at combining a hearty acceptance of critical principles with loyalty to the Catholic Faith.

The series will be less elementary than the Cambridge Bible for Schools, less critical than the International Critical Commentary, less didactic than the Expositor's Bible ; and it is hoped that it may be of use both to theological students and to the clergy, as well as to the growing number of educated laymen and laywomen who wish to read the Bible intelligently and reverently.

Each commentary will therefore have

(i) An Introduction stating the bearing of modern criticism and research upon the historical character of the book, and drawing out the contribution which the book, as a whole, makes to the body of religious truth.

(ii) A careful paraphrase of the text with notes on the more difficult passages and, if need be, excursuses on any points of special importance either for doctrine, or ecclesiastical organization, or spiritual life.

But the books of the Bible are so varied in character that considerable latitude is needed, as to the proportion which the various parts should hold to each other. The General Editors will therefore only endeavour to secure a general uniformity in scope and character : but the exact method adopted in each case and the final responsibility for the statements made will rest with the individual contributors.

By permission of the Delegates of the Oxford University Press and of the Syndics of the Cambridge University Press the Text used in this Series of Commentaries is the Revised Version of the Holy Scriptures.

WALTER LOCK.
D. C. SIMPSON.

# PREFACE

ONLY within, comparatively speaking, recent years has it been fully realized to how large an extent Israelite thought was affected by extraneous influences. The most recent recognition of the exercise of such influences has been its presence in the domain of the Wisdom Literature. It is because only during the last few years the material has become available for proving the existence of this influence that attention has not been drawn to it before. The distinctive feature, therefore, of this commentary is that it attempts to show that the Hebrew Wisdom Literature was part of a world literature, and that the Hebrew Sages were largely influenced by Babylonian, and especially by Egyptian, thought. By saying this it is not meant to imply that the Hebrew Wisdom writers were mainly indebted to the Sages of other lands; far from that. What especially emerges from the comparison between Hebrew and non-Hebrew wisdom is that the former is of a very distinctly superior character. But the broad and sympathetic outlook of the Hebrew Sages was such that they welcomed everything, whatever its source, which contributed to enrich their conception of the true nature of Wisdom. They were universalistic in their ideas. Therefore they sought out the wisdom of other lands; studied it, submitted to its influence, appropriated it, and often ennobled it with a deeper and fuller content. This twofold element of indigenous Hebrew Wisdom and the adapted wisdom of foreign lands, whether Egyptian, Babylonian, or Greek—and for all we know at present the wisdom of other lands, Edom and Arabia for example, may also be represented—is to be found in all the books of Hebrew Wisdom which have come down to us; not least in the book of *Proverbs*.

It is, therefore, hoped that an added interest will be imparted to *Proverbs* in studying it in the light of this newly discovered non-Israelite literature, so far as at present available.

In one respect the arrangement of subject-matter in this commentary differs slightly from that of the others belonging to this

Series. The Introduction has been reduced to a minimum in order that more space could be devoted to a number of Excursuses. Several of these, it is true, would ordinarily form part of an Introduction; but others, especially the first, would hardly come under that head. They might, on the other hand, have taken the form of Additional Notes; but some of them are rather more than notes; besides, Additional Notes are apt to be regarded as subsidiary, with the risk of their being passed over as not of primary importance. It seemed, therefore, to be the best course to gather together these Excursuses under a separate head, and by placing them in the forefront to indicate that they are of primary importance.

In transliterating Hebrew letters vowels, short or long, are indicated in the ordinary way. As regards consonants ו is transliterated by *w*, ז by *z*, ח by *ch*, ט and ת by *t*, י by *j*, כ by *k*, פ by *ph*, ק by *q*, צ by *tz*, ס and שׁ by *s*. There are one or two exceptions in the case of proper names, such as Achikar, the form of which has become familiar.

To the genial General Editors the writer would wish to express his sincere appreciation and thanks for their kind advice and guidance on various matters connected with the work.

W. O. E. O.

*January, 1929.*

# CONTENTS

# INTRODUCTION

## I

### THE BOOK OF PROVERBS

The book forms part of the *Chokmah* or Wisdom Literature of the Hebrews; to this literature belong also the book of *Job, Ecclesiastes*, and some of the Psalms, in the canonical scriptures, and *Ecclesiasticus* ('The Wisdom of Ben-Sira') and the *Book of Wisdom* in the Apocrypha; to these should certainly be added 'The Sayings of the Fathers' (*Pirqe 'Abôth*), and possibly one or two other books of less importance.

The *literary* form of a collection of proverbs presupposes a previous period of indefinite length during which short popular sayings, based upon observation and the experiences of life, have gradually become proverbial. These form the original background of thought from which the carefully constructed literary proverbs are developed. Taken as a whole, though there are exceptions, the artificially constructed types of proverbial sayings in our book suggest that a less developed *literary* form may have preceded that now represented by *Proverbs*. One thing which points to this is the occurrence of single-lined proverbial sayings which occur in the book. It is not unnatural to suppose that if, as will be granted, written proverbs followed the stage of oral sayings, which were always simple, consisting of one sentence, the *first* stage of written proverbs would follow the traditional pattern, and take the form of one line; the distich would then represent a second literary stage. That there are examples of such one-line proverbs in other parts of the Old Testament, as well as in *Proverbs*, is well known (see Excursus VI); and that some of these were traditional, oral proverbs is certain; but there are others with an advanced thought-content which mark them out as literary proverbs, i. e. not the spontaneous utterance of one of the populace, but the thought-out product of the mind of a writer.

But, however this may be, the difference in structural form of the proverbs in our book makes it certain that proverbial literature went through stages of development. One has but to compare the simplest couplets with the elaborately constructed miniature essay form, both of which occur in *Proverbs*, to become convinced that one represents an earlier literary form than the other.

It is, therefore, not fanciful to discern in the body of material contained in the book of *Proverbs* three stages of development in the form of proverbial literature: the single-line saying, which follows the traditional pattern, the distich which demands more thought, and the more elaborate treatment of the distich which takes the form of a miniature essay.

This, quite apart from other reasons, would point to collections belonging to different periods having been incorporated in the book of *Proverbs*. It is possible to discern ten collections which were originally quite independent. That some of these had a history behind them is likely, but, with two exceptions, we are not in a position to trace their history as *data* are wanting.

## II

## THE COLLECTIONS INCORPORATED IN *PROVERBS*

These collections are thrown together in a somewhat haphazard fashion. The general arrangement of the material is to a large extent quite arbitrary. Here and there some attempt at co-ordination of subject-matter is to be discerned, e. g., xvi. 12–15, xxv. 1–7, xxvi. 13–16; but, generally speaking, the desire seems to have been to gather material of all kinds, provided it were relevant, and to incorporate it without troubling to place together what, according to subject-matter, belonged together. This idea of getting as much material together as possible seems to have been undertaken without much attention as to whether it all really deserved a place in the book; only on this supposition can one explain the incorporation of matter differing so widely in quality, as e. g., viii or xv, on the one hand, and xxx. 18–31 or xxxi. 1–7, on the other.

Sometimes there are small groups of proverbs beginning with the same letter, at others with the same word; thus xi. 9–12 has four verses each of which not only begins with ב (*b*) but the second clause also always begins with ב preceded by an adversative particle, excepting in the final clause of the group; again, xviii. 20–22, xx. 7–9, xx. 24–26: each group contains three verses beginning with מ (*m*); xv. 13, 14: each verse begins with לב ('heart'), 16, 17 with טוב ('good'); once more, xvi. 27–29: each verse begins with איש ('man'). There are other instances; but most of these small groups belong to the earliest collection in the book as we now have it. Such groups point clearly to literary composition; but it is possible that they did not originally belong to any collection, and that they were gradually gathered together by the sage who was responsible for this earliest collection.

We will now proceed to look a little more closely into the ten collections contained in *Proverbs*.

The *first* collection, which is by no means the earliest, is comprised in i. 7–ix. 18; the first six verses are introductory. The outstanding point of difference between this collection and the others contained in the book is the way in which Wisdom is personified. This is seen most clearly in such passages as i. 20–33, viii. 1–36, ix. 1–6, but there are others, though less striking, in which the personification of Wisdom is implied, e. g. the whole of chap. ii, and iv. 5–9. Such a conception of Wisdom as is presented in this collection is not found elsewhere in the book, and, as the highest development concerning Wisdom, marks the collection which contains it as the latest portion of the book. This late date is also borne out by the literary structure of the material; with the exception of chap. xxxi, this collection is the only one in the book which presents us with a series of short sections approximating to a miniature essay-form; a structure which marks the latest development in the literary form of the Wisdom Literature; a similar structure is characteristic of the *Wisdom of Ben Sira*.

There are, therefore, good grounds for assigning this first collection to the middle of the 3 cent. B. C. as it stands. But there is one strong reason for believing that not the whole material in the collection belongs to this late date. The reason is that two different points of view regarding the motive of well-doing occur in the collection. The advanced conception of Wisdom presented is purely religious (see i. 7, ii. 5–8, iii. 19, 20, viii. 13, 22 ff., ix. 10), so that the motive-power conducing to right living is, from this point of view, wholly religious. But in various passages (e. g. vi. 1–5, 6–11, 25–26, vii. 25–27, ix. 13–18) the avoidance of a wrong course is advocated on purely prudential grounds and by means of a worldly wisdom which has no religious content. This latter is quite in accordance with the earlier idea of wisdom, which, though it partook of a certain element of religion in so far as all wisdom in its various forms was the gift of God, was a very different thing from the conception of wisdom here portrayed. The conclusion, therefore, is that two such different points of view cannot have come from the same mind, and that the compiler of this collection gathered some material from other sources, perhaps small wisdom books, and with that inconsequence so characteristic of the ancient Hebrew mind, incorporated it into his collection. It is difficult to account otherwise for such a difference of point of view in one and the same collection.

The *second* collection (x. 1–xxii. 16) forms the central part of the book. The general rule in this collection is that each verse consists of a self-contained couplet wholly independent of its neighbours. Exceptions to this are to be accounted for in two ways; sometimes a single line, complete in itself, occurs; this may be a derelict, having originally formed the first or the second line of a couplet; but it may also be an original one-line proverb, and therefore following the pattern of the earliest, oral, type. Another form of exception is when something more than a couplet occurs; in such cases it is probably safe to say that a later scribe has made an addition, though in the very rare instances of an obviously complete triplet there is no reason to deny that it belonged to the collection as originally compiled. The couplets in this collection are of three kinds: Antithetic parallelism, e. g.:

> He becometh poor that dealeth with a slack hand,
> But the hand of the diligent acquireth wealth (x. 4).[1]

Comparative parallelism, e. g.:

> As vinegar to the teeth, and as smoke to the eyes,
> So is the sluggard to them that send him (x. 26).

Synonymous parallelism, e. g.:

> Pride goeth before destruction,
> And a haughty spirit before a fall (xvi. 18).

Continuous sentence, e. g.:

> The blessing of Jahweh, it maketh rich,
> And he addeth no sorrow thereto (x. 22).

There are reasons for believing that this collection is made up of smaller ones; for it is to be noticed, in the first place, that, with few exceptions, chaps. x–xv consist entirely of couplets containing antithetic parallelisms, whereas this form occurs but rarely in xvi–xxii. 16, which consists in the main of the other types of couplets. This difference between the two sections cannot be accidental, but points rather to their having belonged originally to distinct collections. But apart from this there is the somewhat puzzling fact that over and over again the same, or an almost identical line or couplet, occurs twice over in this collection; and this not merely as between x–xv, and xvi–xxii. 16, but also *within* each of these. A few examples of this will be instructive; first, identical or similar lines or couplets occurring in each of these two divisions:

The rich man's wealth is his strong city (x. 15a and xviii. 11a).
He that goeth about as a talebearer revealeth secrets (xi. 13a and xx. 19a).
Before honour goeth humility (xv. 33b and xviii. 12b).

---

[1] Where quotations differ from the R. V. rendering, the reason will be found in the Commentary.

*He that oppresseth the poor reproacheth his Maker* (xiv. 31[a], almost identical with xvii. 5[a] which has 'whoso mocketh . . .').

*Of a truth, the evil man shall not be unpunished* (xi. 21[a], almost identical with xvi. 5[b] which omits 'the evil man').

*There is a way which seemeth right unto a man;*
*But the end thereof are the ways of death* (xiv. 12 and xvi. 25).

*The poor is hated even of his own neighbour;*
*But the rich hath many friends* (xiv. 20;) this is not quite identical with, but very similar to, xix. 4:

*Wealth addeth many friends;*
*But the poor is separated from his friend.*

The same is true of the next two couplets:

*He that is surety for a stranger shall smart for it;*
*But he that hateth those that strike hands is sure* (xi. 15).
*A man void of understanding striketh hands,*
*And becometh surety in the presence of his neighbour* (xvii. 18).

It is interesting to note how on these couplets the miniature essay in vi. 1–5 is formed.

Instances of identical or similar lines or couplets occurring in the section x–xv are:

*Violence covereth the mouth of the wicked* (x. 6[b] and 11[b], but it is possible that in the former the text is corrupt, see note in Comm.).

*The prating fool shall fall* (x. 8[b] and 10[b]; probably in each case the line is out of place; but that does not affect the subject under consideration).

*In the multitude of counsellors there is safety* (xi. 14[b] and xv. 22[b], excepting that the latter has 'they are established', in reference to 'purposes' in the first line).

*By the fruit of the mouth of a man shall he be satisfied* (xii. 14[a] and xiii. 2[a], the latter has 'eat' for 'satisfied,' probably wrongly; see the notes on each verse in the Comm.).

*A wise son maketh a glad father,*
*But a foolish son is the heaviness of his mother* (x. 1).
*A wise son maketh a glad father,*
*But a foolish man despiseth his mother* (xv. 20; here 'despiseth' is probably a textual corruption, and the line should run as in the former couplet; see note in the Comm.).

*Treasures of wickedness profit nothing;*
*But righteousness delivereth from death* (x. 2).
*Riches profit nothing in the day of wrath,*
*But righteousness delivereth from death* (xi. 4).

What appears to be an interesting case of deliberate alteration occurs in the following:

*The teaching of the wise man is a fountain of life,*
*To depart from the snares of death* (xiii. 14).

*The fear of Jahweh is a fountain of life,*
  *To depart from the snares of death* (xiv. 27).

The latter would seem to be the original form of the couplet; a sage apparently altered 'the fear of Jahweh' to 'the teaching of the wise man' in the interests of the *Chăkāmim.*

In the section xvi–xxii. 16 we have the following instances:

*The king's wrath is as the roaring of a lion* (xix. 12).
*The terror of a king is as the roaring of a lion* (xx. 2).

There does not appear to be sufficient reason to regard 'terror' as due to textual corruption, see below.

*All the ways of a man are clean in his own eyes,*
  *But Jahweh weigheth the spirits* (xvi. 2).
*Every way of a man is right in his own eyes,*
  *But Jahweh weigheth the hearts* (xxi. 2).

On the slight variations here of an original form of a couplet, see below.

*A false witness shall not be unpunished,*
*And he that uttereth lies shall not escape* (xix. 5 and 9, excepting that the latter verse has 'shall perish').

*Divers weights, and divers measures,*
  *Both of them alike are an abomination to Jahweh* (xx. 10).
*Divers weights are an abomination to Jahweh,*
  *And a false balance is not good* (xx. 23).

Another instance of two couplets of identical meaning being in close juxtaposition occurs in xxi. 9 and 19:

*It is better to dwell in the corner of the housetop,*
*Than with a contentious woman in a wide house.*
*It is better to dwell in a desert land,*
*Than with a contentious and fretful woman.*

The passages cited raise some interesting points for consideration. The first few examples show identical, or almost identical, sayings in different contexts; all of them are self-contained single-line sayings, and since they occur in different contexts the probability is that they were originally intended to be only single-line sayings; that this was the form of a proverb in the pre-literary stage needs no insisting upon (see Excursus V). But the content of the single-line sayings which have been quoted show that they cannot have belonged to the pre-literary stage, because they presuppose advanced social conditions. We may, therefore, conclude that in the literary stage of the development of the proverb, or *māshāl*, the single-line saying preceded the couplet form, following therein the traditional oral pattern. And if this is so we may expect to find other instances of single-line sayings in *Proverbs*, remnants of the earlier mode. This is a point of some importance as it helps to explain some difficult passages. There are cases in which scholars have been at pains to emend the text of a line in order to make it appropriate to its context; but it is just possible that sometimes, at least, no emendation is required, and that a single-line saying was inserted in a collection with which a later scribe, accustomed to the couplet form, was not satisfied, and to which he added, not always very skilfully, a second line.

This leads to a further consideration: there are a great many instances of the first line of a couplet being self-contained, and no doubt the great mass of these were intended to be couplets from the beginning; but in view of what has been said the question may be asked as to whether we may not, in fact, have in *Proverbs* many more originally single-line sayings to which a line has been added later than is generally supposed. It is impossible now to decide in individual cases whether the couplet-form is original, or whether it is originally a single-line saying with a line added later; but from the point of view of the history of the development of proverbial sayings the question is not without interest.

In the passages cited we have cases of the identical, or almost identical, saying occurring in each of the sections x–xv and xvi–xxii; as different writers are not likely to have hit independently on the same proverb, the probability is that these two sections represent two collections which have been joined together here. But as the compiler of each of these has some identical sayings, they must both have made independent use of some common source. The interest of this is that our present form of *Proverbs* marks a third step in the history of the compilation, a fact which has a certain bearing on the original date of portions of our book.

The existence of identical, or almost identical, lines or couplets in the *same* section (x–xv or xvi–xxii. 16) is more puzzling, and is not always easy to account for. Several explanations suggest themselves. The most obvious would be that within these sections, representing collections, there are smaller collections which have been joined together. But while this is possible, it is rather a large assumption, and not always necessary; it will certainly not suit all cases, e.g. when one gets the same line in verses quite close together. Each case must be considered separately. One or two suggestions may be offered here. It is possible that a sage may have purposely used the same saying more than once in order to adapt it to a different context; thus, assuming that 'In the multitude of counsellors there is safety' was originally a one-line saying, it may well have been used

b

to point a moral in circumstances of two different kinds, viz. when the people fall into calamity for want of wise guidance (xi. 14), and when an undertaking fails owing to a similar cause (xv. 22); the saying is quite appropriate in either context, and there is no reason why the same writer should not have used it twice over. Again, a well-known saying might have been used twice over by the same collector, but altered slightly in order to suit a different context; e.g. ' the king's wrath is as the roaring of a lion'; in xix. 12 this describes the attitude of a king; but the slight alteration, ' the terror of a king is as the roaring of a lion' in xx. 2 describes the effect which the king's wrath has on a subject. In the former case it is used for the purpose of an antithesis, in the latter to act as a deterrent to a presumptuous courtier.

Slight alterations of this kind may in other cases be due to another cause; it is possible that a saying may have been an oral one originally, and have been inaccurately quoted.

Further, the possibility of textual corruption must also be considered. In xii. 14 and xiii. 2 it is probable that the same saying was originally used, 'By the fruit of the mouth of a man shall he be satisfied'; in the former passage the blessing of congruity between word and deed is declared; in the latter it is used for an antithesis; but apparently the antithesis did not appear sufficiently marked to some later copyist, who altered the text accordingly. But here again there is no reason why originally the same sage should not have used a saying in two different contexts.

Cases in which sayings are identical, or sufficiently similar to be regarded as originally identical, occur in closely contiguous verses ; these must either be due to carelessness, or they may be the work of a later scribe who overlooked the fact that they had already been utilized, e.g. x. 6 and 11, xix. 5 and 9, xx. 10 and 23, xxi. 9 and 19.

But there are other cases in which the hypothesis of originally smaller collections having been incorporated seems justified, e.g. x. 2 and xi. 4, x. 1 and xv. 20, x. 27 and xix. 23, xiii. 14 and xiv. 27, xvi. 2 and xxi. 2 ; these must have figured in collections which were originally quite distinct, each collector having apparently utilized the same source; when they were incorporated in *Proverbs* the compiler failed to notice that in a number of instances the different collections contained the same sayings. On the passages which contain a reference to the king, see below, pp. xxiii ff.

The *third* collection is represented by xxii. 17–xxiii. 14, but most commentators hold that this collection includes xxii. 17–xxiv. 22, with xxiv. 23–24 as an appendix. For reasons to be given in the

Commentary we believe that we have here *three* originally distinct collections. These three collections differ in form from the rest in the book in that they are composed of quatrains; but further details need not be given here as they are dealt with in the Commentary. The extraordinary parallelism between the third collection (xxii. 17–xxiii. 14) and the recently published Egyptian Wisdom-book, *The Teaching of Amen-em-ope*, is illustrated below (Excursus I).

The *sixth* collection comprises chaps. xxv–xxix. In general form it is similar to the second collection (x. 1–xxii. 16). A number of lines and couplets, some identical and some nearly so, occur in both these collections; so that what has been said regarding the second collection applies largely to this one. In this collection, too, there are signs that it consisted originally of two compilations which have been merged into one. There are some marked differences between the sections xxv–xxvii and xxviii–xxix; the latter consists only of couplets, the observance of the Law receives emphasis, and the religious element is much more prominent. These differences lead to the conclusion that the work of two compilers has been incorporated in this collection.

The remaining four collections are very short; xxx. 1–14, and 15–33, xxxi. 1–9, and 10–31; but that they are all independent pieces is proved not only by their great differences in content, but also by the fact that they stand in different and independent positions in the Septuagint (for details see the Commentary). The probability is that these four pieces are excerpts from other Wisdom-books, not necessarily all from Hebrew books. They may be compared with the third collection, which consists of excerpts from the Egyptian Wisdom-book, *The Teaching of Amen-em-ope*, adapted to Hebrew readers. Indeed, as will be seen below (Excursus I), there is every reason for believing that in the case of all the collections in *Proverbs* use has been made of extra-Israelite sources. This is often obscured by the skilful way in which the Hebrew compilers have adapted the material utilized to their readers; but when comparison is made with the extra-Israelite sources at our disposal, the underlying identity of thought is too pronounced and too frequent to blind us to the fact that the Hebrew sages were often indebted to foreign authors. In saying this it is not intended to imply that the Hebrew Wisdom writers were mainly dependent on others; very far from that; in their way they were unique, and emphatically superior to all their compeers in other countries; but that did not prevent them studying and utilizing what others had to say on the subject of Wisdom. Nor must it be supposed that the Hebrew sages were borrowers only; there are distinct signs that Hebrew thought influenced the minds of foreign sages. This subject, which cannot be pursued here, is further dealt with in the present writer's *The Wisdom of Egypt and the Old Testament*, pp. 75 ff. (1927).

## III

### DATES OF THE COLLECTIONS

With the exception of the *Psalms* there are no books in the Old Testament which lend themselves more easily to additions by later scribes than those belonging to the sapiential literature. And of these the book of *Proverbs*, with its numbers of short couplets of the most varying content, quite independent of their context in most cases, is the one more likely than any of the others to receive additions; indeed, one might almost say that its aphoristic character invites them. While this facilitates the fixing of an approximate date for the book in its present form, it complicates the question of the dates of the various collections in their original form. Precise dates cannot, in any case, be given because there is insufficient evidence for determining them. The question turns upon whether any parts of the book are pre-exilic. Most modern commentators answer this in the negative; we hope to show grounds for believing otherwise.

First, there are some reasons for believing in the *a priori* probability of the oldest collections in *Proverbs* (apart from additions from later hands) belonging to pre-exilic times:

(i) There existed a body of popular sayings in oral form long before the Exile (see further Excursus VIII), indeed, before the foundation of the monarchy; these were, without doubt, all short sayings consisting of a single sentence, many of which easily lent themselves to enlargement by the addition of a second line, thus forming a couplet; and the couplet is the earliest literary form of the proverb. Thus the *material* for the formation of collections was in existence centuries before the Exile.

(ii) Wise men, or *Chăkāmim*, likewise existed before the Exile. From the writings of both Isaiah and Jeremiah one can see that the term *Chăkāmim* had already in their day become a technical one; they form an order as distinct as the priestly and the prophetical orders. This proves that they must have been long in existence at the end of the 8 cent. B.C. (see further Excursus VII). The *Chăkāmim*, as will be shown later (see Excursus VII), are to be identified with the Scribes, in the early sense in which this term is used; and this vouches for the fact that written collections of proverbs were made during the time of the monarchy; the Israelite Wisdom-scribes herein following in the wake of Egyptian and Babylonian teachers. As an illustration of the way in which extra-Israelite Wisdom writings influenced Israelite thinkers the following parallel between the Egyptian Wisdom-book, the *Teaching of Amen-em-ope* IV. vi. 1–12 and Jer. xvii. 5–8 will be found instructive; both give a description of the lot of the wicked and the righteous respectively:

> 'The passionate man in the temple,—
> He is like a tree that groweth in the forest;
> In one moment it loseth its branches,
> And it findeth its end in [. . . ?].[1]
> It is swept away from its place,
> And the flame is its winding-sheet.
> But the truly silent one, when he standeth aside,
> He is like a tree that groweth in a plot.
> It groweth green, and the fruit thereof increaseth,
> It standeth in the presence of its Lord;
> Its fruits are sweet, its shade is pleasant,
> And it findeth its end in the garden.'

The Jeremiah passage runs: ' Cursed is the man that trusteth in man, and maketh flesh his arm, and whose heart departeth from Jahweh. For he shall be like a tamarisk in the desert, and shall not see when good cometh; but shall inhabit the parched places in the wilderness, a salt land and not inhabited. Blessed is the man that trusteth in Jahweh, and whose hope Jahweh is. For he shall be as a tree planted by the waters and that spreadeth out his roots by the river, and shall not fear when the heat cometh, but his leaf shall be green; and he shall not be careful in the year of drought, neither shall cease from yielding fruit.'

The international character of the pursuit of Wisdom makes it difficult to believe that the Israelite sages did not form collections of wise sayings and write them down in pre-exilic times, just as the sages of other lands did, and had done for many centuries.

If, then, the material for making collections of proverbial sayings existed long before the Exile, and the type of man who would make such collections was likewise in existence long before the Exile, we are justified in saying that there is, at the least, a high probability that collections of proverbial sayings existed in literary form before the Exile. And this conclusion is supported by some further considerations.

(iii) Most modern critics reject entirely the tradition that Solomon

---

[1] The omitted word seems to be of uncertain meaning; it is rendered 'harbour' by some Egyptologists; Ll. Griffith renders it 'dockyard'.

composed a number of proverbs. The record of this is as follows:
'And Solomon's wisdom excelled the wisdom of all the children
of the east, and all the wisdom of Egypt. For he was wiser than all
men; than Ethan the Ezrahite, and Heman, and Calcol, and
Darda, the sons of Mahol; and his fame was in all the nations
round about. And he spake three thousand proverbs; and his songs
were a thousand and five. And he spake of trees, from the cedar that
is in Lebanon even unto the hyssop that springeth out of the wall;
he spake also of beasts, and of fowl, and of creeping things, and of
fishes. And there came of all peoples to hear the wisdom of Solomon,
from all kings of the earth, which had heard of his wisdom' (1 Kgs.
iv. 30–34 [v. 10–14 in Hebr.]). Then, again, we read of the visit of
the queen of Sheba, who came to prove Solomon with 'hard questions', and was overwhelmed by his wisdom and wealth (1 Kgs. x.
1–9). It may well be asked where these ideas came from; there must
have been some reason for connecting wisdom with Solomon in this
way; it cannot, so to say, have been grasped out of the air! And the
mention of the wisdom of Egypt and Arabia cannot be without
significance. On the former passage Gressmann remarks: 'Against
the reliability of this record nothing can be urged, likely enough
though it may be that utterances of others were put into the mouth
of the king, as the general custom was in court circles, especially in
the ancient east.'[1] Similarly Eissfeldt, in his recent work on the
*Books of Kings*, says in reference to the passage: 'On the historicity
of this piece of information it is hardly possible to throw doubt.
Moreover, the description of the proverbs and songs given in verse 13
(33) is much to the point; analogies from the literatures of other
lands enable us to picture to ourselves the character of this kind of
poetry.'[2] Even if it be granted that a minimum of these compositions
is to be ascribed to Solomon himself, the fact still remains that, like
some other oriental monarchs both previous and subsequent to his
day, he was a patron of such literature. This tradition, therefore,
points to the fact that collections of proverbs existed as early as the
time of Solomon; and though it is not suggested that the earliest
collections incorporated in *Proverbs* belong to this early date, it is
not too great an assumption to say that they contain elements which
in their origin go back to the time of Solomon. This will apply to
the collections x–xxii. 16 and xxv–xxix, but more especially to
x–xv because in so many cases in these chapters the first line of a
couplet is self-contained and may well have stood alone originally;

---

[1] In the *Zeitschrift für die alt-test. Wissenschaft*, p. 282 (1924).
[2] In Kautzsch's, *Die heilige Schrift des A. T.* i. 503 (4 ed. 1922).

the single-line proverb, as we have seen, was the earliest form, being based on the oral pattern.

(iv) Next, we must consider the mention of the king in its bearing on the question of dates. It would, of course, be absurd to suppose that the reference to the king necessarily presupposes a pre-exilic date for the collection in which it occurs. For example, once in the first collection the king is mentioned. 'By me [i. e. Wisdom] kings reign, and princes decree justice' (viii. 15); as Toy rightly says: 'The rulers of the world are here conceived of ideally as governing by wisdom.' Nobody would take a general statement of this kind as referring necessarily to Israelite kings, especially as there are over-whelming reasons for regarding the collection in which this saying occurs as one of the latest in the book. The same applies to the men-tion of the king in the eighth collection (xxx. 22, 27), and in the ninth (xxxi. 4). It is different in the second collection (x–xxii. 6), and in the sixth (xxv–xxix). A few of the passages in which the king is spoken of must be quoted:

> *A divine oracle is in the lips of the king,*
> *His mouth doth not deal treacherously against justice* (xvi. 10).
> *It is an abomination to kings to commit wickedness,*
> *For the throne is established by righteousness.*
> *Righteous lips are the delight of a king,*
> *And they love him that speaketh right.*
> *The wrath of a king is as messengers of death;*
> *But a wise man will pacify it.*
> *In the light of the king's countenance is life;*
> *And his favour is as a cloud of the latter rain* (xvi. 12–15).
> *A king that sitteth on the throne of judgement*
> *Scattereth away all evil with his eyes* (xx. 8).
> *A wise king winnoweth the wicked,*
> *And bringeth upon them their own iniquity* (xx. 26).[1]
> *Mercy and truth preserve the king,*
> *And he upholdeth his throne by equity* (xx. 28).[1]
> *The king's heart is in the hand of Jahweh as the watercourses;*
> *He turneth it whithersoever he will* (xxi. 1).
> *Jahweh loveth the pure in heart,*
> *He maketh gracious his lips, a king is his friend* (xxii. 11).[1]

These are from the second collection; one or two examples from the sixth may also be given:

> *It is the glory of God to conceal a thing;*
> *But the glory of kings is to search out a matter.*
> *The heaven for height, and the earth for depth,*
> *And the heart of kings is unsearchable* (xxv. 2, 3).

---

[1] For the justification of this rendering see the note on the verse in the Comm.

*As a roaring lion, and a ranging bear,*
*So is a wicked ruler over a poor people* (xxviii. 15).
*The king by justice establisheth the land;*
*But he that exacteth gifts overthroweth it* (xxix. 4).
*The king that faithfully judgeth the poor,*
*His throne shall be established for ever* (xxix. 14).

These do not exhaust the passages in the two collections in which reference is made to the king; but they are amply sufficient to give us a good insight into what the Sages have to say on the subject. The question therefore arises as to whether the king thought of is a Jewish ruler or the king of some foreign land. If the latter, it will point to a post-exilic date for these collections; but if the former, it will be an unanswerable argument for their belonging to pre-exilic times. For these passages are part and parcel of the text, they affect the collections as a whole, they are not of the type which a later scribe would add.

It must be emphasized, first of all, that these collections were written for Jews, by Jews, in a Jewish land; what would be the point of such frequent references to a king for people who had not a king of their own, and who could hardly be expected to take much interest in foreign potentates? It is not as though, in these passages, it were a question of a general statement of the kind which occurs in the collections of demonstrably late date referred to previously.

If in even one of the passages cited above it can be shown that it must be a Jewish king to whom reference is made, that will be presumptive evidence that this is the case in the others. Now, is it conceivable that a Jew would speak of a Gentile king as one who uttered a divine oracle, or as one whose heart was in the hand of Jahweh? We do not forget that an exilic writer could speak of a Gentile king as Jahweh's anointed (Isa. xlv. 1); but the cases are hardly parallel; the circumstances in which Cyrus is spoken of in this way do not bear comparison with those under which the kind of passages in question were written. It is, therefore, most difficult to believe that a king other than a Jewish one can have been in the mind of the writer of these passages. Similarly in the other collection; the parallel mention of 'the glory of God' and the 'glory of kings' is not what one would look for in a Jewish sage writing in reference to Gentile kings, who, from the sage's point of view, did not believe in God at all; whereas the thought would be an appropriate one in reference to a king who was a worshipper of Jahweh. Such phrases as 'a wicked ruler over a poor people', 'the king by justice establisheth the land', 'the king that faithfully judgeth the poor', give the impression of referring to the home-land. Sellin makes an interesting

point in saying that 'in the first collection (i. e. x–xxii. 16) enthu-
siasm for the Monarchy and confidence in it is everywhere apparent,
cf. xiv. 28, 35, xix. 12, xx. 2, 8, 26, 28, xxi. 1, xxii. 11, and especially
xvi. 10–15; in the second (i. e. xxv–xxix) there is scepticism, xxviii.
15 f., xxix. 4, 12, 14, 26; in xxviii. 2 there is perhaps even a side
glance at the rapid changes on the throne of the Northern Kingdom.
It is exactly the same kind of relationship as between the two
sources of the books of Samuel.'[1] On the subject of these 'royal'
proverbs Gressmann says 'that they originated during the period of
the monarchy is self-evident; to make them refer to extra-Israelite
kings appears to me as a *resource d'embarras* (Verlegenheitsaus-
kunft).'[2]

The two collections, x–xxii. 16 and xxv–xxix, may therefore be
dated, at any rate, not later than 700 B.C.

(v) The collection xxi. 17–xxiii. 14, as will be seen in the Commentary (cf. also Excursus I), is, in the main, based on the Egyptian
Wisdom-book, the *Teaching of Amen-em-ope*. The best expert opinion
dates this work as belonging to the middle of the 8 cent. B.C. or later;
some authorities date it considerably earlier; the question is still unsettled.[3] The fact, therefore, that it was utilized for this collection is
not decisive so far as the date is concerned, for it might have been
utilized by a Hebrew sage centuries after its composition. One thing
can, however, be stated; this collection differs from the two collections just dealt with in being composed of quatrains; it is recognized
on all hands that, generally speaking, this form is a development of
the couplet form, and therefore of later date. But in the case before
us the quatrain form does not *necessarily* denote a post-exilic date,
because this form was taken over from the Egyptian book mentioned;
the quatrain form of composition is characteristic of it. What does
definitely mark this collection as pre-exilic is xxii. 29: 'A man who is
skilful in his office shall stand before kings.' Here it is not only the
mention of kings which marks the date, but also the reference to the
man who is skilful in his office; for, as is explained in the Commentary, this is a reference to the scribe in the early sense of the term,
and this points to pre-exilic times.

The two shorter collections (xxiii. 15–xxiv. 22 and xxiv. 23–34),
which are closely connected with that just considered (see p. xviii),
may be assigned to approximately the same period, viz. shortly

---

[1] *Intro. to the Old Testament*, p. 209 (1923). With what Sellin says about xxviii. 2
we are unable to agree; see the notes on this verse in the Commentary.
[2] *Op. cit.*, p. 286.
[3] For details see the present writer's *The Wisdom of Egypt and the Old Testament*,
pp. 8–10 (1927).

before the Exile; the words of xxiv. 21, 'My son, fear thou Jahweh and the king', are decisive for a pre-exilic date.

(vi) The four small collections contained in chaps. xxx, xxxi do not offer any certain indications of date, though in the first three (xxx. 1–14, 15–33, xxxi. 1–9) there is nothing which points necessarily to post-exilic times; but the style of the last (xxxi. 10–31) suggests a considerably later date. The ethical-religious ideal of woman here portrayed is not found elsewhere in the Old Testament. Toy may be right in assigning it to the second cent. B.C., but it is difficult to understand why he regards the whole of these four collections as belonging to the same late date.

(vii) Finally, we have the first collection in the book (i–ix). There is a general consensus of opinion that, apart from xxxi. 10–31, this is the latest portion of the whole book. That this section is intended to be an introduction to the 'Proverbs of Solomon', beginning at chap. x, has been clearly shown by Budde.[1] An unanswerable argument in favour of its late date is the developed conception of Wisdom which is constantly exhibited, e.g. i. 20–33, ii, iii. 11–20, vii, x, and, above all, viii. This is of itself amply sufficient to assign the collection, in the main, to the third cent. B.C., though it is exceedingly probable that some earlier elements have been incorporated. This date is supported by a certain number of late Hebrew words and expressions, to which reference is made in the Commentary.

To sum up; it may be stated with some confidence that the collections were made, approximately, as follows:

II (x. 1–xxii. 16) and VI (xxv–xxix), the middle of the 8 cent. B.C.; III (xxii. 17–xxiii. 14), IV (xxiii. 15–xxiv. 22), and V (xxiv. 23–34), during the 7 cent. B.C.; a more precise date cannot be given; VII (xxx. 1–14), VIII (xxx. 15–33), and IX (xxxi. 1–9), uncertain, but in all probability pre-exilic; I (i. 7–ix) and X (xxxi. 10–31), the 3 cent. B.C., and quite possibly later still. The Preface, i. 1–6, was prefixed perhaps some time after the whole compilation had been made, but it is also possible that it was due to the collector of i. 7–ix.

# IV

## THE TITLES OF THE COLLECTIONS

The title of the book itself is *Mishlê*, 'Proverbs', an abbreviation of *Mishlê Shĕlōmōh*, 'The Proverbs of Solomon'. In the Septuagint the title is Παροιμίαι, thus agreeing with the abbreviated Hebrew title,

---

[1] *Geschichte der hebräischen Literatur*, pp. 269 f. (1906).

which must therefore be old; but in the three Codd. אAC the subscription adds the name of Solomon; Cod. B, however, omits this. The Vulgate MSS. have *Proverbia*, others *Liber Proverbiorum*. 'The name might naturally have been suggested', says Toy, 'by 1 Kgs. iv. 32 (v. 12), but would originally have been given to the collection x. 1–xxii. 16, whence it would have been extended to the whole book as additions were made to it from time to time.' This may well be the case.

As to the titles within the book, all the collections indicated, with three exceptions, have them. The exceptions are: IV (xxiii. 15–xxiv. 22), VIII (xxx. 15–33), and X (xxxi. 10–31).

The first occurs in i. 1: 'The proverbs of Solomon the Son of David, king of Israel', which presumably applies to i–ix since other collections have titles of their own. The words 'king of Israel', which would be so unnecessary for Jews, shows that this collection was intended for the edification of Gentiles as well as Jews; and as the former did not constitute part of the population of Jerusalem until well into the Greek period,[1] this title is a further indication of the late date of the collection.

The second occurs in x. 1: 'The Proverbs of Solomon'. Apart from the evidence of the Solomonic tradition, this title has no importance; but there is a curious little point of interest about it discovered by Behnke.[2] The collection at the head of which it stands (x. 1–xxii. 16) contains 375 proverbs; this corresponds with the numerical value of the Hebrew letters forming the name of Solomon. It is doubtful whether this means anything more than that some scribe purposely made the number of proverbs in the collection correspond with the name of Solomon. But it seems to show that at a relatively late period this collection circulated independently.

The fact that the next, the third, collection (xxii. 17–xxiii. 14) has no title in the Hebrew text as it stands must not blind us to the fact that originally it did have one; this is evident both from the Septuagint, which has the title 'Sayings of the Wise' (Λόγοις σοφῶν is obviously a case of dittography; it should be Λόγοι σοφῶν), and from the present form of the Hebrew text (see note in Comm.); there is no doubt that the title is there, only it has been mistakenly put into the text. From what we now know about the origin of this collection (see Excursus I) there is much significance in the form of this title. It must be old, comparatively speaking, as its incorporation

---

[1] See further F. C. Grant, *The Economic Background of the Gospels*, pp. 25 ff. (1926).

[2] *Zeitschrift für die alttest. Wissenschaft* for 1896, p. 122.

into the text shows. The scribe who prefixed it—and there is really no decisive reason why it should not have been put there by the original collector—regarded the wise men of all lands as belonging to a confraternity. It is worth emphasizing that where a collection of proverbs is of Jewish origin it is definitely said so in the titles (i. 1, xi. 1, xxv. 1); where there is reason to suspect a non-Jewish origin the titles are vague (xxii. 17, xxiv. 23, xxx. 1, xxxi. 1).

The next collection (xxiii. 15–xxiv. 22) has no title, and perhaps never had one, the collection having been subjoined to the preceding one at the first; indeed, most commentators regard iii and iv as one collection; but for the reasons given on p. 188 we believe them to have been originally distinct.

The fifth collection (xxiv. 23–34) has the title: ' Also these (belong) to the Wise men'; the emphatic 'also' must be in reference to the title in the third collection. In the Septuagint this collection occurs in quite a different context, showing that it was entirely independent originally; and although it has no title there, it is easy to see that it existed separately once, and has now been incorporated in the text; the reverse process to that of the title of the third collection. On the analogy of the title of the third collection, it may be assumed that this one indicates the non-Jewish origin of the little collection.

The sixth collection (xxv–xxix) has the title: 'These are also proverbs of Solomon, which the men of Hezekiah king of Judah copied out', which occurs also in the Septuagint. The nature of this title stamps it as belonging to the time when the collection was made. Gressmann regards it as decisive for the date of the collection. 'The unique statement regarding the men of Hezekiah,' he says, ' although not confirmed by any mention elsewhere, can clearly only be accounted for on the supposition that it rests on sound tradition; at any rate, nobody has as yet been able to explain for what purpose and at what period it is supposed to have been invented!' [1] On some further details regarding this title see pp. 219 f.

The titles to the VII collection (xxx. 1–14) and the IX (xxxi. 1–9) are dealt with in the Commentary (pp. 267 f., 281). The two remaining ones (xxx. 15–33 and xxxi. 10–31) have no titles.

# V

## THE HEBREW TEXT

A few words must be said about the state of the Hebrew text in the form in which it has come down to us.

---

[1] *Op. cit.*, p. 286.

There is a marked difference here between the collections, and it is interesting to note that, upon the whole, the state of the text of the different parts of the book tends to confirm the conclusions arrived at regarding their respective dates. Thus, the Hebrew text of the second collection (x–xxii. 16), which is the earliest portion of the book, is in a much worse condition than any other part. This is what might be expected, since as the oldest part, and therefore with a longer history behind it, it is likely to have suffered more in transmission at the hand of copyists. The number of verses in which textual corruption of one kind or another exists is great; in a few cases the corruption is so deep-seated as to defy emendation; but, generally speaking, it is possible to reconstruct the text with reasonable certainty, especially as not infrequently the change of a letter, as a rule fairly obviously demanded, gives the indication as to how the whole sentence should be emended. But the mere change of a letter does not by any means always suffice; for what has evidently happened in some cases is that one copyist has made a mistake in copying one or more letters wrongly, and this, by bringing into the text a wrong word, has misled a later copyist who has tried to emend the text from the point of view indicated by this wrong word; by this means confusion was made worse confounded, though the procedure was a very natural one. At the same time, one cannot help often wondering at the ineptitude at one time, the carelessness at another, of copyists. Over and over again one asks oneself whether a copyist read over what he had written, and if so, what he himself supposed that the line or the verse meant! It is, however, very possible that many mistakes arose from a different cause. And here we have the very interesting case of the copying out of the Egyptian Wisdom book, the *Teaching of Amen-em-ope*; in discussing a certain passage from this book which has been copied out on what is known as the 'Turin tablet', Prof. Ll. Griffith says: 'It looks very much as if the teacher had dictated from the British Museum papyrus [i.e. of the *Teaching of Amen-em-ope*] to the scholar who wrote on the Turin tablet. But if so, the teacher in his dictation corrected some of the mistakes of the papyrus, and of course the scholar made further mistakes.'[1] It is possible that some of the mistakes in this collection in *Proverbs* arose in a similar manner, i.e. through having been dictated to a youthful scribe who was not altogether *au fait* with his subject.

However this may be, the mistakes are there, and in some chapters, e.g. xiv and xvi, they are more prevalent than in others. There are also a certain number of cases of displacement, e.g. x. 6, 8, 10, 13, xi.

---

[1] *The Journal of Egyptian Archaeology*, XII, parts iii and iv, p. 193 (1926).

7, 9; but it is, of course, possible that these are not really displacements, but merely additions by some more or less contemporary scribe.

In the collection xxv–xxix the text is not in such a bad state, though in some cases a verse is hopelessly corrupt, e.g. xxvi. 9, xxvii. 9; and in xxviii there are more corruptions than in the other chapters of this collection. In the collections comprised in xxii. 17–xxiv. 34 the text is also better, though a number of emendations are required here too.

In the first collection (i–ix) the corruptions are far less, and with two or three exceptions, such as vii. 22, 23, they are of a minor character. Here and there some verses seem to be out of place, e.g. viii. 13, 32–34. The notable difference in the state of the text between this section and the central part of the book is to be accounted for partly by the difference of their date, as already pointed out, but partly also because of the difference in the form of composition. In the miniature essay form of the later collection the sense of a passage is clearer, and therefore mistakes are more easily avoided; while in the very short but pregnant clauses of the earlier collections mistakes would be more likely to creep in because it often happens that the sense is not immediately apparent, and a copyist would not stay to think it out.

The four short collections comprised in the last two chapters are remarkably free from textual corruption; exceptions to this are the titles at the beginning of each of the chapters; on these see the previous section.

## VI

### THE ANCIENT VERSIONS

By far the most important of these is the Septuagint; indeed, it is quite indispensable for the study of *Proverbs*, though for the correction of the Hebrew it requires to be used with caution as its own text is in anything but good condition. In a great number of cases, however, it helps us to reconstruct the Hebrew text. Often, even when it clearly does not represent what stood in the original, it gives valuable hints for the purpose of reconstruction.

It is found that the Septuagint gives more help for emending the Hebrew text of the central part of the book than for that of i–ix.

In comparing the Septuagint with the Massoretic text the following points, put very briefly, are to be noted:

There are many passages in which the text of the Septuagint is preferable to that of the Hebrew, notably in viii, xiv, xv; and in most of the other chapters several instances occur. In the central part of the book there are a number of verses the Greek form of which evidently presupposes a Hebrew text superior to that of the Massoretes.

The Septuagint contains a certain amount of material not represented at all in the Hebrew; this material may be divided into two classes: part of it reads as if it had been translated from Hebrew; this does not necessarily mean that it represents anything that has fallen out of the Hebrew text, though the possibility of this must not be lost sight of (see e.g. vii. 22, 23, xvi. 5, 17, xix. 7); but it may well have been taken from some extant Hebrew collection now lost (see e.g. the couplets after ix. 12). That material from other sources has been incorporated is shown by the fact that after xxvi. 11 a saying from Ben-Sira (Ecclus. iv. 21) has been inserted. The other part of this material is in all probability not translated, but has been taken from a collection of proverbs written in Greek.

In some cases the Septuagint omits verses contained in the Hebrew (e.g. x. 13, xv. 31); this may be due to accident, but it may also be that the verse did not figure in the Hebrew text before the translator.

There are verses which it appears the translator did not understand, or only understood in part; this would account for the number of paraphrases in the Septuagint (see e.g. x. 18, xi. 31).

In some cases the order of passages in the Septuagint differs from that of the Hebrew: see e.g. xv. 28–xvi. 9 and the positions of the four different collections in xxx, xxxi; this suggests that originally the various collections circulated separately.

The other Versions are only of minor importance, and rarely give much help, though the Targum is sometimes useful. The Syriac (Peshitta) is a very precarious aid; it is evidently based on the Hebrew, but often agrees with the Septuagint against it. The Latin followed the Hebrew, and is of very little help.

# VII

## SELECTED BIBLIOGRAPHY

*Commentaries:*

Wildeboer, *Die Sprüche*, in Marti's 'Kurzer Hand-Commentar zum Alten Testament' (1897).

Frankenberg, *Die Sprüche*, in Nowack's 'Göttinger Handkommentar zum Alten Testament' (1898).

Toy, *A Commentary on the Book of Proverbs*, in 'The International Critical Commentary' (1914).

Volz, *Sprüche der Weisen*, in 'Die Schriften des Alten Testaments' (1921).

Steuernagel, *Die Sprüche*, in 'Die heilige Schrift des Alten Testaments' (1923).
For the earlier Commentaries see Toy, pp. xxxv f., and the Bible Dictionaries.

## *Other works bearing on the subject:*

Bernstein, *Jüdische Sprichwörter und Redensarten* (1908).

Bickell, *Kritische Bearbeitung der Proverbien*, in the 'Wiener Zeitschrift für die Kunde des Morgenlandes' (1891).

Cheyne, *Job and Solomon* (1887).

Cohen, *Ancient Jewish Proverbs* (1911).

Dyserinck, *Kritische Scholien*, in 'Theol. Tijdschrift' (1883).

Elmslie, *Studies in Life from Jewish Proverbs* (2nd impression, undated).

Goldman, *Proverbs of the Sages* (1911).

Meinhold, *Die Weisheit Israels* (1908).

Wünsche, *Die Räthselweisheit bei den Hebräern* (1883).

See also the works referred to in Excursus I, and in the notes in the Commentary.

# EXCURSUSES

## I

## THE WISDOM LITERATURE OF THE ANCIENT ORIENTAL WORLD

### I

The Wisdom Literature of the Hebrews, in the form of proverbial sayings, has a twofold origin. It is the outcome, on the one hand, of everyday experience; while, on the other, it is based on religious experience. What is unique and specific in Hebrew Wisdom Literature will be considered later. Regarding the first of these, it is obvious that in its origin there is not necessarily anything specifically Hebrew about it, since the ordinary experiences of life are common to humanity in general. When, for example, the ancient proverb is quoted: 'Out of the wicked cometh forth wickedness' (1 Sam. xxiv. 13, in Heb. 14), it expresses a truth of general experience. Regarding the second, it must also be said that in its origin it was not necessarily specifically Hebrew, however much it was developed in course of time by religious Hebrew thinkers. We have, for example, the proverbial saying: 'Like Nimrod a mighty hunter before Jahweh' (Gen. x. 9); in so far as the name of the deity is brought in this must be regarded as a religious saying; but this proverb can hardly have originated among the Hebrews; Nimrod was either an Arabian or a Babylonian hero, so that in its original form a non-Israelite god must have stood in place of Jahweh. The proverb must thus be regarded as having been adapted from an extra-Israelite source. Originally both types of proverbs would have circulated orally.

Later evidence, moreover, as we shall see, leads to what amounts to proof of the fact that in its literary form the wisdom of the Hebrews was part of a world literature; and this being so, it is *a priori* probable that in its earliest forms it partook of what might be called an international character. Indeed, the Old Testament offers further indications of the truth of this. Balaam, the diviner, is stated to have come from Pethor (Num. xxii. 5); whether this place was in Babylonia or elsewhere, it was, in any case, not in Palestine. Familiarity with extra-Israelite wisdom is indicated in 2 Sam. xx. 18, where it is said: 'They were wont to speak in old time, saying, They shall surely ask counsel at Abel'; this place, called also Abel-beth-Maacah, is now 'generally admitted to be identical with the northern Abil, near Hūnīn, on one of the brooks which unite to

c

compose the Jordan' ;[1] it was, therefore, in Aram (Syria). Again, in
1 Kgs. iv. 30, 31 (v. 10, 11) it is said that 'Solomon's wisdom
excelled the wisdom of all the children of the east, and all the wisdom
of Egypt. For he was wiser than all men ; than Ethan the Ezrahite,
and Heman, and Calcol, and Darda, the sons of Mahol.' The 'children of the east' refer to the Bedouin Arabs, the 'sons of Mahol'
were Edomites. The tradition of the wisdom of Edom is mentioned
in Jer. xlix. 7 ; and 'the wise men of Edom' are spoken of in Obad. 8.
In Job. ii. 11 the names of Job's friends show that they were non-
Israelite; Teman was in Edom, Shuah in Assyria, and though
Naamah was in south-west Judah, it is most probable that Zophar
was thought of as an Edomite because the clan which settled in
Naamah, viz. the Calebites (see 1 Chron. iv. 15, where Naam is the
same as Naamah), was of Edomite extraction. Further, in Prov.
xxx. 1 it is possible that 'Massa' is a proper name (but see the Commentary on this verse), and if so, we have in Prov. xxx. 1–14 a collection of sayings which came originally from an Arabian source;
the same will apply to Prov. xxxi. 1–9.

We have, thus, definite indications that the Hebrews were not
unfamiliar with the wisdom of Babylonia, Egypt, Arabia, Syria, and
Edom.

When we come to compare the *Book of Proverbs* (which contains
the earliest known Hebrew collections, as well as later ones) with the
extant Wisdom Literature of Egypt and Babylonia, we shall find
indubitable proof that that of the Hebrews formed part of a world
literature. It is obvious that the interest of the *Book of Proverbs* is
greatly enhanced when studied in the light of this fact.

Unfortunately nothing of the wisdom of the other countries mentioned has yet come to light.

## II

Before coming to a detailed comparison it will be well to indicate,
in the briefest possible way, the material at our disposal for this purpose. We will begin with *Egyptian Wisdom Literature* as being the
most ancient.

*The Teaching of Ptah-hotep.* Known also as the 'Prisse Papyrus',
after the name of the French Egyptologist who acquired it at Thebes.
It belongs to about the middle of the third millennium B.C., possibly
even earlier. It contains moral precepts and guidance for conduct
of life, together with warnings against various vices (Erman, *Die*

---

[1] *Encycl. Bibl.*, i. 279.

*Literatur der Aegypter*,[1] pp. 86–99 [1923]. English transl. by F. Ll. Griffith in the *World's Best Literature*, 5329–5340 [1897]).

*The Teaching of Ka-Gemni*. This belongs also to the 'Prisse Papyrus'. Only a fragment of it is extant. It teaches the need of modesty, and of good behaviour at a feast (Erman, *op. cit.*, pp. 9 f. Engl. transl. by Griffith, *op. cit.*, 5327–5329).

*The Teaching of Amenemhet*. Oldest copy about 1300 B.C., but the original was older. The contents are of a somewhat different character from the other Wisdom books; it does not contain moral teaching, but recounts the experiences of the writer and a few exhortations to caution arising out of them (Erman, *op. cit.*, pp. 106–109. Engl. transl. by Griffith, *op. cit.*, 5323–5327).

*The Teaching for King Meri-Ka-re*. About the middle of the 15 cent. B.C. in its present form. With one exception (see below) this is the most important of the Egyptian Wisdom books so far discovered. Especially noticeable is its religious tone. It was written for the guidance of Meri-Ka-re by his father, whose name, however, is not known. A king of this name lived in the second half of the 3 millennium B.C., but otherwise nothing is known of him. The book is full of admirable moral precepts. Great stress is laid on right living; and there are various references to the deity. A striking saying is: 'The virtue of a right-minded man is more acceptable (to God) than the ox [i.e. for sacrifice] of an evil-doer' (Erman, *op. cit.*, pp. 109–119. Engl. transl. by Gardiner in the *Journal of Egyptian Archaeology*, i. 20 ff.).

*The Teaching of Duauf*. About 1300 B.C. in its present form; but the personal names mentioned in it show that the original was much older. It describes the lot of different kinds of artisans, the mason, barber, gardener, peasant, weaver, &c.; so that it is full of interest from the point of view of social life in ancient Egypt among the labouring classes. It does not, however, offer much of value regarding wisdom (Erman, *op. cit.*, pp. 100–105. Engl. transl. by Griffith, *op. cit.*, 5342–5343).

*The Wisdom of Anii*. Probably after 1000 B.C. in its present form. It was originally written by the scribe Anii. Unfortunately the pupil who wrote the present copy made so many mistakes that, as Erman says, there are long passages of which no sense can be made. Nevertheless, there is still a good deal which experts have been able to translate. Like most of the extant Egyptian Wisdom books, it is a

---

[1] It was not until the present writer had completed his work that he discovered that an English translation of Erman's book had been published by Messrs. Methuen & Co., under the title Erman, Adolf, *The Literature of the Ancient Egyptians* (translated by Aylward M. Blackman), 1927.

treatise on how to live rightly and therefore wisely. A religious element appears here and there (Erman, *op. cit.*, pp. 294–302. Engl. transl. by Griffith, *op. cit.*, 5340–5342).

*The Teaching of Amen-em-ope.* This is by far the most important of the Egyptian Wisdom books hitherto discovered. It is fuller, and of much greater interest; moreover, it is characterized by a religious tone which, according to all authorities, is unique in Egyptian literature. Its importance for the study of Hebrew Wisdom Literature will be seen by its numerous points of contact with the *Book of Proverbs.* The question of its date is not yet settled; we may, at any rate provisionally, accept Griffith's opinion that it belongs approximately to 600 B.C. in its present form; the original, he believes, cannot be earlier than the middle of the 8 cent. B.C. For details on this and on other subjects concerning this profoundly interesting book, see the present writer's *The Wisdom of Egypt and the Old Testament* (1927). Engl. transl. of the whole text by Griffith in *The Journal of Egyptian Archaeology,* xii, parts 3 and 4 (1926), to which is added a comparison of the book with certain parts of *Proverbs,* by Canon D. C. Simpson.

Of *Babylonian Wisdom Literature* not so much has, so far, been discovered; but there is amply sufficient to show how highly it was estimated.

*The Babylonian Job.* This is not the title of the work, but it is that given to it by modern scholars on account of its striking similarity in some essential points to the Hebrew *Book of Job.* It is a poem of great antiquity. Concerning it C. J. Ball says: 'The purpose of this venerable relic of ancient piety is to glorify the god Merodach as a healer and saviour, and to attract sufferers to his temple in hope of deliverance.' (Engl. transl. by C. J. Ball in *The Book of Job,* pp. 12–30 [1922]).

*The Bilingual Book of Proverbs.* Later than the 9 cent. B.C. What remains of this, together with fragments of similar texts of Babylonian wisdom, has been gathered and translated into English by Langdon, *Babylonian Wisdom* (1923); see also Ebeling, *Ein Babylonischer Koheleth* (1924).

*The Proverbs of Achikar.* These proverbs form part of *The Story of Achikar.* 'We make the acquaintance of the story, first of all, in the supplementary pages of the *Arabian Nights*; we then trace it through the legends of a variety of peoples, with a growing sense of the antiquity of the common nucleus which underlies the traditions, and finally, as an interesting combination of good luck and good learning, the original story turns up in an Aramaic papyrus of the fifth century B.C. among the ruins of Elephantiné; in a language, that is, which had been conjectured as its original, and of antiquity even greater than had been assigned to it by any of its investigators.' Of the four parts which make up the book, the *Proverbs* and the *Parables*, are the two with which we are concerned. The quotations here given are from the Syriac A version, of which an English translation is given in Charles's *The Apocrypha and Pseudepigrapha of the Old Testament*, ii. 728–38 (1913).

An English translation of the Aramaic papyrus is given by Cowley, *Jewish Documents of the time of Ezra*, pp. 87–95, in 'Translations of Early Documents' (1919), from which the quotations are taken.[1]

### III

We shall now proceed to give the parallels and similarities in thought and word between *Proverbs* and the various extra-Israelite Wisdom books mentioned. They are for the most part quoted in the Commentary, where references to chapters and verses, or sections, will be found; but it is thought advisable to gather together the whole material here as this will show at a glance the community of thought and teaching. Where the wording of the quotations from *Proverbs* differs from that of the Revised Version, justification for the change will be found in the Commentary.

It will be seen that these similarities differ considerably in closeness, but for our present purpose this is not of great moment, for our main object is to show the *milieu* to which the Hebrew Wisdom Literature belongs. The question of indebtedness on one side or the other cannot be discussed here.

i. 8, 9: *My son, hear the instruction of thy father.*

'How beautiful it is when a son hearkens unto his father, and how happy is he to whom this is said. . . . If a son accepts what his father says, he will not go wrong in his thoughts' (*Teaching of Ptah-hotep*).

[2] 'Give thine ears, hear the words that are said,
    Give thine heart to interpret them.
It is good to place them in thine heart;
—Be woe to him that neglecteth them—
Let them rest in the casket of thy belly,
That they may be a threshold (?) in thine heart.'

(*Teaching of Amen-em-ope.*)

'Hear, O my son Nadan,[3] and come to the understanding of me, and be mindful of my words, as the words of God' (*Proverbs of Achikar*).

---

[1] See also the same writer's *Aramaic Papyri of the Fifth Century B.C.* (1923).

[2] The words are addressed by Amen-em-ope to his son.

[3] One of the Syriac texts speaks of Nadan as the son of Achikar's sister; but in the original text Achikar is Nadan's father (see Charles, ii. 728).

iii. 2:     *For length of days, and years of life,*
        *And peace shall they add unto thee.*
   'He that is wise attaineth to old age' (*Bilingual Book of Proverbs*).

iii. 25, 26:    *Be not afraid of sudden fear,*
        *Neither of the destruction of the wicked, when it cometh ;*
        *For Jahweh shall be thy confidence,*
        *And shall keep thy foot from being taken.*
        'Be thou courageous before other people
        For one is safe in the hands of God' (*Teaching of Amen-em-ope*).

iii. 28:    *Say not to thy neighbour, 'Go, and come again,*
        *And to-morrow I will give,' when thou hast it by thee.*
   'My son, though the thresholds of thy house were high, and thy neighbour lay sick, say not, "What shall I send him?" But go upon thy feet, and see with thine eyes; that were better for him than a thousand talents of gold and silver' (*Words of Achikar*).

iv. 23, 24:   *Keep thy heart with all diligence ;*
        *For out of it are the issues of life.*
        *Put away from thee a froward mouth,*
        *And perverse lips put far from thee.*
   'With more than watchfulness watch thy mouth, and over what thou hearest harden thy heart; for a word is like a bird, and when he hath sent it forth a man doth not recapture it' (*Words of Achikar*).

v. 3–11:    *For the lips of a strange woman drop honey,*
        *And her mouth is smoother than oil . . .*
        *Remove thy way far from her,*
        *And come not nigh the door of her house,*
        *Lest thou give thine honour unto others,*
        *And thy years unto strangers . . .* (See also vi. 24–35.)
   '. . . Into whatsoever place thou enterest, beware of approaching the women. The place where they are is not good. On their account a thousand go to ruin; a man is but mocked by their glistening limbs, which soon become as Herset-stones.[1] A little moment, and what was like a dream became death in the end' (*Teaching of Ptah-hotep*).

   ' Beware of the strange woman, who is not known in her city. Ogle her not, and have no intercourse with her. She is a deep expanse of water, and her turning is not known. A woman who is away from her husband says daily unto thee, "I am beautiful," when no witness is present. That is a great crime worthy of death. . . .' (*Wisdom of Anii*).

   'My son, lift not up thine eyes and look upon a woman that is bedizened and painted; and do not lust after her in thine heart; for if thou shouldst give her all that is in thine hands, thou findest no advantage in her; and thou wilt be guilty of sin against God' (*Proverbs of Achikar*; the same subject is mentioned elsewhere in the book).

---

[1] A sign of grief (Erman).

vi. 16–19: See Commentary for similarity of thought with a passage from the *Teaching of Amen-em-ope* which is too long to quote in full.

vi. 25:     *Lust not after her beauty in thine heart;*
        *Neither let her take thee with her eyelids.*
        'My son, go not after the beauty of a woman,
        And lust not after her in thine heart' (*Proverbs of Achikar*).

vi. 32:     *He that committeth adultery with a woman is void of understanding,*
        *He that destroyeth his own soul doeth it.*
        'My son, commit not adultery with the wife of thy neighbour,
        Lest others should commit adultery with thy wife.'
                           (*Proverbs of Achikar.*)

vii. 25–27: See under v. 3–11.

ix. 7–9:     *He that correcteth a scorner getteth to himself shame,*
        *And he that reproveth a wicked man getteth himself a blot.*
        *Reprove not a scorner, lest he hate thee,*
        *Reprove a wise man, and he will love thee.*
        *Impart to a wise man, and he will be yet wiser;*
        *Teach a righteous man, and he will increase in learning.*

'My son, smite the (wise) man with a wise word, that it may be in his heart like a fever in summer; (but know) that if thou smite a fool with many blows, he will not understand' (*Proverbs of Achikar*).

x. 18:     *He that hideth hatred is of lying lips;*
        *And he that uttereth a slander is a fool.*
        'Slander shalt thou not speak, nor counsel which is not sure;
        He that maketh gossip, despised is his head.
        Nor shalt thou deal in slander, but speak what is pure.
        Evil shalt thou not utter, but say what is good.
        Of him that dealeth with slander, speaking evil,
        Shamash shall wait for his head with recompense.'
                           (*Babylonian Book of Proverbs.*)

x. 19:     *In the multitude of words there wanteth not transgression,*
        *But he that refraineth his lips doeth wisely.*
        'Make not wide thy mouth, but guard thy lips;
        The thoughts of thy mind thou shalt not speak at once,
        For then quickly what thou hast spoken thou wilt take back again.'
                           (*Babylonian Book of Proverbs.*)

xi. 2:     *When pride cometh, then cometh shame;*
        *But with the lowly is wisdom.*
'My son, cast down thine eyes, and lower thy voice, and look from beneath thine eyelids' (*Proverbs of Achikar*).

xi. 13:     *He that goeth about as a talebearer revealeth secrets;*
        *But he that is of a faithful spirit concealeth the matter.*
'Let not thy words be spread abroad among others' (*Teaching of Amen-em-ope*).
'My son Nadan, if thou hast heard a word, let it die in thy heart, and reveal it to

no man. . . . My son, do not tell all that thou hearest, and do not disclose all that thou seest. . . . My son, if thou hear an evil matter, put it seven fathoms deep underground' (*Proverbs of Achikar*).

'My son, do not chatter overmuch till thou reveal every word which comes into thy mind, for in every place are their eyes and their ears; but keep watch over thy mouth, let it not be thy destruction' (*Elephantiné Words of Achikar*).

**xi. 28:**    *He that trusteth in his riches shall fall;*
       *But the righteous shall flourish as the green leaf.*

'When thou hast become great after having been of no account, and hast amassed wealth after having previously suffered penury in thine own city, forget not thy former state. Trust not in thy riches, which were granted thee as a gift from the God' (*Teaching of Ptah-hotep*).

'One is rich, while another is poor. He who in the past year was wealthy, hath in this year become a stable-boy' (*Wisdom of Anii*).

**xii. 7:**    *The wicked are overthrown and are not;*
       *But the house of the righteous shall stand.*

'My son, the wicked falleth and riseth not; but the just man is not moved, for God is with him' (*Proverbs of Achikar*).

**xii. 19:**    *The lip of truth shall be established for ever,*
       *But a lying tongue is but for a moment.*

'My son, lie not in thy speech before thy lord, lest thou be convicted, and he shall say to thee, "Away from my sight." My son, let thy words be true, in order that thy lord may say to thee "Draw near", and thou shalt live.'

                                        (*Proverbs of Achikar.*)

**xii. 22:**    *Lying lips are an abomination to Jahweh,*
       *But they that deal truly are his delight.*
       'Speak not to a man in falsehood,
       The abomination of God;
       Sever not thy heart from thy tongue,
       That all thy ways may be prosperous.'   (*Teaching of Amen-em-ope.*)

**xii. 23:**    *A prudent man concealeth knowledge,*
       *But the heart of fools proclaimeth foolishness.*
       'He who concealeth his speech within himself
       Is better than he who uttereth it to his hurt.'
                                        (*Teaching of Amen-em-ope.*)

**xiii. 3.**    *He that guardeth his mouth keepeth his life;*
       *But he that openeth wide his lips shall have destruction.*
       'Sleep a night before speaking,
       Lest the tempest arise as a flame in the straw.'
                                        (*Teaching of Amen-em-ope.*)

**xiii. 7:**    *There is that maketh himself rich, yet hath nothing;*
       *There is that maketh himself poor, yet hath great wealth.*

'My son, put not a gold ring on thy finger when thou hast not wealth, lest fools make mock of thee' (*Proverbs of Achikar*). See also next quotation.

xiii. 11: *Wealth gotten in haste shall be diminished,*
*But he that gathereth slowly shall have increase.*

'Better is poverty that gathereth, than wealth that scattereth' (*Proverbs of Achikar*).

xiii. 17: *A wicked messenger falleth into evil,*
*But a faithful envoy (bringeth) security.*[1]

For the similar thoughts in the *Teaching of Ptah-hotep*, and in the *Teaching of Amen-em-ope*, see under xxvi. 6.

xiii. 20: *Walk with wise men, and thou shalt be wise;*
*But the companion of fools shall smart for it.*

'My son, associate with the wise man, and thou shalt become wise like him; and associate not with a garrulous and talkative man, lest thou be numbered with him' (*Proverbs of Achikar*).

xiii. 22: *A good man leaveth an inheritance to his children's children.*

'My son, while thou hast shoes on thy feet, tread down the thorns and make a path for thy son and for thy son's sons' (*Proverbs of Achikar*).

xiii. 24: See under xxiii. 13, 14.

xiv. 20: *The poor is hated even of his own neighbour,*
*But the rich hath many friends.*

'My son, he whose hand is full is called wise and honourable;
But he whose hand is scant is called abject and foolish.'

(*Proverbs of Achikar.*)

xv. 3: *The eyes of Jahweh are in every place,*
*Keeping watch upon the evil and the good.*

' . . . His eye travels round the Two Lands [i.e. Upper and Lower Egypt];
If he sees him that perverts with his finger [in reference to the scribe],
He takes away his provisions in the deep waters' (*Teaching of Amen-em-ope*).

xv. 4: *A wholesome tongue is a tree of life,*
*But perverseness therein is a breaking of the spirit.*

'If thy words are soothing to the heart, then will the heart incline to receive them' (*Wisdom of Anii*).

xv. 16: See under xvi. 8.

xv. 17: *Better is a dinner of herbs where love is,*
*Than a stalled ox and hatred therewith.*

'Better is bread with a happy heart,
Than wealth with trouble' (*Teaching of Amen-em-ope*).

xv. 21: *Folly is joy to him that is void of wisdom.*

'(The fool) regardeth wisdom as ignorance, and what is excellent as evil.'
(*Teaching of Ptah-hotep.*)

xv. 27: *He that is greedy of gain troubleth his own house;*
*But he that hateth gifts shall live.*[2]

'Bring no man into misfortune in a court of justice,
And disturb not the just man' (*Teaching of Amen-em-ope*).

---

[1] See notes in the Commentary. [2] The reference is to a judge.

xvi. 3: *Commit thy works unto Jahweh.*

'Place thyself in the arms of God' (*Teaching of Amen-em-ope*, where the same words occur more than once).

xvi. 8: *Better is a little with righteousness,*
*Than great revenues with injustice.*

'Better is poverty (being) in the hand of God,
Than wealth in the storehouse (i.e. without God).
Better is bread with a happy heart,
Than wealth with trouble.'

.    .    .    .    .    .    .

'Better is one bushel given thee by God,
Than five thousand unjustly gained.' (*Teaching of Amen-em-ope.*)

xvi. 9: *A man's heart deviseth his way,*
*But Jahweh directeth his steps.*

'The words which men say are one thing,
The things which God doeth are another.' (*Teaching of Amen-em-ope;* see further the notes in the Commentary.)

xvi. 11: *Balance and scales are Jahweh's,*
*All the weights of the bag are his work.*

'Move not the scales
And diminish not the part of the corn-measure.
The Ape [the symbol of the God Thoth] sitteth by the balance,
His heart being the plummet.[1]
Where is a god so great as Thoth,
Who discovered these things and made them!'

(*Teaching of Amen-em-ope.*)

xvi. 14: *The wrath of a king is as messengers of death;*
*But a wise man will pacify it.*

'In presence of a king, if (a thing) is commanded thee, it is a burning fire; hasten, do it; let it not kindle upon thee and hide (?) thy hands; for also the word of a king is with wrath of heart; why should wood strive with fire, flesh with a knife, a man with a king?' (*Wisdom of Achikar*, [Elephant. pap.])

xvi. 28: *A froward man scattereth abroad strife;*
*And a whisperer separateth chief friends.*

'My son, restrain a word in thy heart, and it shall be well with thee; because when thou hast exchanged thy word, thou hast lost thy friend' (*Proverbs of Achikar*).

xvii. 1: See under xvi. 8.

xvii. 5: *Whoso mocketh the poor reproacheth his Maker,*
*And he that is glad at him that is perishing shall not be unpunished.*

'Mock not at a man who is in the hand of God,
And be not wrath (?) with him when he hath transgressed.'

(*Teaching of Amen-em-ope.*)

---

[1] The plummet of Egyptian scales was often made in the form of a heart (Ranke).

xvii. 14: *In a multitude of words is the beginning of strife,*
*Therefore before contention breaketh out cease (words).*
'Do not join in wrangling with the hot-mouthed,
Nor goad with words;
Pause before an intruder [or adversary],
And give way unto him that attacketh.'

(Teaching of Amen-em-ope.)

xvii. 15: *He that justifieth the wicked, and he that condemneth the righteous,*
*Both of them alike are an abomination to Jahweh.*
'Do not pervert (?) a man in the law-court,
Nor disturb the just man.'
'Justice is a great gift of God,
He will give it to whom He will' (*Teaching of Amen-em-ope*).

xviii. 2: *A fool hath no delight in understanding,*
*But only that his heart may reveal itself.*
' . . . He regardeth wisdom as ignorance, and what is excellent as evil. He doeth that which is blameworthy, and daily he is reproached' (*Teaching of Ptah-hotep*).

xviii. 6, 7: *A fool's lips enter into contention,*
*And wrath calleth for stripes.*
*A fool's mouth is his destruction,*
*And his lips are the snare of his soul.*
'He is ruined and he is built up by his tongue,
Yet he maketh an ugly (?) speech;
He maketh an answer worthy of stripes,
For its burden is of evil' (*Teaching of Amen-em-ope* [1]).

xviii. 13: *He that giveth answer before he heareth,*
*It is folly and shame unto him.*
'Leap not to go in and meet him,
When thou hast not seen what he doeth.' (*Teaching of Amen-em-ope;* the reference is to the attitude to be adopted towards an opponent in debate.)

xviii. 21: *Death and life are in the power of the tongue,*
*And they that love it shall eat the fruit thereof.*
'My son, sweeten thy tongue, and make savoury the opening of thy mouth; for the tail of a dog giveth him bread, but his mouth getteth him blows.' (*Proverbs of Achikar.*)

xviii. 24: *He that maketh many friends doeth it to his own destruction.*
'If thou seekest the companionship of a friend . . . prove his heart through speaking with him. If he betrayeth something that he hath seen, or doeth something whereof thou art ashamed, take heed. . . .' (*Teaching of Ptah-hotep*).

---

[1] See notes in the Commentary.

xix. 7: *All the brethren of the poor do hate him;*
*How much more do his friends go far from him.*

'Friends exist not for a man on the day of troubles' (*Teaching of Amenemhet*).

'Friendship is of a day, but posterity is of eternity' (*Babylonian Proverb*).

xix. 11: *It is discretion in a man to restrain his anger,*
*And it is his glory to forgive transgression.*

'Be not angry; to be friendly is good. Let the memory of thee abide because of thy lovingkindness' (*Teaching for Meri-Ka-re*).

xix. 18: *Chasten thy son, seeing there is hope;*
*And set not thy heart on his destruction.*

'My son, subdue thy son while he is yet a boy, before he wax stronger than thee and rebel against thee, and thou be shamed in all his corrupt doing' (*Proverbs of Achikar*).

xx. 3: *It is an honour for a man to keep from strife;*
*But every fool will be quarrelling.*

'My son, stand not in the house of those that are at strife; because from a word there cometh a quarrel, and from a quarrel is stirred up vexation, and from vexedness springeth murder' (*Proverbs of Achikar*).

xx. 9: *Who can say, I have made my heart clean,*
*I am pure from my sin?*

'Say not, "I have no sin,"
And be not at pains to seek to (conceal it).' (*Teaching of Amen-em-ope*; see the notes on this passage in the Commentary.)

xx. 10: *Divers weights and divers measures,*
*Both of them alike are an abomination to Jahweh.*

'Move not the scales and falsify not the weights,
And diminish not the parts of the corn-measure.'

(*Teaching of Amen-em-ope.*)

xx. 19: *He that goeth about as a talebearer revealeth secrets;*
*Therefore meddle not with him that openeth wide his lips.*

' Utter no secret words, nor speak insolent words' (*Teaching of Duauf*).

' Utter not what is in thine heart to man. A wrong word, having issued from thy mouth, will, if he repeat it, make thee enemies. A man perisheth because of his tongue' (*Wisdom of Anii*).

'Let not thy words be spread abroad among others,
And have thou nothing to do with the chatterbox.'

(*Teaching of Amen-em-ope.*)

'My son, if thou hast heard a word,
Let it die in thy heart, and reveal it to no man' (*Proverbs of Achikar*).

' My son, do not chatter overmuch till thou reveal every word which cometh into thy mind; for in every place are their eyes and their ears; but keep watch over thy mouth, and let it not be thy destruction' (*Elephantiné Version of Achikar*).

xx. 20: *Whoso curseth his father or his mother,*
*His lamp shall he put out in the blackest darkness.*

'Give a double portion of bread to thy mother who bore thee' (*Wisdom of Anii*).

'Give food to eat and wine to drink,
Seek justice, feed and honour parents.
In such an one will his god have pleasure.
It is pleasing unto Shamash who will reward him with good.'
                (*Babylonian Book of Proverbs.*)

'My son, bring not upon thee the curses of thy father and of thy mother, lest thou rejoice not in the blessings of thy children' (*Proverbs of Achikar*).

'He who is not proud of the name of his father and the name of his mother, let not the sun shine upon him, for he is an evil man' (*Elephantiné Version of Achikar*).

xx. 22:    *Say not thou, I will recompense evil;*
            *Wait on Jahweh, and he shall save thee.*

'God knoweth the sinner, God punisheth him for the transgression in blood' (the meaning is a little uncertain; but according to Erman, the implication is that recompense is in the hand of God; *Teaching for Meri-Ka-re*).

'Say not, "Find me a strong chief,
For a man in thy city hath injured me."
Say not, "Find me a redeemer,
For a man whom I hate hath injured me."'
                (*Teaching of Amen-em-ope.*[1])

xx. 23:    See under xvi. 11.

xx. 24:    *A man's goings are of Jahweh,*
            *How then can man understand his way?*

'The counsel of God is full of knowledge, who understandeth it?'
                (*Babylonian Wisdom.*)

'Who the minds of the gods in heaven can learn?
The counsel of God full of subtlety who can comprehend?'
                (*Babylonian Book of Job.*)

xx. 27:    See the Commentary.

xx. 28:    *Mercy and truth preserve the king,*
            *And he upholdeth his throne by equity.*

'Do what is just as long as thou abidest on the earth. Comfort the weepers, worry not the widow, drive no man from his father's possession, and harm not the judges in their seat. Beware of punishing unjustly' (*Teaching for Meri-Ka-re*).

xxi. 1:    See the Commentary.

xxi 3:    See the Commentary.

xxi. 6:    *He that getteth treasures by a lying tongue . . .*
'My son, if thy will is to be wise, refrain thy tongue from lying, and thy hand from theft, and thou shalt become wise' (*Proverbs of Achikar*).

xxi. 23:   See under xiii. 3.

---

[1] See further the notes in the Commentary.

xxii. 1:    *A good name is rather to be chosen than great riches,*
              *And favour is better than silver and gold.*
              'Better is a good name than much beauty,
              Because a good name standeth for aye,
              But beauty waneth and wasteth away' (*Proverbs of Achikar*).

xxii. 9:    *He that hath a bountiful eye shall be blessed,*
              *For he giveth of his bread to the poor.*
'Eat no bread if another suffereth want, and thou hast not offered him bread in thine hand' (*Wisdom of Anii*).

The collection contained in xxii. 17–xxiii has so much in common with the *Teaching of Amen-em-ope*, the parallelism in some cases being extraordinarily close, that it will be best to set forth these in parallel columns. Passages of similar import from other Wisdom books will also be added in the right-hand column.

The rendering here given is taken from the German translations of Ranke and Lange together with Griffith's variations from them. It is very necessary that the explanatory notes in the commentary should be read.

| *Proverbs* | *The Teaching of Amen-em-ope* |
|---|---|
| xxii. 17. *Incline thine ear, and hear my words,* <br> *And apply thine heart to apprehend (them);* <br> 18. *For it is pleasant if thou keep them in thy belly,* <br> *That they may be fixed like a peg upon thy lips.* | I. iii. 9. 'Give thine ear, and hear what I say, <br> 10. And apply thine heart to apprehend. <br> 11. It is good to place them in thine heart, <br> 12. —Woe to him that refuseth them— <br> 13. Let them rest in the casket of thy belly, <br> 14. That they may be a threshold in thine heart; <br> 15. That if a hurricane of words arise, <br> 16. They may act as a peg upon thy tongue.' <br><br> Cp. also the *Teaching of Ptah-hotep*: <br> 'Instructing the ignorant to knowledge <br> And to the rules of good speech; <br> A profitable thing to him who shall obey, <br> (But) baneful to him that shall transgress it.' <br><br> Cp. also the *Proverbs of Achikar* ii. <br> 1: 'Hear, O my son Nadan, and come |

*Proverbs*     *The Teaching of Amen-em-ope*

to the understanding of me, and be mindful of my words, as the words of God.'

19. *That thy trust may be in Jah-weh,*
*I have made known to thee the ways of life.*

17. 'If thou spend thy lifetime with these things in thine heart,

18. Thou wilt find it bringeth prosperity,

iv. 1. Thou wilt find my words a storehouse of life,

2. And thy body will prosper on earth.' Cp. also:

Intr. i. 7. 'To direct (a man) upon the ways of life,

8. And to make him prosper on earth.'

20. *Have I not written for thee thirty sayings*
*Of counsels and knowledge!*

XXX. xxvii. 7. 'Consider these thirty chapters;

8. They delight, they instruct;

9. They are the chief among all books,

10. They make the unlearned wise!'

21. *That thou mayest make known truth to him that speaketh,*
*That thou mayest carry back words to him that sent thee.*

Intr. i. 5. 'Knowledge how to answer him that speaketh,

6. And (how) to carry back a report to one that sent him.'

Cp. the *Teaching of Ptah-hotep:*

'If thou art one of those trusted ones sent from one noble to another, do thy duty conscientiously if thou art sent. Thou must carry out thy commission as it is commanded thee. Of what he tells thee keep nothing secret, and beware of forgetting anything. Keep to the truth, and transgress it not, even though what thou hast to tell be unpleasant. Beware of making bad blood which would cause one noble to despise the other through the talk of people.'

See also under xxvi. 6.

22. *Rob not the poor, because he is poor,*
*Neither oppress the lowly in the gate.*

II. iv. 4. 'Beware of robbing the poor

5. And of oppressing the afflicted.'

| *Proverbs* | *The Teaching of Amen-em-ope* |
|---|---|
| 23. | No parallel |

| 24. *Associate not with a passionate man,* *Nor go with a wrathful man,* | IX. xi. 13. 'Associate not with a passionate man, |
|---|---|
| | 14. Nor approach him for conversation.' |

| 25. *Lest thou learn his ways,* *And get a snare to thy soul.* | xiii. 8. 'Leap not to cleave to such an one, |
|---|---|
| | 9. That the terror carry thee not away.' Cp. also: |
| | xi. 17. 'For he is able to ensnare thee with his words, |
| | 18. (Therefore) give not free rein to thine answer.' |

| 26, 27. | No parallel. |
|---|---|
| 28. | See under xxiii. 10, 11 below. |

| 29. *A man who is skilful in his business* *Shall stand before kings.* | XXX. xxvii. 16. 'A scribe who is skilful in his business |
|---|---|
| | 17. Findeth himself worthy to be a courtier.' |

| xxiii. 1. *When thou sittest to eat with a ruler,* *Consider diligently what is before thee;* | XXIII. xxiii. 13. 'Eat not bread in the presence of a ruler, |
|---|---|
| 2. *And put a knife to thy throat,* *If thou be a man given to appetite.* | 14. And do not lunge forward (?) with thy mouth before a governor (?). |
| 3. *Be not desirous of his dainties,* *Seeing they are deceitful meat.* | 15. When thou art replenished with that to which thou hast no right, |
| | 16. It is only a delight to thy spittle. |
| | 17. Look upon the dish that is before thee, |
| | 18. And let that (alone) supply thy need.' |

Cp. the *Teaching of Ptah-hotep:*
'If thou art one who sitteth where the table of a greater man than thou standeth, take what is set before thee when he giveth it. Do not dart many glances at him. . . . Look downwards till he greet thee, and only speak after he hath greeted thee. Laugh when he laugheth. That will greatly

*Proverbs*

*The Teaching of Amen-em-ope*

cheer his heart; and what thou doest will be pleasant to him. One knoweth not what is in his mind.'

The *Teaching for Ka-Gemni:*

'When thou sittest (at table) with many others, refuse the food, even when thou likest it. It only meaneth self-control for a moment; and it is horrid to appear greedy.'

The *Proverbs of Achikar* :

'My son, eat thy portion, and despise not thy neighbours.'

4. *Toil not to become rich,*
   *And cease from thy dishonest gain ;*
5. *For wealth maketh to itself wings,*
   *Like an eagle that flieth heavenwards.*

VII. ix. 14. 'Toil not after riches,
   15. When thy needs are made sure to thee.
   16. If stolen goods are brought to thee,
   17. They remain not over the night with thee;
   18. At daybreak they are no more in thy house.
   19. One seeth where they were, but they are not (there).
   20. The earth hath opened its mouth and swallowed them ;

x. 1. They are drowned in the underworld ;
   2. (Or) They have made them a great hole which fitteth them ;
   3. They are sunk in the treasure-house ;
   4. (Or) they have made for themselves wings like geese,
   5. And have flown into the heavens.'

6. *Eat thou not the bread of him that hath an evil eye,*
   *Nor desire thou his dainties.*
7. .    .    .    .
   [*And as one who has choking in his throat*]
   *Eat and drink, saith he to thee,*
   *But his heart is not with thee.*

XI. xiv. 5. 'Covet not the goods of a dependent,
   6. And hunger not after his bread.
   7. The property of a dependent is a choking for the throat,
   8. And as a vomiting for the gullet.
      [Four lines follow]
   13. When thou failest before thy chief,

d

| *Proverbs* | *The Teaching of Amen-em-ope* |
|---|---|
| 8. *The morsel which thou hast eaten shalt thou vomit up, And lose thy sweet (things).* | 14. And art embarrassed in thine utterances, |
| | 15. Thy flatteries are answered by curses, |
| | 16. And thine obeisance by beating. |
| | 17. Thou swallowest (indeed) thy too great mouthful, and must vomit it forth again, |
| | 18. And thus be emptied of thy good.' |
| 9. *Speak not in the hearing of a fool, For he will despise the wisdom of thy words.* | XXI. xxii. 11. 'Empty not thine inmost soul to everybody, |
| | 12. Nor spoil (thereby) thine influence.' |
| 10. *Remove not the widow's landmark, And enter not into the fields of the fatherless;* | VI. vii. 12. 'Remove not the landmark from the bounds of the field, |
| | 13. Nor shift the position of the measuring-cord. |
| 11. *For their redeemer is strong, He shall plead their cause against thee.* | 14. Covet not (even) a cubit of land, |
| | 15. And violate not the widow's boundary. |
| | 16. A furrow ... worn by time, |
| | 17. He who wrongfully seizeth it in a field, |
| | 18. Though he claim it with false oaths, |
| | 19. Will be taken captive by the might of the Moon (-God).' |
| 12. *Apply thine heart unto instruction, And thine ears to the words of knowledge.* | I. iii. 8. 'Give thine ears, hear (the words) that are said, Give thine heart to interpret them.' |

xxiii. 13, 14: *Withhold not correction from the child; Though thou beat him with the rod, he will not die. Thou shalt beat him with the rod, And shalt deliver his soul from Shĕól.*

'Withhold not thy son from the rod if thou canst not keep him from wickedness. If I smite thee, my son, thou wilt not die, but if I leave thee to thine own heart thou wilt not live' (*Proverbs of Achikar, Elephantiné Version*).

xxiii. 35: *They have stricken me, shalt thou say, and I was not hurt, They have beaten me and I felt it not.*

'My son, withdraw at the first cup, and tarry not for lickerish draughts, lest there be to thee wounds in thy head' (*Proverbs of Achikar*).

xxiv. 1:     *Be not thou envious against evil men,*
            *Neither desire to be with them.*
'Keep far from an unfriendly man, and take him not as a companion' (*Wisdom of Anii*).

xxiv. 11:     *Deliver them that are carried away to death,*
            *And those who are tottering to slaughter hide.*
        'Cry not "Crime" at a man.
        Hide the manner of (a fugitive's) flight' (*Teaching of Amen-em-ope*).

xxiv. 12:     *Doth not he that weigheth the hearts consider it?*
See the reference to the *Teaching of Amen-em-ope* in the Commentary.

xxiv. 17:     *Rejoice not when thine enemy falleth,*
            *And let not thine heart be glad when he is overthrown.*
        'My son, envy not the prosperity of thine enemy,
        And rejoice not at his adversity.'
        'My son, if thine enemy meet thee with evil,
        Meet thou him with wisdom' (*Proverbs of Achikar*).

xxiv. 29:     *Say not, 'I will do so to him as he hath done to me,*
            *I will render to the man according to his work.'*
See the quotation from the *Teaching of Amen-em-ope* under xx. 22.
        'Unto him that doeth thee evil shalt thou return good,
        Unto thine enemy justice shalt thou mete out' (*Babylonian proverb*).

xxv. 15:     *A soft tongue breaketh the bone.*
'Soft is the tongue of a king, but it breaketh the ribs of a dragon' (*Proverbs of Achikar*, Elephantiné version; the similarity is only in expression; the application is quite different).

xxv. 17:     *Let thy foot be seldom in thy neighbour's house,*
            *Lest he be weary of thee and hate thee.*
        'My son, let not thy foot run after thy friend,
        Lest he be surfeited with thee and hate thee' (*Proverbs of Achikar*).

xxv. 18:     *A man that beareth false witness against his neighbour*
            *Is a maul, and a sword, and a sharp arrow.*
        'There was a cruel witness against me,
        And who then has justified me?' (*Proverbs of Achikar*.)

xxv. 21:     *If thine enemy be hungry, give him bread to eat,*
            *And if he be thirsty, give him water to drink.*
See the quotations under xx. 22, xxiv. 17, 29.

xxvi. 6:     *He that sendeth a message by the hand of a fool,*
            *He cutteth off (his) feet, and drinketh in wrath.*
'My son, send a wise man, and give him no orders; but if thou wilt send a fool, go rather thyself, and send him not' (*Proverbs of Achikar*).

xxvi. 16:     *The sluggard is wiser in his own eyes*
            *Than seven men that answer discreetly* (cf. xxvii. 2).
        'My son, count not thyself to be wise,
        When others count thee not to be wise' (*Proverbs of Achikar*).

xxvi. 21: *As bellows are to hot embers and wood to fire,*
*So is a contentious man to inflame strife.*
'His lips are sweet, his tongue bitter,
But flame burns in his belly' (*Teaching of Amen-em-ope*).

xxvii. 1: *Boast not thyself of to-morrow,*
*For thou knowest not what a day may bring forth.*
'Of a truth thou knowest not the design of God,
Thou canst not realize the morrow.'
'Man knoweth not how the morrow will be,
The events of the morrow are in the hands of God.
(*Teaching of Amen-em-ope.*)
'He who was alive yester-eve died on the morrow;
In a moment was he troubled, quickly was he crushed.'
(*Babylonian Book of Job.*)

xxvii. 2: See under xxvi. 16.

xxvii. 5, 6: *Better is open rebuke*
*Than love that is hidden;*
*Faithful are the wounds of a friend;*
*But the kisses of an enemy are* [*untrue*, lit. *perverse* (?)].
'My son, let the wise man strike thee with many blows,
And let not the fool salve thee with sweet salve' (*Proverbs of Achikar*).

xxvii. 7: *The full soul loatheth an honeycomb;*
*But to the hungry soul every bitter thing is sweet.*
'Hunger sweeteneth what is bitter,
And thirst [text mutilated].'
(*Proverbs of Achikar, Elephantiné Version.*)

xxvii. 8: *As a bird that wandereth from her nest,*
*So is a man that wandereth from his place.*
'My son, the flock that maketh many tracks
Becometh the portion of wolves' (*Proverbs of Achikar*).

xxvii. 10: *Thine own friend, and thy father's friend, forsake not;*
*And go not to thy brother's house in the day of thy calamity;*
*Better is a neighbour that is near than a brother far off.*
'My son, remove not from thy father's friend,
Lest perchance thy friend come not near to thee.'
'My son, better is a friend that is at hand,
Than a brother who is far away' (*Proverbs of Achikar*).

xxvii. 14: *He that greeteth his friend with a loud voice,*
*It shall be counted a curse to him.*
'Salute not thy passionate (opponent), forcing thyself,
Nor grieve thine own heart (thereby);
Say not to him, 'Hail to thee,' in falsehood,
When there is terror in thy belly.'
(*Teaching of Amen-em-ope*; see the notes in the Commentary.)

xxvii. 17: *Iron sharpeneth iron,*
*So a man sharpeneth his friend.*
'My son, with a wise man thou wilt not be depraved,
And with a depraved man thou wilt not become wise.
My son, associate with the wise man, and thou wilt become wise
like him;
And associate not with a garrulous and talkative man, lest thou be
numbered with him.' (*Proverbs of Achikar*; see the notes in
the Commentary.)

xxvii. 20: *Shĕôl and 'Abaddôn are never satisfied,*
*And the eyes of man are never satisfied.*
'My son, the eye of man is like a fountain of water,
And it is not satisfied with riches until filled with dust' (*Proverbs of Achikar*).

xxvii. 22: *Though thou bray a fool in a mortar,*
*Yet wilt thou not remove his foolishness from him.*
'(Even) if thou smite the fool with many blows,
(Yet) will he not understand' (*Proverbs of Achikar*).

xxviii. 5: *Evil men understand not judgement;*
*But they that seek Jahweh understand all things.*
'My son, every one who doth not judge right judgement angereth God'
(*Proverbs of Achikar*).

xxviii. 19: *He that tilleth his land shall have plenty of bread.*
'Plough thine own fields, then wilt thou find what is needful,
And wilt obtain bread from thine own threshing-floor.'
(*Teaching of Amen-em-ope.*)

xxviii. 20: See under xiii. 11.

xxix. 5: *A man that flattereth his neighbour,*
*Spreadeth a net for his steps.*
'Like a net trouble hath covered me' (*Babylonian Book of Job*).

xxxi. 30: *Favour is deceitful, and beauty is vain,*
*But a woman of intelligence, she shall be praised.*
'My son, go not after the beauty of a woman, and lust not after her in thy
heart; because the beauty of a woman is her good sense, and her adornment is
the word of her mouth' (*Proverbs of Achikar*).

We have thus well over a hundred instances of community of
thought, and at times something more, between passages in *Proverbs*
and sayings from other Wisdom books, which are extra-Israelite.

In reading these it is impossible to get away from the conviction
that the whole of this material, Hebraic and non-Hebraic, belongs,
in its essence, to one and the same mould; in other words, that the
Wisdom Literature of the Hebrews formed a part of the much larger
Wisdom Literature of the ancient east as a whole.

In some of the parallels given above the resemblance may appear
to be superficial at first sight, but, as a rule, a careful scrutiny in

comparing them shows some underlying community of thought; and this occurs too often to be fortuitous. Allowance must, moreover, be made for the difference in the mode of expression of a similar thought by writers of different nationality writing in a different language. It is not too bold to assert that in many cases the similarity is, in all probability, much closer in reality than appears upon the surface. Take, for example, an Egyptian sage and a Hebrew sage, each formulating an identical thought according to his individual mode of linguistic expression; this must necessarily differ in each case, both when common floating material is being utilized, as well as when one is directly indebted to the other. But this difference in outward form will not blind one to the essential *identity of thought* underlying each when this is to be discerned; and it is this latter which must be looked for as the really important factor in all the examples given.

But there are other instances in which in addition to identity of thought there are verbal parallels; and here the question naturally arises as to which of the two is indebted to the other. It is not denied that here a certain amount of subjectivity is almost inevitable; at the same time, some *criteria* of a definite character are not altogether wanting. When, for example, an un-Hebraic thought occurs in a Hebrew saying, a parallel to which is found in an Egyptian saying, doubt as to who is the borrower can hardly arise; so that in such a saying as occurs in Prov. xvi. 11 it is quite obvious that the Hebrew is indebted to the Egyptian sage. Conversely, in the case of Prov. xx. 9 it is pretty evident that the Egyptian is indebted to the Hebrew sage.

But in most cases the issue is not so clear, and probably common material has been utilized and there is no indebtedness on either side. Each instance must be decided on its merits; and that is where the subjective element is almost bound to come in; we recognize the danger.

Of special interest are the quite obvious parallels between Prov. xxii. 17–xxiii. 14 and the *Teaching of Amen-em-ope*, and here, for a variety of reasons, we are forced to the conclusion that the Hebrew sage has made copious use of the Egyptian Wisdom book; into these reasons we cannot go now.[1]

Interesting, too, are the parallels between *Proverbs* and the *Proverbs of Achikar*. There are seventy-five sayings in the Babylonian Wisdom book, of which more than half are paralleled in *Proverbs*. The Syriac form of *Achikar* is late, and it seems certain that in its

---

[1] See the present writer's *The Wisdom of Egypt and the Old Testament* (1927).

present from it owes much to *Proverbs*; but even so there is over-
whelming proof that it belongs originally to a time long anterior to
*Proverbs* as now constituted; and there are instances of parallelism
which suggest that the Hebrew sage utilized the Babylonian book.
The Elephantiné form of *Achikar*, when compared with the Syriac
form, raises an interesting problem which, unfortunately, cannot be
dealt with here.

One concluding remark. With one or two exceptions, whenever the
Hebrew sage has utilized some extraneous source for the construction
of a saying, he has not failed to make it his own, and has thereby
transformed it into something much better than it was before.

## II

## THE RELIGIOUS VALUE OF *PROVERBS*

Since the Hebrew Sages regarded wisdom as essentially religious
(i. 7), indeed, as an attribute to God Himself (viii. 22–31), and since,
in consequence, every form of wisdom, according to them,—the less
exalted forms, such as ordinary skill, shrewdness, foresight, &c., as
well as its higher forms,—had a religious content of some kind, it is
evident that, according to their purpose and intention, *all* that they
wrote about wisdom was to be regarded as partaking of a religious
character. To act wisely is to act in accordance with the divine will;
nay, the very object of acting wisely is that God's will may be done;
thus it is true to say that from the Sages' point of view worldly wisdom
is piety. This must be recognized if in seeking to estimate the religious value of *Proverbs* due justice is to be done to the writers.

Now there are many passages in our book which, taken by themselves, as isolated sayings, appear to be entirely devoid of any religious content. To give a few examples:

> He that is surety for a stranger shall suffer for it,
> But he that hateth suretyship is sure (xi. 15).

> A wicked messenger causeth (one) to fall into evil,
> But a faithful envoy is profitable (xiii. 17).

> The appetite of a labouring man laboureth for him,
> For his mouth urgeth him (thereto) (xvi. 26).

> The rich man's wealth is his strong city,
> And as an high wall in his estimation (xviii. 11).

Passages such as these, and there are many of a similar character,
would, as they stand, be quite naturally interpreted and understood
in a purely secular way. Such an interpretation would, however, not
be just to the writer. These collections of proverbs have a very definite

religious foundation, and a no less definite religious atmosphere permeates them; this must soon become evident even to the undis-
cerning reader; and this religious background and environment
must be given due weight if these apparently purely secular sayings
are to be interpreted and understood from the writer's point of view.
The four passages quoted could, apart from their *milieu*, be explained
as expressing such commonplace truths as that ordinary caution in
money matters should be observed, that it pays to employ a reliable
messenger, that a man must work if he wants to eat, and that wealth
is power. All things which must appeal to the most unreligious man
of the world, and which in themselves have not necessarily anything
to do with religion. But if understood and interpreted from the
writer's point of view and in the light of his intention, they all *have*
a religious content. Prudence and reliability are God-given forms of
wisdom; the hunger which impels a man to work belongs to the
divine economy; wealth is a good thing, but entails responsibilities
to God and man. That is the way in which the Sages envisaged these
things; there was a Godward thought at the back of their minds in all
that they wrote which hallowed what we call worldly wisdom, and
which sanctified common sense. It is, therefore, maintained that if
we would be fair to the writers, and understand their sayings from
their point of view and intention, we must recognize that there is a
religious content in all the apparently purely secular utterances
which are scattered among the more explicitly religious ones in these
collections.

Thus, one important element which emphasizes the religious value
of the book is that it teaches that even in the ordinary acts of everyday life men must realize that they cannot separate themselves from
the relationship which exists between God and themselves; they
may ignore that relationship, and often do, with woeful consequences
to themselves, as the Sages are never tired of pointing out; but as beings created by God and therefore with duties to Him, men can per-
form no act in which God is not concerned.

But the type of sayings referred to occur far less frequently than
the very definite religious utterances with which the book abounds;
and it is these which so amply illustrate its religious value.

First we have the *Conception of God*. That a monotheistic faith is
nowhere expressed in the book in so many words cannot excite surprise; it is not called for, partly because belief in One God is taken for
granted, and partly because doctrinal definitions are not to be looked
for in a book on practical ethics. But as to the Divine Personality
the Sages are sufficiently explicit. He is the All-Creator (iii. 19, viii.

22–31, xvi. 4, xx. 12), who is the disposer of all things (xvi. 1, 33);
His purpose stands, whatever man may do (xix. 21, xxi. 30, 31); His
all-seeing eye perceives the doings of men, and their hearts lie open
before Him (v. 21, xv. 3, 11, xvii. 3). His ethical character is insisted
on again and again; the perfect and upright man is His delight (xi.
20, xii. 2, 22, &c.), justice and judgement are more acceptable to
Him than sacrifice (xxi. 3); on the other hand, everything that
offends against righteousness is abhorrent to Him (iii. 33, v. 16 ff.,
xii. 22, xv. 25, xvi. 5, xx. 10, &c.). It is the ethical monotheism as
taught by the prophets.

Further, *the mutual relationship between God and man* is a constant
theme, and is brought out in a variety of ways. The 'Fear of the
Lord' is a phrase which occurs about a score of times, and is inculcated in all parts of the book. It is God who takes care of men (x. 3,
xx. 24, xxii. 22, 23), who is their shield of defence (ii. 7), who hears
their prayer (xv. 29), who rewards righteous dealing (xxv. 22), whose
blessing brings prosperity (x. 22, 29), whose very name is a strong
tower of refuge (xviii. 10); therefore men are bidden to honour Him
(iii 9), to wait on Him (xx. 22, xxii. 12, 19), to put their trust in Him
(iii. 5, 6, xvi. 20, xxii. 19, xxviii. 25, xxix. 25), and to commit all their
works unto Him (xvi. 3).

It will thus be seen that the thoughts about God, and of His intimate relationship with men, whether in regard to their devotion
to Him, or to His direct interest in their everyday affairs of life,—
in a word, the Godward attitude of the writers as expressed in this
book,—show its high religious value in spite of its predominantly
ethical character so far as outward form is concerned.

The subject of *Free-will*, which figures very prominently, is important in considering the religious value of the book. And here
again, if isolated sayings are taken and dealt with apart from the
religious atmosphere which underlies and permeates the book as a
whole, it might well appear that the emphasis placed on human free-
will were not adequately balanced by a sufficient recognition of
divine grace; but this would not be a just estimate. The practice
of such virtues as truth (i. 2, iii. 3), love (x. 12), self-control (vi. 24,
25, xiv. 29), modesty (xi. 2, xviii. 12), moderation (xvii. 1, xxiii. 1–3),
industry (xx. 13, xxi. 5), courage (xxviii. 1), and others, and of such
vices as pride (xiii. 10, xvi. 18), bad temper (xiv. 29), covetousness
(xv. 27), bearing false witness (xix. 9), sloth (xix. 24, xx. 4), drunkenness (xx. 1), lying (xx. 17, xxi. 6), taking revenge (xxiv. 17), slander
(xxv. 23), &c., are mentioned indiscriminately as things in which man
takes the initiative of his own-free will; and that is, of course, in

accordance with fact; but it is implied, and often explicitly stated, that God guides men to good actions and keeps them from evil if called upon, thus showing a belief in divine grace both as an incentive to well-doing, and a preventive in wrong-doing. It is perfectly true that the main stress is laid upon human free-will, just as in later Judaism; but it would not be right on that account to assume that the action of divine grace was believed to be only secondary. As already remarked, in an ethical treatise one must not look for doctrinal definitions, but there could hardly be a more nicely balanced statement on this subject than that expressed in xvi. 6:

> *By mercy and truth iniquity is atoned for,*
> *And by the fear of Jahweh men depart from evil.*

We may not be prepared, in the light of fuller revelation, to endorse altogether what is said in the first line, but in so far as acts of mercy and truth must be accomplished by man's co-operating will we can agree with it; the second line is a very definite statement regarding the action of divine grace.

It is, further, only one side of the truth to say that right-doing is inculcated, and wrong-doing deprecated, solely on utilitarian grounds. While there may be some truth in Toy's statement that 'the motive for good living is individualistic, utilitarian, or eudæmonistic—not the glory of God, or the welfare of men in general, but the well-being of the actor', yet this is not the whole truth; it is impossible to read what is said in *Proverbs* about God's relationship to men without seeing that so far as the Sages themselves were concerned they implicitly assumed a Godward intention among the motives which should impel men to right-doing or which should restrain them from wrong-doing:

> *The fining pot is for silver, and the furnace for gold;*
> *But Jahweh trieth the hearts* (xvii. 3).

> *Every way of a man is right is his own eyes;*
> *But Jahweh weigheth the hearts* (xxi. 2).

Once more, it is true that there is no explicit mention of *Repentance*; but that the Sages regarded the need of this as essential, and took it for granted among right-minded men, is to be gathered from such passages as the following:

> *Who can say, I have made my heart clean,*
> *I am pure from my sin?* (xx. 9).

> *He that covereth his transgressions shall not prosper;*
> *But whoso confesseth and forsaketh them shall obtain mercy.*
> *Happy is the man that feareth alway;*
> *But he that hardeneth his heart shall fall into calamity* (xxviii. 13, 14).

In dealing with the subject of the religious value of *Proverbs* one has to remember that the underlying purpose of the Wisdom writers was to apply the religion of the Law and the Prophets, so far as this had developed, to the practical, everyday life of the individual; if this is done, it will be realized that even though religious expression may not be so prominent as in many other of the Old Testament books, yet the essence of all that is written has a religious basis; and if the main stress is laid on ethics, it must be remembered that to the Sages ethics and religion were inseparable. (See further the next Excursus.)

# III
## THE HEBREW CONCEPTION OF WISDOM

With the origin of the conception of Wisdom we are not concerned here; suffice to say that as conceived of as an elemental principle there is every reason to believe that Hebrew thought was influenced by Babylonian ideas.[1] The few passages in the Wisdom Literature which deal with the transcendental character of Wisdom (Prov. viii. 22–31, Job xxviii, Ecclus. i. 1–10, xxiv, Wisdom vii. 22–viii. 1) are quite exceptional; we are thinking at present of what is ordinarily understood by Wisdom.

In the book of *Proverbs*, and in the Wisdom Literature generally, the Hebrew *Chokmah* ('wisdom') never means pure knowledge. In its earliest meaning wisdom connoted 'the faculty of distinguishing between what was useful or beneficent, and what was harmful; later, more ethically, between what was good and what was bad'.[2] In the Wisdom Literature there is an intermingling of both these ideas regarding wisdom, but with the Sages there is always, or almost always, a *religious* content in it. We may perhaps illustrate this in the following way: as an example of a purely secular wise saying let us take 1 Kgs. xx. 11: *Let not him that girdeth on his armour boast himself as he that putteth it off*; to do this is not wise because it may result in a man bringing ridicule upon himself, i. e. it is harmful; wisdom here is to refrain from doing what is harmful. In this case there is no religious content whatsoever in the idea of wisdom. But the Wisdom writers, owing to the conception of Wisdom which was one of their special contributions to the subject, viz. its essentially religious character, make the most secular proverb partake of a

---

[1] See the present writer's *The Books of the Apocrypha: their origin, teaching, and contents*, pp. 224 ff. (1914); see also the notes to Chap. viii in the Commentary.

[2] *The Books of the Apocrypha*, p. 234.

religious content. So that when one of them says: *The simple believeth every word, but the prudent man looketh well to his going* (Prov. xiv. 15)—a proverb which in itself might be purely secular—he sees in it a religious saying because to him *every* form of wisdom is from God and therefore every wise act is a religious act; while every form of un-wisdom is opposed to the divine will and therefore an irreligious act. To the Wisdom writers every form of wisdom, as just remarked, comes from God; therefore, although the highest form of it is the knowledge and fear of the Lord, the lower forms of wisdom are none the less also part of the great gift of God; in other words, worldly wisdom in its manifold forms does not differ in kind, but only in degree, from wisdom at its highest. Thus it is that the Wisdom writers see in the most diverse kinds of wisdom something in the nature of a religious act, whether it be diligence whereby a man may become rich (x. 4), or industry which brings its reward (xii. 11, Ecclus. vii. 15), or reticence (xii. 8, xxi. 23), or a word in due season (xv. 23), or pleasant speech (xvi. 24), or forethought (Ecclus. xxxii. 12 ff.), or knowledge (xiv. 8), or self-control (xxiii. 1, 2), or good behaviour in society (Ecclus. xxxiv. 12 ff.), or the physician's art (Ecclus. xxxviii. 1 ff.), or the care of flocks (xxvii. 23), or the work of the craftsman (Ecclus. xxxviii. 32 ff.), and so on. So that the Wisdom writers with their wide-embracing idea of the essence of wisdom in its endless forms, bring religion into every nook and cranny of daily life. That this is what they were bent upon is evident from the fact that all such things as those just mentioned—and there are many others of a similar kind—things which in themselves are purely secular, are interspersed among the far greater number of sayings in which the directly religious note is definitely expressed.

If the lowest forms of wisdom have a religious content it is unnecessary to emphasize the fact that every higher form must have the same, and of course in a greater degree; in the great mass of the sayings these higher forms of wisdom are dealt with, for it was the Sages' striving to inculcate all the virtues, and to make people understand that to lead a sensible, that is a wise, life was to lead a religious life. That was the special *métier* of the Wisdom writers. Other things indispensable to leading a religious life,—and indeed the highest things,—are not dealt with by them. Prayer, worship, keeping the divine commandments, are only incidentally referred to; they are taken for granted; they are the highest of all forms of wisdom; they would be included under 'the fear of the Lord' which is the zenith of all wisdom. That these are not more fully dealt with does not mean that the Wisdom writers were wanting in deep religious feeling;

it is simply that they were called upon to emphasize one aspect of the religious sense; and it was one which was peculiarly required, since it meant the religious education of adolescents. This teaching of wisdom in its manifold forms was primarily addressed to young men; and the Sages' presentation of wisdom was calculated to appeal especially to them. However, what we have more especially desired to point out here is the wide sense in which ' wisdom ' was used by the Sages.

# IV

## THE DOCTRINE OF RETRIBUTION AND REWARD

The teaching of the Sages on this subject is presented in two forms; one rationalistic, the other religious.

As to the former, it is emphasized again and again that there is an inevitable correspondence between what a man says or does and what he experiences in consequence:

> *Poverty and shame (are the lot of) him that refuseth instruction,*
> *But he that regardeth reproof shall be honoured* (xiii. 18).

> *Slothfulness casteth into a deep sleep,*
> *And the idle soul shall suffer hunger* (xix. 15).

And so too with grosser sins; of murderers it is said:

> *These lay wait for their own blood,*
> *They lurk privily for their own lives* (i. 18).

And of the adulterer:

> *He that committeth adultery with a woman is void of understanding,*
> *He doeth it that would destroy his own soul* (vi. 32).

In the same way, right doing brings advantage:

> *The liberal soul shall be made fat;*
> *And he that watereth shall be watered also himself* (xi. 25).

> *The high way of the upright is to depart from evil,*
> *He that keepeth his way preserveth his soul* (xvi. 17).

> *He that is slow to anger is better than the mighty,*
> *And he that ruleth his spirit than he that taketh a city* (xvi. 32).

This kind of teaching occurs very often; to the mature man it would, of course, appear as self-evident; but it was for youths without knowledge of life, and without the foresight born of experience, of whom the Wisdom writers thought primarily. The appeal is always to self-interest; it is rarely, if ever, that a higher motive is put forth; to refrain from evil because it is evil, or to do good for good's sake, is never held up as an ideal. Nor is it hinted that an evil course should be avoided because of the harm it might do to others, either by example or by more direct effect; and, in the same way, right action is not inculcated because others might benefit from it. This continual appeal to self-interest may strike one as ignoble; but in extenuation it must be remembered that *practical* pædagogics was the *métier* of the Sages; they never profess to be idealists; to make a young man a sensible and decent member of society was their main object. Further, there is the fact that this practical, common-sense, and purely secular form of wisdom was the earliest form; and, as such, there is no doubt whatsoever that it was the heritage of much earlier times, and probably largely based on extraneous sources, as can be seen by a reference to the older Egyptian Wisdom books with their purely ethical teaching. And, therefore, the Hebrew Sages had a tradition before them which they very naturally followed; and, moreover, there was, in later days, no need to modify the forms of these precepts, the product of an earlier tradition, because since the Sages taught that Wisdom in its most diverse forms was of divine origin, therefore even those precepts which inculcated nothing more than common prudence, caution, forethought, &c., were regarded as containing a religious element.

However, in the first instance, the Sages' teaching on Retribution partook of a non-religious character.

The other form of this teaching presented is of a religious character. Right or wrong action, with its respective consequences, is not only a question of cause and effect; and it is difficult to resist the conviction that this must be a later stage in the doctrine of Retribution among the Wisdom teachers, although it is true that there is no evidence to show this. This side of the teaching points to *divine* retribution or reward as the result respectively of an evil or a righteous course:

> *Jahweh will not suffer the soul of the righteous to famish,*
> *But he thrusteth away the desire of the wicked* (x. 3).

> *They that are perverse in heart are an abomination to Jahweh;*
> *But such as are perfect in their way are his delight* (xi. 20).

> *Jahweh is far from the wicked;*
> *But he heareth the prayer of the righteous* (xv. 29).

> *When a man's ways please Jahweh,*
> *He maketh even his enemies to be at peace with him* (xvi. 7).

> *The reward of humility and the fear of Jahweh*
>   *Is riches, honour, and life* (xxii. 4, see also *v.* 12, xxv. 21, 22,
>   xxviii. 25).

What is very noticeable about this side of the Sages' doctrine of retribution is that it receives vastly less attention than the purely rationalistic view. Perhaps it is rash to hazard the suggestion, but sometimes one receives the impression that the references to God in this connexion were the work of some more pious scribes who added them because the secular tone of the sayings was (generally speaking) felt to be unsatisfactory.

However this may be, the predominantly secular tone of this very prominent element in *Proverbs* points to a pre-exilic rather than to a post-exilic time; in the latter religion came to occupy a larger place in the life of the people, and therefore the comparative absence of an explicit religious tone in so much of the teaching of the book indicates the earlier period.

One other thing in connexion with this subject demands brief notice. In various passages the Wisdom writers, in conformity with traditional belief, assert as a fact that the righteous enjoy prosperity, while the reverse is the lot of the wicked, e.g.:

> *There shall no mischief happen unto the righteous;*
> *But the wicked shall be filled with evil* (xii. 21).

> *The righteous shall never be removed;*
> *But the wicked shall not dwell in the land* (x. 30).

> *The house of the wicked shall be overthrown;*
> *But the tent of the upright shall flourish* (xiv. 11).

> *Evil pursueth sinners;*
> *But the righteous shall be recompensed with good* (xiii. 21).

In these and all other similar passages, the reward or punishment always takes place in this life (ch. xi. 31); there is never any thought of recompense or retribution beyond the grave because of the undeveloped belief concerning the Hereafter (see Excursus V).

That the facts of life constantly contradicted what was here taught did not seem to trouble the Wisdom writers any more than it did many of the Psalmists. The attitude they took up towards this problem was twofold. Sometimes there is the frank recognition that they do not understand it:

> *A man's goings are of Jahweh,*
> *How then can man understand his way?* (xx. 24).

If perplexity of this kind arises it is but the more necessary for a man to put his trust and hope in God:

> *Let not thine heart envy sinners,*
> *But fear Jahweh all the day long,*[1]
> *For if thou keepest it there is a reward,*[1]
> *And thy hope shall not be cut off* (xxiii. 17, 18, see also xxiv. 19, 20).

---

[1] For the justification of these renderings see the Commentary.

And in any case there was the knowledge that the wicked were hateful to God, but that He was a friend to the righteous:

> *Envy not thou the man of violence,*
> *And choose none of his ways;*
> *For the perverse is an abomination unto Jahweh,*
> *But his friendship is with the upright* (iii. 31, 32).

It was, moreover, pointed out that in the case of a good man his posterity would reap the reward:

> *A good man leaveth his inheritance to his children's children* (xiii. 22).
>
> *The seed of the righteous shall be delivered* (xi. 21).

But there was another attitude which the Sages sometimes adopted in face of this perplexity, and that was that things would sooner or later right themselves to the advantage of the godly:

> *The evil bow before the good,*
> *And the wicked at the gates of the righteous* (xiv. 19);

and that punishment might overtake the wicked at any moment:

> *He that being often reproved hardeneth his neck,*
> *Shall suddenly be broken, and that without remedy* (xxix. 1).
>
> *Therefore shall calamity come suddenly,*
> *On a sudden shall he be broken, and that without remedy* (vi. 15).

In these ways the Wisdom writers faced this problem, until, with the rise of a fuller belief in the Hereafter, it was taught that final recompense and retribution would be meted out in the world to come.

# V

## THE DOCTRINE OF IMMORTALITY

The ethical teaching of the Sages was of such a practical character, and their thoughts were consequently so concentrated on the present world, that from the nature of the case we should not look for many references to the Hereafter. Apart from this, however, all the writers of our book have the same ideas about the next world that are found, with few exceptions, in the rest of the Old Testament. Death is the end of all things; it is, therefore, not dwelt upon, and only mentioned as indicating the punishment of the wicked; the punishment consisting in the fact that death overtakes the wicked *sooner* than the righteous, not that there is any difference between the good and the bad in the Hereafter. *Shĕôl*, the place to which the departed go, is only incidentally referred to, and is used synonymously with death, e.g. in v. 5:

> *Her feet go down to death,*
> *Her steps reach unto Shĕôl* (cf. vii. 27).

It is situated deep down in the earth (xv. 24, though on this passage
see below), which is implied by the use of another synonym for it,
the 'Pit':

> Let us swallow them up alive as Shĕól,
> And whole, as those that go down into the pit (i. 12).

Yet another synonym is 'Abaddón:

> Shĕól and 'Abaddón are before Jahweh,
> How much more then the hearts of the children of men (xv. 11).

> Shĕól and 'Abaddón are never satisfied;
> And the eyes of man are never satisfied (xxvii. 20).

With this personification of Shĕól cf. Isa. xxviii. 18, Ps. cxli. 7. A
few words in reference to these two synonyms for Shĕól, as apparently
they are in this book, may be offered. It is just possible that they
reflect some slightly developed ideas of the underworld. In Isa. xiv.
15 it is said: 'Yet thou shalt be brought down to Shĕól, to the uttermost parts of the Pit'; the uttermost parts of the Pit suggest something more than Shĕól itself; and in verse 19 of the same chapter
there is the curious expression of going down to 'the stones of the
Pit'. It may be that there existed here in the mind of the writer the
idea of the Pit being some special place in Shĕól which was reserved
for the worst enemies of Jahweh; this impression is also gained from
such passages as Ezek. xxxii. 23, 25, 28–30. If this is so, then we may
perhaps be justified in seeing in the use of this expression the idea of
some differentiation between the dwellers in Shĕól. A synonym is
often used in order to express a slightly different point of view about
one and the same thing, which may be the point of departure for some
new idea regarding it. Possibly this is the case with Shĕól and the
Pit. In this connexion there may be some significance in the words:

> Shĕól and 'Abaddón are before Jahweh.

The very fact that the name of Jahweh is brought into connexion
with the world of the Hereafter denotes the beginning of some fuller
thought in regard to it. As long as God was conceived of as being
wholly unconcerned about Shĕól and its dwellers it could not be a
subject of much interest to Israel's religious thinkers. But when
once a more developed conception of God arose, owing in the first
instance to the teaching of the prophets, the way was paved for the
belief that His power over and interest in men extended beyond the
grave. For this to germinate in the minds of the religious thinkers,
and finally to come to fruition, would take centuries, owing both to
the tenacity of traditional belief and to other causes such as the

e

popular conceptions about the departed,[1] which had to be counter-
acted, and the general Semitic belief, outside of Israel, that there was
a special god of the underworld.[2] The passage before us points to the
early beginnings, certainly subconscious, of such development.

The expression *'Abaddôn*, which means 'destruction', suggests
something more than what is connoted by the term *Shĕôl*, and likewise points conceivably to the beginnings of what later became some
extended conception regarding the place of the departed.

The state of the departed is expressed by the term *Rephaim*, applied
to them:

> *Her way leadeth down to death,*[3]
> *And her paths unto the Rephaim* (ii. 18).
> *But he knoweth not that the Rephaim are there,*
> *That her guests are in the depths of Shĕôl* (ix. 18; cf. xxi. 16).

This word is usually translated 'Shades', and there is no doubt that
according to orthodox Jewish belief this was intended to describe the
condition, without body, without soul (in the Hebrew sense of individuality), silent, inactive, and yet existing, of the departed. That this
is quite incompatible with much else that is said about the *Rephaim*
in the Old Testament, and is not borne out by the probable derivation of the word ('healers') is certain; but into this subject we cannot
go now.[4] The writers of the passages quoted no doubt understood by
the term what had come to be the orthodox connotation.

The passages xi. 7, xiv. 32, xv. 24, which in their English form
might seem to point to a somewhat developed thought concerning
the Hereafter, cannot bear such an interpretation, as a reference to
the notes in the Commentary will show.

In *Proverbs*, therefore, the doctrine of immortality is the same as
that held normally by the religious teachers of Israel. If we are justified in seeing, as in some other books of the Old Testament, the faint
adumbration of what in later ages became a development of belief
on the subject, it is highly improbable that the writers of *Proverbs*
were themselves conscious of anything of the kind. The *beginnings*
of mental evolutionary processes are not perceived.

---

[1] See further the present writer's *Immortality and the Unseen World*, pp. 202 ff.
(1921).

[2] Among the Babylonians Nergal was the god of the underworld; see Jensen,
*Kosmologie der Babylonier*, pp. 476 ff. (1890); Jeremias, *Das A.T. im Lichte des alten
Orients*, pp. 45 ff. (1904); Jastrow, *Die Religion Babyloniens und Assyriens*, i. 63 ff.
(1905).

[3] For the justification for this rendering see the Commentary.

[4] It is dealt with in *Immortality and the Unseen World*, pp. 63 ff., 92 ff.

# THE ATTITUDE OF THE SAGES TO WORSHIP

References to worship in *Proverbs* are rare; but what is taken for granted does not require frequent mention. No word about Circumcision or the Sabbath ever occurs in this book; but nobody would for that reason suppose that the Wisdom writers repudiated them. For one thing, what concerned the *cultus* it was the duty of the priestly teachers to give instructions about; it did not come within the scope of what the Sages taught. To suppose, therefore, that the *Chăkāmim* were opponents of the sacrificial system, or of liturgical worship generally, would be a great mistake. They had not the remotest desire to depreciate these, nor do they ever utter a word to this effect; had such a thing ever been suspected by the religious authorities it is certain that our book would never have been admitted into the Canon.

The words in iii. 9, though belonging to the latest portion of the book, reflect what would have been in the mind of any religious teacher in Israel in earlier days:

> *Honour Jahweh with thy substance,*
> *And with the firstfruits of all thine increase.*

How it is taken for granted that everybody recognized what was incumbent upon them in this respect is seen from the fact that even a harlot is represented as stating that she has fulfilled her obligations (vii. 14). But that offerings of such a kind were looked upon with horror would have been the case with the Sages of later generations as it was with those of earlier days, one of whom says:

> *The sacrifice of the wicked is an abomination unto Jahweh* (**xv.** 8).

It is thoroughly in the prophetic spirit and doubtless a mark of the influence of the teaching of the prophets that it is said elsewhere:

> *To do justice and judgement*
> *Is more acceptable to Jahweh than sacrifice* (**xxi.** 3).

But that does not imply any wish to see the abrogation of the sacrificial system, any more than in the case of the prophets. To avoid such an erroneous conclusion one has only to ask oneself, when considering such a passage as the one before us and similar ones in the prophetic books: What did either the prophets or the Sages propose to put in its place? Both classes of teachers knew well enough that the bulk of the people, whose religious conceptions were still of a somewhat undeveloped character, were not yet capable of purely spiritual worship. A preliminary step in that direction would be to show that sacrifices *per se* were useless and thus to inculcate the right spirit

e 2

in offering them; that is what they did. And that is what is meant in the passage quoted. This is further borne out by the words of xxi. 27:

> *The sacrifice of the wicked is an abomination to Jahweh;*
> *How much more when he bringeth it for wickedness.*

The meaning of the second line is that a sacrifice was brought with the idea that it would atone for a wicked act; that such a thought regarding sacrifice was in vogue in later days too there is clear evidence (see the note in the Commentary). It is against this that the Wisdom writers inveigh; but not against the sacrificial system itself. In one passage, indeed, we have an implicit recognition of the sacrificial system, for in xvii. 1 it is said:

> *Better is a dry morsel and quietness therewith,*
> *Than a house full of the sacrifices of strife.*

Although 'the sacrifices of strife' here refers to feasting, the word used (*Zebach*, the ordinary one for 'sacrifice') shows that the reference is to one of those private sacrifices which was accompanied by a feast; so that the writer here takes the sacrificial system for granted.

That there are very few references to prayer in *Proverbs* is not because the writers were lacking in devotional feeling, but because they were primarily concerned with ethical teaching. Prayer, like the sacrificial system, and like belief in God, is taken for granted; thus, in the passage xv. 8, part of which has already been quoted, it is said:

> *The sacrifice of the wicked is an abomination to Jahweh,*
> *But the prayer of the upright is his delight.*

So, too, in xv. 29:

> *Jahweh is far from the wicked;*
> *But he heareth the prayer of the righteous* (cf. xxviii. 9).

# VII

## THE *CHĂKĂMIM* ('WISE MEN')

The origin and development of the *Chăkămim* is an interesting study; and although the Old Testament does not give a great deal of information on the subject, there are certain *data* which, when studied in the light of what is known about the Wise men of Egypt and Babylon, enable us to reach some definite conclusions.

From Egyptian Wisdom books we learn that the teachers of wisdom, who were called scribes, were important State functionaries; they wrote their books for the purpose of instructing those who would in course of time fill offices of trust and importance such as they themselves were holding. There is ample evidence to show that regular schools existed in ancient Egypt which were attended by pupils for the purpose of receiving instruction in the various things necessary for those who looked forward to move in court and government circles. First and foremost, of course, writing was taught; but also what was understood by wisdom, viz. respect for one's superiors, behaviour in the presence of nobles, duty, truthfulness, reliability, manners, &c. One way whereby these things were inculcated was by making the pupil copy out the writings of the Wise men; the remains of such copies, full of school-boy mistakes, are still in existence. That the office of these Egyptian teachers or scribes was in a real sense a religious one can be gathered from the fact that scribes were under the special care of the god Thoth.

While the evidence is not nearly so full regarding Babylon and Assyria, there is sufficient to show that things were similar. Here, too, the teachers of Wisdom were State functionaries; similarly, they went under the name of *Shapiri*, 'Scribes'; Achikar, for example, who occupied a position somewhat corresponding to that of prime minister, as well as commander-in-chief of the army, is spoken of as 'the wise and skilful scribe'. Moreover, scribes were closely connected with the temples, and were under the protection of Nebo, the divine scribe.

When we turn to the Old Testament we find that the evidence, though somewhat meagre, is significant in the light of what has been said. It is in the nature of things that there must have been institutions of some kind, however primitive, where instruction in one form or another was given; but nothing direct is said about such so far as the earlier periods are concerned. At the same time a slight indication is afforded by such a passage as 2 Sam. i. 18, where it is said: 'And he bade them teach the children of Judah the song of the bow; behold, it is written in the book of Jashar'; this presupposes both scribal activity as well as some place of instruction. In this connexion it is also worth pointing out that the place Kiriath-sepher (Josh. xv. 15) means 'the city of the book' (or perhaps it should be Kiriath-sopher, following the Sept., in which case it would be the 'Scribe city', or, as translated in the Sept.,'the city of the scribes'), and that another name for it was Kiriath-sannah (Josh. xv. 49), 'the city of the palm-leaf', i.e. it preserved the name of the material on which the scribes wrote.[1] This certainly suggests a centre of some kind in which the scribal art was pursued and in which instruction would be given. That the scribe, in this early sense, occupied a position somewhat analogous to

---

[1] See Fries, in the *Zeitschrift des Deutschen Pal. Vereins*, xxii. 125; cp. also Jeremias, *Das Alte Testament im Lichte des alten Orients*, p. 5 (1904).

the Egyptian and the Babylonian scribe may be gathered from such
a passage, e. g., as 2 Sam. viii. 17, where among David's high officers
of State Seraiah the scribe (*sôphēr*) is mentioned; see also 2 Sam. xx.
25, 1 Kgs. iv. 3, 2 Kgs. xix. 2. Nor can we doubt that the Israelite
scribe also fulfilled some religious function as in the cases of the
Egyptian and the Babylonian scribes, although this is not specifically
stated so far as this early type of scribe is concerned; for the Israelites
were assuredly not less religious in this matter than their Gentile
neighbours.

When we come to later times and obtain more definite evidence
we find that it supports the earlier indications. The first time the
Wise men, or *Chăkāmim*, are mentioned it is quite obvious that they
must have been long in existence, for the word is used as a technical
term, and they are spoken of as a well-known institution. Thus, in
Isa. xxix. 14 it is said that, owing to the evil state of country and
people, the wisdom of the *Chăkāmim* shall perish. More pointed is
Jer. xviii. 18, where the *Chăkām* is mentioned, as belonging to an
order, alongside of the priest and the prophet: '. . . the law shall not
perish from the priest, nor counsel from the wise, nor the word from
the prophet'; while Jer. viii. 8, 9 reads as though the *Chăkāmim* and
the *Sôphĕrim* ('Scribes') were identical: 'How say ye, We are wise
men (*Chăkāmim*), and the law of Jahweh is with us? But, behold,
the false pen of the scribes (*Sôphĕrim*) hath wrought falsely.' That
the scribe was also, as in Egypt and Babylon, a state functionary is
again definitely stated; according to Jer. xxxvi. 20, 21 the scribe
Elishama has charge of the State archives; and from 2 Kgs. xxii. 3–7
it is evident that the scribe Shaphan occupied a position something
like that of a minister of finance.

From these *data* we are justified in inferring that among the
Hebrews, just as in Egypt and Babylon, the *Chăkāmim* or 'Wise men'
were one and the same as the *Sôphĕrim* or 'Scribes'; and that this
was actually the fact is proved by the case of Ben-Sira, who combined in himself the calling of a wise man and a Scribe (see especially
Ecclus. xxxviii. 24–xxxix. 11); this, it is true, is evidence of a rather
later date, but taken with what we gather from the *data* of earlier
times, the conclusion does not admit of doubt that the *Chăkāmim*
came originally from the circle of the Scribes, not in the later sense
of those who were occupied with the study and copying of the
Scriptures, but in the earlier sense of the State functionary.

It must have been at a relatively early period, at any rate while
the monarchy was still in existence, that men, drawn at first from
the circles of the Wisdom-Scribes, gradually narrowed down their

activity to the study and collecting and writing of Wisdom material, thus forming themselves into a distinct body and becoming *Chăkā-mim* in the technical sense of Sages. Not that, at any rate in the case of some, more secular duties played no part; for Prov. xxii. 29 shows that the Wise man (the term *māhîr* being applied to him proves that he was a scribe, see note in Commentary) was still at times occupied with State affairs; and as late as the time of Ben-Sira we find that the Scribe (identical with the Wise man, cf. Ecclus. xxxix. 1–3, see below) is spoken of thus:

> *He serveth among great men,*
> *And appeareth before a ruler;*
> *He travelleth in the land of foreign nations,*
> *And hath had experience of both good and evil things among men*
> (xxxix. 4).

As Wise men in the more restricted sense they appear as the public teachers of religion and ethics; to them the two were inseparable. While in no sense theologians, their teaching necessarily touched upon theological questions, if but incidentally. The basis of their teaching was Scripture, the influence of the prophetical writings being especially noticeable. But, as is becoming more and more recognized, they also went further afield and gathered material from extra-Israelite sources. The Hebrew Scriptures, however, formed the real foundation of all their teaching; and this is what would naturally be expected; for while, as we have seen, the Wise men are to be identified with the Scribes in the earlier sense of State func-tionaries, they were undoubtedly also concerned with religious matters, as was the case with Egyptian and Babylonian scribes; this is seen by the fact that the scribe Ezra was also a priest. There is much in the writings of the Sages to show their sympathy with the priesthood (see, e. g., Ecclus. vii. 29–31). There can be no doubt that at one time the Wise men shared with the priests the duties of teaching both the observance of legal precepts and also of moral instruction. But in course of time each specialized in his particular domain, the priests becoming more and more occupied with the functions of their calling, while the Wise men concentrated on the teaching of ethics. Mutual sympathy, however, continued. It was not until after the Maccabæan struggle, when the anti-Hellenistic attitude of the religious leaders became dominant, that there was no place for the Wise men, who consequently became absorbed in the Scribes in the later sense of the term. But that belongs to a time later than that with which we are dealing.

The main efforts of the Sages were concentrated on the education and instruction of young men in all that appertained to right living, and this in the religious as in the secular domain. At the same time, much of their teaching was adapted to wider circles; and their interests covered every grade in social life.

Their indebtedness to the teaching of the prophets and their study of the Wisdom literature of other lands gave them a broad outlook on things in general. The quality of common-sense is strikingly exhibited in their writings, a thing which they show to be in no way incompatible with high ideals.

Ben-Sira, in describing the pursuits of the Wise man, says that:

> He meditateth in the Law of the Most High;
> He searcheth out all the wisdom of the ancients,
> And is occupied in prophecies;
> He preserveth the discourses of men of renown,
> And entereth into subtleties of parables;
> He seeketh out the hidden things of proverbs,
> And is conversant with the dark things of parables (Ecclus. xxxix. 1–3).

This expresses equally the striving of the Sages of earlier times, and tells of the way in which they prepared themselves for their task of teaching.

Indications occur in the Wisdom books of the way in which pupils were gathered together for instruction. The picture of personified Wisdom inviting all and sundry to come and be taught of her doubtless reflects what was done in the case of teachers:

> Doth not wisdom call,
> And understanding put forth her voice?
> In the top of high places upon the road,
> In the midst of the pathways, she standeth;
> Beside the gates at the entry of the city,
> At the coming in at the doors, she crieth aloud:
> Unto you, O men, I call;
> And my voice is to the sons of men (Prov. viii. 1–4).

While, no doubt, instruction was given in open spaces where crowds assembled, there were also houses to which the pupils came; and here, too, we may take it for granted that the picture of Wisdom's house, where she prepares a feast for her devotees, reflects in an idealized form what was actually the case:

> Wisdom hath builded her house,
> She hath hewn out her seven pillars (ix. 1).

Many teachers would have regular gatherings in their own houses where they gave lectures to their pupils. Ben-Sira mentions this;

and in his day such places of meeting had technical names, which may, of course, be much older than his time; he says:

> *Turn in unto me, ye unlearned,*
> *And lodge in my house of instruction* (Ecclus. li. 23).

The 'house of instruction' is the *Beth-ha-Midrash*, the technical name for an academy of learning. He also speaks of his *Yĕshĭbah*, likewise a technical name for a larger place of instruction (li. 29).

It goes without saying that the instruction was oral (cp. Ecclus. li. 25); the written form of the Sages' teaching gives the condensed *résumé* of their lectures. It was, we may surmise, when the teaching of the Sages assumed a literary form that additions were made from other collections of sayings; these included traditional proverbs in the literal sense, as well as longer sayings gathered from both Hebrew and foreign sources.

# VIII

## THE MEANING AND USE OF THE TERM *MĀSHĀL* ('PROVERB')

There are a number of passages in the book of *Proverbs*, some extending over several verses (e.g. ii. 1–22, xxii. 17–21, xxvii. 23–27, xxx. 1–6 and many others) in regard to which the word 'proverb' does not appear appropriate; it will therefore, be well to examine the connotation of the Hebrew term *māshāl*[1] and its usage in the Old Testament.

(i) The earliest meaning of *māshāl* is that of a *popular proverb*; the word is directly applied to such in 1 Sam. x. 12: 'Therefore it became a proverb (*māshāl*), "Is Saul also among the prophets?"' Again, in 1 Sam. xxiv. 13 (14 in Hebr.):

'As with the proverb (*māshāl*) of the ancients, "Out of the wicked cometh forth wickedness".' These two passages are old; but in much later times we also find a popular proverb spoken of as a *māshāl*; thus, in Ezek. xii. 22 it is said: 'Son of man, what is this proverb that ye have in the land of Israel, saying, "the days are prolonged, and every vision faileth"?' Similarly in Ezek. xviii. 2: 'What mean ye, that ye use this proverb in the land of Israel,

---

[1] The root from which this word comes means 'to be like' (in all probability a primitive, not a denominative root). There is an identical root meaning 'to rule'; the attempts which have been made to show that the two ideas 'to be like' and 'to rule' came originally from one and the same root are not convincing; it is more probable that the two roots were in their origin distinct. A root (*m-sh-l*) meaning 'to be like' is common to all Semitic languages.

saying, "the fathers have eaten sour grapes, and the children's teeth are set on edge"?'

A number of instances occur in which what is evidently a popular proverb is quoted, though the term *māshāl* is not directly applied to it. These are introduced by such words as, 'wherefore it is said', or 'wherefore they say', clearly pointing to the saying being well known and current among the people. Thus, in Gen. x. 9 we have: 'He was a mighty hunter before Jahweh; wherefore it is said, " Like Nimrod a mighty hunter before Jahweh".' Again, in 2 Sam. v. 8: 'And David said on that day, whosoever smiteth the Jebusites, let him get up to the watercourse. . . . Wherefore they say, "The blind and the lame shall not enter into the house".' One other early example is found in 2 Sam. xx. 18: 'They were wont to speak in old time, saying, "They shall surely ask (counsel) at Abel and at Dan "' (so, according to the Sept.)

Besides these there are many sayings which read like proverbs though the word *māshāl* is not applied to them, nor are they introduced by any formula; a few of these are worth quoting. One occurs in Gen. xvi. 12, where the terseness of the Hebrew has more the ring of a popular proverb than the R.V. rendering would imply; literally it runs: 'A wild ass of (i. e. among) men, his hand against all, the hand of all against him'. Another, which is quite unmistakeable, is: 'Let not him that girdeth on (his armour) boast himself as he that putteth it off'; in the original this consists of three words (1 Kings. xx. 11). The same is true of the proverb in Isa. xxii. 13: 'Let us eat and drink, for to-morrow we die' (cf. 1 Cor. xv. 32); and of that in Isa. xxxvii. 3: 'The children are come to the birth, and there is no strength to bring forth' (cf. lxvi. 9). In the case of Jer. viii. 22, and the same applies to others, the context shows that a proverb is being quoted: 'Is there no balm in Gilead? Is there no healer there?' Other instances are in all probability the following: 'They have sown wheat and reaped thorns' (Jer. xii. 13); 'What is straw to wheat?' (Jer. xxiii. 28); 'They sow the wind, and shall reap the whirlwind' (Hos. viii. 7); 'A living dog is better than a dead lion' (Eccles. ix. 4).

To these must be added a few examples from the book of *Proverbs* which from their nature may be regarded as ancient popular proverbs incorporated by the sages in their collections. These, as one would expect, are found mainly in the second collection (x–xxii. 16), which is the oldest part of the book; thus, in xvi. 18 we have: 'Before destruction Pride', i. e. Pride precedes a fall (cf. xviii. 12). 'Hope deferred maketh the heart sick' (xiii. 12). 'Where no oxen are there is no corn' (xiv. 4). 'A man's heart deviseth his way; but Jahweh directeth his steps' (xvi. 9, probably adapted from some earlier form). 'Wine is a mocker, strong drink a brawler' (xx. 1). And there are, doubtless, others. These by no means exhaust the number of sayings in the Old Testament which are to be reckoned as ancient popular proverbs, and to which the term *māshāl* is either directly applied or which from their form and content may be regarded as such. This, therefore, is the earliest and simplest form of what is understood by a *māshāl*; and it may be taken for granted that the *māshāl* of this type in its origin always circulated orally.

Now it has been pointed out that the root from which this word *māshāl* comes means 'to be like', so that the term in its essence means 'likeness' or 'comparison'. But it will be seen that while in some cases the word 'likeness' or 'simile' can be appropriately applied to these sayings, in the case of many others this is not so. For example, the idea of comparison clearly underlies such a saying as, 'Is Saul also among the prophets?' i. e. there is an incongruity in the companionship between these two. Just as one would not expect men of different station and temperament to consort, so one would not expect the presence of Saul among the prophets; hence this interrogative proverb. Saul among the prophets is like a man mixing in the society of uncongenial fellows. Again the idea of likeness is obvious in the saying: 'Out of the wicked cometh forth wickedness',—like proceeding from like. So, too, in the case of, 'Like Nimrod a mighty hunter before Jahweh'. These, which are certainly among the oldest of the proverbs which have been preserved in the Old Testament, contain the idea of likeness or comparison; and there are, no doubt, a few others. But this is not the case with the great majority of these sayings; by far the greater number contain no idea of likeness, nor is there any thought of a comparison in them. So that there seems to be a difficulty about the root-idea of *māshāl* being that of 'likeness' or 'comparison'. But the solution of this difficulty probably is that the use of the term *māshāl* has gone through several stages. While its original form and connotation was a short popular saying which contained a comparison, the history of the term entered upon a second stage when it came to be employed of any short popular saying which contained a truth gained from general experience.

So far, then, the term *māshāl* corresponds to what we understand by a 'proverb' in the ordinary sense of the word.

(ii) But the term receives a wider connotation when it enters from the oral into the literary stage. Judging from the examples which have come down to us, the ancient popular proverb, as we have seen, was quite a short saying consisting usually of a single sentence; in those cases in which it was something more than this, it was still very terse and concise, e. g. in such two-lined sayings as:

> *Let us eat and drink,*
> *For tomorrow we die.*
>
> *They sow the wind,*
> *And shall reap the whirlwind.*

But when they come to be composed as literary pieces their simple character gradually alters. It may be surmised that the oral popular proverb was the original pattern upon which the more elaborate form was based, whether it consisted of one line or two; and judging from various proverb-like sayings in the prophetical books, it was the prophets who first utilized this pattern. They seem both to have introduced popular proverbs in their teaching and also to have composed others for the purpose of driving home some truth. And thus with the writing down of prophetic utterances the literary stage of proverbs first began. In support of this contention it is only necessary to emphasize the fact that in the prophetical writings we find examples both of proverbs which had been current in oral form, as well as some which were apparently composed by the prophets themselves; though with the exiguous material which has come down to us it would be precarious to distinguish between the two with any degree of certainty.

When we come to the Wisdom writers we find this process greatly elaborated. Although one cannot speak positively, there is certainly reason to believe, as we have seen, that in the book of *Proverbs* there are instances of a single-lined saying of the early popular type having been utilized for the purpose of constructing a two-lined proverb which was the form characteristic of the Wisdom writers. The borrowed saying was sometimes the first, sometimes the second line in the newly-formed distich; examples will be found in the Commentary.

In course of time further elaborations were made, the miniature essay-form being the final development. In the book of *Proverbs* every stage, from the simple single-lined saying to the elaborated essay-form, is represented; and each of these is called a *māshāl*; for the proof of this it is sufficient to point to such passages as Prov. i. 1, x. 1, xxv. 1, where the term is applied in each case to all that is contained in the collection that follows.

(iii) But the term *māshāl* is further applied to sayings of an entirely different character. It must strike one as extraordinary that *māshāl* should be used in reference to the oracular utterances of Balaam;

in Num. xxiii. 7, e. g. it is said: 'And he took up his parable (*māshāl*) and said'; the same occurs in xxiii. 18, xxiv. 3, 15, 20, 21, 23. These 'parables' are of very varying length; xxiv. 20 is a simple distich; xxiv. 21, 22, and xxiv. 23, 24 consist each of two couplets; while the others are much longer. In content these are all oracles or prophecies; and the term *māshāl* applied to them is in so far inappropriate since the idea of likeness or comparison does not enter in. What is to be gathered, therefore, from this is that in course of time a greatly extended meaning came to be attached to the term *māshāl*. And this is borne out by the way in which it is applied to yet other kinds of literary composition.

(iv) Among these, though only few in number, and confined to the prophetical books, is the prophecy of woe. In Isa. xiv. 4–6 there is a *māshāl* against the king of Babylon consisting of three distichs the content of which is that Jahweh has brought to nought the power of the wicked under whose tyrannical sway the peoples had suffered. In Mic. ii. 4 the *māshāl* is in the form of a lamentation in two distichs which, it is said, will be uttered by the people of Israel. In Hab. ii. 6, 7, it is again a prophecy of woe against the Chaldæans which, apparently, consisted originally of two distichs. Although these are the only three instances in which this type of utterance is directly called a *māshāl*, it is highly probable that many others of a similar character in the prophetical books had the same term applied to them even though *māshāl* is not used in reference to them.

(v) Three times in the book of *Ezekiel* (xvii. 2, xx. 49 [in Hebr., xxi. 5], xxiv. 3), an allegory is called a *māshāl*; these are of greater length (xx. 49 only mentions the prophet as a 'speaker of parables', i. e. of allegories).

It will thus be seen that *māshāl* is used in a variety of ways in the Old Testament, and its derivation does not explain its somewhat wide connotation. We must conclude that it is a case, occurring in other languages too, of a word being used originally in quite a restricted sense and coming by degrees to have a much wider meaning.

# IX

## THE CONNOTATION OF *LĒB* ('HEART') IN *PROVERBS*

To the ancient Hebrews, as is well known, though some exceptions occur even in the early books, the heart was the seat of the understanding, and therefore the organ whereby wisdom was apprehended. It was the same among the Egyptians and Babylonians (see, e. g. the quotations on p. xlvi). But there are some passages in *Proverbs*, though not confined to this book, in which 'heart' is used with a slightly different connotation, the various shades of meaning being suggested by the context; in most of these, however, the word *is* more or less connected with the understanding. A brief consideration of the passages in question will not be without interest. It is realized that there is the danger here of sometimes reading into a particular usage of the word a meaning which perhaps it was not intended to bear; but the danger must be risked, especially as there can be no doubt that in the case of the Wisdom writers, who were more especially concerned with the intellect, one may reasonably expect some extension and development of the meaning of such a word as 'heart' beyond that which had been traditionally assigned to it.

Doubtless the ordinary meaning attached to 'heart' is predominant; when, e.g. it is said:

> *In the lips of him that hath discernment wisdom is found,*
> *But the rod is for the back of him that is void of understanding (lēb; x. 13),*

it is clear that 'heart' is used for the understanding, or the mind; and so very often. But a slightly different shade of meaning is to be noticed in those cases in which 'heart' is used in the sense of *reflection*; thus in vi. 18, it speaks of:

> *An heart that deviseth wicked imaginations;*

here 'heart' is not simply the understanding, but the seat of reflection, which of course is a mental faculty, but it is an extension of mere understanding. The same is true of the words in xv. 28:

> *The heart of the righteous studieth to answer,*

and xxiv. 2:

> *For their heart studieth oppression;* see also xvi. 9, xix. 21.

In some other passages 'heart' is used as synonymous with *memory*; e.g. iii. 3:

> *Let not mercy and truth forsake thee;*
> *Bind them about thy neck,*
> *Write them upon the table of thine heart;* see also vii. 3;

so also vi. 21:

> *Bind them continually upon thine heart,*
> *Tie them about thy neck.*

Sometimes the word is used as synonymous with wisdom:

> *Folly is joy to him that is void of wisdom (lēb),*
> *But a man of understanding maketh straight his going (xv. 21).*

*He that getteth wisdom (lēb) loveth his own soul;*
*He that keepeth understanding shall find good* (xix. 8).

In the examples so far given, 'heart', although not used directly of the understanding, connotes things connected with the mind. We come next to its use in a somewhat different connexion.

Not infrequently it is represented as the *seat of the emotions*; thus, of joy in xv. 30:

*The light of the eyes rejoiceth the heart,*
*And good tidings make the bones fat* (see also xvii. 22, xxvii. 9, 11).

Of sorrow:

*The heart knoweth its own bitterness* (xiv. 10).
*Even in laughter the heart is sorrowful* (xiv. 13).

Of pride:

*Every one that is proud in heart is an abomination to Jahweh* (xvi. 5).
*Before destruction the heart of man is haughty,*
*And before honour goeth humility* (xviii. 12, see also xxi. 4).

Of obstinacy:

*He that hardeneth his heart shall fall into calamity* (xxviii. 14, see also xvii. 20).

Of evil:

*Silver laid over an earthen vessel,*
*(So are) flattering lips and a wicked heart* (xxvi. 23).

Closely connected with these are passages in which the heart is synonymous with *character*; the contrast between one who has wisdom and one of bad character is contained in xii. 8.

*A man shall be commended according to his wisdom;*
*But he that is perverse* (lit. 'twisted') *of heart shall be despised* (see also xi. 20).

'Heart' is also used in the sense of *disposition* in much the same way as of character, e. g. in xxv. 20:

*. . . So is he that singeth songs to an heavy heart.*

A rather different usage is that in which 'heart' is used as synonymous with the *inner man*; e. g.:

*Trust in Jahweh with all thine heart,*
*And lean not upon thine own understanding* (binah; iii. 5);

here there is a direct contrast between 'heart' and 'understanding' in the ordinary sense; the two words might almost be expressed respectively, by 'spiritual being' and 'intellect'. A similar connotation of 'heart' is contained in xv. 11:

*Shĕól and 'Abaddón are before Jahweh;*
*How much more then the hearts of the children of men!*

Here it is clearly the inner man that is meant, thus giving a much fuller content to the word than merely the understanding. One more example of this usage is in xxv. 3, where the context gives it special significance:

> *The heaven for height, and the earth for depth,*
> *And the heart of kings is unsearchable.*

Much the same idea is expressed by 'heart' in iv. 23, where perhaps it has even the fuller sense of man's entire individuality:

> *Keep thy heart above all that thou guardest,*
> *For out of it are the issues of life* (see also **xxxi. 11**).

One or two exceptional uses of the word may also be referred to. In xiv. 30 it expresses that which is opposed to the flesh:

> *A tranquil heart is the life of the flesh.*

Twice it is used as synonymous with the inner ear; both passages are probably of Egyptian origin (see notes in the Commentary):

> *Incline thine ear, and hear the words of the wise,*
> *And apply thine heart unto my knowledge.*

The heart as parallel to the outward ear suggests the sense of the inner ear; similarly in xxiii. 12:

> *Apply thine heart unto instruction,*
> *And thine ears to the words of knowledge.*

A quite exceptional use of the word, though not confined to *Proverbs*, is found in xxiii. 34, xxx. 19, where it is used of the 'midst' of the sea; see a similar use in Exod. xv. 8 and cf. Ezek. xxvii. 4, 25 ff.

It will thus be seen that while the normal use of the word 'heart' is that of the seat of the understanding, it undergoes considerable development in *Proverbs* and comes to have a much wider meaning.

## X

### THE SUBJECT OF WOMAN IN *PROVERBS*

In the Old Testament, speaking generally, woman is thought of and spoken of almost wholly from the point of view of man. Marriage is for the man's benefit, not the woman's; she is useful to him, she looks after the household, ministers to his comfort, bears children; all for the man; the woman is not considered; she can be divorced, but she cannot divorce her husband; he can have a couple of wives or more, and concubines if he can afford to keep them all; she may only have one husband.

This animal egotism, however, the remnant of savage life, was

worse in theory than in practice; there is no reason to believe that
the lot of Hebrew women was as bad as the theory might lead one to
suppose; indeed, as soon as we are afforded some insight into woman's
real domain, namely family life, it is seen that the theory is discarded.
That the part played by woman in the life of the people finds scarcely
any place in the books of the Old Testament (with few exceptions) one
can understand from the nature and contents of the books themselves,
for they deal with phases and aspects of the national life which
were outside woman's sphere. In the prophetical books women are
rarely referred to; when this is the case they are not presented in a
very flattering light (see, e.g. Am. iv. 1, Hos. iii. 1–3, Isa. iii. 16—iv. 1),
but the same is true of men. It was the prophets' task to lay bare
the darker side of national life in their efforts to purge it.

But when we come to the book of *Proverbs* we find that it gives
really a lot of information about the part played by women, and a
good deal can also be gathered from what is implied. The Sages tell
of bad women, and they tell of good women, just as they do of bad
men and good men; but there are clearly not so many types of 'fools'
among the former as among the latter.

Although polygamy was permitted by the Law it is never hinted at
or implied in *Proverbs*; all that is said in the frequent references to
a wife gives one the distinct impression that the Wisdom writers
regarded monogamy as the ideal; this will be seen from the following
passages:

> *A virtuous wife is a crown to her husband* (xii. 4).

This, assuredly, could not have been said in reference to a man who
had more than one wife; he could only wear one crown! The Sage's
thought is a beautiful one, and presents woman in a position very
different from that usually found in most books of the Old Testament.

> *Whoso findeth a wife findeth prosperity,*
> *And obtaineth favour of Jahweh* (xviii. 22).

True, there is a touch of male egotism here again; but at any rate the
wife is prized; and what is noticeable here especially is that marriage
is thought of as something sacred. This is clearer still in xix. 14:

> *House and riches are an inheritance from fathers;*
> *But a prudent wife is from Jahweh.*

In the late portion of the book marriage is spoken of as a covenant of
God (ii. 17), and monogamy is directly taught (v. 15–19).

There are various references to family life from which one sees that
the mother occupies as important a part as the father:

> *A wise son maketh a glad father;*
> *But a foolish son is the heaviness of his mother* (x. 1).

f

A variant to this occurs in xv. 20, but as shown in the Commentary, the text is probably corrupt and should be read as in x. 1. The way in which both parents are mentioned together shows the mother's position in the house to be equal to that of the father. The mention in xvii. 25 of their joint sorrow at their son's folly points to the true relationship between a man and his wife, and implies monogamy:

> *A foolish son is a grief to his father,*
> *And bitterness to her that bare him* (see also xxiii. 25, where their mutual joy is spoken of).

Under very different circumstances this joint mention of father and mother, indicating a oneness which is well worth noting, occurs in xix. 26:

> *He that spoileth his father, and chaseth away his mother,*
> *Is a son that causeth shame and bringeth reproach.*

This is further illustrated by the very stern denunciation against one who curses his parents, or who robs them:

> *Whoso curseth his father or his mother,*
> *His lamp shall be put out in the blackest darkness* (xx. 20).

> *Whoso robbeth his father or his mother, and saith, It is no transgression,*
> *The same is the companion of a destroyer* (xxviii. 24).

But on this latter quotation see the note in the Commentary; it is possible that the insertion of 'mother' is due to a later scribe; this would not detract from the pointedness of the words, though it may bring them, as they stand, to a somewhat later date. At any rate, the passage is entirely in keeping with the ideas expressed elsewhere in the earliest collection on the subject.

A life-long union seems to be implied in the words:

> *Hearken unto thy father which begat thee,*
> *And despise not thy mother when she is old* (xxiii. 22).[1]

The predominant position of the woman in the home is concisely but strikingly expressed in the words:

> *Every wise woman buildeth her house* (xiv. 1).

The reference is, of course, not to literal building, but to the successful management and arrangement of household matters in general, including persons as well as things. Regarding the former, we have an interesting indication of the mother's part in educating her children in the later portion of *Proverbs*, but there is no reason to doubt that the same applies to earlier times as well; thus in i. 8, 9, it is said:

> *My son, hear the instruction of thy father,*
> *And forsake not the teaching of thy mother;*

---

[1] See also xi. 16, but the note on this verse in the Comm. should be consulted.

*For they shall be a chaplet of grace unto thy head,*
*And chains about thy neck* (so, too, in vi. 20, and cf. iv. 3).

The noble panegyric on woman contained in xxxi. 10–31 is fully dealt with in the Commentary.

The picture of Woman as presented in *Proverbs* would not be complete without a reference to the less pleasing side of the subject. In part, this also bears out, however, the anything but submissive and inferior position generally implied in the Old Testament books. In fact, it is the man rather than the woman who is the victim according to some passages. Thus, in xix. 13 a husband is contemplated who is unfortunate both as regards his son and his wife:

*A foolish son is the calamity of his father;*
*And the contentions of a wife are a continual dropping.*

And in xxi. 9 it is thought to be wiser for a man to retire to the attic than to be worried by a quarrelsome wife:

*It is better to dwell in the corner of the housetop,*
*Than with a contentious wife in a wide house* (cf. verse 9, and in xxv. 24 the passage is repeated; and for a similar thought see xxvii. 15).

It is noteworthy that the Sages with all their outspokenness and their fearlessness in laying bare the frailties of human nature very rarely find it necessary to refer to adultery. This is hinted at in xi. 22:

*A golden ring in a swine's snout!*
*A fair woman that turneth aside from modesty!* [1]

And in xii. 4ᵇ it is directly referred to. With the exception of the latest collection in the book (i–ix), these are the only places in which the subject is spoken of; and the delicacy with which this is done is worth remarking. Noticeable, too, is the fact that there is no mention of divorce either for incompatibility of temper or for adultery. The Sages had a high ideal regarding the marriage bond.

Prostitutes are referred to in the warnings to young men against sins of the flesh (xxii. 14, xxiii. 27, xxvii. 13, xxix. 3).

In the latest collection of the book the sin of unchastity occupies an abnormal amount of space. It is evident that in later days this form of vice, owing largely to foreign influences, became more pronounced.

Apart, therefore, from this darker side of the picture, which is quite exceptional in the body of the book, Woman is presented in *Proverbs* in a manner which is in pleasing contrast with what is found in most of the other Old Testament books. No doubt the nature of our book gives more scope for dealing with the subject and reflects

---

[1] See the note on this verse in the Commentary.

the true facts of which the other books are for the most part silent, or in which the existence of a theory is implied which, being out of date, no longer worked in practice. But the fact remains that *Proverbs* is the only Old Testament book in which a rational estimation of Woman is found.

## XI

### THE TYPES OF THE 'FOOL' IN *PROVERBS*

The Hebrew Wisdom teachers regarded humanity as consisting of two strongly opposed divisions. The fundamental antagonism between these two lay, according to the Sages, in a difference of world-outlook, a difference of attitude towards men and things, which was determined in the last instance by what may be described in general terms as sensibleness, as characteristic of the one, and foolishness, as characteristic of the other. Under the former would be included such virtues, among others, as forethought, discernment, caution, tact, self-control, self-respect, &c.; under the latter such common failings as thoughtlessness, carelessness, and that general weakness of character which involves inability, or at least unwillingness, to resist momentary impulses to wrong-doing, and which therefore will finally often result in floundering into the worst excesses.

The Wisdom writers were mainly concerned in placing in relief these two mental attitudes—being at pains to emphasize the contrast between them—for the purpose of showing the wisdom of the one, and the folly of the other; they also never tire of declaring the reward or punishment, respectively, which will inevitably be the lot of those who follow in the steps of the one or the other.

So far as it goes this is, of course, admirable. But one cannot fail to realize that there is an incompleteness here; there is something lacking. Contrast is always instructive; sometimes it will be helpful; but it is not often encouraging. True, some 'fools' may not be so irretrievably foolish as not to find some incentive in seeing the reward of the wise; but there is that in human nature which is much inclined to resent the advantage gained by one who has shown himself to be wiser than his fellows; at any rate, most 'fools' are so constituted. Or again, there are 'fools' whom stripes will reform; but experience shows that it is the exception. In a word, the Wisdom writers, in seeking to reclaim 'fools', only use the means and methods of contrast and deterrent, but fail to appeal to those better instincts possessed by every mortal, whereby they are drawn on their own initiative to contemplate and follow the better way. They evince none of that love and sympathy for the individual

which is so vastly stronger in its effect than all the threatenings
in the world. However the absence of this *trait* be accounted for,
the fact is that it is not there. This must be recognized in discussing
the various types of those for whom the Wisdom Literature was
primarily written.

What the Wisdom writers say about the various types of 'fools'
for whom they write applies to their literature as a whole; but we are
concerned now only with *Proverbs*.

The first type to be considered goes under the name of *Pethi*; a
few passages may be quoted to show what is understood by this term:
the writer of the first collection says that among the purposes for
which he has written his proverbs is:

> *To give prudence to the simple ones (pĕtha'im),*
> *To the young man knowledge and discretion* (i. 4).

Three points regarding this type of 'fool' come out here: he is
without experience, he is one who is young, and he is thought of as
teachable. As the most hopeful type one can understand that the
*Pethi* is the most frequently occurring term for 'fool' in *Proverbs*; in
addition, the type is often referred to without the actual word being
used.

But though capable of learning better the *Pethi* has no anxiety
to do so; that is where the essence of his folly lies; in that respect
he is mentioned in the same category with 'fools' of a much worse
type; thus, in i. 22 it is said:

> *How long, ye simple ones (pĕthaim), will ye love simplicity?*
> *And scorners delight them in scorning,*
> *And fools hate knowledge?* (cf. viii. 5, ix. 6).

Further, the *Pethi* is described as unstable, of weak will, and therefore
easily led into temptation:

> *And I beheld among the simple ones (pĕtha'im),*
> *I discerned among the youths*
> *A young man void of understanding,*
> *Passing through the street near her corner,*
> *And he went the way to her house* (i. e. of the harlot; vii. 7, 8, see

further i. 32, ix. 16–18).

Quite in accordance with this is the quality of stupidity in not
even taking the trouble to keep out of harm's way:

> *A prudent man seeth the evil and hideth himself,*
> *But the simple (pĕthaim) pass on and suffer for it* (xxii. 3, xxvii. 12).

Another *trait* of the *Pethi* is his credulity:

> *The simple (pethi) believeth every word,*
> *But the prudent man looketh well to his going* (xiv. 15).

Once only is it said that the *Pethi* is deliberate in his folly, otherwise he is always stupid rather than actively vicious; this is in xiv. 18:

> *The simple (pĕtha'im) inherit folly,*
> *But the prudent are crowned with knowledge.*

The force of the word translated 'inherit' here is rather 'take possession of', implying purposeful action.

A redeeming quality regarding the *Pethi* is that he has at least the sense to take warning when he sees others punished:

> *Smite a scorner, and the simple (pethi) will learn prudence* (xix. 25);
> *When the scorner is punished the simple (pethi) is made wise* (xxi. 11).

So that this type of 'fool' is the man of weak character with no will of his own; he is by no means a hardened sinner, for he is teachable; and in the right hands may be made to go right. He was the kind of young man with whom the Wisdom writers were especially concerned.

In the next place we have two types of 'fools' of a distinctly worse character than the *Pethi*. They are the *Kĕsîl* and the *'Evîl*; although there does not seem to be much difference between the two, the latter, if anything, represents the more depraved type. Of the *Kĕsîl* it may be said that he is characterized by obstinate stupidity; and of the *'Evîl* that he is, in addition, licentious; both are always morally bad. Both differ from the *Pethi* in being avowedly and of set purpose wicked. If the *Pethi* is weak of will and silly, these two are strong-willed and use their brains for bad ends. This may be illustrated by a few quotations illustrating both types. Both have an ingrained dislike for every form of wisdom; thus, of the *Kĕsîl* it is said: *Fools hate knowledge* (i. 22), and of the *'Evîl*, that *they despise wisdom and instruction* (i. 7, cf. xv. 5). The *Kĕsîl* takes a delight in wrong-doing:

> *It is as sport to a fool (kĕsîl) to do wickedness* (x. 23).
> *A fool (kĕsîl) hath no delight in understanding,*
> *But only that his heart may reveal itself* (xviii. 2).

And he is shameless in being quite content that all the world should know of his folly:

> *A prudent man concealeth knowledge;*
> *But the heart of fools (kĕsîl) proclaimeth foolishness* (xii. 23).
> *The tongue of the wise uttereth knowledge aright;*
> *But the mouth of fools (kĕsîl) poureth out folly* (xv. 2, cf. xv. 14).

That the *'Evîl* is thought of as even worse may be gathered from the following:

> *It is an honour for a man to keep aloof from strife;*
> *But every fool ('evîl) will be quarrelling* (xx. 3).

And it is probable that the whole section vii. 7–23 has the *'Evîl* type
of fool in mind, for although verse 22 has a corrupt text, the fact that
*'Evîl* was written (whether rightly or wrongly, see note in the Comm.)
shows that it was believed that this type was intended. He is thus
represented as licentious.

Both types are regarded as incorrigible:

> *A rebuke entereth deeper into one that hath understanding,*
> *Than a hundred stripes into a fool (kĕsîl) (xvii. 10).*

> *Though thou shouldest bray a fool ('evîl) in a mortar,*
> *Yet will not his foolishness depart from him (xxvii. 22).*

But perhaps the most objectionable type of all is that known under
the name of *Lētz* ('scorner'), for he is as much an enemy to God and
men as to himself. Like the last two types spoken of he takes a
delight in his folly (i. 22), and will not listen to wisdom (xiii. 1, xv. 12).
But there are other things said about this type which marks it out as
worse than these. There is a supercilious arrogance about him which
men naturally resent:

> *The proud and haughty man, scorner is his name,*
> *He worketh in the arrogance of pride (xxi. 24).*

His quarrelsomeness and mischief-making are dangerous on account of
their far-reaching effect, because it is not only within small circles that
the evil of this is felt, but he sets a whole community at loggerheads:

> *Cast out the scorner, and contention shall go out;*
> *Yea, strife and ignominy shall cease (xxii. 10).*

> *Scornful men set a city in a flame;*
> *But wise men turn away wrath (xxix. 8).*

Such a one may seek wisdom, for he has aptitude, but the constitution
of his evil nature makes it impossible for him to acquire it (xiv. 6).
Any attempt to improve him only results in making matters worse:

> *He that correcteth a scorner getteth to himself shame;*
> *And he that reproveth a wicked man getteth himself a blot.*
> *Reprove not a scorner, lest he hate thee;*
> *Reprove a wise man, and he will love thee (ix. 7, 8).*

It is small wonder that this type of 'fool' is not only an abomination
to men (xxiv. 9), but is scorned by God Himself (iii. 34).

Finally, there are three references to the type called the *Nābāl*, the
dull-witted, churlish man in whose mouth sensible words are out of
place (xvii. 7), who is a cause of grief to his father (xvii. 21), and of
whom it is humorously said that if such an impossible thing should
happen that he became prosperous, it would make the earth tremble
(xxx. 21, 22).

These are, then, the five types of 'fools' dealt with in *Proverbs*.

# THE BOOK OF PROVERBS

## THE FIRST COLLECTION OF PROVERBS

### I. 1—IX. 18. *The Proverbs of Solomon*

THIS collection is in the nature of an introduction to the central part of the book (x. 1—xxii. 16), especially on account of the climax reached in chap. viii, in which the writer's conception of Wisdom finds expression.

More than any other of the collections, the sections in this one approximate, by the comparative length of the discourses, to the miniature essay-form. The exhortations, admonitions, and warnings contained in it are addressed primarily to young men (cf. i. 4); they constitute, in effect, an elaborate reply to the Psalmist's question: *Wherewithal shall a young man cleanse his way?* (Ps. cxix. 9). The two sins against which the sage more particularly warns are highway robbery, which may lead to the shedding of blood, and adultery; the latter is the more fully dealt with as being the extreme form of folly. The key-note of the collection is that by following wisdom a man is walking righteously in the sight of God; it is by inculcating this truth that the sage's deeply religious mind is revealed. The fundamental purpose of the Wisdom writers, of which this opening section offers a good illustration, is not to impart knowledge, but to lay down precepts of guidance for the formation of character.

**I. 1** THE proverbs of Solomon the son of David, king of Israel:

### CHAPTER I

**I. 1-6.** *General Introduction.*

**1.** *Title.* In the Hebrew Bible the title is simply *Mishlē* ('Proverbs'). The words *Proverbs of Solomon, son of David, king of Israel,* are probably meant to be the title of this first collection, and not of the book as a whole, because the other collections each have their own title, see x. 1, xxv. 1, xxx. 1, xxxi. 1. There is, it is true, no title to the third collection, beginning at xxii. 17, but the 'Appendix' to this collection (xxiv. 23–34) begins with: 'These also are (sayings) of the wise men,' which suggests that the collection itself had originally the title 'Words of the Wise men' (see the opening verse). See further, Intr. § iv.

*The Proverbs.* Cf. Eccles. xii. 9., 1. Kgs. iv. 32. On the meaning of the word *māshāl* ('proverbs') see note on *v.* 6 and Excursus VIII. *Son of David, king of Israel,* cf. the title in Eccles. i. 1; the Sept. has 'who reigned in Israel'. The superfluousness of these words suggests their being a later addition; on the other hand, it is quite possible

B

2 To know wisdom and instruction;
  To discern the words of understanding;
3 To receive instruction in wise dealing,

that the writer contemplated the use of the book by non-Israelites, in which case the addition of the words can be understood.

**2.** *To know* ... The apparently faulty syntax in the R.V. does not occur in the Hebrew, which reads: 'Proverbs of Solomon (written) that men may know . . .', i. e. the whole of *vv.* 1–4 form a single sentence. To 'know' here means to 'recognize', 'discern', or the like; this is demanded by the parallel, to 'discern', in the next line. Toy explains it as meaning to 'acquire', but the usage of the word (*yāda*') in the O.T. scarcely seems to justify this. There is a special word used for acquiring knowledge or wisdom, which, in this connexion, is peculiar to *Proverbs* (*qānah*), see i. 5, iv. 7, xv. 32, xvii. 16, &c. A man must recognize wisdom before he can acquire it.

*wisdom.* See Excursus III.

*instruction.* Hebr. *mūsār*; this word is one of the most characteristic among the Wisdom writers; the different meanings attached to it give some insight into the methods and procedure of what the sages understood by education. The root idea is that of chastisement, see xiii. 24, where it occurs as a mark of love on the part of a father towards his son, in antithesis to a father's hate for his son if he spares the rod, so that there 'chastisement' and 'the rod' are parallel terms (cf. also i. 8, iv. 1, xiii. 1, 24). Then the meaning becomes modified and it is used to describe 'admonition', as for example in viii. 33, 'Listen to instruction, and be wise'; in this sense the meaning would be best expressed by 'correction', see also vi. 23; chastisement by the tongue thus taking the place of corporal chastisement. A further step in the connotation of the word is seen in the many instances where 'discipline' is its best equivalent in English; in xxiii. 12, e. g. 'Apply thy heart (mind) to instruction', i. e. the mental discipline for acquiring wisdom. And, finally, it means the result of these efforts, as, e. g. in xxiv. 32: 'I saw, and received instruction'. So that this word *mūsār* may be said to connote the means to and acquisition of knowledge, the course of education as well as its attainment.

*discern.* This refers to the faculty of perception, whether of the eyes (vii. 7), of the ears (xxix. 19), or, as here, of the mind (ii. 5, 9, xxix. 7). The root meaning of the word is 'to be separated'; the man of understanding is one who can distinguish between things, and is thus able to discern what is right.

*understanding.* From the same Hebr. root as 'discern' (*bīnāh*). Like Wisdom it is sometimes personified (ii. 8, vii. 4, viii. 14).

**3.** *Wise dealing. Sēkel* (cf. iii. 4); the root idea is 'good sense'; the man who is willing to benefit by the teaching contained in the

In righteousness and judgement and equity;
4 To give ¹ subtilty to the simple,
  To the young man knowledge and discretion:

¹ Or, *prudence*

proverbs here put forth will know how to direct his conduct of
life on sensible lines; cf. x. 5, 19, xiv. 35, xv. 24, xvii. 2. In xix. 11,
where R.V. renders it 'discretion', it is said to restrain a man from
anger; in xii. 8, where R.V. renders it 'wisdom', it is declared that
the exercise of it brings approbation. Such 'wise dealing' is seen, as
the next line says, in righteousness, judgement, and equity, practised
in daily conduct.

*righteousness.* 'Rightness' better expresses the Hebr. *zedeq* when
applied, as here, to conduct; while the closely allied word *zĕdāqāh* is
properly expressed by 'righteousness'; the latter is the natural outcome of the former.

*judgement.* Hebr. *mishpāt*; in its origin this refers to customary
law, and therefore always connotes what is right. As a divine decision it occurs in xvi. 33, xxix. 26; and as equivalent to 'righteousness' (*zĕdāqāh*) it is used in xii. 5; as such it is a joy to the righteous
(xxi. 15), and always distasteful to the wicked (xix. 28, xxi. 7,
xxviii. 5).

*equity.* The meaning of the Hebr. word, used only in the plural
(*mēshārīm*), is well illustrated by Isa. xxvi. 7, where it refers to the
evenness of the path of the righteous; the root meaning is to be
'smooth' or 'straight'. Hence when used in an ethical sense it is
equivalent to 'rightness', as here, and in ii. 9, cf. viii. 6, xxiii. 16. As
Toy well points out, *v.* 2 'declares that knowledge of right principle
is the basis of true life; *v.* 3 assumes that this knowledge necessarily
leads to action controlled by moral principle'.

**4.** *subtilty.* In *Proverbs,* and the Wisdom literature generally,
this word (*'ormah*) is always used in a good sense, of 'shrewdness', or
'prudence' (cf. viii. 5, 12, xii. 23, xiv. 15, xv. 5, xix. 25); but elsewhere it is found in a bad sense, 'craftiness' (Exod.xxi.14; Josh.ix.4).

*the simple.* More exactly 'the inexperienced'; the root meaning
suggests that the reference is to one who is open to every influence;
the corresponding word in Arabic means a 'youth' (Wildeboer), see
further, Excursus XI.

*the young man.* Parallel to the foregoing, and very apt since this
word is also used of a babe or child (cf. Exod. ii. 6; 2 Kings iv. 29).

*knowledge.* Synonymous with wisdom in ii. 10, xiv. 6, and cf. xxi.
11, xxii. 17.

*discretion.* The Hebr. word (*mĕzimmāh*) suggests the idea of pur-
posefulness; in a good sense, as here, it is used in ii. 11, iii. 21, v. 2,
viii. 12, in an evil sense in xii. 2, xiv. 17, xxiv. 8.

5 That the wise man may hear, and increase in learning;
   And that the man of understanding may attain unto sound
      counsels:
6 To understand a proverb, and [1]a figure;

[1] Or, *an interpretation*

**5.** A new sentence begins here: 'Let the wise man . . .', the verse
being in parenthesis; the writer feels it necessary to add in passing
that although what he has just said has been in reference to the inexperienced and the young, yet even wise men and those of mature
mind can also derive benefit from studying what is to follow. Cf. ix. 9.

*wise man.* See Excursus VII.

*and increase in learning.* The word for 'learning' (*lekach*) here used
is comparatively rare, but well illustrates the Jewish method of
acquiring knowledge; it comes from the root meaning 'to take', or
'receive', referring to that which is received by being handed down.
Cf. iv. 2, ix. 9, xvi. 21, 23. In Rabbinical literature it is used in the
sense of a 'lesson' delivered by the teacher to his pupil; the highest
praise which one Rabbi can utter of another is contained in the
Mishna tractate *Pirqê 'Abôth* ii. 11, where it is said: 'Eliezer ben
Hyrcanos is a cistern (plastered) with lime which loseth not a drop;'
i. e. everything which he had received from his teachers he retained;
the further implication being that he was therefore in a position to
hand it down to others. In vii. 21, the word is used in a bad sense
(ironically, according to Wildeboer) of the persuasive argument of the
adulteress.

*the man of understanding.* Or 'discernment'. See note on i. 2.

*attain.* Better 'acquire', or 'gain'.

*sound counsels.* The root meaning of the Hebr. word means 'rope',
the idea being that of pulling a rope, or steering; another word from
the same root means 'sailor'; so that the underlying thought here is
that of steering a boat. The Septuagint renders the word 'steers-
man'. Sound counsels direct a man aright on the sea of life. In xi. 14
the R.V. translates it by 'wise guidance'. The word, which is only
used in the plural, occurs, with the exception of Job. xxxvii. 12, only
in *Proverbs*, five times.

**6.** *proverb.* The root-meaning of the Hebr. word *māshāl* means 'to
be like'; but the word is used in various ways, the more important
being (1) as a poem composed of parallel sayings, Num. xxiii. 7–10,
18–24 ('He took up his parable') and others. (2) as a taunting poem,
e. g. Isa. xiv. 4 ff., cf. Mic. ii. 4; Hab. ii. 6. (3) as a didactic poem or
psalm, Ps. xlix. 4 (5 in Hebr.), lxxviii. 2; but more commonly (4) as a
pithy saying in reference to men and affairs, and often expressed in
figurative language, e. g. 1 Sam. x. 12, xix. 24, xxiv. 13; Jer. xxxi. 29;

The words of the wise, and their ¹dark sayings.

7 The fear of the LORD is the ²beginning of knowledge:

> ¹ Or, *riddles*     ² Or, *chief part*

Ezek. xviii. 2, &c.; (5) as a short ethical saying; these last two are those of which *Proverbs* consists in the main. See further, Excursus VIII.

*figure.* The Hebr. word for this (*mĕlitzāh*) comes from a root meaning 'to scorn' or 'taunt', in which sense the word is mostly used in the O.T. In Gen. xlii. 23, where the participle is used, it means 'interpreter', and in 2 Chron. xxxii. 31 'ambassador', but lit. 'interpreter', cf. also Isa. xliii. 27; Job. xxxiii. 23. The word means a mocking or satirical saying. The Sept. rendering, ' a dark saying', would imply that the satire was concealed. The form of the word as here used is only found elsewhere in Hab. ii. 6. In later Hebrew *mĕlitzāh* means a 'metaphor', i.e. something which requires an interpretation.

*dark sayings.* The root meaning of this word (*chîdāh*) is 'to turn aside', the idea being that of something indirect, not straightforward, the sense of which does not lie upon the surface, and therefore requires probing before it can be understood; hence 'riddle' in Judg. xiv. 12, cf. Num. xii. 8. This is the only occurrence of the word in our book. With this *v.* cf. Ecclus. xlvii. 1, 17; and with the whole introductory section should be compared the somewhat similar thoughts in the first chapter of Amen-em-ope's book (see Excursus I, p. xxxvi); among other things he says:

> 'Give thine ears, hear (the words) which are said,
> Give thine heart to interpret them'. (I. iii. 9, 10.)

See further the note on i. 9.


**I. 7–19.** *An exhortation to follow parental guidance, followed by a warning against pursuing evil courses for the sake of gain.*

The picture given in these verses doubtless represents one aspect of the conditions of the time. The lust for gain among certain sections of the people led them into the worst excesses; and the temptation to some of the wilder youths to enrich themselves by laying violent hands on travellers and others, and robbing them, was increased by the chance of doing this with impunity, owing to the unsettled times. It is for this reason that the sage emphasizes at the close of the section that retribution comes, though in an unexpected form, upon those who enrich themselves in this way, viz. they fall out among themselves and are the instruments of their own undoing.

**7.** This *v.* is a kind of *leit-motif* to the whole collection; it stands quite by itself, being unconnected with what precedes and follows. It is, as various commentators have pointed out, in the nature of a

*But* the foolish despise wisdom and instruction.

8 My son, hear the instruction of thy father,
   And forsake not the [1]law of thy mother:

              [1] Or, *teaching*

motto similar to those which Arabian Wisdom-writers placed at the head of their collections of proverbs.

*The fear of* . . . Cf. Ecclus. i. 14, 16, 20, 27, xxv. 10; Job. xxviii. 28; Ps. cxi. 6; and with the whole *v.* cf. *Pirqê 'Abôth* iii. 24: 'If (there be) no wisdom (there is) no fear (of the Lord); if (there be) no fear (of the Lord) (there is) no wisdom.' Towards the end of this collection the words are repeated, see ix. 10.

*the Lord.* i.e. Jahweh; this name of the national God of the Jews, here, of course, thought of as the One and only God, was in later times not pronounced; but instead *Adōnai*, 'Lord', was used. When this usage first began is not known for certain.

*beginning.* The Hebrew *rêshîth* is a derivative from *rōsh*, 'head'; the word therefore means both 'the starting-point', essence, and chief part, or 'zenith'.

*the foolish.* Cf. xv. 5; the root meaning of this word (*'ĕwîl*) contains the idea of sluggishness. As those who despise Wisdom they are *ipso facto* godless. The word is always used of those who are morally bad, see e.g. vii. 22; Ecclus. xxxi (xxxiv) 7, and refers to the worst type of 'fool' in the Wisdom Literature; see further on this and other types of 'fools', Excursus XI.

*wisdom and instruction.* See notes on i. 2.

**8, 9.** These *vv.* form a hortatory introduction to the warning which follows.

*My son.* The usual mode of address of the Wise man to a pupil; but it is not specifically Jewish; the *Babylonian Book of Proverbs* is 'characterized by the phrase "My son", being cast in the form of instructions by a father'.[1] In the *Words of Achikar*,[2] too, most of the sayings are introduced by 'My son'. It is also used in the Egyptian Wisdom book *The Proverbs of Anii*,[3] which is a dialogue between Anii and his son Chons-hotep. This form of address is specially characteristic of this collection (i–ix) but does not occur often in *Proverbs* elsewhere; Ben-Sira frequently uses it, Ecclus. ii. 1, iii. 12, 17, vi. 8 &c.

*hear.* The Hebrew word also means to 'obey', which is probably its force here, cf. vi. 20.

*instruction.* See note on i. 2.

*thy father.* It was commanded in the Law that fathers should teach

---

[1] Langdon, *Babylonian Wisdom*, pp. 88 ff.; *PSBA* 1916, pp. 105–116, 131–137; the book may be as old as the 22 cent. B.C.

[2] Belonging to the 5 cent. B.C.

[3] Griffith in *The World's Best Literature*, pp. 5340 ff. Erman gives it the title of 'The Wisdom of Anii' (*Die Literatur der Aegypter*, pp. 294 ff. 1923); it is not later than about 1000 B.C. in its present form.

9 For they shall be a chaplet of grace unto thy head,
　　And chains about thy neck.

their children, see Deut. vi. 6, 7, and cf. Exod. xii. 26 ff., xiii. 14, 15. This teaching concerned religious belief and practice primarily; but here the reference is also to guidance in general conduct of life. The sage has in mind what his pupils had been taught in childhood by their fathers; as a *Chākhām* (or 'Wise man') he is addressing young men who are no longer under parental authority.

With the precept here uttered cf. *The Teaching of Ptah-hotep*:

> 'How beautiful it is when a son hearkens unto his father, and how happy is he to whom this is said ... If a son accepts what his father says, he will not go wrong in his thoughts' (Erman p. 97). Cf. also the opening words of the *Proverbs of Achikar*; see Excursus I.

*the law.* The Hebr. word here is *Tōrah*, and it is necessary to understand what the word connotes. 'The term Law or *Nomos* is not a correct rendering of the Hebrew word *Tōrah*. The legalistic element, which might rightly be called the Law, represents only one side of the *Tōrah*. To the Jew the word *Tōrah* means a teaching or instruction of any kind. It may be either a general principle, or a specific injunction, whether it be found in the Pentateuch, or in the other parts of the Scriptures, or even outside the Canon.'[1] In the passage before us the word is to be understood in a general sense of teaching. Its root meaning may be discerned in vi. 13, where 'he maketh signs with his fingers', meaning literally 'he points out with his fingers' (cf. Gen. xlvi. 28 where the word is used of directing or pointing out the way, i.e. to Goshen). Pointing out something has reference to some particular thing or spot, and one can therefore understand how this meaning of the word came to be derived from its original sense of to 'throw', or 'shoot', because one throws or shoots at some specified objective; see further, the note on iii. 1.

*thy mother.* See Excursus X. In most respects the mother's position was inferior to that of the father's, for in strictly legal or ritual matters she had no say; but where the teaching of ethics and general behaviour were concerned the mother's authority in regard to children was scarcely less important than the father's, see Deut. xxi. 18, 19; Prov. xxx. 17. The book of *Proverbs* has more to say about the love and respect due to the mother than any other book in the Bible; see vi. 20 where this verse occurs again, x. 1. which is practically repeated in xv. 20, xix. 26, xx. 20, xxiii. 22, 25, xxx. 17; in all these passages the mother's claim to consideration is equal with the father's.

**9.** *a chaplet of grace.* This *v.* is quoted in *Pirqê 'Abôth* vi. 7; the same expression occurs in iv. 9.

*thy neck.* The Hebr. word occurs only in *Proverbs*, see iii. 3, 22, vi. 21. It is always used in the plural because of the different parts

---

[1] Schechter, *Some Aspects of Rabbinic Theology*, p. 47 (1909).

10 My son, if sinners entice thee,
  Consent thou not.

11 If they say, Come with us,
  Let us lay wait for blood,
  Let us lurk privily for the innocent without cause;

12 Let us swallow them up alive as ¹Sheol,
  ²And whole, as those that go down into the pit;

  ¹ Or, *the grave*   ² Or, *Even the perfect*

included—throat, neck, nape, and either side; cf. the Hebr. word *'aph* which, when used in the sense of 'face' has the dual form because it includes both sides of the face. With *vv.* 8, 9, cf. Ecclus. iii. 2–6, and the following quotation from Amen-em-ope, where the Egyptian sage, at the beginning of his book, admonishes his son to accept his words of wisdom and treasure them up:

> *Give thine ears, hear (the words) that are said;*
> *Give thine heart to interpret them.*
> *It is good to place them in thine heart;*
> *But woe to him that neglecteth them—*
> *Let them rest in the casket of thy belly,*
> *That they may be a threshold (?) in thine heart (I. iii. 9–14).*

The word in the original rendered 'threshold' is uncertain.

**10.** *My son* . . . That a disciple of the Hebrew sage should be exhorted to refrain from the course of action in these verses is remarkable; it points to a lawless condition of society. Ben-Sira in Ecclus. xxxiv. (xxxi.) 25–27 depicts a somewhat similar state, though he is speaking generally, and is not addressing one of his own followers. In the passage before us the writer evidently has in mind an organized band of robbers (see *v.* 14). Such a condition of affairs suggests perhaps a period, as Toy points out, 'when, under Persian and Greek rule Jerusalem and Alexandria sheltered a miscellaneous population, and a distinct criminal class became more prominent'.

*sinners.* The Hebrew root from which this word comes (*chātā'*) means literally, like the corresponding Greek word ἁμαρτάνω 'to miss the mark', see e.g. Prov. xix. 2. The word is used normally of sinning against God, sometimes of sinning against man; whereas the other frequently occurring word for sin (*rāshā'*) is used equally of 'doing wickedly' either against God or man.

**11.** *for blood.* A parallel with 'the innocent' in the next line is what one would naturally expect, and a very slight change in the Hebr. gives the word 'for the perfect' (man) (לחם instead of לדם); this is to be preferred. The reading 'for blood' may well have arisen under the influence of *vv.* 16, 17. Cf., however, Ecclus. xi. 32.

*without cause.* The word is meaningless here and spoils the rhythm in the Hebr.; it should be deleted.

**12.** *Sheol.* For the personification of *Shĕōl* as a devouring monster, see Isa. v. 14. See further, Excursus V.

13 We shall find all precious substance,
   We shall fill our houses with spoil;
14 [1]Thou shalt cast thy lot among us;
   We will all have one purse:
15 My son, walk not thou in the way with them;
   Refrain thy foot from their path:
16 For their feet run to evil,
   And they make haste to shed blood.
17 For in vain [2]is the net spread,
   In the eyes of any bird:
18 And these lay wait for their own blood,
   They lurk privily for their own lives.

   [1] Or, *Cast in thy lot*     [2] Or, *the net is spread in the sight &c.*

*whole.* The Hebr. word can mean either morally perfect, or physically whole; the parallel 'alive' favours the latter sense here. The general thought is that of a sudden murderous assault.

*the pit.* See Excursus V.

**13.** *substance.* Or 'wealth' (הוֹן), cf. viii. 18 'riches', Ecclus. iv. 14.

**14.** *Thou shalt cast.* Read with R.V. marg., following the Sept., 'Cast in thy lot'.

**15.** *My son.* This is rightly omitted by the Sept. for it is not wanted; the sentence begins at *v.* 11, 'If they say', the supposed words of the robbers follow, and the primary sentence continues in *v.* 15, 'walk not thou. . . .'

**16.** *For their feet . . . to shed blood.* This quotation from Isa. lix. 7 breaks the connexion between *vv.* 15 and 17; it is omitted by the best Sept. MSS, and is evidently not part of the original form of the text.

**17, 18.** These *vv.* belong together. The point of *v.* 17 is not easy to determine, and various interpretations have been offered; we suggest the following:

**17, 18.** By 'bird' is meant 'my son' (*v.* 10); the spreading of the net, i.e. the snare laid before the intended victim, is in vain because the sage explains (*v.* 18) that by their act the robbers are in reality planning their own destruction. Knowing this, his disciples will not be caught should the trap be laid.

The Sept. reads: 'For not in vain'; the negative was no doubt added in order to make the *v.* more in accord with actual fact, for generally speaking it is not in vain that the net is spread, whether in the sight of a bird or not. But the writer of the passage is not using 'bird' in a literal, but in a figurative, sense. The negative would spoil the point of *v.* 18.

*bird.* Lit. 'lord, or possessor, of wings'; it is not the usual word for 'bird', and occurs only here and in Eccles. x. 20.

19 So are the ways of every one that is greedy of gain;
    It taketh away the life of the owners thereof.
20 Wisdom crieth aloud in the street;
    She uttereth her voice in the broad places;
21 She crieth ¹in the chief place of concourse;
    At the entering in of the gates,
    In the city, she uttereth her words:

¹ Heb. *at the head of the noisy* streets.

**19.** *So are the ways* . . . i. e. this is ultimately the fate of every one that is greedy of gain. This is in accordance with the doctrine of retribution found elsewhere in the Wisdom Literature. See the introductory paragraph to this section.

**I. 20–33** *The voice of Wisdom proclaiming judgement.*

*Vv.* **20, 21** tell of the lifting-up of the voice of Wisdom in the streets and broad places; *vv.* 22, 23 contain Wisdom's question to the unwise as to how long they will continue to be deaf to her appeal, and an exhortation to turn to her. *Vv.* 24–32 announce their refusal to listen to the appeal, and the dire consequences. *V.* 33 declares the happiness of those who hearken to Wisdom. With the whole section cf. Ecclus. i. 1–10. It is in accordance with the view of the Wisdom writers in general that in *vv.* 24 ff. it is taken for granted that the mass of mankind do not follow Wisdom's precepts in spite of the obvious advantages to be gained by doing so, and in spite also of the equally obvious penalties entailed by refusal. Their knowledge of human nature had taught them this. Hence there is no need to suppose any incongruity in the abruptness of *vv.* 24 ff., and the appeal in *vv.* 22, 23. The general tone of this section recalls the utterances of the prophets; like the prophets of old, Wisdom goes out into the broad places of the city with denunciation and the prophecy of doom.

**20.** *Wisdom.* See Excursus III. With this section should be read viii, ix. 1–6, and Ecclus. i. 1–10, xxiv. The Hebr. form for 'Wisdom' here is in the plur., as in ix. 1, xiv. 1, xxiv. 7 (and not elsewhere), the force of the plur. is to express the fulness and perfection of Wisdom.

*crieth aloud.* The word is used of shouting with exultation, especially as an act of praise to God.

*street.* The Hebrew word refers to the space outside the walls of a city. The Sept., no doubt rightly, has the plural, corresponding with 'broad places' in the second line.

*broad places.* The open spaces within the city about the gates where the people were wont to assemble, cf. Jer. v. 1, ix. 20; Nah. ii. 5.

**21.** *the chief place of concourse.* In Isa. xxii. 2 a 'tumultuous city' is spoken of where the same Hebr. word is used; it also describes

22 How long, ye simple ones, will ye love simplicity?
   And scorners delight them in scorning,
   And fools hate knowledge?
23 Turn you at my reproof:
   Behold, I will pour out my spirit unto you,
   I will make known my words unto you.

the noise of the multitude (Isa. xvii. 12; Jer. vi. 23, l. 42), as well as
the roaring of the waves (Jer. v. 22, xxxi. 35; Isa. li. 15).

*In the city she uttereth her words.* Read: 'At the entering in of the
gates she speaketh'; then follow her words in *vv.* 22 ff.

**22.** For the meaning of the different types of 'fools' here mentioned see Excursus XI.

*And scorners . . .* Read, 'And, ye scorners, will ye delight in
scorning'; the corruption in the Hebr. text (חָמְדוּ לָהֶם) is emended
(חֲמַרְתֶּם) to correspond better with the first clause of the verse.

*and fools . . .* Read, 'And, ye fools, will ye hate knowledge',
(reading תִּשְׂנְאוּ for יִשְׂנְאוּ). Steuernagel would omit the two last lines
of the verse; their form certainly suggests that they are a copyist's
addition. As the next verse has three lines instead of the usual two,
he takes the first line of *v.* 23 as belonging to *v.* 22, and reads:

     'How long will ye love simplicity,
      And turn from my reproof?'

This has much to commend it.

**23.** *Turn you.* If we follow the R.V. rendering the meaning will be
that since the 'fools' mentioned in the preceding *v.* have hitherto
turned their back upon Wisdom, they are now exhorted to turn
round and face her in order to listen to her words (but see note on the
preceding *v.*). In the prophetical literature the word occurs often in
the sense of repenting, but that is not the case here.

*reproof.* 'Admonition' is perhaps a better rendering of the Hebrew
word (*tôkachath*), though the word undergoes different shades of
meaning according to the context in which it stands. Thus, in vi. 23
'reproof', i.e. for the sake of discipline, is the best rendering; in xv.31,
'the reproof of life' means the kind of 'admonition' which, if acted
upon, ensures prosperity; in xii. 1, too, the word means 'admonition';
while in xxix. 1 the slightly stronger word 'rebuke' would be appropriate, cf. xxix. 15. Sometimes, though not in *Proverbs*, the word is
used in the sense of 'reasoning', or 'argument', see Job xiii. 6,
xxiii. 4. The verse means that the rebuke which Wisdom has hitherto
refrained from uttering will now be poured forth; this rebuke is contained in the verses which follow.

*pour out.* Lit. 'Cause to bubble forth', cf. xv. 2, 28, xviii. 4.

*my spirit.* Cf. Ecclus. xvi. 25 (Hebr.).

24 Because I have called, and ye refused;
   I have stretched out my hand, and no man regarded;
25 But ye have set at nought all my counsel,
   And would none of my reproof:
26 I also will laugh in *the day of* your calamity;
   I will mock when your fear cometh;
27 When your fear cometh as ¹a storm,
   And your calamity cometh on as a whirlwind;
   When distress and anguish come upon you.

¹ Or, desolation

**24.** *stretched out my hand.* i. e. for the purpose of beckoning them to her.

*no man regarded.* Perhaps better, 'and none paid attention', cf. iv. 20, v. 1, vii. 24.

**25.** *set at nought.* The root idea of the Hebrew word is that of 'letting loose' (see Exod. xxxii. 25); the restraint which Wisdom's counsel might have had is thrown to the winds.

*would none.* The meaning is: 'ye would not yield to', cf. *v.* 30.

*reproof.* See note on *v.* 23.

**26.** Now follows the description of the consequence of having turned a deaf ear to the voice of Wisdom.

*I also will laugh.* The force of the Hebr. is, 'I, on my part, will laugh'.

*in* the day of *your calamity.* 'The day of' is not expressed in Hebr. but has to be supplied.

*I will mock.* Stronger than laughing in that it implies utterance.

*your fear.* Parallel to 'calamity', it means that which causes the fear, or dread. What the nature of the calamity is does not appear; but it is taken for granted that those who ignore Wisdom will be overtaken by grievous harm, the reference being, of course, to something that will happen in this world. The attitude of the personified Wisdom here does not appeal to us, being neither dignified nor wise, according to our ideas; but the enemies of Wisdom are regarded in the same light as ordinary enemies, and to exult over them in the day of their defeat was the natural thing to do, cf. ii. Chron. xx. 27; Mic. vii. 8; Prov. xxiv. 17.

**27.** *storm.* R.V. marg. 'desolation' is a better rendering of the Hebr., but 'storm' corresponds better with 'whirlwind' in the next clause; both come suddenly in the east, and it is the suddenness of the calamity which is the thought of the passage; cf. vi. 15, xxiv. 22, xxix. 1.

*when distress . . .* It is possible that this line is a later addition, it overloads the verse which corresponds better with the preceding verse without it.

28 Then shall they call upon me, but I will not answer;
    They shall seek me [1]diligently, but they shall not find me:
29 For that they hated knowledge,
    And did not choose the fear of the LORD:
30 They would none of my counsel;
    They despised all my reproof:
31 Therefore shall they eat of the fruit of their own way,
    And be filled with their own devices.
32 For the backsliding of the simple shall slay them,
    And the [2]prosperity of fools shall destroy them.
33 But whoso hearkeneth unto me shall dwell securely,
    And shall be quiet without fear of evil.

       [1] Or, *early*       [2] Or, *careless ease*

**28.** This and the following verses describe the *nemesis* which over-takes those who have been deaf to the call of Wisdom.

*they shall seek me diligently.* The idea underlying the Hebr. word is seeking in the morning, at day-break, hence the R.V. marg. 'early'. It is taken for granted that calamity will necessarily induce the search for Wisdom, but that it will be a vain search. The religious outlook of the Wisdom writers falls short of that of the prophets, see e.g. Ezek. xxxiii. 11.

**29.** *knowledge : the fear of the Lord.* Both are synonymous with Wisdom.

**30, 31.** These verses bring out the truth of the Pauline *dictum*, 'Whatsoever a man soweth that shall he also reap' (Gal. vi. 7).

**32.** *backsliding.* This refers to the turning away from the precepts of Wisdom, which are the condition of right living; this results in their undoing.

*the simple.* See Excursus XI.

*the prosperity.* Read with R.V. marg. 'careless ease'; the meaning of the line is well illustrated by Lk. xii. 19.

**33.** A final invitation after all the menaces of the preceding verses; it describes the happy lot of him who accepts what Wisdom offers, cf. Ecclus. iv. 15 (Hebr.).

*without fear of evil.* The reference is to external calamity or mis-fortune.

## CHAPTER II

**II. 1-22.** *The blessings of giving heed to Wisdom.*

THIS section is a unity, but is divided into two clearly defined parts: the acquisition of Wisdom is the means of attaining to the knowledge of God, and thereby of leading a righteous life (1-11); it is also the means whereby a man is enabled to avoid evil ways. *Vv.* 1-4 form a

**II.** 1 My son, if thou wilt receive my words,
  And lay up my commandments with thee;
 2 So that thou incline thine ear unto wisdom,
  And apply thine heart to understanding;
 3 Yea, if thou cry after discernment,
  And lift up thy voice for understanding;
 4 If thou seek her as silver,
  And search for her as for hid treasures;

protasis, to which 5–8 are the apodosis, 9–11 being closely connected. To this is joined *vv.* 12–22 as an integral part; 12–15 contain the assurance that Wisdom will be a protection against temptations from evil-disposed men, 16–19 against those of 'the strange woman', while 20–22 tell of how the follower after Wisdom will live uprightly, and how the wicked will come to an untimely end.

**1.** *My son.* The speaker is now no longer Wisdom, but the sage. On the expression 'My son' see note on i. 8.

*my words.* Unlike the prophet, who speaks in the name of God ('Thus saith Jahweh'), the sage speaks in his own name. Not that he is lacking in religious feeling, for the whole object of his teaching is that men may attain to the fear of Jahweh (*v.* 5).

*lay up.* This is the further step after the words have been accepted; the word means properly to 'hide or treasure up' (cf. Josh. ii. 4.) something of value, cf. x. 14.

*my commandments.* These, again, are more than words. 'Commandments' (*mitzwōth*) is the technical term for legal precepts; the Wisdom writers, while not ignoring the Law and its demands, were more concerned with the commandments of Wisdom; the writer speaks of them as 'my commandments' because he has so thoroughly assimilated what Wisdom demands.

*with thee.* i.e. in thine own keeping.

**2.** *incline thine ear.* i.e. listen, cf. Ecclus. iii. 29.

*apply.* The Hebr. word means lit., to 'stretch out' or 'extend'. As in the preceding verse there was the gradation: 'receive my words', 'lay up my commandments', so here; there is first, 'incline thine ear', then the further step 'apply thine heart'.

*heart.* See Excursus IX.

**3.** *Yea.* The Hebr. expression has the force of 'Nay, further', or the like. Once more there is a gradation: 'lift up thy voice', in the second strophe being stronger than 'cry' in the first.

**4.** *search.* The cognate word in Aramaic means 'to dig'; the idea here is that of searching for something hidden; treasures were often buried in the earth for the sake of security, cf. Job iii. 21 and Matt. xiii. 44.

5 Then shalt thou understand the fear of the LORD,
   And find the knowledge of God.
6 For the LORD giveth wisdom;
   Out of his mouth *cometh* knowledge and understanding:
7 He layeth up sound wisdom for the upright,
   [1] *He is* a shield to them that walk in integrity;
8 [2] That he may guard the paths of judgement,
   [3] And preserve the way of his saints.

[1] Or, And *a shield for &c*     [2] Or, *That they may keep*     [3] Or, *Yea, he preserveth*

**5.** Now follows the apodosis; the result of seeking Wisdom is to attain to the fear of Jahweh and the knowledge of God; one implies the other. This and the following *vv.* offer one illustration of many shewing a deeply religious conception of Wisdom.

*the knowledge of God.* This phrase occurs only once in this book, and in Hos. iv. 1, vi. 6.

**6.** *Out of his mouth.* This anthropomorphism occurs here only in the book; the Sept. tones it down by saying 'from his presence'.

**7.** *sound wisdom.* This well represents the force of the Hebr. word (*tushiyyah*) which is a technical one in the Wisdom Literature; apart from Isa. xxviii. 29; Mic. vi. 9, which are held by most scholars to be late passages, the word occurs only in *Job* and *Proverbs*.

He is *a shield.* 'He is' is not expressed in Hebr.; one would expect a verb, and the Versions have a verb or a participle; but the form of the Hebr. word can only be a noun. Cf. Ps. xxxiii. 20, lxxxiv. 12, lxxxix. 19, see also the Psalm of Thanksgiving, verse 10, which occurs after li. 12 in the Hebr. of Ecclus.

**8.** *That he may guard.* The Hebr. construction makes it possible for either Jahweh or 'those who walk in integrity' to be the subject; but as Jahweh is the subject in the next line, as well as in *vv.* 6, 7, it is best to read as in the text of R.V., not as in the marg.

*judgement.* See note on i. 3.

*saints.* Hebr. *Chassidim*; the graecized form Assidæans (also written Hasidæans) occurs in i. Macc. ii. 42 ff., vii. 12 f.; they are often spoken of in some of the later psalms. The mention of them here (the only time in the book) stamps the passage as late. They were the 'pious' ones who clung tenaciously to the Law, both written and oral, when, from the third century B.C. onwards, many of the Jews were becoming lax owing, largely, to Hellenistic influences. 'They were animated by a strong antipathy towards every one who was Hellenistically inclined; they were legalists in the strictest sense of the word, and particularists. Although in existence beforehand, it was only during the Maccabæan struggle that they commenced to play an important *rôle* in the political life of the nation' (Oesterley, *The Books of the Apocrypha*, p. 125 [3. ed. 1921]).

 9 Then shalt thou understand righteousness and judgement,
   And equity, *yea*, every good path.
10 For wisdom shall enter into thine heart,
   And knowledge shall be pleasant unto thy soul;
11 Discretion shall watch over thee,
   Understanding shall keep thee:
12 To deliver thee from the way of [1]evil,
   From the men that speak froward things;
13 Who forsake the paths of uprightness,
   To walk in the ways of darkness;
14 Who rejoice to do evil,
   And delight in the frowardness of [1]evil;
15 Who are crooked in their ways,
   And perverse in their paths:

[1] Or, *the evil* man

**9.** *And equity*...   The Hebr. text of this line can hardly be in
order; a verb is expected to correspond with 'then shalt thou understand'; by a slight emendation the text can be read: 'and shalt keep'.
   *every good path.*  Better, 'every path of good'. The Hebr. word
means lit. a 'wagon-track'; it is only used figuratively, both in a good
sense (iv. 11, 26, v. 21) and in a bad sense (see *vv.* 15, 18, and v. 6).
Cf. Ecclus. iv. 17, vi. 20 (Hebr.).
   **10.** *For wisdom shall enter* . . . With this thought cf. Wisd. i. 4–7,
xi. 17; in later Jewish teaching Wisdom was identified with the holy
Spirit of God.
   **11.** *discretion.* See note on i. 4. Knowledge, discretion, understanding, are all manifestations of Wisdom.
   **12.** *from the way of evil.* The Hebr. can mean either this, or 'from
the way of the evil man'; the latter accords better with the context.
   *froward things.* The word occurs only in *Prov.* (vi. 14, viii. 13, &c.)
and in Deut. xxxii. 20; it means lit. that which is turned upside down.
The cognate word in Arabic means a 'lie' (Wildeboer).
   **13.** *the ways of darkness.* Cf. Ps. lxxxii. 5.
   **14.** *in the frowardness of evil.* Read 'in froward things'; the
second 'evil' is perhaps due to dittography; in any case 'froward
things of evil' is pleonastic, and if we take the Hebr. text as it stands
we must read 'froward things of evil men', as in *v.* 12. Cf. xv. 21.
   **15.** The Hebr. text is not quite in order; read, following the Versions, 'whose ways are crooked, and their paths perverse'. The Hebr.
word for 'perverse' comes from the root (*lūz*) meaning to 'bend' from;
it is therefore a very appropriate parallel to 'crooked'. Cf. xiv. 2; in
iii. 32 the word is used of one who is the antithesis to the upright man.

16 To deliver thee from the strange woman,
   Even from the stranger which [1]flattereth with her words;
17 Which forsaketh the [2]friend of her youth,
   And forgetteth the covenant of her God:
18 For [3]her house inclineth unto death,
   And her paths unto [4]the dead:
19 None that go unto her return again,
   Neither do they attain unto the paths of life:

[1] Heb. *maketh smooth her words.*     [2] Or, *guide*     [3] Or, *she sinketh down unto death,* which is *her house*     [4] Or, *the shades* Heb. *Rephaim.*

**16.** *the strange woman.* Cf. vii. 5, which is almost identical with this verse. It is possible that 'strange' is to be taken in the sense of 'foreign', i.e. a non-Jewess; cf. vi. 24–26, where a 'whorish woman' (stranger) is differentiated from an adulteress. In the Talmud a harlot is called an *'Arāmīth,* an 'Aramæan woman' (Wildeboer); but from what is said in the next *v.* it is more likely that an adulteress is meant here.

*flattereth.* Lit. 'maketh smooth her words'; in xxviii. 23 there is the similar phrase, 'maketh smooth the tongue' for flattering, cf. Ps. v. 9 (10 in Hebr.). Cf. with the verse Ecclus. ix. 2, 3.

**17.** *the friend of her youth.* 'Friend' refers to her husband, cf. Mal. ii. 14. R.V. marg. can be ignored, the word (*'allūph*) never has the sense of 'guide' in the O.T.

*the covenant of her God.* The reference is to Exod. xx. 14, 'thou shalt not commit adultery.' The Sept., no doubt rightly, omits 'her'.

**18.** As it stands the Hebr. cannot be correct; a slight alteration enables us to read: 'Her house (in the sense of those who consort with her) leadeth down (lit. sinketh down) to death.' For 'her house' (בֵּיתָהּ), however, Steuernagel suggests 'her way' (נְתִיבָתָהּ), cf. i. 15, viii. 2, which offers a better parallel with the second line.

*the dead.* Hebr. *Rěphā'im* ('shades'); see further on these the present writer's *Immortality and the Unseen World,* pp. 63 ff. (1921), and Excursus V.

**19.** *None that go . . .* Cf. the Babylonian description of the land of the dead in the 'Descent of Ishtar', which is described as:

> 'the house which whosoever enters never leaves again,
> the path from which there is no return,
> the house which whosoever enters is taken from the light.'

*the paths of life.* As in x. 17 the reference is to this world, cf. v. 6; Ps. xvi. 10, 11; the 'path of life' is that which leads to a life made happy through the fear of the Lord.

c

20 That thou mayest walk in the way of good men,
   And keep the paths of the righteous.
21 For the upright shall dwell in the ¹land,
   And the perfect shall remain in it.
22 But the wicked shall be cut off from the ¹land,
   And they that deal treacherously shall be rooted out of it.

**III.** 1 My son, forget not my ²law;
   But let thine heart keep my commandments:

¹ Or, earth        ² Or, teaching

**20.** See note on *v.* 9.

*the righteous.* Hebr. *Zaddîqîm*; i.e. such as do what is right in ordinary life (*zedeq*), and practice the divine precepts in righteousness (*zĕdaqah*).

**21.** *the land.* i.e. Canaan; cf. Exod. xx. 12; Deut. v. 16; the R.V. marg. 'earth' can be ignored.   So, too, in the next verse.

**22.** *cut off.* Cf. Ps. xxxvii. 38.

*rooted out.* Cf. xv. 25; Deut. xxviii. 63; Ps. lii. 5 (7 in Hebr.).

CHAPTER III

THE central point of this section is to warn young men against the belief in their own infallibility, one of the prime failings in youth. They are bidden not to rely on their own understanding, and not to be wise in their own eyes. The sage, who must have been in very close touch with his pupils, and who therefore knew how ingrained this failing is in the young, leads up to his central point with skill and tactfulness, being anxious not to wound the susceptibilities of his youthful hearers. He begins with a personal note by referring to his own teaching, this being the object for which the pupils have come to him; he then leads their thoughts on to God, the Fount from whom all truth proceeds; and thus, having brought them into touch with divine teaching, contrasts the trust to be placed in God with the self-reliance of immature youth. Not in the light of their own understanding, but in the acknowledgement and acceptance of God's guidance, will they discern the right way. And he concludes with the words of promise and encouragement to all who act on this principle.

**III. 1–10.** *Exhortations to follow the teaching of the Sage.*

**1.** *my law.* i.e. teaching; cf. iv. 2. Jer. xviii. 18 speaks of three kinds of teaching, the law of the priest, the counsel of the wise men, and the word of the prophet. That 'law' is here used of the teaching of the sage and points to the development which was gradually taking place in the standing and profession of the Wise men, or *Chăkāmîm*;

2 For length of days, and years of life,
   And peace, shall they add to thee.
3 Let not [1] mercy and truth forsake thee:
   Bind them about thy neck;
   Write them upon the table of thine heart:

[1] Or, *kindness*

for ultimately they became identified with the Scribes, one of whose main duties was the teaching of the Law, in the narrower sense. As yet, however, the law, or teaching, of the sage was mainly concentrated on moral precepts for right conduct of life; he addresses himself to the individual, not to the nation, which was the *rôle* of the earlier prophets; and he is not concerned with teaching on ritual and worship, which was exclusively the priest's concern.

*my commandments.* This further illustrates what has just been said. The term used, *Mitzwōth* ('commandments'), became later the technical one for legal precepts. That the word is used of the sage's counsels shows that we are still within the period of a freer atmosphere than that of the later scribal activity.

**2.** *length of days . . .* i. e. increase of days (cf. Exod. xx. 12; Isa. lxv. 20, 22); 'years of life' is not synonymous with this, for the idea of 'life' meant earthly felicity and well-being (cf. xvi. 15); these, together with peace (the word connotes both inward and outward tranquillity), constituted all that a man could wish for. They are the reward of the true follower of Wisdom. Cf. the saying in *The Bilingual Book of Proverbs*, 31: 'He that is wise attaineth to old age.'[1] This verse is quoted in *Pirqê 'Abôth* vi. 7, where the Law is identified with Wisdom.

**3.** *mercy and truth.* The Hebr. words are perhaps better expressed by 'kindness and faithfulness', or 'steadfastness'; the two are often mentioned together (xiv. 22, xvi. 6, xx. 28; Ps. lxxxv. 10 (11 in Hebr.), and elsewhere; they sum up a man's duty to his neighbour.

*Bind them.* Cf. Exod. xiii. 9, 16; Deut. vi. 8, xi. 18, and Ecclus. vii. 8 for the converse, 'Bind not up sin'. The idea is illustrated by the *Tĕphillin* (the 'phylacteries' of the Gospels), which were little black boxes, bound on the head and hand, containing the '*Shĕma*'' ('Hear, O Israel . . .'); they were worn, and still are, in the Synagogue (see further, Oesterley & Box, *The Religion and Worship of the Synagogue*, 2. ed., pp. 447 ff. [1911]).

*Write them upon . . .* Cf. Jer. xxxi. 33; the words occur also in Prov. vii. 3. The line is wanting in the Septuagint, and is probably a later addition; a third line is not found in the original form of any other verse in this section.

---

[1] Langdon, *op. cit.*, p. 83.

4 So shalt thou find favour and [1]good understanding
  In the sight of God and man.
5 Trust in the LORD with all thine heart,
  And lean not upon thine own understanding:
6 In all thy ways acknowledge him,
  And he shall [2]direct thy paths.
7 Be not wise in thine own eyes;
  Fear the LORD, and depart from evil:
8 It shall be health to thy navel,
  And [3]marrow to thy bones.

[1] Or, good repute    [2] Or, make straight or plain
[3] Or, refreshing  Heb. moistening.

**4.** *So shalt thou find.* The Hebr. has the imperative, 'and find'.
*favour and good understanding.* This is a strange combination; the variety of renderings in the Versions shows the difficulty felt. The Hebr. text is probably corrupt. By a slight emendation the word for 'understanding' can be made to read 'name' (שֵׁם for שֵׂכֶל, cf. xxii. 1); this would certainly make better sense.
**5.** With the first line cf. Ecclus. iii. 21–24, and with the whole verse cf. Jer. ix. 23, 24 (22, 23 in Hebr.). The second clause is quoted in *Pirqê 'Abôth* iv. 20.
**6.** *direct.* The Hebr. word is used of making a path smooth by clearing it of obstacles, so in Isa. xl. 3; the figurative use of this form (*pi'el*) of the verb occurs only in *Prov.*, see ix. 15, xi. 5, xv. 21; in iv. 25 it is used of looking straight before one. Cf. Ecclus. ii. 6.
**7.** *Be not wise in* ... Cf. xxvi. 12, and Isa. v. 21.
*Fear the Lord and* ... The one is the necessary consequence of the other.
**8.** *health.* The form of the word is Aramaic, it comes from the root meaning to 'heal', and occurs here only in the O.T.
*to thy navel.* The Hebr. word occurs elsewhere only in Ezek. xvi. 4, and Song of Songs vii. 3. As a parallel to 'bones' it is inappropriate; by a slight change in the Hebr. we may read the word for 'flesh' (בְּשָׂר for שֵׁר, cf. iv. 22, 'health to all thy flesh'); the Septuagint reads 'body', the Hebr. word for which is similar to that in the text. The combination flesh and bone occurs in xiv. 30, and in Gen. ii. 21 ff., xxix. 14; Judg. ix. 2; 2 Sam. v. 1; Job ii. 5. In *Pirqê 'Abôth* vi. 7, however, this verse is quoted as in the text.
*marrow to thy bones.* The Hebr. word for 'marrow' means lit. 'drink', see Hos. ii. 5 (7 in Hebr.); Ps. cii. 9 (10 in Hebr.), the only other occurrences of the word in the O.T. Here it is used figuratively for 'refreshment'. The human bones (Hebr. *'ăzāmōth*), according to Hebr. ideas, occupied a peculiarly important place, difficult for the modern mind to understand. They were identified with a man's

9　Honour the LORD with thy substance,
　　And with the firstfruits of all thine increase:
10　So shall thy barns be filled with plenty,
　　And thy fats shall overflow with new wine.

personality (cf. Job iv. 14, xx. 11; Ps. xxxv. 19; Jer. xxiii. 9); hence
the importance attached to their burial (cf. Gen. l. 25; Exod. xiii. 19;
Josh. xxiv. 32); and the direst punishment which could be inflicted
on a man was not only to leave his body unburied, but also his bones,
even long after the flesh had decayed, see 2 Kings xxiii. 16; Jer. viii.
1, 2; cf. Am. ii. 1. The reason why this importance was attached to
the bones, as distinct from the flesh, is nowhere directly stated in the
O.T., but it is hinted at in such a passage as Ezek. xxxvii (the vision
of the dry bones), and in Isa. lxvi. 14, '... your bones shall flourish
like the tender grass'. Thus, there was the belief that life resided in
the bones after death, or even permanently. In two striking passages
Ben-Sira speaks of the bones of the Judges flourishing again out of
their place (Ecclus. xlvi. 11, 12), and of the bones of the prophets,
that 'they may sprout beneath them' (xlix. 10). This conception of
the life of the deceased lying dormant in the bones is widespread
among uncultured peoples.

**9.** *Honour the Lord* ... Cf. Isa. xliii. 23; Ecclus. xxxv. 8.

*substance.* Properly 'riches' or 'wealth', as in viii. 18; a very
common word in *Proverbs*.

*with the firstfruits.* The Hebr. has 'from' or 'of', because the Law
commanded only part of these to be offered, see Deut. xviii. 4, xxvi. 2;
cf. also Ecclus. vii. 31. This is one of the rare references in *Proverbs*
to the ceremonial Law; not that the Wisdom writers were unmindful
of what was demanded; it was only that their special preoccupation
was in a different direction; see Excursus VI.

*increase.* The next verse shows that the reference is to agricultural produce.

**10.** *plenty.* The Septuagint reads 'corn', which is perhaps better;
the Hebr. words for 'plenty' and 'corn' are very similar.

*overflow.* Lit. 'burst'; the vats will be so full that they will burst,
and thus overflow. With the promise contained in this *v.* cf. Deut.
xviii. 4, xxviii. 8; Mal. iii. 10–12.

### III. 11–20. *The blessings of Wisdom.*

The first two verses of this section are, in all probability, out of
place, since they deal with an entirely different subject from that
of the rest of the section. Here we have another of the many ways in
which the Wisdom teachers sought to commend Wisdom to the youth
of their day. As in all ages, the acquisition of wealth was a primary
occupation of thought and action. The sage knew, therefore, that he

11  My son, despise not the ¹chastening of the LORD ;
    Neither be weary of his reproof:
12  For whom the LORD loveth he reproveth ;
    Even as a father the son in whom he delighteth.
13  Happy is the man that findeth wisdom,
    And the man that ²getteth understanding.

¹ Or, instruction          ² Heb. draweth forth.

would at once gain the attention of his hearers by touching upon a
topic of such universal interest.  So he teaches that none of the things
so much desired, silver and gold and jewels, are to be compared with
the kind of wealth which can be procured by means of Wisdom.  With
Wisdom as a possession a man is placed in the position of being able to
gather not only riches, but, in addition, that which all the world craves
for, length of days and a life of pleasantness and peace.  Verses 19, 20
are not altogether appropriate, it is possible that they were placed here
from elsewhere for the purpose of giving a more definitely religious
tone to the section.  It was hardly necessary, for the sages were no
materialists, and they make it abundantly clear that they believed
every form of Wisdom to come from the divine Giver, so that there
was no need to be constantly repeating what was regarded as self-
evident.

**11.** *My son.*  In Hebr. the sentence does not open with this form
of address, as is always the case when it is used; it evidently did not
belong to the original text, but was inserted later, though why it was
not put in its proper place at the opening of the sentence is difficult
to say.

*chastening.*  See note on i. 2.  Cf. Heb. xii. 5.

*Neither be weary.*  A stronger expression in Hebr. than 'despise'
in the first line; the word means lit. to 'feel an abhorrence' or 'loath-
ing' for something, see Lev. xx. 23; Num. xxi. 5, &c.

**12.**  Cf. Job v. 17, 18.

*the Lord.*  The repetition of Jahweh here breaks the rhythm; it
is not required as the preceding *v.* shows that 'the Lord' is the
subject.

*Even as a father* ...   The Hebr. text of this line is awkward, and can
hardly be in order.  The words 'and as a father the son' should be
emended to read, with the Sept., 'and afflicteth him'; both being
very similar in Hebr.  The Sept., it is true, has 'son'; but this seems
to have been put into the Hebr. by mistake because of the misreading
'as a father'.  God is never spoken of as 'father' in *Proverbs*.  The
line should thus run: 'And afflicteth him in whom he delighteth', cf.
Job v. 18 (Hebr.); Ecclus. ii. 1, 5.

**13.** *Happy.*  The Hebr. expression is lit. 'Oh the blessedness of'

14 For the merchandise of it is better than the merchandise of
      silver,
    And the gain thereof than fine gold.
15 She is more precious than ¹rubies:
    And none of the things thou canst desire are to be compared
      unto her.

¹ See Job. xxviii. 18.

(cf. Ps. i. 1), but has come to be used almost as an exclamation; see
also viii. 34.

*that findeth.* The Hebr. has 'that hath found'.

*that getteth.* The Hebr. word means to 'bring forth', or 'produce',
and here it is not the perfect as in the previous verb; the difference
in tense between the two is not without purpose. In the first case the
man is blessed because he has found God's gift of Wisdom; but the
possession of this divine gift is of little benefit unless it is utilized; so
in the second case the man is blessed if he draws forth, or produces,
from his possession discernment.

**14.** *merchandise.* The Hebr. word means properly 'gain' through
commerce, see Isa. xxiii. 3 (rendered 'revenue' in R.V.); the second
'merchandise' is really not wanted (there is nothing parallel to it in
the second clause), it is self-understood. One might paraphrase the
line by: The gain which Wisdom brings in is better than the profit
made by means of silver.

*gold.* The Hebr. word for 'gold' used here is not the ordinary one,
and occurs only in *Prov.* and the *Psalms*; it comes from a root
meaning 'to be yellow'. It is the Phoenician word for 'gold', and
occurs on the Tabnith inscription (see Driver, *Notes on the Hebrew
Text of the Books of Samuel*, p. xxviii [1890]).

**15.** *She.* The subject is Wisdom.

*rubies.* The meaning of the Hebr. word is uncertain. 'Rubies', in
any case, can hardly be right, since 'there is no proof that the ruby,
which is found only in Ceylon and in Burmah, was known to the
Hebrews any more than it was to the Greeks till after the time of
Theophrastus' (Prof. Ridgeway, 'The Ruby Mines in Upper Burmah',
in the *Cornhill Magazine* for December 1901, quoted in the *Encycl.
Bibl.* iv. 4163). Some scholars render the word by 'pearls', but this
is excluded by Lam. iv. 7, where they are referred to as 'ruddy'. The
most probable conjecture is that the word means 'corals'; a cognate
Arabic word means 'branch' of a tree (see *Oxf. Hebr. Lex.* s.v.). See
further *Encycl. Bibl.* 1. 895 f. The word occurs also in Prov. xiii. 11,
xx. 15, xxxi. 10; Job xxviii. 18.

*And none . . .* Read, following viii. 11 and the Sept.: 'And all
things that may be desired are not to be compared unto her.'

16 Length of days is in her right hand;
  In her left hand are riches and honour.

17 Her ways are ways of pleasantness,
  And all her paths are peace.

18 She is a tree of life to them that lay hold upon her:
  And happy is every one that retaineth her.

19 The LORD by wisdom founded the earth;
  By understanding he established the heavens.

20 By his knowledge the depths were broken up,
  And the skies drop down the dew.


21 My son, let not them depart from thine eyes;
  Keep sound wisdom and discretion;


**16, 17.** Wisdom is personified and lavishes with both hands the things desired, long life and riches, to those who are attached to her. A pleasant life of peace is also the lot of those who follow her ways. If this verse strikes one as somewhat materialistic, it must be remembered that there are a far greater number of passages which present higher ideals. *V.* 16 is quoted in *Pirqê 'Abôth* vi. 7.

**18.** *a tree of life.* i.e. she prolongs life to those who partake of her fruits, cf. viii. 19. For the expression cf. xi. 30, xiii. 12, xv. 4, which show that it is in no way connected with the idea of 'the tree of life' in Gen. ii. 9. The text is quoted in *Pirqê 'Abôth* vi. 7. In Rabbinical literature *vv.* 17, 18 are interpreted as referring to the *Tōrah*, e.g. *T. B. Sukkah.* 32 *a.*

**19, 20.** With these *vv.* cf. viii. 22 ff.; Job xxviii. 24-28; Ecclus. xxiv. 1 ff.; Wisd. ix. 9.

*the dew.* According to the old Hebrew idea the dew, like the rain, comes from the clouds.


## III. 21-35. *Precepts of Wisdom.*

**21.** *let them not depart* ... The identical words occur in iv. 21 in R.V., the Hebr. is very slightly different. The subject of 'let them not ...' is clearly wisdom and discretion, but as it is against Hebr. usage to have a subject in the second clause like this, it is likely that the two clauses have become displaced, and that we should read: 'My son, keep ..., let them not depart from thine eyes.'

*depart.* The Hebr. word, which is not the usual one for to 'depart', occurs only in the Wisdom literature, cf. iii. 32, iv. 21, xiv. 2.

*sound wisdom.* See note on ii. 7.

*discretion.* See note on i. 4.

22 So shall they be life unto thy soul,
And grace to thy neck.

23 Then shalt thou walk in thy way securely,
And ¹thy foot shall not stumble.

24 When thou liest down, thou shalt not be afraid:
Yea, thou shalt lie down, and thy sleep shall be sweet.

25 Be not afraid of sudden fear,
Neither of the ²desolation of the wicked, when it cometh:

26 For the LORD shall be thy confidence,
And shall keep thy foot from being taken.

¹ Heb. *thou shalt not dash thy foot.*       ² Or, *storm*

**22.** *life unto thy soul.* Cf. iv. 22. Life means physical life, cf. iii. 2. 'Unto thy soul' is the Hebr. way of saying 'unto thee'; the soul is equivalent to the individual.

*grace to thy neck.* Cf. i. 9. 'Grace' here means properly 'elegance'; Wisdom adorning a man's character is compared to a beautiful ornament on a woman's neck.

**23.** *And thy foot...* See R.V. marg. The Hebr. word for 'stumble' is not used intransitively as here (see Ps. xci. 12); it means to 'strike' or 'smite', cf. e.g. Isa. xix. 22.

**24.** Cf. vi. 22. The force of the Hebr. tenses is lost in the R.V.; lit. we should read: 'When thou shalt lie down thou shalt not be afraid; and when thou hast lain down, sweet is thy slumber.'

*thy sleep shall be sweet.* Cf. Jer. xxxi. 26.

**25.** *sudden fear.* Precisely the same phrase occurs in Job xxii. 10.

*desolation.* See note on i. 27. Here the word means 'destruction' or 'ruin', cf. Isa. x. 3, xlvii. 11.

**26.** *thy confidence.* Cf. Job viii. 14, xxxi. 24; Ps. lxxviii. 7. The Sept. has 'in all thy ways'.

*from being taken.* Hebr. 'from capture'; the Hebr. word is used here only; for the thought cf. Ps. ix. 15 (16 in Hebr.).

With these two *vv.* we must compare the *Teaching of Amen-em-ope* X. xiii. 19–xiv. 1:

> Be thou courageous before other people,
> For one is safe in the hand of God.

If we take the first line of *vv.* 25, 26 respectively we get this couplet:

> Be not afraid of sudden fear
> For Jahweh shall be thy confidence.

This is, in essence, parallel to the Egyptian couplet. It looks as though the compiler of *Proverbs*, in adapting Amen-em-ope's words, expanded them to form two couplets, just as has sometimes been done with a single-lined popular proverb.

27 Withhold not good from them to whom it is due,
   When it is in the power of thine hand to do it.
28 Say not unto thy neighbour, Go, and come again,
   And to-morrow I will give;
   When thou hast it by thee.

*Vv.* 27–30 deal with a man's duty to his neighbour; they come in here somewhat inappropriately, being out of harmony with the context. There is, however, nothing surprising in this. The Wisdom writers were all to some extent compilers; they gathered their material from different quarters; and they composed sayings of their own, partly original and partly based on those of other thinkers, not necessarily of their own nation. So that it is natural enough if in the arrangement of accumulated material of various content there should not always be a strictly logical sequence. This explains also the frequent repetitions which occur in the book, both in the subject-matter and form of a verse. A careful co-ordination of subject-matter on the part of the compiler would, it is likely enough, have resulted in the deleting of a good many superfluous verses, to the advantage of the book as a literary composition; but the compiler was not so much concerned with the niceties of composition as with recording all that he could gather from every source, including con-tributions from his own mind. A still more striking illustration of what has been said is offered by the *Wisdom of Ben-Sira (Ecclesiasti-cus)* and, on a less extensive scale, by the Egyptian Wisdom book, the *Teaching of Amen-em-ope.*

**27.** *from them to whom it is due.* The Hebr. has 'from the owners (baals) thereof', i.e. of good; the R.V. paraphrases this. The Sept. apparently understood the Hebr. in a way similar to that of the Revisers, rendering it 'from the poor'. But it is doubtful whether the Hebrew will bear this meaning. Toy justly remarks that 'in ex-pressions of position or quality *baal* always signifies one who employs or controls the thing in question'; he then illustrates this, main-taining therefore that there is no authority in Hebrew usage for the statement that the expression before us may mean 'not him who does good, but him to whom good is done'. He therefore suggests that the Hebrew word is a corruption for one meaning 'thy neigh-bour' (the two words are not unlike in Hebrew, read רעיך for בעליו), and this is supported by the context, 'Say not unto thy neighbour' (*v.* 28), and *v.* 29.

*in the power of thine hand.* For the phrase cf. Gen. xxxi. 29; Deut. xxviii. 32; Mic. ii. 1.

**28.** Cf. Ecclus. iv. 3, Jas. ii. 16, and the following words of Achikar: 'My son, though the thresholds of thy house were high, and thy neigh-bour lay sick, say not, " What shall I send him? " But go upon thy

29 Devise not evil against thy neighbour,
  Seeing he dwelleth securely by thee.

30 Strive not with a man without cause,
  If he have done thee no harm.

31 Envy thou not the man of violence,
  And choose none of his ways.

32 For the perverse is an abomination to the LORD:
  But his [1] secret is with the upright.

33 The curse of the LORD is in the house of the wicked;
  But he blesseth the habitation of the righteous.

[1] Or, *counsel*  Or, *friendship*

feet, and see with thine eyes; that were better for him than a thousand talents of gold and silver' (quoted by Volz, *op. cit.*, p. 176).

**29.** *Devise not evil.* In this usage the Hebr. word has mostly a bad meaning, cf. vi. 14, xi. 20, xiv. 22, but in this last passage it is also used in a good sense. The ordinary meaning of the word is to 'engrave' and then to 'plough', which is the commonest use of the word; cf. Ecclus. vii. 12.

*securely.* i.e. trustfully.

**30.** *without cause, If he have done thee no harm* is tautologous; the latter seems to be an unskilful addition, a second line being required for the sake of symmetry. The original line must have dropped out.

**31.** *Envy thou not.* One might be inclined to take the Hebrew word rather in the sense of 'emulate not', cf. Ps. xxxvii. 1, since there is nothing to envy in the violent man; but what is probably meant is illustrated by Ps. lxxiii. 3–5, 'I was envious of the arrogant when I saw the prosperity of the wicked ...'; cf. Ecclus. ix. 11.

*the man of violence.* Cf. x. 6, 11, xiii. 2, xxvi. 6, &c.

*choose* ... The Hebrew word, by the change of one letter, should probably be read 'fret not thyself because of all his ways'; so the Sept., the verse seems to be based on Ps. xxxvii. 1, cf. Prov. xxiv. 19.

**32.** *the perverse.* See note on ii. 15.

*his secret* ... The Hebr. word means familiar or confidential intercourse, such as exists between God and those who fear Him, cf. Ps. xxv. 14, lv. 14 (15 in Hebr.).

*upright.* Lit. 'straight'.

**33.** *The curse of* ... Cf. Ps. xxxvii. 22; Zech. v. 3, 4; Mal. ii. 2.

*habitation.* The Hebr. word means, in its origin, the abode of a shepherd of flocks (cf. Isa. xxvii. 10); it usually refers to a dwelling-place in the country; so that the contrasting ideas underlying the two clauses are those respectively of the noisy city where the wicked congregate, and the peace and quietude of the country-side.

34  [1]Surely he scorneth the scorners,
      [2]But he giveth grace unto the lowly.
35  The wise shall inherit glory;
      But [3]shame shall be the promotion of fools.

      [1] Or, *Though*          [2] Or, *Yet*          [3] Or, *fools carry away shame*

**34.** *Surely he scorneth* ... The Hebrew text is slightly out of order;
read, 'With the scorners he will be scornful', cf. Ps. xviii. 26 (27
Hebr.).

*But he giveth* ... Cf. xvi. 19.

**35.** *The wise.* See Excursus VII. This clause is quoted in *Pirqê
'Abôth* vi. 3.

*shall inherit.* The Hebr. word also means to 'get possession of',
'acquire'; and this is the meaning it has here. Cf. Ecclus. iv. 13.

*glory.* i. e. honour, referring to the respect in which they will be
held by others for their wisdom.

*shall be the promotion.* The Hebr. word is difficult, and a number
of suggestions have been offered regarding it; Wildeboer, by the
alteration of one letter, reads 'bear' (as their portion), cf. xiv. 29 b;
Steuernagel suggests the emendation 'inherit' (מוֹרִישִׁים for מֵרִים),
'but fools inherit shame'; this is the most probable. The general
sense of the line is, without doubt, that fools shall have shame as
their possession.

*fools.* See Excursus XI.

# CHAPTER IV

**IV. 1–27.** *Exhortations to follow the instruction of the Wise Man.*

THE sage addresses his pupils as a father instructing his son. He
teaches them that Wisdom is first of all moral conduct of life. He
speaks as one who has had his own experience; he knows what the
temptations of life are; he has chosen the path of virtue, and the
reward has been very precious. He lays special stress on the need of
avoiding the first step on the way of wrongdoing; that way must be
passed by. To those who walk upon it wickedness becomes second
nature, and without some daily act of wrongdoing they are ill at ease.
How different it is with those who follow the precepts of Wisdom
which he inculcates; for them prosperity and health are in store.
The passage well illustrates the intense seriousness of the Wisdom-
teachers; they are consumed with anxiety for the moral welfare of
their pupils. The instruction given, it is true, is purely ethical; there
is no mention at all here of the name of God, nor of religion as such;
but it must be remembered that in the mental background of the
Wise men *all* wisdom, of which moral living is one form, is religious.
Besides this, however, the Wisdom writers knew human nature well,
and they were perfectly aware that to young men in the heyday of

**IV.** 1 Hear, *my* sons, the instruction of a father,
  And attend to know understanding:
2 For I give you good doctrine;
  Forsake ye not my [1]law.
3 For I was a son unto my father,
  Tender and [2]only beloved in the sight of my mother.
4 And he taught me, and said unto me,
  Let thine heart retain my words;
  Keep my commandments, and live:
5 Get wisdom, get understanding;

[1] Or, *teaching*      [2] Heb. *an only one.*

life the over-emphasizing of religion defeats its own end; when once
stedfast in the way of moral conduct the higher things will come in
due course. This was the practical common-sense characteristic of
the Wisdom-teachers.

**IV. 1–9.** *Wisdom must be striven after.*

**1.** my *sons*. Omit 'my'; it is better to render 'children' here because the sage is for the moment addressing his hearers not so much
as pupils, but rather as children who are to receive fatherly admonitions.

*a father.* The speaker is referring to himself as assuming the
character of a father.

**2.** *doctrine.* See note on i. 5.

*my law.* See note on iii. 1. In *Pirqê 'Abôth* vi. 3, where this verse
is quoted, *Tôrah* is used in reference to the Law of God; it is also
quoted in iii. 23, where the *Tôrah* is spoken of as the instrument
whereby the world was created, being thus identified with Wisdom,
cf. Wisd. viii. 22 ff.

**3.** *For I was a son* ... Or 'I have been'; the sage is merely giving
himself as an illustration and example of one who has had experience; he would say to his hearers that he has been in their
position, and learned from his father; therefore they are to learn
from him who has for the time being assumed the character of father
to them.

**4.** *And he taught me.* The force of the Hebr. form of the word is,
'and he used to teach me'.

*thine heart.* See Excursus IX.

*and live.* See note on iii. 2. The Sept. omits.

**5.** The Hebr. text is undoubtedly somewhat out of order; various
suggestions for emendations are proposed, but there is necessarily
uncertainty about them all; and as, in any case, the general sense of

Forget *it* not, neither decline from the words of my mouth:

6 Forsake her not, and she shall preserve thee;
Love her, and she shall keep thee.

7 ¹Wisdom *is* the principal thing; *therefore* get wisdom:
Yea, with all thou hast gotten get understanding.

8 Exalt her, and she shall promote thee:
She shall bring thee to honour, when thou dost embrace her.

9 She shall give to thine head a chaplet of grace:
A crown of ²beauty shall she deliver to thee.

10 Hear, O my son, and receive my sayings;
And the years of thy life shall be many.

¹ Or, *The beginning of wisdom* is, *Get wisdom*          ² Or, *glory*

the verse is not affected by them, it will be better to take it as it
stands.

*Get wisdom* . . . This line is omitted in the Sept. though some later
MSS. place it after 'forget it not' in the next line. The repetition of
'get' (i.e. 'acquire', cf. xvii. 16, xxiii. 23) suggests the sage's insistence on the need of possessing wisdom, cf. Ecclus. li. 25.

*Forget* it *not*. This is omitted by the Syriac Version. The 'it' is not
required.

*neither decline*. Better, 'neither turn aside', see Num. xxii. 23.

**6.** *Love her* . . . Cf. viii. 17.

**7.** It is clear that this *v*. interrupts the connexion between *vv*. 6
and 8, so that there is justification in following the Sept. in omitting
it. It cannot well be part of the original text, and looks like a (later)
expansion of the first clause of verse 5.

*Wisdom* is *the principal thing*. Neither this nor the R.V. marg.
represents the Hebrew; the 'is' in the marg. rendering is not justified.
The Hebrew text has simply two isolated phrases: 'The beginning of
Wisdom', 'Get Wisdom'.

*with all thou hast gotten*. Hebr. 'with all thy possession'.

**8.** *Exalt her*. Cf. Exod. ix. 17 for this use of the Hebr. word
which also means to 'cast up', of a highway, cf. Isa. lvii. 14.

*promote*. Lit. 'set up on high', to correspond with 'exalt'.

*She shall bring thee to honour*. Cf. Ecclus. i. 19.

*embrace*. Cf. Song of Songs ii. 6; Eccles. iii. 5.

**9.** See notes on i. 9; cf. Ecclus. vi. 29 ff.; the verse is quoted in
*Pirqê 'Abôth* vi. 7.

**IV. 10–19.** *Exhortations to follow the instruction of the Wise
Men: contrast between those who follow Wisdom and those who
walk in the path of the wicked.*

**10.** Cf. iii. 2, 16, ix. 11.

11 I have taught thee in the way of wisdom;
   I have led thee in paths of uprightness.

12 When thou goest, thy steps shall not be straitened;
   And if thou runnest, thou shalt not stumble.

13 Take fast hold of instruction; let her not go:
   Keep her; for she is thy life.

14 Enter not into the path of the wicked,
   And walk not in the way of evil men.

15 Avoid it, pass not by it;
   Turn from it, and pass on.

16 For they sleep not, except they have done mischief;
   And their sleep is taken away, unless they cause some to fall.

**11.** *paths of uprightness.* i.e. moral living. The *v.* illustrates the stress laid by Wisdom teachers on the value of Wisdom for conduct of life.

**12.** *thy steps shall not* ... Cf. Job xviii. 7; Ps. lvi. 13 (14 in Hebrew); Ecclus. xxxiv. 16 d.

**13.** Note the piling-up of expressions: take fast hold, leave not go of her, guard, because Wisdom is all in all to a man, cf. Ecclus. vi. 27.

*life.* See note on iii. 2.

**14.** *Enter not* ... Cf. i. 15.

*walk not.* The Sept. reads 'envy not' (cf. iii. 31), but the Hebr. is preferable.

**15.** *Turn from it.* Hebr. 'from upon it', implying that one must not even stand on it, let alone walk in it.

**16.** Concerning the type of men portrayed in these *vv.* Toy says: 'The writer may have in mind the foreign and native oppressors of the Jews in the fourth and third centuries B.C., as in Pss. xiv, liii, lxiv, lxxiv, &c.; more probably he is thinking of a class of men that was numerous in the great cities of that period, unscrupulous government agents, revenue farmers, grasping and desperate men of all sorts, some of whom are described by Josephus. The conditions of the society of the time were favourable to violence and oppression, and it is on these conditions that the writer bases his description, which must thus be taken as a local picture of life. His division of men is simple; they are wholly good or wholly bad, or ignorant and stupid; he does not recognize the nicer and more complicated experiences of the soul. There is a certain justification for this general point of view; evil, it may be said, whatever its degree, is always evil, and therefore to be avoided; dallying with transgression of assured moral rules is dangerous. This is the sharply defined, objective old-Hebrew view, which stands in contrast with the modern disposition to distinguish and divide, to recognize good and evil in all things' (*op. cit.*, pp. 92 f.).

17 For they eat the bread of wickedness,
   And drink the wine of violence.

18 But the path of the righteous is as ¹the shining light,
   That shineth more and more unto the perfect day.

19 The way of the wicked is as darkness:
   They know not at what they stumble.

20 My son, attend to my words;
   Incline thine ear unto my sayings.

21 Let them not depart from thine eyes;
   Keep them in the midst of thine heart.

22 For they are life unto those that find them,
   And health to all their flesh.

¹ Or, *the light of dawn*

**17.** *bread of wickedness.* i.e. food obtained by violence or fraud, cf. xx. 17.

**18, 19.** These *vv.* read better if transposed, as *v.* 19 follows logically after *v.* 17.

*the shining light.* The R.V. marg. is to be preferred because of what is said in the next line.

*that shineth more and more.* Lit. 'going and shining'.

*unto the perfect day.* Lit. 'until the day is firmly established', i.e. when the sun is at its zenith. The idea of the *v.* is that the way of the righteous goes on increasing in its brightness as the sun from dawn to mid-day. Isa. ii. 5 was possibly at the back of the writer's mind; cf. also Job xxii. 28. Divine guidance is, of course, what is meant by the light.

**19.** *darkness.* It is not the ordinary word for darkness, but one which means 'thick darkness', as in Exod. x. 22; Deut. xxviii. 29, and elsewhere.

*They know not . . .* The reference is to evil or misfortune which suddenly overtakes them.

## IV. 20–27. *Further exhortations of the Wise Man.*

**20.** *attend.* As these *vv.* show, ears, eyes, and heart are all to be concentrated on the teacher.

**21.** *Let them not depart.* Cf. iii. 21; Ecclus. xxxix. 2.

*thine heart.* This and vi. 25 are the only two occurrences of the word *lēbāb* for 'heart' in Prov.; otherwise it is always *lēb*.

**22.** *life.* See notes on iii. 2, 22. In *Pirqê 'Abôth* vi. 7 this *v.* is quoted as illustrating the following saying: 'Great is Torah, which

23  Keep thy heart [1]with all diligence;
    For out of it are the issues of life.
24  Put away from thee a froward mouth,
    And perverse lips put far from thee.
25  Let thine eyes look right on,
    And let thine eyelids look straight before thee.
26  [2]Make level the path of thy feet,
    And let all thy ways be [3]established.
27  Turn not to the right hand nor to the left:
    Remove thy foot from evil.

[1] Or, *above all that thou guardest*      [2] Or, *Weigh carefully*
[3] Or, *ordered aright*

gives life to those who practise it, in this world and in the world
to come, as it is said,' then follows this *v.*

**23.** *Keep thy heart* . . . Lit. 'more than all guarding keep thy
heart', i. e. keep watch over thy heart more than over anything else
that thou guardest, cf. Matth. xv. 19.

*For out of it* . . . The line means that the things which happen
during a man's life-time depend upon what the heart thinks and
prompts. On the connotation of 'heart' in *Proverbs* see Excursus IX.
With the thought of this verse and 24 cf. *The Words of Achikar*:
'With more than watchfulness watch thy mouth, and over what thou
hearest harden thy heart; for a word is (like) a bird, and when he
hath sent it forth a man doth not (recapture it).' This is from the
Aramaic Elephantiné fragments, the rendering is a little uncertain
on account of the mutilated state of the text.

**24.** *Put away.* The Hebr. word means lit. 'cause to depart'.

*a froward mouth.* Lit. 'crookedness of mouth' (cf. vi. 12); the
word for 'crookedness' is an Aramaism; the reference is, of course,
to what is said by the mouth, i. e. things which are not straightforward and true.

*perverse lips.* Lit. 'crookedness of lips', also an Aramaism; the
word is similar in meaning to the previous one, a deviation, i. e. from
right speaking.

**25.** *Let thine eyes* . . . In contrast to the 'crookedness' of mouth
and lips. He who speaks the truth can look a man straight in the face.

**26.** *Make level.* For the R.V. marg. cf. *v.* 21. For the picture cf.
Isa. xl. 3, 4.

*be established.* The Hebr. word means to 'make firm'; after the
road is levelled it must be made firm.

**27.** *Turn not* . . . When once on the level and firm road it must be
kept to; to deviate from it is to incline into a wrong path.

D

**V.** 1 My son, attend unto my wisdom;
Incline thine ear to my understanding:
2 That thou mayest preserve discretion,
And that thy lips may keep knowledge.
3 For the lips of a strange woman drop honey,
And her mouth is smoother than oil:
4 But her latter end is bitter as wormwood,
Sharp as a two-edged sword.

### Chapter V

**V. 1–23.** *Warning against consorting with a 'strange woman', and an exhortation to conjugal fidelity.*

With this chapter cf. vii. 5–27 and Ecclus. ix. 3–9, xviii. 30, 31, xxiii. 16–37, xlii. 12–14. The section is a self-constituted whole; it begins with a few words of general exhortation (*vv.* 1, 2), and then plunges into the main subject of warning (*vv.* 3–14). The disciple is then called upon to be faithful to his own wife (*vv.* 15–20), and the section closes with a reference to the calamity which overtakes the wicked.

**1.** *wisdom . . . understanding.* See Excursus III.
**2.** Cf. ii. 11.
*discretion.* The Hebr. word is in the plur. in which form it usually has a bad sense when referring to men (though not in viii. 12), see xii. 2, xiv. 17, xxiv. 8; Job xxi. 27; Ps. x. 2, 4. Here it is used in a good sense, 'wise thoughts' or the like.
*And that thy lips . . .* It is obvious that the Hebr. text is out of order here, for 'lips' do not 'keep knowledge'. The Sept. reads: 'And the knowledge of my lips (i.e. uttered by my lips) I command thee' (or is 'commanded thee', according to another reading). But the mention of 'lips' here is, in any case, inappropriate; it doubtless got in from the next verse by mistake. The simplest way is to delete 'lips' and read: 'and that thou mayest keep knowledge.'
**3.** *strange woman.* See note on ii. 16.
*drop honey.* Properly, honey that is flowing, i.e. from the comb, cf. Ps. xix. 10 (11 in Hebr.). See also xvi. 24; Song of Songs iv. 11.
*mouth.* Lit. 'the roof of the mouth', or 'palate', cf. Job xii. 11, xxxiv. 3; Song of Songs ii. 3; see also Prov. xxiv. 13.
*smoother.* Smoothness of tongue denotes flattery, cf. xxix. 5; Ps. v. 9 (10 in Hebr.).
**4.** *latter end.* The word connotes ultimate punishment; cf. for the thought xxiii. 32.
*bitter as wormwood.* Note the antithesis between this and the sweet honey. Wildeboer points out that the word for wormwood means a 'curse' in Arabic.

5 Her feet go down to death;
 Her steps take hold on [1]Sheol;
6 [2]So that she findeth not the level path of life:
 Her ways are unstable *and* [3]she knoweth *it* not.
7 Now therefore, *my* sons, hearken unto me,
 And depart not from the words of my mouth.

[1] Or, *the grave* [2] Or, *Lest thou find the level &c.* Or, *Lest thou weigh carefully the path of life* [3] Or, *thou canst not know* them

*Sharp*. Antithesis to 'smooth' in *v.* 3.

*a two-edged sword*. Lit. 'a sword of mouths', cf. Ecclus. xxi. 3; the blade of a sword is called a mouth because it devours, see e.g. Jer. xlvi. 10, 14; Nah. ii. 13; the plur. is used because the blade is two-edged.

**5.** *Her feet* ... Cf. ii. 18, vii. 27; Ecclus. xix. 3.

*take hold on*. This is the usual meaning of the word, but it can hardly have this meaning here; Sheol as the abode of the departed cannot be grasped; it must mean 'attain' or 'reach' here.

*Sheol*. See Excursus V.

**6.** The Hebr. text as it stands does not make sense, and must be corrupt. In the first clause a negative is expected, and is so read by the Versions. It is evident from *v.* 5 that the strange woman is the subject of this *v.*, so that, even if one reads the negative, sense is still lacking ('She doth not make level the path of life'); in any case the strange woman would not do that; moreover, the sentence is contradictory, for the path of life *is* level just because it is the path of life. The Sept. renders, 'She cometh not upon . . .', which follows well upon the preceding *v.*, and may well have stood in the text translated by the Sept. (cf. Isa. xli. 3, or Job xvi. 22 for the Hebrew).

*and she knoweth* it *not*. Here again the Hebr. text cannot be in order. Toy rightly insists on the strangeness of the phrase, for 'whether it be taken to mean that she knows not that her ways are unstable, or that she knows not whither her ways wander, the point indicated by the connexion is not her ignorance, but the evil character of her paths'; and he regards the whole *v.* as a contrast to iv. 26, in which case his suggestion that we should read 'not firm' or 'not established' is much to the point. The whole *v.* should therefore run: 'She entereth not upon the path of life, her ways are unstable and not established', or 'ordered aright'.

**7.** *sons*. Clearly an error, it should be the sing. as the discourse is addressed to 'my son' (verse 1), and in the *vv.* which follow it is always 'thy' ('thy way', 'thine honour', 'thy years', &c.). The Sept. has the sing., the verbs should also be in the sing. as in the Sept. and as they are in the Hebr. in the *vv.* which follow.

D 2

 8 Remove thy way far from her,
　　And come not nigh the door of her house:
 9 Lest thou give thine honour unto others,
　　And thy years unto the cruel:
10 Lest strangers be filled with thy [1]strength;
　　And thy labours *be* in the house of an alien;
11 And thou [2]mourn at thy latter end,
　　When thy flesh and thy body are consumed,
12 And say, How have I hated instruction,
　　And my heart despised reproof;
13 Neither have I obeyed the voice of my teachers,
　　Nor inclined mine ear to them that instructed me!
14 I was well nigh in all evil
　　In the midst of the congregation and assembly.

　　　　　　[1] Or, *wealth*　　　　　　[2] Or, *groan*

**9.** *thine honour.* The Sept. reads 'thy life', which is a better parallel to 'thy years' in the next clause; the two words in Hebr. are similar.

*the cruel.* A very unusual word in such a connexion; the Targum reads 'strangers', which is a better parallel to 'others' in the preceding line; cf. *v.* 20.

**10.** *strangers.* *Zārīm*, a different word from that suggested in the preceding note, which is *Nŏkrīm*.

*strength.* Read with R.V. marg. 'wealth', cf. Job vi. 22.

*labours.* Cf. x. 22, where the same word is rendered 'sorrow' (R.V. marg. 'toil').

With verses 5–8 cf. *The Proverbs of Achikar*, ii. 5:

> *My son, lift not up thine eyes and look upon a woman that is bedizened and painted ; and do not lust after her in thine heart ; for if thou shouldst give her all that is in thine hands, thou findest no advantage in her ; and thou wilt be guilty of sin against God.* See further note on vii. 27 and Excursus I.

**11.** *And thou mourn.* Read with R.V. marg. 'groan', cf. Ezek. xxiv. 23; the word is used of the roaring of the sea in Isa. v. 30, and of the growling of a lion in Prov. xix. 12, xxviii. 15, and Isa. v. 30. The Sept. reads 'and thou repent'.

*consumed.* As the result of dissolute living; similarly in Ecclus. xxiii. 16, 17.

**12.** *How.* The Hebr. expression is better rendered by 'Alas!', and belongs to the whole of *vv.* 12, 13.

*instruction . . . reproof.* See notes on i. 2 and i. 23.

**14.** *I was well nigh . . .* The Hebr. idiom is difficult to render literally; it means that (through his folly) he had nearly fallen a victim to 'all evil', which presumably includes the worst evil, i. e. death; this would be in accordance with Deut. xxii. 22 (cf. Lev. xx. 10). But

15 Drink waters out of thine own cistern,
   And running waters out of thine own well.
16 ¹ Should thy springs be dispersed abroad,
   And rivers of water in the streets?
17 Let them be for thyself alone,
   And not for strangers with thee.
18 Let thy fountain be blessed;
   And rejoice in the wife of thy youth.
19 *As* a loving hind and a pleasant doe,
   Let her breasts satisfy thee at all times;
   And ² be thou ravished always with her love.
20 For why shouldest thou, my son, ² be ravished with a strange
      woman,
   And embrace the bosom of a stranger?

¹ Or, *Let*          ² Heb. *go astray.*

from vi. 33 ('wounds and dishonour shall he get') it seems clear that
the death sentence for adultery was no more enforced at the time at
which this was written, for had it still been in vogue it would assuredly have been mentioned as the most efficacious deterrent. This
was certainly so in the time of Ben-Sira, for in speaking of the
adulterer he says that 'he shall be punished in the streets of the city'
(xxiii. 21); but neither in regard to him or his companion in crime
is anything said of the death sentence. It is more than probable
that the official abolition of the death penalty altogether in Jewish
law, which took place during the first half of the first century A.D.,
was but the tardy recognition of what had obtained for generations.
The punishment for an adulterer was public scourging, while the
adulteress was divorced and lost all her rights under the marriage
contract (Mishnah, *Sotah* vi. 1). So that by 'all evil' here it seems
that we must understand the public scourging and the ignominy
which would be indelibly attached to the adulterer; vi. 33 precisely
describes this. The second half of the *v.* speaks of the 'congregation
and assembly', which are synonymous terms; the congregation in its
judicial capacity inflicted the penalty just as in earlier times it
carried out the death sentence (see Lev. xxiv. 16; Deut. xvii. 7). The
adulteress is not mentioned in this connexion, but see Ecclus. xxiii. 24.

**15.** The reference is to lawful intercourse with his own wife; see
Song of Songs, iv. 11 ff., where the poet is speaking of his bride, and
cf. v. 15 with this passage; cf. also Ecclus. xxvi. 12.

**16.** *Should thy springs* . . . Read with a number of Sept. MSS.:
'Let not thy springs . . .'; it is a prohibition against unlawful intercourse with other women.

**18-20.** 'This group repeats and interprets the exhortation of the

21 For the ways of man are before the eyes of the LORD,
    And he [1]maketh level all his paths.
22 His own iniquities shall take the wicked,
    And he shall be holden with the cords of his sin.
23 He shall die for lack of instruction;
    And in the greatness of his folly he shall go astray.

[1] Or, *weigheth carefully*

preceding in literal terms,—the erotic expressions (cf. *Canticles*) are partly explained by the fact that women did not in ancient times form part of the audiences addressed by men, or of the public for which books were written' (Toy). It must also be remembered that there was not the remotest idea of there being anything indecent in expressing things which in these days would be regarded as extremely indelicate. One finds the same thing in later Jewish books; not only in Ben-Sira, but also in Rabbinical writings.

**21.** *before the eyes.* Cf. Jer. xvii. 16, 'before thy face', i.e. absolutely plain before Him.

*maketh level.* Cf. *v.* 21. Here the R.V. marg. is the better rendering, the Sept. has 'observes'; the thought is that God scrutinizes the ways of men.

**22.** *His own iniquities* ... The construction of this sentence in the original points to late Hebrew. It is probable that 'the wicked' should be deleted as a later gloss of emphasis. The Sept. has 'a man' for 'the wicked'.

*take.* 'Entrap' expresses the meaning perhaps better, cf. Ps. xxxv. 8.

*shall be broken.* The same word is used in xxxi. 19 of grasping a distaff.

*the cords of his sin.* Cf. the phrases 'the cords of death' (Ps. xviii. 4; Hebr. 5, cxvi. 3), 'the cords of Sheol' (xviii. 5, Hebr. 6). In reference to this *v.* it is said in the Midrash on Proverbs: 'As man throws out a net whereby he catches the fish of the sea, so the sins of man become the means of entangling and catching the sinner' (quoted by Schechter, *Some Aspects of Rabbinic Theology*, p. 247 [1909]).

**23.** *He shall die* ... Cf. Job iv. 21. Just as the possession of wisdom ensures a long life (iii. 16), so the lack of it brings death.

*he shall go astray.* This does not offer a good parallelism with 'he shall die' in the preceding clause; a slight change in the Hebr. would give the word 'he shall perish', which is the reading of some Sept. MSS.; cf. Job iii. 11, iv. 10, where the suggested word occurs as a parallel with 'die'.

**VI. 1** My son, if thou art become surety for thy neighbour,

## Chapter VI

**VI. 1–19.** *Warnings against Suretyship* (1–5); *against Sloth* (6–11); *against Insincerity* (12–15); *and against seven other sins* (16–19).

**1–5.** Cf. xi. 15, xvii. 18, xx. 16, xxii. 26, 27, xxvii. 13; Job xvii. 3; Ecclus. viii. 13, xxix. 14–20.

It was not until later times that banks and a credit system on business lines had a place among the Jews. In pre-exilic and early post-exilic times if any one lent money it was not with the object of investment which paid interest, but only in order to help some one in temporary need. Jewish law forbade the receiving of interest from a fellow Jew. The Jews, therefore, differed entirely in this from other nations among whom a high interest on money lent was ordinarily demanded and paid. The law says nothing about suretyship. A reference to it occurs in Gen. xliii. 9, where Judah tells Jacob that he will be surety for Benjamin's safe return. Otherwise it is mentioned only in post-exilic literature (Job xvii. 3; Ps. cxix. 122). The Hebr. word for 'to go surety' ('*arab*) and its derivative '*ērābōn*, 'pledge', are borrowed from Phoenician (for the latter cf. the Grk. ἀρραβών 2 Cor. i. 22, v. 5; Eph. i. 14). In this section, as elsewhere in the Wisdom Literature, it is therefore a question of lending or borrowing money without interest. This came under the category of charitable acts; the sages exhort their disciples to do it with willingness, and yet with caution; and, on the other hand, the borrower is bidden to be punctual in repayment; that was a question of honour. But while lending is reckoned as a duty, to go surety is folly; an exception to this is Ecclus. xxix. 14: 'A good man becometh surety for his neighbour.' Probably it is not a question here of a legal transaction, but of a friend going surety for another in a private capacity, though this does not in any way mitigate the responsibility of the man who goes surety for another. But however that may be, it is foolish, so the sages taught, when an emotional and impulsive man lets his feelings over-ride his common-sense by standing surety; the wise man will hesitate before committing himself, and will do better still to refuse. Experience of men and matters impelled the Wisdom writers to adopt an attitude here which, after all, was the most sensible; and in seeking to prepare young men for their life-struggle it was well to warn the generous-hearted that undiscriminating and impulsive benevolence may often defeat its own end.

**1.** *become surety.* In this sense the word is Neo-Hebr., the ordinary meaning is 'to exchange', or 'give in pledge'.

If thou hast stricken [1]thy hands for a stranger,

2 Thou art snared with the words of thy mouth,
  Thou art taken with the words of thy mouth.

3 Do this now, my son, and deliver thyself,
  Seeing thou art come into the hand of thy neighbour;
  Go, [2]humble thyself, and importune thy neighbour.

4 Give not sleep to thine eyes,
  Nor slumber to thine eyelids.

5 Deliver thyself as a [3]roe from the hand *of the hunter*,
  And as a bird from the hand of the fowler.

[1] Or, *thy hand with a stranger*          [2] Or, *bestir*          [3] Or, *gazelle*

*stricken thy hands*. Read 'hand' with many MSS. and the Versions. This use of the word, of an act ratifying a bargain, is late Hebr.; and occurs only in *Proverbs*.

*for a stranger*. As in xxvii. 2 the word means 'another'.

**2.** *Thou art snared*. One must supply 'if' in both clauses of this *v.*, for it does not necessarily follow that he for whom a man stands surety will default; it is only if this is the case that the surety will have to keep his word and pay.

*with the words of thy mouth*. It is better to read with the Sept. 'with thy lips', since it is improbable that the identical word in both clauses is original.

**3.** The advice given in this *v.* is contingent upon the conditions mentioned in *v.* 2.

*and deliver thyself*. This is unnecessary and should be deleted. In the Hebr. there is only one clause, not two as in R.V., viz. 'Do this then, my son, since thou art come into thy neighbour's hand'.

*into the hand*. i.e. 'power'; the more usual expression is to 'fall into the hand' of some one, cf. Judg. xv. 18; 2 Sam. xxiv. 14.

*Go, humble thyself*. Lit. 'trample upon thyself', i.e. humble thyself; but the word is probably corrupt. Read with the Sept., 'and be not slack', i.e. bestir thyself.

*importune*. The word is used in Ecclus. xiii. 8 (Hebr.) of 'acting violently', almost 'madly'; a stronger word than 'importune' is required; 'overwhelm', or 'storm', would express the Hebr. better.

**4.** *Give not* ... A rhetorical way of urging that nothing must come in the way of extricating himself out of the difficulty into which he has got himself.

**5.** *roe*. Better 'gazelle' (= R.V. marg.), cf. Isa. xiii. 14.

*from the hand*. A textual error; following the Versions and Ecclus. xxvii. 20 ('a gazelle out of a snare'), read 'out of a snare' (מִפָּח). The words 'of the hunter' are an addition made in the R.V. in order to try to make sense out of the text as it stands; they can be ignored.

*as a bird* ... Cf. Ps. xci. 3.

6 Go to the ant, thou sluggard;
  Consider her ways, and be wise:
7 Which having no ¹chief,
  Overseer, or ruler,
8 Provideth her meat in the summer,
  And gathereth her food in the harvest.
9 How long wilt thou ²sleep, O sluggard?
  When wilt thou arise out of thy sleep?
10 *Yet* a little sleep, a little slumber,
  A little folding of the hands to ²sleep:
11 So shall thy poverty come as a ³robber,
  And thy want as ⁴an armed man.

¹ Or, *judge*          ² Heb. *lie down.*          ³ Or, *rover*
          ⁴ Heb. *a man with a shield.*

**6–11.** Cf. xxiv. 30–34; Ecclus. xxii. 1, 2.

**6.** *Go to the ant.* Cf. Job xii. 7, 'But ask now the beasts, and they shall teach thee'; see also 1 Kings iv. 33 (v. 13 in Hebr.), and for the ant see Prov. xxx. 25.

*sluggard.* The word ('*āzēl*) occurs only in *Proverbs* (though the verb is used in Judg. xviii. 9) and 'sluggishness' once in Eccles. x. 18; see, for an extreme example of the type, xix. 24.

*be wise.* Or 'in order that thou mayest be wise'.

**7.** *chief.* The word (*katzín*) means originally 'judge', cf. Isa. i. 10; Mic. iii. 1, it is also used in this sense in Prov. xxv. 15. Here it means 'leader' as in Josh. x. 24; Judg. xi. 6; Deut. xi. 18.

*Overseer.* (*shôtēr*) translated 'officer' in Exod. v. 6, 14. The original meaning is 'scribe', cf. the Assyrian word *shataru* 'writer' (Wildeboer).

*ruler.* (*mōshēl*) the usual word. It is not to be surprised at that the writer shows so little knowledge of the organization among ants. The second couplet of the *v.* has fallen out.

**8.** The force of the tenses in this *v.* is worth noting, viz. 'is wont to provide . . . and hath gathered . . .'. After this *v.* the Sept. adds several *vv.* about the busy bee; but there is no reason to suppose that these *vv.* represent anything that ever stood in the Hebr. text.

**10.** *folding the hands.* Cf. Eccles. iv. 5, x. 18.

**11.** This *v.* occurs again in xxiv. 34, the only difference being that it has 'one who goeth quickly' for 'robber' (the two words are from the same verb, and are very similar in Hebr.), cf. Ecclus. xxxvi. 26 (31 in Hebr.).

*robber.* R.V. marg. 'rover' is better, the thought is that of a highwayman.

*an armed man.* Lit. 'a man of shield', cf. R.V. marg.; this suggests the idea of a soldier.

12 A worthless person, a man of iniquity;
 He walketh with a froward mouth;
13 He winketh with his eyes, he [1]speaketh with his feet,
 He [2]maketh signs with his fingers;
14 Frowardness is in his heart, he deviseth evil continually;
 He [3]soweth discord.
15 Therefore shall his calamity come suddenly;
 On a sudden shall he be broken, and that without remedy.
16 There be six things which the LORD hateth;
 Yea, seven which are an abomination [4]unto him:
17 Haughty eyes, a lying tongue,
 And hands that shed innocent blood;

[1] Or, *shuffleth*   [2] Or, *teacheth*   [3] Heb. *letteth loose*
[4] Heb. *of his soul*

**12–15.** Cf. Ecclus. xxvii. 22–24.

**12.** *A worthless person.* Lit. 'a man of Belial'; the word means 'degradation' or 'depravity'.

*with a froward mouth.* See note on iv. 24.

**13.** *winketh with his eyes.* A sign of malicious insincerity, cf. x. 10; Ps. xxxv. 19; Ecclus. xxvii. 22.

*speaketh.* This is the lit. meaning of the Hebr. word, and is better than the R.V. marg. 'shuffleth'; the Sept. paraphrases by the rendering 'giveth signs'. The expression denotes insincerity, the movement or 'language' of the feet indicating something different from that uttered by the tongue.

*maketh signs* . . . Here again there is reference to the language of signs illustrating the froward mouth which says one thing while the motion of the fingers points to something else.

**14.** It is better to divide the verse thus: 'Frowardness doth the evil man devise in his heart, continually doth he send forth discord'.

*deviseth.* Lit. 'engraveth' or 'fashioneth', cf. iii. 29.

*soweth.* Lit. 'sendeth forth', or as R.V. marg. 'letteth loose', cf. xvi. 28.

**15.** *Therefore shall* . . . Cf. i. 26–32.

*broken.* i.e. destroyed, cf. Isa. i. 28; Jer. xvii. 18.

*without remedy.* Lit. 'and no healing', cf. xxix. 1.

**16–19.** For this 'numerical' form of proverb cf. xxx. 7, 15, 18, 21, 24, 29; and Job v. 19; Ecclus. xxiii. 6, xxv. 7, xxvi. 5, 28, l. 25, and *Pirqê 'Abôth* v. It occurs also in the *Proverbs of Achikar* (Elephantiné version): 'Two things are godly, and of three there is pleasure to Shamash' (Cowley 92, 93).

**17.** *Haughty eyes.* Cf. xxx. 13, Ps. xviii. 27 (28 in Hebr.), cxxxi. 1.

*a lying tongue.* Cf. xii. 19, xxi. 6, xxvi. 28; Ps. cix. 2.

*innocent blood.* Cf. i. 11.

18 An heart that deviseth wicked imaginations,
   Feet that be swift in running to mischief;
19 A false witness that ¹uttereth lies,
   And he that ²soweth discord among brethren.

20 My son, keep the commandment of thy father,
   And forsake not the ³law of thy mother:
21 Bind them continually upon thine heart,
   Tie them about thy neck.

    ¹ Heb. *breatheth out.*      ² Heb. *letteth loose.*      ³ Or, *teaching*

**18.** *in running.* The Sept. omits this; it is not required, and disturbs the rhythm.

**19.** *A false witness.* Cf. Ps. xxvii. 12.

*uttereth.* Lit. 'breatheth out'; the same expression occurs in xiv. 5, 25, xix. 5, 9.

*soweth discord.* As in 14ᵇ.

With *vv.* 16–19 cf. a passage in the *Teaching of Amen-em-ope* IX. xii. 1–xiii. 9, which contains some identical thoughts; the reference is to one who is 'laden with false words', who is guilty of 'calumnious speech', who 'layeth snares with words', who 'setteth men to wrangling', and who 'goeth before every breeze like clouds' ( = 'feet that are swift in running to harm' of verse 18ᵇ). Such a close connexion between the Hebrew and the Egyptian passages points to an influence of one on the other, for five similar thoughts found together in each cannot be fortuitous. On the question of which influenced the other see Excursus I, p. liii f.

## VI. 20—VII. 27. *Warnings against the wiles of the adulteress.*

This section continues the subject dealt with in v. 1–23, cf. also ii. 16–19, ix. 13–18; Ecclus. vi. 2–4, xxiii. 16–27, xxv. 2, xxvi. 9–12. The prevalence of sins of the flesh to which these passages bear witness is further borne out by many prophetical utterances, e. g. Hos. iv. 2; Jer. vii. 9, xxiii. 10; Mal. iii. 5, &c. The frequency of the references to the subject in the Wisdom Literature has suggested to some scholars the idea that the 'strange woman' is intended to be the personification of Folly as opposed to Wisdom; but in view of what is so often said about adultery in the prophetical writings this opinion cannot be regarded as justified. The facts of life are what the sage is dealing with.

**20, 21.** See notes on i. 8, iii. 3, and cf. the quotation from the *Teaching of Amen-em-ope* in the note on i. 6.

22 When thou walkest, it shall lead thee;
　　When thou [1]sleepest it shall watch over thee;
　　And when thou awakest, it shall talk with thee.

<sub>1</sub> Heb. *liest down.*

**22 ff.** Unlike nearly all the other *vv.* in this section verse 22 has
three lines. There is a difficulty regarding the subject; in verse 22 it
says *it shall lead thee,* but in the preceding verses 'commandment and
law' are the subjects, and the pupil is told to bind 'them' upon his
heart &c., but in this *v.* 'it' has no subject. Moreover, a logical connexion between *vv.* 23 and 24 is wanting. Clearly there must be
something out of order here. Various remedies are proposed, by
addition, deletion, or transposition, for rectifying the text. But
from the nature of the case there is bound to be uncertainty about
these. The fact must be recognized that we have in *Proverbs* a
medley; not only have various collections been laid under contribution, so that there are repetitions of the same proverbs, but isolated
sayings are inserted which may or may not be relevant to the context; it is also probable enough that editors have put in here and
there proverbs of their own composition, and with perfect justification. The repetition of subject-matter scattered about the book
instead of being grouped together shows that the main object has
been to collect material and not necessarily to classify it. This being
so it is small wonder if we find, as for example in *vv.* 22, 23, sayings
which have been culled from somewhere and put into the text without a great regard for their appropriateness to the context. The
Eastern has not the same love for logical sequence that is so largely
characteristic of the Western mind; a single point of attachment
suffices for him to place a saying, otherwise not necessarily congruous,
within a new environment. Like *Proverbs* the *Wisdom of Ben-Sira*
illustrates this seemingly somewhat haphazard method of compilation in an even more pronounced way, so much so that one sometimes
receives the impression that it must have been a first draft, which
later the author intended to put into final form, but for some reason
or other was prevented from doing so.

**22.** This *v.* consists of a triplet, the normal form in this collection
(i–ix) being a couplet; but the triplet is complete and satisfying in
itself, so that it does not seem necessary to delete the third line in
order to bring the *v.* into conformity with the rest, it may well be an
excerpt from some other collection, which would also account for the
indefinite 'it' as the subject; in the original context the subject was
doubtless Wisdom which has been mentioned in some preceding
verse; there was a point of contact between Wisdom and Torah (in
verse 20) which would account for the insertion of the *v.* here.

*walkest.* Cf. iii. 23.
*sleepest.* Lit. 'liest down', cf. iii. 24.

23 For [1]the commandment is a lamp; and the [2]law is light;

*watch over thee.* Cf. ii. 11.

**23.** This *v.*, again, seems to have been inserted from elsewhere as it does not belong logically to the context. Although the 'law' here has a different connotation from the 'law of thy mother' in verse 20, the word was a sufficient justification to the compiler, as a point of contact for inserting the *v.* in its present position.

*commandment . . . law.* Hebr. *Mitzwah . . . Torah*; there is a particular interest in finding these two expressions close together as early as the time at which this collection was made, for when placed in juxtaposition like this they have always had a specific significance among the Jews. Maimonides (he died in 1204 A.D.) in his Preface to the *Yād ha-Chăzāqah* ('the Strong Hand'), clearly indicates what has been held by the Jews since pre-Christian times to represent the facts of the Oral Tradition; he says: 'All the commandments which were given to Moses on Sinai were given with their interpretation; for it is said (Exod. xxiv. 12), "And I will give thee the tables of stone, and the *Torah* (Law) and the *Mitzwah* (Commandment)". *Torah*: that is the written Law; *Mitzwah*: that is its interpretation. He commanded us to observe the *Torah* in accordance with (עַל-פִּי lit. "according to the mouth of") the *Mitzwah*. And this *Mitzwah* is called the "Oral Law". Moses our teacher wrote down the whole Law with his own hand before he died . . . the *Mitzwah*, that is the interpretation of the Law, he did not write down, but he commanded it to the elders and to Joshua, and to the rest of Israel; for it is written, "All the words which I have commanded you, these shall ye observe and do" (Deut. xii. 28). And therefore this is called the "Oral Law" (תּוֹרָה שֶׁבְעַל פֶּה lit. "the Law which is according to the mouth").'

However fantastic this theory may appear it is an ineradicable tenet of Judaism, and there can be little doubt but that in this *v.* it already finds implicit expression, and the words of Ps. cxix. 105 are adapted to illustrate it. The 'commandment' (*Mitzwah*) is the 'lamp' to illuminate the path, but the source from which it comes is the 'light' of the 'Law' (*Torah*). The Hebrew form brings this out more clearly: 'For a lamp (is) Mitzwah, but Torah (is) light.' (It is interesting to note the contrast between John the Baptist as the lamp, in John v. 35, and Jesus as the Light, in i. 8, 9.) These two constitute 'the way of life', to them correspond 'admonition' (*tōkachath = Torah*) and 'instruction' (*mūsār = Mitzwah*). The order of the corresponding words has a significance of its own: *Mitzwah*, *Torah*, first the lesser, then the greater; and in the practical application: *Tōkachath*, *Mūsār*, first the greater, then the lesser. Both 'lamp' (*nēr*) and light ('*ôr*) are used in reference to the Law in Rabbinical literature.

And reproofs of instruction are the way of life:
24 To keep thee from the evil woman,
   From the flattery of the stranger's tongue.
25 Lust not after her beauty in thine heart;
   Neither let her take thee with her eyelids.
26 For on account of a whorish woman *a man is brought to a*
      *piece of bread*:
   And [1]the adulteress hunteth for the precious life.

   [1] Heb. *a man's wife.*

*reproofs of instruction.* Read, with the Sept., Syr., and Targum,
'reproof (better "admonition") and instruction'; one Hebr. MS. also
reads the singular.

**24.** *To keep thee* . . . This should come immediately after verse 21;
it is the 'binding' of the parental commands and teaching upon the
heart and neck which will keep him from evil ways.

*the evil woman.* The Sept. reads 'the wife of another'; a very
slight change in the Hebr. would give this reading; cf. verse 29
'neighbour's wife', which justifies the Sept. rendering.

*flattery.* Lit. 'smoothness'.

*the stranger's tongue.* As the Hebr. text stands it is 'the strange
tongue'; but some Sept. texts, as well as the Syr., Vulg., and Targ.,
read 'the stranger's tongue', which no doubt represents the true
reading. 'Stranger' is used of an adulteress in v. 3, vii. 5; though a
different word is used in these two passages; cf. also ii. 16.

**25.** *with her eyelids.* The reference is to the lustful look of the
half-closed eyes, cf. Ecclus. xxvi. 9, where this is contrasted with the
'lifting-up of the eyes'.

With the verse cf. the *Proverbs of Achikar,* ii. 19:

> *My son, go not after the beauty of a woman,*
> *And lust not after her in thine heart.*

**26.** Cf. Ecclus. ix. 6 ff. Commentators differ as to whether in this
verse two types of immoral women are referred to, the prostitute and
the unfaithful wife, or whether both clauses refer to the latter.
Syntactically the Hebr. offers difficulties, though they are not in-
superable. If interpreted of two types of immoral women the verse
may mean that while he who consorts with a prostitute is brought to
poverty, he who has intercourse with the wife of another risks his
life (i. e. from the outraged husband). This interpretation is, however,
unsatisfactory; the subject of this section is the adulterous wife, and
nowhere in all these chapters is a prostitute mentioned; it does not
at all follow that a harlot would bring a man to penury, though this
might well be the case through misconduct with a married woman.
In Hosea 'harlot' and 'adulteress' are both applied to the unfaithful

27 Can a man take fire in his bosom,
  And his clothes not be burned?
28 Or can one walk upon hot coals,
  And his feet not be scorched?
29 So he that goeth in to his neighbour's wife;
  Whosoever toucheth her shall not be ¹unpunished.

¹ Heb. *held innocent.*

wife (ii. 5, iii. 1). It is, therefore, far more likely that both clauses
of the verse refer, like the whole context, to the adulterous wife.

*on account of.* For the unusual use of the Hebr. preposition cf. Isa.
xi. 14 (though the reading is uncertain), Job ii. 4.

*a whorish woman.* For the Hebr. expression cf., among other
passages, Jer. iii. 3; Ezek. xvi. 30, both in reference to an adulterous
wife (fig. of the nation).

*a piece of bread.* Lit. 'a round loaf of bread', cf. 1 Sam. ii. 36, the
usual form of bread in the East; the dough was pressed with the
hands so that the 'loaf' was somewhat thin; to be reduced to nothing
but this for sustenance would be a sign of dire poverty.

*the adulteress.* Lit. 'the wife of a man'.

*hunteth . . . life.* Lit. '. . . soul'; for the expression see Ezek. xiii.
18–20.

**27.** *take fire.* Cf. Isa. xxx. 14.

*bosom.* The Hebr. word means both 'breast' and the fold of the
garment at the breast; the latter is the meaning here and in xvi. 33,
xxi. 14 (cf. Exod. iv. 6, 7); the former in v. 20 (cf. Gen. xvi. 5).

**28.** *coals.* Not, of course, in the modern sense; glowing wood is
meant, see Ps. xxvi. 21, cxx. 4.

**29–31.** These *vv.* may well be insertions by some later sage who
wished to add a few thoughts of his own. The reasons for regarding
them as early additions rather than as belonging to the original text
are these: (1) The punishment for consorting with a neighbour's wife
has already been indicated in *v.* 26, and is further developed in *vv.*
32 ff., so that the original writer is unlikely to have dealt with this in
*v.* 29 too. (2) The interrogations in *vv.* 27, 28, which are thoroughly
in the style of the Wisdom writer, are in the nature of reflexions upon
what has just been said in *v.* 26; to enlarge upon them, as *v.* 29 does,
spoils their effect. So much for *v.* 29. As to *vv.* 30, 31; these form
a digression not at all in the style of the author of this collection (i–ix);
they are presumably intended to offer either an analogy or a contrast,
but whichever it may be it is not *à propos.* And lastly, if one reads
*v.* 32 immediately after *v.* 28 the words are more pointed, and nothing
is lost by omitting the intervening verses.

**29.** *goeth in.* A euphemism, like 'toucheth' in the next clause,
for the act of adultery; the phrase may have originally come, as
Wildeboer suggests, from going into the women's part of the tent.

30 Men do not despise a thief, if he steal
    To satisfy his soul when he is hungry:
31 But if he be found, he shall restore sevenfold;
    He shall give all the substance of his house.


**30.** *Men do not . . .* Some Hebrew MSS. reads: '*Do not men despise . . .*' But this was probably done because it was felt that theft under any circumstances was a sin, and therefore not to be excused. Taking the text as it stands it must be confessed that it is not in accordance with O.T. teaching. Some commentators hold that the point of this verse is that a hungry thief is not despised, but an adulterer is; that is purely gratuitous; there is nothing in the text to support it. Steuernagel emends the text so as to read:

> 'Do not men despise a thief
> If he steal to satisfy his greed (lit. "soul", i.e. desire)?'

The words 'when he is hungry' overload the line and should in any case be deleted; they also spoil the sense of the passage, of which the point is this: For an ordinary theft a man is despised, how much more then for stealing another man's wife!

**31.** In this *v.* the thief is represented as a man of property, while in the preceding *v.* he is excused for stealing because he is hungry. There is obviously something wrong here. Toy, following some other commentators, is inclined to take *v.* 30 as a question, and says: 'The contrast will then be, "A thief suffers disgrace, but escapes with loss of money; an adulterer gets disgrace and blows, and no money payment atones for his offence". This seems to be the better interpretation of the contrasted fortunes of thief and adulterer. The discrepancy between *v.* 30 and *v.* 31 remains; it must be regarded as an oversight of the author.' To this it must be replied that a contrast, inept as it is, occurs already between the two verses, i.e. between the hungry thief who gets off scot free if not found, but has to give all the substance of his house if he is found. There is nothing in the *vv.* to suggest a contrast between the thief and the adulterer. Indeed, such a contrast would be quite out of place in this section where the writer is concentrating on the one subject of adultery. The simplest and most natural solution of the difficulty occasioned by the presence of these *vv.* is to regard them as some tentative reflexions of a sage jotted down on the margin of the MS., which have either been misread or have suffered corruption in transmission, and which were never intended to have been inserted in the text; the Hebr. MSS. of *Ecclesiasticus* offer some good illustrations of this; though they are very much later in date, they show what a natural procedure it was to make these marginal notes; there is no reason to doubt that the Wisdom writers of earlier ages did likewise.

32 He that committeth adultery with a woman is void of
        [1] understanding:
   He doeth it that would destroy his own soul.
33 Wounds and dishonour shall he get;
   And his reproach shall not be wiped away.
34 For jealousy is the rage of a man;
   And he will not spare in the day of vengeance.
35 He will not regard any ransom;
   Neither will he rest content, though thou givest many gifts.

**VII.** 1 My son, keep my words,
    And lay up my commandments with thee.
   2 Keep my commandments and live;
    And my [2] law as the apple of thine eye.

             [1] Heb. *heart*.              [2] Or, *teaching*

**32.** Here we come to the real sequel to verses 27–29; who but a
man void of understanding would put fire in his lap (*v.* 27), or walk
on hot coals (*v.* 28) ? This, nevertheless, is the type of man who
commits adultery; and he is void of understanding because by doing
this he destroys his own soul, i.e. himself.
   *void of understanding.* Lit. 'lack of heart', cf. Eccles. x. 3.
   *would destroy.* It is 'doth destroy'.
   With the verse cf. the *Proverbs of Achikar* ii. 6:
      *My son, commit not adultery with the wife of thy neighbour,*
      *Lest others should commit adultery with thy wife.*
**33.** See note on v. 14.

### Chapter VII

**VII. 1–5.** These verses form an introduction to what follows; the
subject is a continuation of what has preceded.
   **1.** *My son* . . .   Cf. ii. 1, iii. 1.
   **2.** *Keep my* . . .   The same line as in iv. 4[c].
   *law.* See note on iii. 1.
   *the apple of thine eye.* Cf. Deut. xxxii. 10; Ps. xvii. 8, where, as here,
it is a metaphor for something precious, see also Ecclus. xvii. 22.  In
Lam. ii. 18; Zech. ii. 8 (12 in Hebr.), where the same phrase occurs in
the R.V., the Hebr. form is different, lit. 'daughter of the eye'.  For
the word 'apple', cf. Prov. vii. 9, where it means the 'middle' (i. e.
of the night), and xx. 20, where it is used to express intensiveness
(i. e. depth of darkness).  The Hebr. word is *'ishôn* (אישׁוֹן); according to Gesenius-Kautzsch § 86 g (26th ed.) the termination *-ôn* signifies a diminutive; so that what the word means lit. is the 'little man'.

E

3 Bind them upon thy fingers;
  Write them upon the table of thine heart.
4 Say unto wisdom, Thou art my sister;
  And call understanding *thy* [1]kinswoman:
5 That they may keep thee from the strange woman,
  From the stranger which [2]flattereth with her words.
6 For at the window of my house
  I looked forth through my lattice;
7 And I beheld among the simple ones,
  I discerned among the youths,
  A young man void of understanding,

----

[1] Or, *familiar friend*          [2] Heb. *maketh smooth her words.*

----

This must originally have had reference to the widespread belief that
the soul resided in the pupil of the eye (see the writer's *Immortality
and the Unseen World*, pp. 169f., 1921); the reflection of any one
looking into the eye of another suggested the presence there of the
'little man', i.e. the soul.

**3.** *Bind* . . . See note on iii. 3.

*table of thine heart.* If, as seems unquestionable, the allusion in the
preceding line is to phylacteries, the 'table' must allude to the
*mezûzah*, or 'door-post' symbol (on this see Oesterley and Box, *op.
cit.*, pp. 454 f.).

**4.** *Thou art my sister.* Cf. Wisdom viii. 2.

*kinswoman.* The word, which implies the intimate knowledge
which exists between relations, occurs elsewhere only in Ruth ii. 1,
iii. 2.

**5.** See notes on ii. 16, vi. 24, and cf. Ecclus. ix. 3.

**VII. 6–27.** The wiles of the adulteress are described in these
verses together with the fatal consequence to him who is ensnared
by them. The account of what follows professes to be given by an
eye-witness; its vividness certainly bears out the claim.

**6.** *my house.* One expects a verb in the line; it is therefore suggested by some commentators that 'my house' (בֵּיתִי) is a corruption
of 'I looked' (הִבַּטְתִּי). The verse would then run: 'For at the
window I looked, through my lattice I peered.'

*lattice.* See Judg. v. 28

**7.** There must be something not quite in order with this *v.*; its
structure differs from all the *vv.*, with the exception of 22, 23, in the
section. To delete the first two Hebr. words (='And I beheld among
the simple ones') as Toy suggests, would make the verse too short.
It is perhaps best to transpose 'a young man' by placing it after 'the
simple ones', and reading: 'And I saw among the simple ones a
young man, I discerned among the youths one void of understanding.'

8 Passing through the street near her corner,
  And he went the way to her house;
9 In the twilight, in the evening of the day,
  In the ¹blackness of night and the darkness.
10 And, behold, there met him a woman
  With the attire of an harlot, and ²wily of heart.

¹ Heb. *pupil* (of the eye).        ² Or, *close* Heb. *guarded*.

It is just possible that the parallels (cf. i. 4) 'simple ones'='youths', 'young men', 'one void of understanding', was intentional.

*simple ones.* See note on i. 4 and Excursus XI.

**8.** *her corner . . . her house.* The reference must be to the 'strange woman' in *v.* 5, as the particular woman of the section has not yet been mentioned.

*he went the way to . . .* This reads as though the young man were intentionally making straight for the woman's house, but this is not the idea in the original, where he is simply represented as strolling about the streets and happening to pass along by her house. Cf. the following couplet from Ecclus. ix. 7 (the first line is from the Greek, the Hebrew being hopelessly corrupt, the second from the Hebrew):

> *Look not round about thee in the streets of the city,*
> *And wander not in the broad places thereof.*

**9.** *In the twilight.* The Hebr. word comes from the root meaning 'to blow', its force therefore is the 'twilight breeze', cf. Gen. iii. 8, 'in the cool (lit. "wind") of the day'; but the word is not the same one as here.

*in the blackness.* The Hebr. is the same word as 'apple' (of the eye), see note on *v.* 2. Here the meaning is the centre of the night, i.e. midnight. The *v.* represents the young man as strolling about in the streets from twilight to midnight.

**10.** *there met him a woman.* We should expect 'the woman', as the Greek renders; probably the definite article has dropped out.

*With the attire . . .* Cf. Gen. xxxviii. 14; the word occurs elsewhere only in Ps. lxxiii. 6. The woman in question, the adulteress, is thus distinguished from the harlot.

*wily of heart.* The meaning of the word rendered 'wily' is uncertain. The Versions give no help. In Isa. xlviii. 6 it has the sense of something hidden or secret; here it may therefore refer to her deceit towards her husband (Wildeboer), though that meaning in this context is hardly appropriate. The word comes from the root meaning to 'guard' or 'protect'; and if the word for 'heart' (לֵב), be emended, as some suggest, to read 'a covering', or 'garment' (לֹט), cf. Isa. xxv. 7, the phrase could be read 'enveloped in a garment', or the like; cf. Gen. xxxviii. 14, where it is said of Tamar that she 'covered herself with her veil, and wrapped herself . . .'

E 2

11 She is ¹clamorous and wilful;
   Her feet abide not in her house:
12 Now she is in the streets, now in the broad places,
   And lieth in wait at every corner.
13 So she caught him, and kissed him,
   ²*And* with an impudent face she said unto him:
14 Sacrifices of peace offerings ³are with me;
   This day have I paid my vows.
15 Therefore came I forth to meet thee,
   Diligently to seek thy face, and I have found thee.
16 I have spread my couch with ⁴carpets of tapestry,
   With striped cloths of the yarn of Egypt.

¹ Or, *turbulent*           ² Heb. *She hardened her face, and said.*
³ Or, *were due from me*        ⁴ Or, *cushions*

**11.** *clamorous.* The meaning of the Hebr. word is uncertain, though judging from its use in Isa. xxii. 2, and of a similar, though not identical word in 1 Kgs. i. 41, 'clamorous' seems as good a rendering as any; it occurs also in Prov. ix. 13.

*wilful.* The Hebr. word סֹרֶרֶת is used in Hos. iv. 16 of a 'stubborn' heifer, cf. also Ps. lxvi. 7, lxviii. 6 (7), 18 (19), of 'rebellious' people; but as this could only be understood as in reference to her attitude towards her husband, it is inappropriate here, where the thought is of her gadding about the streets (see the second line and the next *v.*); so that those commentators are justified who follow the Vulg. *vaga* and read סֹבֶבֶת as in Canticles iii. 2, 3, 'going about'; cf. Ecclus. xlii. 11.

*Her feet abide not* ... Cf. Ecclus. xxv. 25, 26.

**12.** *Now she is* ... The terseness of the Hebr. is more telling: 'Now in the street, now in the broad places, she lieth in wait ...'

**13.** *So she caught him* ... The Hebr., more graphically, has the verbs in the present tense: 'And she seizeth him and kisseth him ...'
*with an impudent face.* Lit. 'hardeneth her face', cf. xxi. 29.

**14.** *Sacrifices of peace offerings.* See Excursus VI.

**15.** *Therefore came I forth* ... This *v.* seems to suggest that an illicit relationship was already in existence.
*Diligently to seek.* The same word occurs in Ps. lxiii. 1 (2 in Hebr.).

**16.** *carpets of tapestry.* The Hebr. word comes from the same root as that for 'I have spread', it must mean 'coverings'; the only other occurrence of the word is in xxxi. 22. The R.V. marg. 'cushions' can scarcely be the meaning.

*striped cloths.* The Hebr. word occurs here only, an Aramaism, according to Wildeboer; the similar word in Ps. cxliv. 12, 'hewn', comes from a different root.

17 I have [1]perfumed my bed
   With myrrh, aloes, and cinnamon.
18 Come, let us take our fill of love until the morning;
   Let us solace ourselves with loves.
19 For the goodman is not at home,
   He is gone a long journey:
20 He hath taken a bag of money with him;
   He will come home at the full moon.
21 With her much fair speech she causeth him to yield,
   With the flattering of her lips she forceth him away.
22 He goeth after her [2]straightway,
   As an ox goeth to the slaughter,
   Or as [3]fetters to the correction of the fool;
23 Till an arrow strike through his liver;
   As a bird hasteth to the snare,
   And knoweth not that it is for his life.

> [1] Or, *sprinkled*                [2] Heb. *suddenly.*
> [3] Or, *one in fetters*  The text is probably corrupt.

*yarn*. This word, too, occurs only here; the Hebr. is *'etun*, and may be borrowed from the Greek, *ὀθόνη*; on the other hand, the Greek word may be the borrowed one.

*of Egypt*. On the subject of imports of this kind from Egypt see Nowack, *Hebräische Archäologie*, i. 123, 240 f. (1894).

**17.** *I have perfumed*. Lit. 'sprinkled'; the word occurs here only.
*myrrh* . . . Cf. Cant. iv. 14. On myrrh and aloes see Nowack, *op. cit.*, i. 133, on cinnamon ii. 123.

**18.** *let us take our fill*. Cf. v. 19, 'let her breasts satisfy thee . . .'
*Let us solace ourselves*. The Hebrew has, 'let us delight ourselves'. 'Until the morning' is probably a redactor's addition, it overloads the line.

**19.** *the goodman*. Hebr. 'the man', Greek 'my husband'.

**20.** *a bag of money*. Implying that he will be absent for some time.
*at the full moon*. i.e. the full moon feast; the word occurs only here and Ps. lxxxi. 3 (Hebr. 4).

**21.** *fair speech*. Lit. 'learning', see note on i. 5.

**22, 23.** These two verses must be taken together. As they offer, from the text-critical point of view, one of the most difficult passages in *Proverbs*, a somewhat detailed examination of them may be permitted; it will also afford a good illustration both of how easily corruptions in the text arise through the similarity of the Hebrew letters—this can be appreciated even without any knowledge of Hebrew—and also of what importance the Septuagint often is for the study of the Hebrew text. The first two lines of verse 22 are not difficult; for 'straightway' (R.V. marg. more correctly 'suddenly' פְּתְאֹם) it is preferable to read 'the foolish one' (הַפֶּתֶה = Sept. κεπφωθείς) as the preceding verse has made it quite clear that the man has not followed the 'strange woman' suddenly. It is also perhaps better to read for 'as an ox *goeth*' (יָבֹא), 'As an ox *is led*' (יָבֹא = Sept. ἄγεται). The real difficulty begins with the third line. The R.V. rendering is a heroic attempt to make sense out of the meaningless Hebrew text. The word translated 'fetters' is in the singular, but only occurs elsewhere (in the plural) in Isa. iii. 18 as the ornamental bangles worn by ladies on their ankles. But apart from this the text is quite corrupt. Toy offers a drastic emendation, but his ingenuity must be acknowledged, and it makes admirable sense; the similarity between his emendation and the Hebrew as it stands will strike the eye at once; the latter runs: כְּעֶכֶס אֶל־מוּסָר אֱוִיל 'As fetters to the correction of a fool'; Toy suggests: כְּעֵגֶל אֶל־מַרְבֵּק יוּבַל : 'As a calf is led to the stall'. This offers a good parallel to the ox being led to slaughter, as the stalled calf was kept ready to be killed at any time, cf. the 'fatted calf' (Lk. xv. 23), and see 1 Sam. xxviii. 4, Am. vi. 4. The fatal objection to this suggested emendation is that it ignores the Sept., for it is impossible to believe that the Sept. does not represent something that stood in the Hebrew text. It looks as though there were a doublet in the Sept. which was due to the fact that the translator was puzzled by a badly written Hebr. text, and was in fact not sure what the words were; two alternatives suggested themselves, and as he could not make up his mind which of the two to choose he put both into his version, and wrote:

'And as a dog (is led) on a lead,
Or as a stag is struck with an arrow through his liver.'

The first point to notice here is that in all probability 'stag' represents a genuine part of the original text, and should be read in place of 'fool'; the latter is quite inappropriate, and in Hebrew the two words are very similar (אֱוִיל 'fool', אַיִל 'stag'). The Hebrew word for 'fetters' is the main difficulty; but in any case it must refer to the stag, as implied by the Hebrew, not to the dog, as rendered by the Sept. The word for 'correction' is also inappropriate. It is, therefore, suggested that in place of the Hebrew as it now stands, we should read: וּכְאֶסֶר אֶל־מָצוֹד אַיָל 'And as a stag is corded (entangled) in a snare'. The word for 'snare' occurs in Job xix. 6 and Eccles. vii. 26: 'And I find a thing more bitter than death, even a woman whose heart is snares (מְצוֹדִים) and nets, and her hands are bands (אֲסוּרִים),' cf. also Gen. xl. 3; 2 Sam. iii. 34; Job xxxix. 5ᵇ; and the thought of a gazelle in a snare, though in a different connexion, occurs in Ben-Sira (Ecclus. xxvii. 20; the Hebr. is unfortunately not extant). It is true that the Hebr. *verb* for 'entangled' is not found in the O.T., but in *Proverbs*, especially in this collection,

24 Now therefore, *my* sons, hearken unto me,
   And attend to the words of my mouth.
25 Let not thine heart decline to her ways,
   Go not astray in her paths.
26 For she hath cast down many wounded:
   Yea, all her slain are a mighty host.
27 Her house is the way to ¹Sheol,
   Going down to the chambers of death.

¹ Or, *the grave*

which is the latest, this should not be an objection. This emendation has in its favour that it is a pointed analogy to the man entangled in the wiles of the 'strange woman'. Another emendation is suggested by Box (in a private communication): וּכְעֶבֶר-לַמוֹסֵר אַיָל ' And as a stag is checked (restrained) by the cord (of the snare)'. In this case, too, the word for 'is checked' does not occur in the O.T., but it has the advantage of accounting for the 'dog' of the Sept., as there is a similarity in the Hebr. letters (כְּלֶב). But there is the further possi-bility that what we have in the Sept. is not a doublet, but that it represents an originally fuller Hebrew text. In the Sept. the illustra-tions 'dog', 'stag', and 'bird' are mentioned; it is interesting to find this curious combination (though in the reverse order) used for illustrative purposes, though in a different connexion, in *The Parables of Achikar* viii. 15–17. Seeing that there are a number of other parallels between Achikar and *Proverbs*, it is quite possible that we have here another; or, at least, that this was originally the case, the Sept. having preserved something that has been lost in the Hebrew.

*liver.* In the sense of the seat of life only here and in Lam. ii. 11; elsewhere always in connexion with sacrificial ritual.

*As a bird.* Cf. i. 17; Eccles. ix. 12.

*that it is for his life.* i. e. that his life is in question.

**24.** This and the following *vv.* give the final exhortation.

*my sons.* Read, with the Sept., 'my son'; the verbs also (as in the Sept.) should be read in the sing., as *v.* 25 shows.

**25.** *decline.* A rare word in Hebr., cf. iv. 15; Num. v. 12, 19, 20, 29; Hos. v. 2, and nowhere else in the O.T.; it means wandering or straying about.

**26.** *For she hath . . . wounded.* Hebr.: 'For many are the dead she hath cast down', i. e. to *Sheol*, see next *v.*

**27.** *Sheol . . . chambers of death.* See Excursus V.

Cf. with this section the following passage from the Egyptian book *The Wisdom of Anii*: 'Beware of the strange woman, unknown in her city. Regard her not, neither have intercourse with her. She is a deep water of wide expanse. A woman who has gone from her hus-band. Daily she saith to thee when no witness is by, "I am well-

**VIII.** 1 Doth not wisdom cry,
    And understanding put forth her voice?
  2 In the top of high places by the way,
    Where the paths meet, she standeth;

liking . . ." That is a great crime, worthy of death, whether others
hear it or not . . .' (Erman, *op. cit.*, p. 296). And again: 'Go not
after a woman that she steal not thine heart' (Erman, *op. cit.*,
p. 300); see Excursus I. Cf. also in the Babylonian wisdom book, *The
Proverbs of Achikar*, these sayings: 'My son, lift not up thine eyes
and look not upon a woman that is bedizened and painted; and do
not lust after her in thy heart; for if thou shouldst give her all that
is in thy hands, thou wouldst find no advantage in her; and thou
wouldst be guilty of sin against God' (ii. 5). Elsewhere the same
writer says: 'My son, go not after the beauty of a woman, and lust
not after her in thy heart; for the beauty of a woman is her good
sense, and her adornment is the word of her mouth' (ii. 19 and
similarly in ii. 72).

## Chapter VIII

**VIII. 1–36.** *The greatness of Wisdom and her works.*

THIS chapter is divided into two parts: *vv.* 1–21, of which *vv.* 1–3
form an introduction, deal with Wisdom among men; *vv.* 22–36, of
which *vv.* 32–36 form the conclusion, speak of her close connexion
with God in His work of creation.

**1–3.** *Introductory words describing her all-embracing appeal.* Cf.
Job xxviii; Ecclus. i. 1–21, xxiv; Wisd. vii. 8–viii. 21. See Excursus III.

**1.** *wisdom . . . understanding.* See notes on i. 2.
*cry.* Better 'call', because Wisdom is making her widespread
appeal and invitation to all men.

**2.** *In the top of high places.* The reference is to any elevated spots
in the city where one is at once seen. The word for 'high places'
(*merōmim*) is a poetical one, and is used often in reference to the
heavens and of the tops of mountains; but, excepting when used of
Zion, which is a special use, it is very unusual to find it mentioned in
connexion with a city as here.

*by the way.* Better 'upon the road'. The thought of the line is that
of Wisdom standing on any conspicuous place alongside the public
thoroughfare. The Sept. omits 'by the way'.

*Where the paths meet.* Better 'in the midst of the pathways', or
streets, following the Sept., and reading בְּתוֹךְ for בֵּית, as in *v.* 20.

3 Beside the gates, at the entry of the city,
  At the coming in at the doors, she crieth aloud:
4 Unto you, O men, I call;
  And my voice is to the sons of men.
5 O ye simple, understand ¹subtilty;
  And, ye fools, be ye of an understanding heart.
6 Hear, for I will speak excellent things;
  And the opening of my lips shall be right things.
7 For my mouth shall utter truth;
  And wickedness is an abomination to my lips.

¹ Or, *prudence*

**3.** *Beside the gates.* The general meeting-place where crowds often collected was by the city gates, cf. Judg. ix. 35; 2 Sam. xv. 2; Jer. xvii. 19. The Hebr. for 'beside' is lit. 'at the hand of'.

*at the entry of the city.* The Hebr. expression for 'at the entry' is again taken from the human body, lit. 'at the mouth of'. The word for city (קֶרֶת) is not the usual one, it occurs elsewhere once in Job xxix. 7, but otherwise only in Prov. ix. 3, 14, xi. 11.

**VIII. 4–21.** *The true things of Wisdom and the reward of those who make them their own.*

**4.** *men . . . sons of men.* The appeal of Wisdom is to all and sundry.

**5.** *simple . . . fools.* See Excursus XI.

*subtilty.* See note on i. 4; it is here parallel to 'heart', the seat of the understanding, as in xv. 32, xvii. 16, xix. 8.

*be ye of an understanding heart.* This does not represent the Hebr. which means 'apprehend wisdom', or the like, 'heart' being a synonym for the 'understanding' here.

**6.** *excellent things.* The Hebr. reads נְגִידִים, 'princes'; it is possible to take it in an abstract sense 'princely things', but the word is never used in this sense; it is better to emend and read נְכֹחִים as in *v.* 9, or 'true things' as in 2 Sam. xv. 3; Isa. xxx. 10; this corresponds better with 'right things' in the next clause, cf. xxiii. 16.

**7.** *mouth.* Strictly 'palate', cf. xxiv. 13.

*shall utter.* The present tense represents the Hebr. better.

*And wickedness is . . .* The Hebr. reads rather strangely; for wickedness as an abomination to the lips is meaningless. It is better to read with the Sept. and the Syr.: 'An abomination to me are the lips of wickedness'; this involves but a slight change in the Hebr. text: וְתוֹעֲבָה לִי שִׂפְתֵי רֶשַׁע, cf. xii. 22. This forms a better contrast to what follows in the next verse.

8 All the words of my mouth [1]are in righteousness;
There is nothing crooked or perverse in them.

9 They are all plain to him that understandeth,
And right to them that find knowledge.

10 Receive my instruction, and not silver;
And knowledge rather than choice gold.

11 For wisdom is better than [2]rubies;
And all the things that may be desired are not to be compared unto her.

12 I wisdom have made [3]subtilty my dwelling,
And find out [4]knowledge *and* discretion.

---

[1] Or, *are righteousness*     [2] See Job. xxviii. 18.     [3] Or, *prudence*
[4] Or, *knowledge of witty inventions*

---

**8.** *in righteousness.* i.e. in accordance with what is righteous.

*crooked.* The underlying meaning of the Hebr. word (נִפְתָּל) is well illustrated by Gen. xxx. 8: 'I have wrestled with . . .', lit. 'I have twisted myself'. The word therefore refers to utterances which are the reverse of 'straight'. This is the only time the word occurs in *Proverbs*; cf. Ps. xviii. 26 (27 in Hebr.).

*perverse.* See note on ii. 15.

**9.** *plain.* Hebr. נְכֹחִים, see note on this word in *v.* 6.

**10.** *my instruction.* The omission of 'my', as in the Sept., Syr., and Targ., accords better with 'knowledge' in the next clause. Cf. iii. 15.

*choice.* The Hebr. word (נִבְחָר) is peculiar to *Proverbs* (viii. 19, x. 20, xvi. 16, xxi. 1, 3).

**11.** *rubies.* See note on iii. 15, and cf. xx. 15.

**12.** At this *v.* Wisdom begins to speak herself; so far it has been the sage who has been exalting her; but now it is 'I, Wisdom', who declares the nature of her activity among men.

*have made my dwelling.* The Hebr. (שָׁכַנְתִּי) can hardly be right, though it is supported by the Sept. (κατεσκήνωσα); the idea that Wisdom dwells in subtilty, or prudence, is not one that the Wisdom writers entertain. The parallel clause suggests some word expressing ownership here; this is supplied by the Syr. and the Targ., which apparently read a Hebr. word meaning both 'I possess', and 'I create' (קָנִיתִי); here it would have the former sense; in *v.* 22 it has the latter sense.

*find out.* The Hebr. word has here, as in vi. 33, the sense of 'acquiring'; cf. Eccles. xi. 1.

*knowledge* and . . . The marg. note in R.V. can be ignored. Although the Hebr. has not the necessary 'and', it occurs in the

13 The fear of the LORD is to hate evil:
   Pride, and arrogancy, and the evil way,
   And the froward mouth, do I hate.
14 Counsel is mine, and [1]sound knowledge:
   I am understanding; I have might.
15 By me kings reign,
   And princes decree justice.
16 By me [2]princes rule,
   And nobles, *even* all the judges [3]of the earth.
17 I love them that love me;
   And those that seek me [4]diligently shall find me.

[1] Or, *effectual working*   [2] Or, *rulers*   [3] Many ancient authorities
read, *of righteousness.*   [4] Or, *early*

Versions, and no doubt dropped out by mistake from the Hebr. text.
The same two words occur together in i. 4.

**13.** It is clear that this *v.* has got in here by mistake; it breaks
the connexion between *vv.* 12 and 14. Not only so, but the clauses of
the *v.* itself do not belong together. The first clause speaks of the
fear of Jahweh, while the last two contain the words of Wisdom.
We have here another illustration of what was said in the note on
iii. 27–30.
   *The fear of the Lord.* Cf. i. 7, ix. 10, x. 27, xiv. 26, 27, xv. 33, xvi. 6,
xix. 23; Job xxviii. 28.
   *the froward mouth.* Cf. ii. 12, vi. 14.

**14.** *Counsel . . . might.* Cf. Isa. xi. 2; Job xii. 13.
   *sound knowledge.* See note on iii. 7.
   *I am understanding . . .* The force of the Hebr. is: 'I (or, "as for
me"), understanding is mine (and) might'; the 'and' has fallen out
in the text.

**15.** *By me kings reign.* The meaning is not that kings reign by the
decree, as it were, of Wisdom (cf. Rom. xiii. 1); but that they carry
out the duties of kingship by means of Wisdom's guidance.

**16.** even *all the judges of the earth.* It gives a better sense and a
more rhythmical line if we follow the Sept. here, and omit 'all', and
read a verb instead of a noun for 'judges' (the word for 'to judge'
has also the meaning 'to rule' or 'govern'); the line then runs: 'And
nobles govern the earth.' For 'earth' (אֶרֶץ) some MSS., the Syr.,
Vulg., and Targum read 'righteously' (צֶדֶק), but this is probably not
the right reading, good as the sense is; for the word ends the preceding *v.*, and was very likely originally copied in mistake for אֶרֶץ
('earth').

**17.** *those that seek . . .* See note on i. 28.

18 Riches and honour are with me;
   Yea, ¹durable riches and righteousness.
19 My fruit is better than gold, yea, than fine gold;
   And my ²revenue than choice silver.
20 I walk in the way of righteousness,
   In the midst of the paths of judgement:
21 That I may cause those that love me to inherit substance,
   And that I may fill their treasuries.

¹ Or, *ancient*          ² Or, *increase*

**18.** *durable.* The Hebr. word means 'surpassing' or 'eminent', it occurs here only in the O.T.; a word from the same root, but different in form, is used in Isa. xxiii. 18 of 'choice' attire.

*righteousness.* This is the usual meaning of the Hebr. word (צדקה), but in the present context it has the sense of 'prosperity' as in Joel ii. 23: '. . . for he giveth you the former rain for prosperity' (not, as the context shows, 'in just measure').

**19.** *My fruit.* Cf. iii. 18 where Wisdom is spoken of as 'a tree of life', and Ecclus. i. 17, vi. 19, xxiv. 16, 17.

*gold.* This word (חָרוּץ) is only found in poetical books (*Psalms* and *Proverbs*); it comes from the root meaning 'to be yellow'; the verb does not occur in the O.T.

*fine gold.* The origin of this word *paz* (פַּז) is uncertain; possibly it comes from a root meaning 'to be refined'. On another poetical word for 'gold', *kethem* (כֶּתֶם), see note on xxv. 12. The ordinary word is *zāhāb* (זָהָב).

*revenue.* This word is used ordinarily of the yield of the crops; here it is used figuratively of what is gained through the possession of Wisdom. See note on iii. 14.

*choice silver.* Cf. x. 20.

**20.** *I walk.* The form of the Hebr. word is intensive, meaning 'I walk steadfastly', or 'continuously'.

*paths of judgement.* i.e. paths of uprightness or justice; the Hebr. *mishpat* is used as a parallel to 'righteousness' also in Ps. cvi. 3; cf. Prov. xii. 5.

**21.** *substance.* This is the only place where the Hebr. word (יֵשׁ) is used in this sense in the canonical Scriptures; it occurs in Ecclus. xxv. 21, xlii. 3, in the sense of 'property'.

**VIII. 22–31.** *Wisdom's presence at the creation of the world.*

The artistic way in which this beautiful poem is constructed is well worth noting: the framework consists of the opening stanza, *vv.* 22,

22 The LORD [1]possessed me [2]in the beginning of his way,
   [3]Before his works of old.

      [1] Or, *formed*        [2] Or, *as*        [3] Or, *The first of*

23, and the closing one, *vv.* 30, 31, in each of which Wisdom speaks of herself; enclosed are the two longer stanzas, *vv.* 24–26, and 27–29; these describe the cosmos, the former negatively, of what had not yet been created when Wisdom was already in being; the latter positively, of what God created by the instrumentality of Wisdom. This descending and ascending movement culminating in the triumphant strain of Wisdom's delight at all the beauty of the Creator's work, is very fine. It is also to be observed how skilfully the danger is avoided of making Wisdom appear in too exalted a position; although present at the Creation, and utilized in the creative work, Wisdom is throughout subordinate; she herself is created, a witness of the divine activity, God's child, His instrument; the Creator is God alone.

The passage, as is well known, has been interpreted from early days in a christological sense. There can be no doubt that *v.* 22 lies at the back of Col. i. 15–18 and Rev. iii. 14. Burney has gathered a number of patristic passages dealing with this crucial verse in the *Journal of Theol. Studies*, xxvii. 160–177 (1926); this article is well worth study; he shows that קנה cannot rightly be rendered 'possessed' me, but that from the context in which it occurs here it must have the sense 'begat' me (cf. the clause in the Nicene Creed, 'begotten of his Father before all worlds'). See further, Lightfoot, *Colossians*, pp. 146–152 (1884), Ottley, *The Doctrine of the Incarnation*, i. 44, 305 (1896).

**22.** *possessed.* The Hebr. word has also the meaning of 'created'; so Gen. xiv. 19, 22, Ps. cxxxix. 13, Sept., Syr., Targ. Cf. Ecclus. i. 4: 'Wisdom hath been created before all things', see also Ecclus. i. 9, xxiv. 8; Wisd. vii. 26; but the word is best translated 'begat me'; see the note at the head of this section.

*in the beginning.* Read 'at the beginning' (*rēshīth*), or as R.V. marg. 'as the . . .'; the point is that Wisdom was the first thing created. *Rēshīth* is written with a capital in many Hebr. MSS.; in the Midrash *Berēshīth Rabba* i. 1, in reference to this verse, it is said that by *Rēshīth* the Torah is to be understood.

*his way.* The Sept. has 'his ways'; the reference is to the acts of Creation, cf. Job xxvi. 14, xl. 19.

*Before.* Read, with R.V. marg., 'the first of'.

*of old.* This does not refer to 'his works', but to 'possessed me'. Cf. Ps. xciii. 2. Sept., Syr. omit.

23  I was set up from everlasting, from the beginning,
       Or ever the earth was.
24  When there were no depths, I was brought forth;
       When there were no fountains abounding with water.
25  Before the mountains were settled,
       Before the hills was I brought forth:
26  While as yet he had not made the earth, nor the fields,
       Nor the ¹beginning of the dust of the world.

¹ Or, *sum*

**23.** *I was set up.* So the Hebr. (נִסַּכְתִּי as in Ps. ii. 6), but the renderings of the Versions presuppose the reading נוֹסַדְתִּי, 'I was founded', i.e. I trace my origin from everlasting. Some commentators suggest the reading נִסַכְתִּי, 'I was woven' (from the root סכך), cf. Ps. cxxxix. 13; Job x. 11, where the word is used in reference to the pre-natal growth in the embryo.

*Or ever the earth was.* Lit. 'from the origins of the earth', cf. Ecclus. xxiv. 9.

**24.** *depths.* i.e. the primeval waters, cf. Gen. i. 2. In the Babylonian cosmogony it is said that before the heaven and the earth received their names, i.e. before they were created, *Apsu* (the ocean) and *Tiamat* (the deep) mingled their waters. It is from this Babylonian mythological conception that the 'depths' here mentioned are ultimately derived, see further Gunkel, *Schöpfung und Chaos in Urzeit und Endzeit*, pp. 21ff. (1895). The Hebrew sage wishes to push back the origin of Wisdom to the farthest possible limits; note the phrases 'as the beginning' of created things, 'the first' of God's work, 'of old', 'from everlasting', 'from the beginning'. This is emphasized in order to show that what the sage taught had come down from a hoary antiquity; the Hebrews placed a high value on what was ancient.

*I was brought forth.* The force of the Hebrew word חוֹלָלְתִּי is 'I was brought forth with travail'.

*abounding with water.* Lit. 'heavy with waters' (נִכְבַּדֵּי־מָיִם), but this use of the Hebr. word is not found elsewhere, and perhaps it is better to read, on the basis of the Sept., 'springs of waters' (נִבְכֵי־יָם) as in Job xxxviii. 16.

**25.** *were settled.* The Hebr. has 'were sunk', i.e. in the waters under the earth; the Hebrew conception was that the mountains rested on foundations which were sunk under the earth in the waters there, cf. Ps. xviii. 7 (8 in Hebr.), civ. 8; Jon. ii. 6 (7 in Hebr.). It is even before the beginning of these that Wisdom existed.

**26.** *nor the fields.* The Hebr. has 'nor the outside places' (חוּצוֹת); possibly the meaning is the 'open places', cf. Job v. 10.

*Nor the beginning.* As it stands the Hebr. text (וְרֹאשׁ) does not

27 When he [1]established the heavens, I was there:
  When he set a circle upon the face of the deep:

            [1] Or, *prepared*

give good sense; it is better to read וְרֹאשׁ, 'nor the green', in the
sense of the green covering of the earth, cf. xxvii. 25; Isa. xv. 6.

*dust.* The Hebr. is in the plur. which is very rare, only elsewhere
in Job xxviii. 6, where it is used in reference to gold. The word does
not necessarily mean 'dust' as we understand it; it has the sense of
clods of soil, and the soil in general in, e.g. Job v. 6, xiv. 8. With
*vv.* 24–26 cf. the opening lines of the Babylonian Creation-myth:

> 'When the heaven above was not yet named,
> And the earth below had not yet been created,
> But the primeval Ocean, the begetter . . .
> When no fields had been formed,
> And no marsh land yet existed;
> When the gods had not come forth, not one,
> And no destinies were decided . . .' [1]

According to Babylonian belief Wisdom dwelt in the depths of the
Ocean with Ea, the creative deity. Apsu, 'the deep', is called the
'house of Wisdom', because out of it came forth the Wisdom of Ea,
and the word of Ea. One of the epithets applied to the god Ea is
'lord of Wisdom'.[2]

One may also compare the Egyptian conception of Isis, who, according to the Greeks, was identified with Sophia. In an ancient
Egyptian poem praise is offered to the highest god, king of all the
heavenly beings; it then continues:

> 'Thee do I greet, holy goddess and mother, the many-named Isis,
> Thee, whom the heavens brought forth on the glittering waves of the sea,
> Who turnedst the darkness to light for all who are children of men;
> Who holdest the sceptre on high as the ancient of days on Olympus,
> Who rulest as mistress divine the earth and the ocean's expanse,
> Whose eye doth discover all things,—much good hast thou given to men.'[3]

**27.** *established.* R.V. marg. 'prepared' is the literal meaning of
the Hebr. word.

*the heavens.* See note on next verse.

*a circle.* This is, of course, what the expanse of the sky would look
like; cf. Isa. xl. 22; Job xxii. 14; Ecclus. xxiv. 5. See next note.

*the face of the deep.* As among the Babylonians so among the
Hebrews the belief was that the deep was not only under the earth,
but also surrounded it; and the 'circle' was placed on this 'deep'.
But clearly the picture here would be that of a semi-circle, not a
'circle', so that it is better to translate this word (חוּג) by 'vault'.

---

[1] Jeremias, *Das alte Testament im Lichte des alten Orients*, p. 52 (1904).
[2] Jeremias, *op. cit.*, pp. 29, 30.
[3] Translated from Erman's German version of the original, *Die ägyptische Religion*,
p. 246 (1909).

28 When he made firm the skies above:
   When the fountains of the deep became strong:
29 When he gave to the sea ¹its bound,
   That the waters should not transgress his commandment:
   When he ²marked out the foundations of the earth:
30 Then I was by him, *as* a master workman:
   And I ³was daily *his* delight,
     ⁴Rejoicing always before him;

¹ Or, *his decree*   ² Or, *appointed*   ³ Or, *had delight continually*   ⁴ Or, *sporting*

**28.** *When he made firm* ... The Hebrews conceived of the skies or firmament as a solid beaten-out expanse; the Hebr. word for 'firmament' (רָקִיעַ) comes from a root meaning 'to beat', or 'hammer out'.

*fountains of the deep.* Here the reference must be to that part of the deep which was believed to have been fixed above; cf. Gen. i. 7, where it is said that 'the waters which were under the firmament' were divided 'from the waters which were above the firmament', but it was originally all one 'deep' (of waters).

*became strong.* So the Hebr. (בַּעֲזוֹז); but in conformity with the form of the verbs in these *vv.*, and following the Versions, we must emend the Hebr. text (בְּעַזֵּז), and read: 'when he made strong', or 'fixed firmly'.

**29.** *When he gave.* Hebr. 'when he set', cf. Gen. i. 9, 10; Job xxxviii. 8–11; Ps. civ. 6–9.

*its bound.* The Hebr. word (חֹק) means something prescribed; here the limits of the place assigned to it is meant. The word also means 'decree' (R.V. marg.), but in other connexions.

*When he marked out.* So the Hebr. (בְּחוּקוֹ); but it gives better sense if, following the Sept., we read בְּחַזְּקוֹ, 'when he made strong'; the word is used in reference to building, in 2 Kgs. xii. 6, 7; Nah. iii. 14, and elsewhere. It is to be taken here in a literal sense, whichever reading is adopted. This verse, unlike the others in this section, has three lines instead of two; it is impossible to say whether a line has fallen out, or whether the second line is an insertion; the *v.* reads better by omitting it.

**30.** *a master workman.* Hebr. *'amōn* (אָמוֹן). The way in which the Rabbis identified the Torah with Wisdom is well illustrated in the Midrash *Bĕrēshith Rabba* i. 1, where it is said that Rabbi Hoshajah (3rd cent. A.D.) was accustomed to open his lecture by quoting this verse, and that he explained this word *'āmōn* as being equivalent to *'ūmān*, 'architect'. (Cf. Cant. vii. 1 [Hebr. 2], אָמֵן.) It then continues: 'The Torah says, "I was God's instrument". When a king builds a palace he does not build according to his ideas, but according to those of an architect; nor does the latter build arbitrarily; but he has parchments and tablets whereon the divisions of the apart-

31 ¹Rejoicing in his habitable earth;
   And my delight was with the sons of men.
32 Now therefore, *my* sons, hearken unto me:
   For blessed are they that keep my ways.
33 Hear instruction, and be wise,
   And refuse it not.

¹ Or, *sporting*

ments and chambers are specified. In the same way God looked into
the Torah, and then created the world.' The word as it stands in the
text occurs nowhere else in the O.T., and its meaning is uncertain.
But if, following the Versions, and Cant. vii. 2, we read אָמֵן ('*ommān*),
which is probably a borrowed Assyrian word, *ummānu* (see the
quotation above), we get a word meaning 'architect' or 'master-
workman'; cf. Wisd. vii. 21: 'For she (i. e. Wisdom) is the artificer
(τεχνῖτις) of all.' Some commentators object to this reading because
it is God Himself who is represented as the architect, and suggest,
after Lam. iv. 5, the reading אֵמוּן ('*ĕmūn*) 'nursling'. As Toy remarks:
'The sense *nursling* accords with the succeeding text, and with the
representation of the whole paragraph.' There is much force in this;
but from what is said by Rabbi Hoshajah, above, it is clear that the
rendering 'architect' is very ancient, and the objection mentioned is
not a fatal one, as Wisd. vii. 21 shows.

*I was daily . . .* The R.V. text is to be preferred to the marg.
according to Hebr. usage of the word for 'delight'.

*Rejoicing.* R.V. marg. 'sporting' better represents the Hebr. word,
cf. Exod. xxxii. 6. This line is very similar to the next one, and may
very possibly be a gloss.

**31.** *in his habitable earth.* Hebr. בְּתֵבֵל אַרְצוֹ, which is a curious
phrase, lit. 'in the inhabited world of his earth'; Wildeboer, on the
basis of the Sept., emends בְּתַכְלִית אָרֶץ, 'at the completion of the
earth'.

## VIII. 32–36. *Concluding exhortation.*

In *vv.* 32–34 both the Hebr. and the Sept. B point to some disloca-
tion in the text (see further below).

**32.** *Now therefore . . .* Hebr. 'And now'. This line does not occur
in the Sept. B.

*For blessed . . .* The 'for' of the R.V. is without any justification;
it is simply 'and', thus suggesting a preceding parallel clause and
therefore not the words which stand in the text now, though what
they may have been cannot be determined now. Probably it is best
to omit the 'and'. In the Sept. this line comes after 'Blessed is the
man that heareth me', in *v.* 34ᵃ.

**33.** This *v.* is omitted by the Sept. altogether.

*refuse.* Better 'reject'.

F

34 Blessed is the man that heareth me,
   Watching daily at my gates,
   Waiting at the posts of my doors.
35 For whoso findeth me findeth life,
   And shall [1] obtain favour of the LORD.
36 But he that [2] sinneth against me wrongeth his own soul:
   All they that hate me love death.

          [1] Heb. *draw forth*.          [2] Or, *misseth me*

**34.** This three-lined *v.* is suspicious as being out of harmony with the strophic formation of the rest of the section.

*heareth me.* Better 'hearkeneth unto me'.

*gates . . . doors.* This idea of Wisdom having her house is developed in ix. 1.

The sequence of the lines of these *vv.* suggested by the Sept. would be:

$\Big\{$ 32ᵃ *And now, (my) sons, hearken unto me,*
     33 *Hear (my) instruction (and be wise), and reject it not.*

$\Big\{$ 32ᵇ *Blessed are they that keep my ways;*
     34ᵃ *Blessed is the man that hearkeneth unto me.*

$\Big\{$ 34ᵇ *Watching daily . . .*
     34ᶜ *Waiting at the posts . . .*

In *v.* 33 the words 'and be wise' overweight the line, and are not required; this order offers an excellent strophic balance, and gives the proper two lines each to *vv.* 33, 34, instead of one and three which they have, respectively, in the present form of the text. With 34ᶜ cf. Ecclus. vii. 36, xiv. 22, 23.

**35.** Cf. iv. 22; Ecclus. iv. 12.

*And shall obtain . . .* Lit. as R.V. marg. 'draweth forth'; the identical line occurs again in xviii. 22ᵇ.

**36.** *he that sinneth against me.* This rendering misses the point of the Hebr.; the root חטא, like the Greek ἁμαρτάνειν, means primarily 'to miss', i.e. the mark. Here it is this original sense which is meant, in contrast to 'whoso findeth' in the preceding *v.* The rendering should, therefore, be as in the R.V. marg.

*death.* This, like 'life' in the preceding *v.*, is to be taken in the physical sense, cf. ii. 21, 22.

### CHAPTER IX

**IX. 1-6.** *The feast which Wisdom offers.*

IN this chapter *vv.* 1-6 and 13-18, respectively, represent Wisdom and Folly as having their houses and inviting guests to come to them. It can scarcely be doubted, therefore, that originally these two sections followed one another immediately; the intervening *vv.* 7-12 have been inserted here somewhat unintelligently by some scribe who did not see that the original writer wished to place in striking

**IX.** 1 Wisdom hath builded her house,
   She hath hewn out her seven pillars:

contrast the choice things which Wisdom had to offer, and the death-bringing food of Folly.

The conception here of Wisdom as a woman presiding over her household affairs is in striking contrast to that of viii. 22 ff., where she appears as a superhuman being utilized in the creation of the world. As a homely virtuous matron she is the embodiment of purity of living, and addresses herself particularly to the younger generation among whom sensuality forms one of the most insidious temptations. Folly, therefore, the antithesis to Wisdom, is represented as a harlot. Volz suggests that the connexion between Wisdom and Virtue, on the one hand, and Folly and Vice, on the other, may have a mythological background. For this corresponds to the dual character of the mother-goddess of the nearer east, the goddess of Love; she appears both as the exalted and pure queen of heaven, as well as the seductive goddess of an impure and immoral worship.

**1.** *Wisdom.* The Hebr. has the plur. form, see note on i. 20.

*hath builded her house.* Cf. Ecclus. xiv. 23, 24. It is possible that the idea of Wisdom having her own house was suggested by something corresponding to the 'House of Learning' (the later *Bēth ha-Midrāsh*, mentioned in the Hebrew of Ecclus. li. 23), to which a sage's disciples resorted for instruction. It is true, we have no direct mention of such places of instruction before the time of Ben-Sira (*circa* 200 B.C.); but he speaks of his 'House of Learning' as of something well known, and the existence of such a technical name as *Bēth ha-Midrash*, mentioned in his book quite incidentally, proves that such institutions cannot have been of recent growth. The repeated occurrence of the address 'My son' in *Proverbs*, the usual one of the sage to his pupils, proves the existence of a place of assembly of some kind. It may be added that Ben-Sira also speaks of his *Yĕshībhah* (li. 29), another technical term for an academy of learning, but on a larger scale than the *Bēth ha-Midrash*. The word comes from the root meaning 'to sit'.

*She hath hewn out.* The Hebr. root (חצב) is used of the stone-mason's work, cf. 2 Kgs. xii. 13; Isa. v. 2, and elsewhere, and is not appropriate here; it is better to follow the Sept. and read, 'she hath set up' (הִצִּיבָה).

*seven pillars.* The houses of the wealthy were mostly rectangular in shape (cf. Job i. 19, 'the four corners of the house'), enclosing a quadrangle surrounded by a gallery supported by pillars (Judg. xvi. 25, 26); in Cant. v. 15 mention is made of 'pillars of marble'. The seven pillars here mentioned would be the ordinary number in a large house, three on either side of the quadrangle, and one at the end farthest from the entrance; the end where the entrance was would have no pillar in order to leave the space at the entry free.

2 She hath killed her beasts; she hath mingled her wine;
  She hath also furnished her table.
3 She hath sent forth her maidens, she crieth
  Upon the highest places of the city,
4 Whoso is simple, let him turn in hither:
  As for him that is void of understanding, she saith to him,
5 Come, eat ye of my bread,
  And drink of the wine which I have mingled.

**2.** *mingled her wine.* The mixing of water with wine (it is not this that is referred to in Isa. i. 22) is probably not so ancient a custom as mixing spices with it in order to increase the flavour (cf. Ps. lxxv. 8 [Hebr. 9]; Isa. v. 22; Cant. viii. 2); it is the latter which is meant here.

*furnished her table.* This is misleading as it suggests that the table is furnished with dishes, but these were not placed on the table until the guests had arrived; it should be 'hath set her table in order' (cf. Isa. xxi. 5; Ps. xxiii. 5). In the earliest times when taking meals people sat on the ground. They did not have tables; the Hebr. word rendered 'table' (*shulchān*) means originally something 'spread out' on the ground, a mat of leather or plaited straw; it was doubtless similar to the old Arabian *sufra*, a skin spread on the ground; this is still in use among the Bedouin Arabs.

**3.** *She hath sent forth* ... i.e. to invite the guests. This is the only place in the O.T. where the mode of invitation to a feast is indicated, though we know from the N.T. (Matth. xxii. 3) that the invitation to a feast was sent by the slaves of the host. Whether the 'maidens' here mentioned are to be thought of as slaves or free women cannot be said with certainty as the Hebr. word includes both; but judging from xxvii. 27, xxxi. 15, they are not thought of as slaves.

*she crieth.* That after having sent forth her maidens to do so Wisdom herself should 'cry' is quite improbable; it is the maidens who would obviously do this. We must therefore emend the Hebr. text and read תִּקְרֶאנָה for תִּקְרָא, making 'maidens' the subject; this is the rendering of the Syr., Vulg., and Targ.

*the highest places of* ... Cf. viii. 2. There is no need for the superlative, see note on *v.* 14.

**4.** *she saith.* So the Hebr. (אָמְרָה), but a slight change in the vowels (אֹמְרָה) makes it, 'I say'; so the Syr., making the whole *v.* the words of Wisdom. This would, however, mean that the 'she crieth' in *v.* 3 is the correct reading, which we have seen reason to doubt. There is no justification for the comma at the end of *v.* 3 in the R.V.; the Hebrew has the usual full-stop. With this *v.* cf. ix. 16.

**5.** *Come, eat* ... Cf. Isa. lv. 1; Ecclus. xv. 3, xxiv. 19 ff., and John vi. 35.

6 ¹Leave off, ye simple ones, and live;
   And walk in the way of understanding.

7 He that correcteth a scorner getteth to himself shame:
   And he that reproveth a wicked man *getteth* himself a blot.

¹ Or, *Forsake the simple.*

**6.** *Leave off, ye simple ones.* This is not a rendering of the Hebr. which has: 'Forsake, ye simple ones'; a noun is expected as the sentence is incomplete without it, the verb is never used without the object. Either a word has fallen out of the text (the Sept. adds ἀφροσύνην, so the other Versions), or the present word (פְּתָאִים) ('ye simple ones') is a corruption of an abstract noun, פֶּתִי 'folly'. This word is used in i. 22, but it is found nowhere else in the O.T.; in *v.* 13 of this chap. another allied word for 'folly' occurs (פְּתִיּוּת), here only in the O.T., but the text is uncertain, see note on the *v.*

## IX. 7-12.    *Some stray Proverbs.*

*Vv.* 7-9 belong together, but the other three *vv.* contain isolated sayings.

**7.** *a scorner.* Cf. Ecclus. iii. 28 (Hebr.).

*shame.* Cf. xi. 2, 'ignominy' or 'disgrace'; in iii. 35, the word is used as the opposite of honour.

*a blot.* The Hebr. word (מוּם) is always used of a physical defect or blemish in the O.T., the only exceptions are Job xi. 15 and this verse (in Deut. xxxii. 5 the text is very uncertain), where it refers to a moral blemish. But in later Hebr. usage it is used of both a physical and a moral defect; e.g. in the Bab. Talm. *Baba Mezia* 59ᵇ it is said: 'Do not reproach thy neighbour with a fault (מוּם) which is also thine own' (Jastrow, *Talmud Dictionary* s.v.). So that it is possible that in a late book like this the word may refer to a moral defect. An allowable rendering would be: 'And he that reproveth a wicked man (getteth to himself) his, i.e. the wicked man's, blemish', meaning that the wicked man would impute his own sin to the reprover. At the same time it is recognized that there is an objection to this rendering because one expects, in conformity with the general usage, a word corresponding to 'shame' in the first clause. It is for this reason that some commentators would emend the text by reading כְּלִמָּה ('reproach') for מוּמוֹ ('his blemish'). Another possible emendation, if it is thought necessary to make one, would be to read חֶרְפָּה ('reproach') as in xviii. 3, where the same word for 'shame' is used as in the *v.* before us.

8 Reprove not a scorner, lest he hate thee:
  Reprove a wise man, and he will love thee.
9 Give *instruction* to a wise man, and he will be yet wiser:
  Teach a righteous man, and he will increase in learning.
10 The fear of the LORD is the beginning of wisdom:
  And the knowledge of the Holy One is understanding.
11 For by me thy days shall be multiplied,
  And the years of thy life shall be increased.
12 If thou art wise, thou art wise for thyself:
  And if thou scornest, thou alone shalt bear it.

**8.** *Reprove not a scorner.* Cf. xv. 12.
*Reprove a wise man* . . . For the thought cf. xxvii. 6; Ps. cxli. 5.
**9.** *Give* instruction. It is hardly necessary to add 'instruction';
as it stands the Hebr. is more telling: 'Give, or impart, to the wise
man . . .' This balances better with the second clause.
With verses 7–9 cf. the *Proverbs of Achikar* ii. 40:

> *My son, smite the [wise] man with wise word,*
> *That it may be in his heart like a fever in summer;*
> *[But know] that if thou smite a fool with many blows,*
> *He will not understand.*

**10.** *The fear of the Lord.* Cf. Isa. xi. 2, 3. In the O.T. to fear
Jahweh has reference to His personality, not to what He may do;
in viii. 13 it is said that 'the fear of the Lord is to hate evil', meaning
that hatred of evil arises through reverence for God.
*the beginning.* The Hebr. word is *techillah* (תְּחִלָּה) 'the first
principle (of Wisdom)', not *rēshīth* (רֵאשִׁית) as in i. 7, viii. 22; Ps. cxi.
10; cf. Ecclus. i. 14, 'beginning' in the sense of head or chief part
(cf. the thought, 'Wisdom is the principal thing', iv. 7, though the
text is corrupt, see note on the *v.*).
*the Holy One.* The Hebr. has the plur. form as in xxx. 3 (cf.
*Elohim* for God, and in Eccles. xii. 1 the 'Creator' is in the plur., so
too in the Aramaic of Dan. iv. 23 [26 in Aram.] 'Heavens' for God),
i.e. the plur. of majesty; but in later Jewish literature, where the
'Holy One', used for God, is very frequent, it is in the singular. The
Versions (except the Targum) read 'holy men', but the preceding
line, 'the fear of the Lord', demands that the reference should be
to God.
**11.** Cf. iii. 2, 16, iv. 10, x. 27, xix. 23. It is better to delete 'thy'
before 'days' and 'life'.
**12.** *shalt bear it.* i.e. the consequence of 'scorning'. With this
teaching on individual responsibility cf. Ezek. xviii. 4. The long
addition (7 lines) in the Sept. does not represent an original part of
the book.

13 [1]The foolish woman is clamorous;
   *She is* [2]simple, and knoweth nothing.
14 And she sitteth at the door of her house,
   On a seat in the high places of the city,
15 To call to them that pass by,
   Who go right on their ways,
16 Whoso is simple, let him turn in hither:
   And as for him that is void of understanding, she saith to
   him,

   [1] Or, *Folly*	[2] Heb. *simplicity*.

## IX. 13–18.	*Folly's invitation to passers-by.*

These *vv.* offer a contrast to *vv.* 1–6, and should come immediately after them.

**13.** *The foolish woman.* The Hebr. reads lit. 'a woman of folly'; but as these *vv.* are clearly meant to stand in contrast to *vv.* 1–6, which begin with 'Wisdom', personified as a hostess, we should expect this section to begin with 'Folly' personified; for, as the following verses show, Folly is, like Wisdom in the former section, represented also as a hostess. It is, therefore, very probable that the mention of the 'woman' was an explanatory gloss intended to indicate that Folly was personified. There was no need to do this in the case of Wisdom, because the personification of Wisdom had already been sufficiently indicated in chap. viii. We must, therefore, read simply 'Folly' with the R.V. marg. But if the word for 'woman' is deleted it makes the line too short; and therefore it is proposed by some commentators, following the Syr. and Vulg., to add the first word of the second line to the first line, reading with these Versions, instead of פְּתַיּוּת, 'simplicity', מְפֻתָּה, 'enticing' (so Toy); for to read 'Folly is loud and simplicity' would be impossible. So the first line should run: 'Folly is clamorous and enticing.' The taking of one word from the second line, however, now makes this line too short; but on turning to the Sept. we find that it has 'shame' for the last word, and must therefore have read כְּלִמָּה ('shame', cf. xviii. 13) instead of the present מָה, which in any case is wrong, as it is always an interrogative pronoun, and therefore out of place here. Moreover, to say that Folly 'knoweth nothing' would not be true, for *v.* 17 shows that she certainly knows how to be enticing. As emended, the line would then run: 'She knoweth no shame' (cf. vii. 11). Each line of the *v.* in the Hebrew would then contain three words.

**14.** *the high places.* See note on viii. 2. In ix. 3 the R.V. renders the same word by 'the highest places'.

**15.** *To call to* . . . As Wisdom does, see i. 20, 21, viii. 1–3.

**16.** The identical words are said in reference to Wisdom in *v.* 4.

17  Stolen waters are sweet,
    And bread *eaten* in secret is pleasant.

18  But he knoweth not that [1]the dead are there;
    That her guests are in the depths of Sheol.

[1] Or, *the shades*   Heb. *Rephaim.*

**17.** Contrast with *v.* 5; cf. Ecclus. xxiii. 17.

**18.** *the dead are there.* Identifying the house of Folly with the abode of the dead. The Hebr. word for 'the dead' is *Rĕphā'īm* or 'Shades'.

*the depths of Sheol.* See Excursus V.

The Sept. has another addition which does not, however, represent anything that stood originally in the Hebr. text.

# THE SECOND COLLECTION OF PROVERBS

## X. 1—XXII. 16. *The Proverbs of Solomon*

THIS collection forms the central part of the book, and, in all probability, stood originally alone. It is, as we have seen, the oldest portion of the book (*Intr.* § III). Each saying consists of two lines, and, as a rule, though there are some exceptions, they are antithetical; here and there synonymous parallels occur. Like the former collection this, too, was put forth primarily for the benefit of young men. The religious atmosphere of this collection is less marked than in i. 1–ix. 18; for the most part the aphorisms are of a secular character; they are mainly what may be termed utilitarian, i. e. right action is recommended because it pays, wrongdoing is deprecated because of its disagreeable consequences. At the same time, as one would expect, a very high moral standard is presented. The many side-lights thrown upon the social life of the times make this collection full of human interest. The various proverbs are massed together in a somewhat haphazard fashion without any attempt at subject-grouping; and there are many repetitions. It is, therefore, impossible to divide the collection into sections; we must be content to follow the chapter divisions, which are, however, quite arbitrary. On the title which stands at the head of the collection, 'The Proverbs of Solomon', see *Intr.* § IV; it is omitted in the Sept. and Syr.

**X.** 1 The proverbs of Solomon.

A wise son maketh a glad father:
But a foolish son is the heaviness of his mother.
2 Treasures of wickedness profit nothing:
But righteousness delivereth from death.

## CHAPTER X

**1.** *A wise son* . . . Cf. xxix. 3[a].
*heaviness.* The Hebr. word (*tūgah*), which means 'grief', occurs elsewhere only in xiv. 13, xvii. 21, and in Ps. cxix. 28; it is the poetical form of the allied word *zāgôn*, 'sorrow', used in prose books, cf. xv. 20.
**2.** *Treasures of wickedness.* i. e. wealth gained by wrong means, such as by lying, see xxi. 6, and cf. Ecclus. v. 8. The almost identical couplet occurs in xi. 4.
*righteousness delivereth* . . . In spite of the contrary experience this tenet was adhered to; Ben-Sira modifies it by saying that 'they profit nothing in the day of wrath'. Righteousness (*zĕdāqāh*) has the meaning of right living here; in the somewhat parallel thought in

3 The LORD will not suffer the soul of the righteous to famish:
  But he thrusteth away the desire of the wicked.
4 He becometh poor that dealeth with a slack hand:
  But the hand of the diligent maketh rich.

Ecclus. xxix. 12 Ben-Sira uses the word in the sense of 'alms' or
'almsgiving', as being righteousness *par excellence*:

> 'Store up alms in thy treasure-chambers,
>   And it shall deliver thee from all affliction';

> cf. iii. 30, xl. 24; Tobit iv. 10, xii. 9.

The words 'righteousness delivereth from death' are repeated in xi.
4[b], cf. xii. 28; they are sometimes to be seen inscribed, in Hebrew, on
the Alms-box in synagogues at the present day.

**3.** *The Lord will not suffer* . . . These words are apt to be misunderstood unless it be remembered that 'soul' in Hebrew is equivalent to personality; the passage does not refer to what might be
described as 'spiritual starvation', but to material want of food.
Daily sustenance was believed to be provided directly from the hand
of God, who would not let a righteous man starve, cf. Ps. xxxiv. 10
(11 in Hebr.), xxxvii. 25; Ecclus. ii. 10. Cf. the Lord's Prayer.

*thrusteth away.* i. e. 'rejecteth'.

*the desire.* When used in this sense the Hebr. word (*havvah*) always
connotes an *evil* desire (see Mic. vii. 3, Ps. lii. 9, if the reading is
correct), which will bring ruin in its train; it is, therefore, also used
to express ruin or destruction, as in xvii. 4, xix. 13, and elsewhere.

*the wicked.* A number of MSS. read 'those who deal treacherously',
but this was probably an explanatory gloss to denote which types of
the more general term 'wicked' were meant; and then the gloss took
the place of the original word.

**4.** *He becometh poor* . . . These words can be read in two ways:
(1) Following the Sept. we can read, 'Poverty maketh (or bringeth
about) slackness of hands'; or else the meaning may be, 'slackness
of hands maketh poor'. In the former case it would mean that
poverty brings a man down (cf. the Sept. ταπεινοῖ) to the state of
having nothing to employ his hands; the latter, that laziness entails
poverty. It is the second which is, no doubt, the meaning here as it
offers a better antithesis to the second line.

*a slack hand.* Lit. 'a palm of slackness'. The idea is that of
hanging loose when applied to the hand; in xix. 15 it is used of the
soul, i. e. a man; the slack or idle man, cf. also xii. 24.

*the hand of the diligent.* 'Hand' here is a different word from that
used in the first line. The original idea of the Hebr. word rendered
'diligent' is that of cutting with an instrument, or of the sharpness
of an instrument, cf. Am. i. 3; Isa. xli. 15; then, since to cut involves
dividing a thing into two, there arose the idea of deciding, so that the
word came to mean a decision between two things, cf. Joel iii. 14

5 He that gathereth in summer is [1]a wise son:
　　*But* he that sleepeth in harvest is a son [2]that causeth shame.
6 Blessings are upon the head of the righteous:
　　But [3]violence covereth the mouth of the wicked.
7 The memory of the just is blessed:
　　But the name of the wicked shall rot.

[1] Or, *a son that doeth wisely*　　　　　[2] Or, *that doeth shamefully*
[3] Or, *the mouth of the wicked covereth violence*

(iv. 14 in Hebr.); and, finally, one who is able to decide must be sharp in the figurative sense; and this, rather than 'diligent', is the sense here and in xii. 24, 27, xiii. 4, xxi. 5, i.e. one who has his wits about him.

*maketh rich.* Or 'acquireth wealth', the reference being to the man himself, not to making others rich.

**5.** *gathereth.* A rare word in O.T. Hebr., occurring elsewhere only in vi. 8, and Deut. xxviii. 39; but common in later Hebrew.

*a wise son.* R.V. marg. more correctly 'a son that doeth wisely'.

*he that sleepeth.* The Hebr. word means 'to sleep deeply', the word in Gen. ii. 21, 'a deep sleep', comes from the same root; in Ps. lxxvi. 6 (7 in Hebr.) it is used of the sleep of death.

*that causeth shame.* The Hebr. can be rendered thus or as the R.V. 'that doeth shamefully'; this latter, however, makes a better antithetic parallel with 'doeth wisely' in the first line. The Sept. is quite different, and either had another text altogether or else is independent of the Hebrew.

**6.** *Blessings.* The Sept. and Vulg. add 'of the Lord', which may have fallen out of the Hebr. text, see *v.* 3.

*upon the head.* Cf. Gen. xlix. 26.

*But violence* . . . So the Hebr., the identical line occurs again in *v.* 11[b]; in this latter it forms a good antithetic parallel to the preceding line; but in the *v.* before us this is not so, and it is quite possible that 11[b] has got in here by some scribal error. Most commentators, however, regard the text as corrupt, and follow the Sept. in reading 'sorrow' for 'violence', and emend the Hebr. word for 'mouth' so as to read 'face'. The line would then run: 'But sorrow covereth the face of the wicked'; this makes a good antithesis to the first line, and is in accordance with the belief then held that the righteous prosper while the wicked are in adversity, see note on *v.* 2.

**7.** *The memory of* . . . Cf. Ecclus. xli. 11[b] (Hebr.): 'The name of the pious shall not be cut off.'

*shall rot.* The use of this word in reference to a name seems incongruous, especially as, when it occurs elsewhere in *Proverbs* (but only as a noun, xii. 4, xiv. 30), it is used of rottenness of bones; hence some commentators, by a slight change in the Hebr. text, read 'will be cursed'. But the word is used figuratively in Hos. v. 12, ' . . . to

8 The wise in heart will receive commandments:
But ¹a prating fool ²shall fall.

9 He that walketh uprightly walketh surely:
But he that perverteth his ways shall be known.

10 He that winketh with the eye causeth sorrow:
³But ¹a prating fool ²shall fall.

11 The mouth of the righteous is a fountain of life:
But ⁴violence covereth the mouth of the wicked.

¹ Heb. *the foolish of lips.*    ² Or, *shall be overthrown* or *laid low*    ³ The Sept. and Syr. read, *But he that rebuketh openly maketh peace.*    ⁴ Or, *the mouth of the wicked covereth violence*

the house of Judah as rottenness', and in Ecclus. xiv. 19 (Hebr.) the same word occurs in reference to the work of man, i.e. in a figurative sense. It is, therefore, likely enough that the text is correct as it stands. The Sept. paraphrases: 'shall be quenched.'

**8.** *The wise in heart.* . . . i.e. the sensible man accepts, and therefore acts in accordance with, commandments. It is obviously not a question here of the commandments of the Law; acceptance of these would be taken as a matter of course; what is referred to are the commandments of Wisdom, as in xiii. 13, xix. 16, not as in vi. 23, where the reference is to the commandment of the Law, see note there.

*will receive.* Better 'receiveth', it is a statement of fact.

*But a prating fool* . . . This line occurs again in *v.* 10ᵇ. That it is out of place here is evident as it forms no proper antithesis to the first line. The Hebr. has lit. 'the foolish of lips', i.e. he who talks folly.

*shall fall.* Better 'is brought to ruin', cf. Hos. iv. 14, where the R.V. has 'shall be overthrown'; the Hebr. word occurs only in these two passages, and in *v.* 10; but in later Hebrew it is more common, and means 'to be troubled'.

**9.** *He that walketh uprightly.* Cf. ii. 7ᵇ.

*surely.* i.e. in security, as e.g. in iii. 23, 'Then shalt thou walk in thy way securely'.

*he that perverteth.* Cf. ii. 15.

*shall be known.* This does not give sense; the Hebr. (וְיִדָּעֵ) should be read (יֵרוֹעַ) as in xi. 15, xiii. 20, 'shall be broken' (cf. Mic. iv. 9) or 'suffer hurt', or possibly 'shall be shaken', the later Hebr. sense.

**10.** *He that winketh.* Cf. vi. 13; Ecclus. xxvii. 22.

*But a prating fool* . . . This line, as in *v.* 8, is again out of place, as it forms no antithesis to the first line, which is the rule in this collection. The Sept. and Syr. have evidently preserved the right reading, and the R.V. marg. should be followed.

**11.** *The mouth . . . fountain of life.* Cf. xiii. 14, xviii. 4; Ps. xxxvi.

12 Hatred stirreth up strifes:
  But love covereth all transgressions.
13 In the lips of him that hath discernment wisdom is found:
  But a rod is for the back of him that is void of ¹under-
    standing.
14 Wise men lay up knowledge:
  But the mouth of the foolish is a present destruction.

¹ Heb. *heart*.

9 (10 in Hebr.); Ecclus. xxi. 13. The Hebr. word for 'fountain'
(*māqōr*) comes from the root meaning to 'dig' or 'bore', so that
'well' would be a better word. This figurative expression for intellectual or spiritual refreshment has always been a favourite one
among the Jews; e.g. in *Pirqê 'Abôth* vi. 1, he who is intent upon the
study of the Law is described as 'a spring that ceaseth not, and as a
river that continueth to flow on'; so, too, in ii. 10 of the same
tractate, Rabbi Eleazar ben Arak is called 'a welling spring' because
of his devotion to the study of the Law. By the 'righteous' here is
meant the man whose life is guided by Wisdom; he is a source of
inspiration and encouragement to his fellows on life's way just as the
wayside well is a source of refreshment and renewed vigour to the
weary traveller.
  *But violence* . . . See note on *v.* 6ᵇ. Violence must be understood
in a figurative sense of injurious language as in xiii. 2. The thought
of 'covering' emphasizes the antithesis as the covering over of a well
must have been in the mind of the writer; to this it may be objected
that he does not contemplate the possibility of the wicked man being
a 'fountain' or well; but inasmuch as the teaching of Wisdom was to
turn the wicked from their way, it must be allowed that they, too,
were regarded as possessing sources of greatness which Wisdom had
the power of drawing forth.
  **12.** *But love covereth* . . . i.e. makes one overlook the shortcomings
of others, cf. xvii. 9; 1 Cor. xiii. 7; 1 Pet. iv. 8; James v. 20.
  **13.** The first line of this verse does not occur in the Sept.; the
second in the Hebr. offers no proper parallel or antithesis. Probably
both lines are out of place here; they certainly do not belong together. It is an example of the somewhat haphazard way in which
some parts of the book have been put together.
  **14.** *lay up.* Better 'conceal', which is equally the meaning of the
Hebr., and gives the proper antithesis, cf. xi. 13; Ecclus. ix. 18, xx.
5–8. The meaning of the verse is that the wise man is reticent
regarding what he knows, whereas the fool, by blurting out the first
thing that comes into his mind, makes mischief as soon as he opens
his lips.

15 The rich man's wealth is his strong city:
   The destruction of the poor is their poverty.
16 The labour of the righteous *tendeth* to life;
   The increase of the wicked to sin.
17 He ¹is in the way of life that heedeth ²correction;
   But he that forsaketh reproof ³erreth.

¹ Or, *is a way*          ² Or, *instruction*          ³ Or, *causeth to err*

**15.** The first line is repeated in xviii. 11ᵃ. Cf. Ecclus. xl. 25, 26. A true saying in all ages, but Ben-Sira shows more discernment in adding that the fear of the Lord is above wealth in value. Cf. also xviii. 23, xix. 4; Ecclus. xiii. 21–23.

**16.** *labour.* The meaning of the Hebr. word (*pĕʿullah*) here is rather the result of labour, i.e. recompense, as in Isa. xlix. 4; or wages, as in Lev. xix. 13. An antithesis is doubtless intended between what the righteous gains as the outcome of work, and the 'increase' (i.e. income) of the wicked, regarding the mode of acquisition of which there is judicious silence; at any rate, it is not by work.

*life.* i.e. prosperity.

*to sin.* The Hebr. (*lĕchatt'āth*) cannot be right; it is the *means* of acquiring wealth which is sinful, otherwise they would not be spoken of as the 'wicked'; so that 'sin' here is by implication tautologous. Moreover, 'sin' does not form the proper antithesis to 'life' in the first line. One expects here some word like 'ruin' (לְמִחְתָּה) (Steuernagel) or 'calamity' (*'eid*, which occurs in i. 26, 27, vi. 15, xvii. 5, xxiv. 22, xxvii. 10); but not 'death', as some commentators suggest, because this is not an antithesis to 'life' in the sense in which it is here used. The contrast is between the well-earned prosperity of the righteous and the dishonestly gained wealth of the wicked which brings calamity.

**17.** *He is in the way* ... Read lit. the Hebr. is: 'A way to life (is) he who heeds instruction'; this can either mean: He who gives heed to instruction enjoys prosperity (cf. first line of the preceding verse); or, He who gives heed to instruction is a means to prosperity for others, i.e. by his example of giving heed to instruction he directs others in the way to prosperity. Both interpretations are permissible so far as the language is concerned; but the former is preferable here on account of the context, for this *v.* seems to be a kind of comment on the preceding one.

*correction.* Hebr. *mūsār*, see note on i. 23.

*erreth.* Or, as R.V. marg., 'causeth to err'. The Hebr. word can mean either, according to the interpretation of the *v.* adopted, see above. With the whole *v.* cf. xii. 1, xv. 10, xix. 16.

18  He that hideth hatred is of lying lips;
     And he that uttereth a slander is a fool.
19  In the multitude of words there wanteth not transgression:
     But he that refraineth his lips [1]doeth wisely.
20  The tongue of the righteous is *as* choice silver:
     The heart of the wicked is little worth.

[1] Or, *is wise*

**18.** *He that hideth hatred* . . . Paraphrased, the translation of the
verse means: If a man conceals hatred he is a liar because his outward profession gives the lie to his inward feelings, but if he spreads
slander he is a fool. The only antithesis here is between concealment
(of hatred) and outspokenness (of a slander); and yet each is a
thoroughly bad thing. Clearly this is not the style and manner of
this collection of Proverbs. Either these two lines are isolated proverbs which have been put together by mistake, or else there is
something wrong with the Hebr. text; but this reads quite naturally
if one takes each line by itself; it is only the combination of them as
parts of one verse which necessitates the emendations suggested by
commentators in order to give sense. Apparently the Sept. had the
present Hebr. text before it, and seeing the incongruity of the verse,
taken as a unit, sought to make sense by rendering the first line
quite unjustifiably: 'Righteous lips conceal enmity'; that is non-
sense, for hypocrisy is not the *rôle* of righteous lips. The most
natural solution of the difficulty is to recognize, as pointed out before,
that our book shows signs of carelessness and want of judgement
here and there in the manipulation of material, and that we have an
instance of this in the verse before us. With the warning against
slander cf. the following sayings from the Babylonian *Book of
Proverbs*:

'Slander shalt thou not speak, nor counsel which is not sure;
He that maketh gossip, despised is his head.'

'Nor shalt thou deal in slander, but speak what is pure.
Evil shalt thou not utter, but say what is good.
Of him that dealeth with slander, speaking evil,
Shamash shall wait for his head with recompense.'
(Langdon, §§ D, M, pp. 88, 91.)

**19.** *multitude of words.* Cf. xiii. 3, xvii. 27; Ecclus. xx. 8. In *Pirqê
'Abôth* i. 17 it is said: 'Whoso multiplieth words occasioneth sin.'
Similarly in the Babylonian *Book of Proverbs* we read:

'Make not wide with thy mouth, but guard thy lips;
The thoughts of thy mind thou shalt not speak at once,
For then quickly what thou hast spoken thou wilt take back again.'
(Langdon, § N, p. 91.)

See further notes on xv. 1, xvi. 24.
**20.** *choice silver.* Cf. viii. 19[b].

21 The lips of the righteous feed many:
   But the foolish die for lack of [1]understanding.
22 The blessing of the LORD, it maketh rich,
   And [2]he addeth no sorrow therewith.
23 It is as sport to a fool to do wickedness:
   [3]And *so is* wisdom to a man of understanding.
24 The fear of the wicked, it shall come upon him:
   And the desire of the righteous shall be granted.
25 [4]When the whirlwind passeth, the wicked is no more:
   But the righteous is an everlasting foundation.

[1] Heb. *heart.*   [2] Or, *toil addeth nothing thereto*   [3] Or, *But a man of understanding hath wisdom*   [4] Or, *As the whirlwind passeth, so is the wicked no more*

**21.** *The lips of* . . . Cf. Ecclus. vi. 5[a] (Hebr.): 'Kindly speech (lit. "a sweet throat") maketh many friends.'

**22.** *The blessing* . . . Cf. Ecclus. xi. 22 (Hebr.): 'The blessing of the Lord is the portion of the righteous.'

*And he addeth* . . . The R.V. marg. can be ignored.

**23.** *as sport.* The Hebr. word comes from the root meaning 'to laugh', and contains the idea of enjoyment, cf. viii. 30.

*And so is wisdom* . . . This is presumably intended to mean that wisdom is sport to a man of understanding; but that does not represent the Hebrew, 'But wisdom to a man of understanding', which, as it stands, means that it is wisdom to a man of understanding to do wickedness; clearly, therefore, there is something wrong with the text; the Versions give no help. Toy suggests the emendation *to'ēbah,* 'abomination', in place of 'wisdom', cf. xvi. 12; this is well worth consideration. Frankenberg would read *kĕchēmah,* 'wrath', on account of the consonants being practically identical with those of 'wisdom' in Hebrew; but the use of the word for 'wrath' in this connexion is improbable.

**24.** *The fear of the wicked.* This is usually interpreted as the fear that is apprehended by the wicked; but it is characteristic of the wicked that they are not troubled with thoughts about the result of their wickedness, otherwise they would forsake it (cf. *v.* 28[b]); so that it seems better to understand the 'fear of the wicked' man in the sense of the fear inspired by him; what others fear from the wicked man will come, not on them, but on the wicked man himself.

*shall be granted.* This is, doubtless, what the Hebr. ought to read (it has 'he shall grant') following the Versions.

**25.** *When the whirlwind* . . . The R.V. marg. can be ignored. With the verse cf. Matth. vii. 24–27.

26 As vinegar to the teeth, and as smoke to the eyes,
   So is the sluggard to them that send him.
27 The fear of the LORD [1]prolongeth days:
   But the years of the wicked shall be shortened.
28 The hope of the righteous *shall be* gladness:
   But the expectation of the wicked shall perish.
29 The way of the LORD is a strong hold to the upright;
   But [2]it is a destruction to the workers of iniquity.
30 The righteous shall never be removed:
   But the wicked shall not dwell in the [3]land.
31 The mouth of the righteous [4]bringeth forth wisdom:
   But the froward tongue shall be cut off.

---

[1] Heb. *addeth*.     [2] Or, *destruction shall be to &c.*     [3] Or, *earth*
[4] Or, *buddeth with*

**26.** The irritation caused by the dilatoriness of a lazy messenger is compared with the teeth being set on edge, and the smarting of the eyes. A forcible comparison. See note on xiii. 17.

**27.** *The fear* ... See note on i. 7, and cf. iii. 2, ix. 11; Ecclus. i. 12.

**28.** *hope.* The root idea of the Hebr. word is 'something for which one is waiting'. The Hebr. of the line is lit. 'the hope ... (is) gladness', i.e. results in gladness. With the second line cf. Ps. cxii. 10c.

**29.** *The way of* ... The Hebr. has: 'A strong-hold to uprightness (is) the way of Jahweh'; but in order to get a proper parallelism to 'the workers of iniquity' in the second line we must follow the Sept., and read 'the upright (man)' for 'uprightness'. Even so the line as translated is not quite satisfactory; it can equally be rendered (with this emendation): 'A stronghold to the upright in way is Jahweh', i.e. Jahweh is a stay or protection to him who walks uprightly, cf. Ps. xxxvii. 39; Joel iii. 16 (Hebr. iv. 16); this is more in harmony with O.T. thought according to which it is Jahweh himself who is the stay of those who are upright in the way.

*But it is* ... The subject is Jahweh, it is He who destroys the workers of iniquity (cf. Isa. vii. 8, xxx. 31). This line, but in a different connexion, occurs again in xxi. 15.

**30.** *The righteous* ... Cf. Ps. xxxvii. 22, 29.

*the land.* Palestine is meant; the R.V. marg. can be ignored. Cf. ii. 21.

**31.** *bringeth forth.* The Hebr. word means to 'bear fruit', see Ps. xcii. 14 (15 in Hebr.): 'they shall still bring forth fruit in old age', cf. lxii. 11. The utterances of the righteous bear the fruit of wisdom, cf. Ps. xxxvii. 30.

*the froward tongue.* Lit. 'the tongue of perverse things', cf. ii. 12, viii. 13, xvi. 28, xxiii. 33.

G

32 The lips of the righteous know what is acceptable:
　　But the mouth of the wicked ¹*speaketh* frowardness.

**XI.** 1 ²A false balance is an abomination to the LORD:
　　But a just weight is his delight.

2 When pride cometh, then cometh shame:
　　But with the lowly is wisdom.

3 The integrity of the upright shall guide them:
　　But the perverseness of the treacherous shall destroy them.

4 Riches profit not in the day of wrath:
　　But righteousness delivereth from death.

　　　　　¹ Or, is　　　　　　　² Heb. *A balance of deceit.*

**32.** *know.* A very slight change of one letter in the Hebr. gives
the word for 'pour forth' (יַבִּיעוּן), which is more appropriate to
'lips'; cf. xv. 2; Ps. xciv. 4; this is supported by the Sept. which has
'drop' (ἀποστάζει, the subject is neuter).

　　speaketh *frowardness.* Read with R.V. marg. 'is' frowardness.


CHAPTER XI

**1.** *A false balance.* Lit. 'balances of deceit'. Cf. xvi. 11, xx. 10, 23,
and Deut. xxv. 15, 16; Am. viii. 5; Mic. vi. 11. On this verse see note
on xvi. 11.

**2.** *shame.* Or 'ignoring'; the fall of the proud man, which comes
sooner or later, brings contempt upon him.

　　*the lowly.* A very rare word occurring elsewhere in the O.T. only
in Mic. vi. 8, where the verb is used of walking humbly before God.
With the verse cf. xiii. 10, xvi. 18, 19, xviii. 12.

**3.** *The integrity of* . . . The thought is that when once a man has
accepted integrity it guides him in the way of life, just as, e.g., a
shepherd guides his lamb along a dangerous path.

　　*perverseness.* The only occurrence of the noun (*seleph*) in O.T.,
though the verb, 'to pervert', or 'overturn', is used several times,
mostly in the Wisdom literature. With the *v.* cf. xiii. 6.

**4.** *profit not.* Or 'avail not'.

　　*the day of wrath.* Not in the prophetic sense of the day of national
overthrow (cf. Zeph. i. 15, 18); but either, as in Job xxi. 30, of a day
of calamity, or else (more probably) of the day of death, being a
parallel to 'death' in the next line. Ben-Sira makes a couplet of
this line:

　　　*Trust not in unrighteous gains,*
　　　*For they profit nothing in the day of wrath* (Ecclus. v. 8, Hebr.).

　　*But righteousness* . . . The same line occurs in x. 2.

5 The righteousness of the perfect shall [1]direct his way:
   But the wicked shall fall by his own wickedness.
6 The righteousness of the upright shall deliver them:
   But they that deal treacherously shall be taken in their own
      mischief.
7 When a wicked man dieth, *his* expectation shall perish:
   And the hope of [2]iniquity perisheth.

---

[1] Or, *make straight* or *plain*          [2] Or, *strong* men

**5.** The verse is similar in thought to *v.* 3.

**6.** Also very similar in thought to *v.* 3.

*in their own mischief.* The emendation of the Hebrew text implied
by the addition of 'their own' (so all the Versions) is undoubtedly
justified, the suffix has fallen out in the Hebr. 'Mischief' is not the
right word to use here; the primary meaning of the Hebr. word is
'desire', see note on x. 3. The meaning of the line is that they who
deal in this way will be ensnared by means of their evil desire; the
treacherous act is always prompted by some bad motive, see the
good illustration in Ps. vii. 15, 16 (Hebr. 16, 17).

**7.** Literally translated this verse runs:

> *When the wicked man dieth hope perisheth,*
> *But (or 'and') the expectation of (or 'in') strength perisheth.*

Clearly the Hebr. text is out of order. The verse was probably
another form of x. 28[b] originally, our book contains a number of
similar repetitions; there is nothing wrong with the first line, excepting that the word for 'man' is unnecessary and overloads the line in
the original; it is therefore better omitted. The passage means that
in the case of a wicked man there is no hope of his leaving a good
name (cf. Ecclus. xl. 11–13), or perhaps posterity (cf. Ps. cix. 13)
behind him when he dies. In the second line the word for 'strength'
('*ōnīm*) is probably a corruption of '*evīlim*, 'wicked'; 'And the
expectation of the wicked perisheth'. The two lines thus express
more or less the same thought; but as such a verse-construction is
not in accordance with that of this collection of proverbs, it is
evident that we have here again two isolated lines which have fallen
out of their proper context and have been carelessly placed together.
The Sept. rendering, which stands quite alone, is interesting; it
runs:

> *When the righteous man dieth hope perisheth not,*
> *But the boast of the ungodly perisheth.*

Here we have an advanced belief in a future life quite out of harmony
with the teaching on the subject in *Proverbs*, showing that the Sept.
form of the verse belongs to much later times.

8  The righteous is delivered out of trouble,
   And the wicked cometh in his stead.
9  With his mouth the godless man destroyeth his neighbour:
   But through knowledge shall the righteous be delivered.
10 When it goeth well with the righteous, the city rejoiceth:
   And when the wicked perish, there is shouting.
11 By the blessing of the upright the city is exalted:
   But it is overthrown by the mouth of the wicked.
12 He that despiseth his neighbour is void of [1]wisdom:
   But a man of understanding holdeth his peace.

[1] Heb. *heart*.

**8.** *And the wicketh cometh* . . . i.e. the wicked enters into the
trouble out of which the righteous has been delivered, see further
on xxi. 18.

**9.** In this verse, again, it looks as though we had two originally
isolated sayings joined loosely together. Even though it be argued
that since it is from the mouth of the godless man that the righteous
man is delivered the two lines are antithetical, it must be conceded
that this is not the type of antithesis characteristic of this collection.
Each line contains an independent statement of fact; in the first,
where the reference is probably to slander, the fact is stated that the
slanderer destroys his neighbour, cf. the words of Ben-Sira:

> Many have fallen by the edge of the sword,
> But not so many as have fallen by the tongue (xxviii. 18, cf. *vv.* 14, 15).

The second line is another general statement of the fact that the
righteous man who has acquired knowledge is delivered, from death
is probably meant, cf. x. 2[b].

**10, 11.** These two verses belong together. Their content is important from the point of view of the date of this collection. What
is said about the city rejoicing at the prosperity of the righteous &c.
could only apply to Israelite cities governed by themselves, i.e. to
pre-exilic times. Toy holds that 'it was in the Greek period that the
city-state became familiar to the Jews, and it seems to be this later
civilization that is here meant'. But there is nothing to show that the
city-state in this sense is here meant; the words of 11[a] would have to
apply to heathen rulers if this were the case, which is incredible in the
mouth of a God-fearing Israelite. It is true that in the Greek period
there were cities in Palestine which were predominantly Jewish; but
though the Jewish elders took part in the government of the city,
they were not independent, and their authority was exercised over
the Jewish element, not the Gentile. Cf. xxix. 2, 16; Ecclus. xvi. 4

**12.** *void of wisdom.* Lit. 'wanting in heart', i.e. lacking in understanding; this is foolish for two reasons, (1) because it is unwise to

13 He that goeth about as a talebearer revealeth secrets:
　　But he that is of a faithful spirit concealeth the matter.
14 Where no wise guidance is, the people falleth:
　　But in the multitude of counsellors there is safety.
15 He that is surety for a stranger [1]shall smart for it:
　　But he that hateth [2]suretiship is sure.
16 A gracious woman retaineth honour:
　　And violent men retain riches.

　　　[1] Heb. *shall be sore broken.*　　　　[2] Heb. *those that strike* hands.

despise any man, and (2) because it makes enemies, and thus recoils
on oneself; cf. xiv. 21[a].
　　**13.** *He that goeth about* ... This line occurs again in xx. 19[a], see
note there. Cf. Ecclus. xix. 7:

　　　　*Never repeat what is said.*
　　　　*Then no one will reproach thee* (see also xxii. 22, xxvii. 16).

The second line of this quotation is from the Syriac. Cf. also *The
Proverbs of Achikar* ii. 2, 3:

　　*If thou hast heard a word, let it die in thy heart, and reveal it to no man* ...
　　*My son, do not tell all that thou hearest,*
　　*And do not disclose all that thou seest.*

In ii. 54 it is said:

　　　　*My son, if thou hear an evil matter,*
　　　　*Put it seven fathoms deep underground.*

A parallel occurs in the *Teaching of Amen-em-ope* XXI. xxii. 13:

　　　*Let not thy words be spread abroad among others.*

A Palestinian proverb runs:

　　　*What is spoken by two is known by two thousand.*

See further Excursus I.
　　**14.** *wise guidance.* See note on i. 5.
　　*in the multitude of* ... Cf. xv. 22; the line occurs again in xxiv. 6[b].
　　**15.** See notes on vi. 1–5, and cf. Ecclus. viii. 13, xxix. 18.
　　**16.** *retaineth.* The Hebr. word means both to 'attain' and 'retain',
the latter seems best here if the text is in order as it stands; but the
couplet is a curious one; a contrast like this between men and women
is very un-Jewish; and there is an inconsistency between the two
lines which shows that they do not belong together; for while in the
first, it is the right and proper thing that the virtuous woman should
retain her honour, in the second it is not right for violent men to
retain wealth, by implication wrongly gained; and yet the point of
contrast is between 'a gracious woman' and 'violent men'. To be
logical the contrast ought to be between a gracious woman who
retains something, and violent men who lose something. It seems,

17 The merciful man doeth good to his own soul:
But he that is cruel troubleth his own flesh.
18 The wicked earneth deceitful wages:
But he that soweth righteousness *hath* a sure reward.
19 [1] He that is stedfast in righteousness *shall attain* unto life:
And he that pursueth evil *doeth it* to his own death.

[1] Or, *So righteousness* tendeth to *life, and he &c.*

therefore, quite clear that the text is out of order, and that either
these two lines have been put in here through carelessness, or else
that something has fallen out of the text. In the latter case it is
quite possible that the Sept. has retained, at any rate, an echo of the
true text; it contains four lines of which the first and last represent
the present Hebrew text:

*A gracious woman raiseth up honour to (her) husband,*
*But a woman who hateth righteousness is a throne of dishonour.*
*They that are slothful become lacking in wealth,*
*But manly men rest secure in their riches.*

With the first couplet cf. Ecclus. xxvi. 26.

*A woman that honoureth her husband appeareth wise to all,*
*But she that dishonoureth him is known to all as one that is godless in her pride.*

Unfortunately the Hebrew of this is not extant. With the second
couplet cf. Ecclus. xiv. 3 (Hebr.):

*To the faint-hearted wealth is unfitting,*
*And why should he of evil eye have gold?*

**17.** The words refer to the result of good or evil action respectively.
*troubleth his* . . . Cf. Ecclus. xiv. 5, 6 (Hebr.).
*cruel.* See note on *v.* 9.

**18.** *deceitful wages.* The meaning is that though the wicked man
earns money and is thus prosperous, they are really deceptive
earnings because, on account of his wickedness, they will not bring
him permanent benefit, see x. 16[b], 25, xi. 4.
*soweth righteousness.* Cf. Hos. x. 12.

**19.** *He that is* . . . The Hebr. text has: 'So righteousness to life',
i. e. leadeth to life; this would connect the line with the preceding
verse, which is entirely against the usage in this collection, each
verse constituting an independent entity. The Versions were evidently puzzled; the Sept. and Syr. read: 'son of righteousness . . .',
the Targ. and the Vulg. both read differently, none of them giving
much help. Some commentators suggest reading *rō'eh*, 'he that
feedeth on (cf. xv. 14) righteousness (attaineth) to life'. Possibly,
seeing how often isolated lines are repeated in our book, the line was
originally the same as xii. 28[a], 'In the way of righteousness is life';

20 They that are perverse in heart are an abomination to the
    LORD:
    But such as are perfect in *their* way are his delight.
21 [1]*Though* hand *join* in hand, the evil man shall not be un-
    punished:
    But the seed of the righteous shall be delivered.
22 *As* a [2]jewel of gold in a swine's snout,
    *So is* a fair woman which [3]is without discretion.

[1] Or, *My hand upon it!* Heb. *Hand to hand.*          [2] Or, *ring*
[3] Heb. *turneth aside from.*

(it is) death (i. e. to him)', omitting the 'to his' before 'death', and
the second line would then read: 'But he that followeth after evil
'to' before 'life' in the first line. With the exception of the first word
of the verse this involves but slight changes in the text.

**20.** Cf. xii. 22, xv. 9.

**21.** Though *hand* join *in hand.* This is an impossible rendering of
the Hebr., which has 'hand to hand', an expression meaning 'of a
truth' or the like (cf. R.V. marg.); it occurs again in xvi. 5[b].

*the seed of the righteous.* The reference is not to the posterity of the
righteous, but to righteous people as a whole, in contrast to the 'evil
man' in the preceding line.

**22.** *As a jewel of gold . . .* In the Hebr. there is no comparison, but
merely two statements of fact illustrating incongruity; each line is
complete in itself, and could be quoted without reference to the other:
'A golden ring in a swine's snout !' 'A fair woman, and she turns
from modesty !' though they undoubtedly belong together. In each
there is something very incongruous, but there can be no question of
comparison. The Hebr. word *nezem* always means a 'ring', either for
the nose, as here, or for the ear, as in xxv. 12, or for the finger, as in
Isa. iii. 21, where the nose-ring is also mentioned. Nose-rings and
ear-rings were worn for ornamentation as well as for the purpose of
warding off evil spirits.

*which is without discretion.* A paraphrase which does not fully express the original, for the verb used, 'to turn from', implies something rather stronger. 'Discretion' is the regular meaning of *ta'am*,
but in connexion with a woman the word may fairly be rendered
'modesty', i.e. that which is fitting, cf. Ecclus. x. 28 (Hebr.). This
verse is illustrated in the *Yalqūt* to *Proverbs* § 14: 'If thou puttest a
vessel of gold into the nose of a swine, he will dirty it with mire and
refuse, so is the student of the Torah if he abandon himself to im-
morality; he makes the Torah dirty' (Schechter, *Some Aspects of
Rabbinic Theology,* p. 234 [1909]).

23 The desire of the righteous is only good:
    *But* the expectation of the wicked is [1]wrath.
24 There is that scattereth, and increaseth yet more;
    And there is that withholdeth [2]more than is meet, but *it*
        *tendeth* only to want.
25 The liberal soul shall be made fat:
    And he that watereth shall be watered also himself.
26 He that withholdeth corn, the people shall curse him:
    But blessing shall be upon the head of him that selleth it.

[1] Or, *arrogance*          [2] Or, *what is justly due*

**23.** *is only good.* i. e. for that which is good.
*is wrath.* The Hebr. word means also 'arrogance', but that can
hardly be the meaning here. Following the Sept. a very slight change
in the Hebr. gives the reading, 'passeth away', or 'perisheth'. This
certainly makes the meaning of the line clearer, which would thus
express the contrast with the 'good', which is permanent, of the
first line.

**24.** *that scattereth.* i. e. 'that disperseth' his money, as in Ps. cxii. 9.
*increaseth.* Hebr. 'is increased', in reference to his wealth.
*more than is meet.* The meaning of the Hebr. word is simply 'what
is meet', cf. Job xxxiii. 23. The meaning of the verse is that some
men spend freely, and in spite of spending they increase in wealth,
while others are very careful with their money, and yet become
poorer. The writer seems simply to be pointing to the facts of life as
he has observed them; there is no reference to almsgiving making a
man richer, and withholding alms making him poorer. Apparently
the moral to be drawn is that if a man has plenty of money let him
spend it and get enjoyment out of it; hoarding does nobody any good.
The sages were deeply religious men; but they were also very human,
with plenty of common sense, and they were well acquainted with
the world. When it is a question of religion and morals they are not
wanting; but in this particular verse the facts of everyday life are
dealt with.

**25.** This is one of the few verses in this collection which is not
antithetical, the second line repeats the sense of the first.
*The liberal soul.* Lit. 'the soul of blessing'; the Hebr. word for
blessing has also the sense of 'gift', cf. Gen. xxxiii. 11; 2 Kgs. v. 15,
and elsewhere.
*shall be made fat.* i. e. shall prosper, cf. xiii. 4, xxviii. 25.
*he that watereth . . .* An agricultural metaphor; the thought is the
same as, e. g., in Luke vi. 38, 'Give, and it shall be given unto you',
where, as the use of μέτρον in the context shows, the thought is
suggested by the picture of an overflowing corn-measure.
**26.** *He that withholdeth . . .* It must be remembered that in

27  He that diligently seeketh good seeketh favour:
　　　But he that searcheth after mischief, it shall come unto him.
28  He that trusteth in his riches shall fall;
　　　But the righteous shall flourish as the green leaf.
29  He that troubleth his own house shall inherit the wind:
　　　And the foolish shall be servant to the wise of heart.

southern Palestine corn was not grown in any great quantities; as it
had to a large extent to be imported, its scarcity was not necessarily
confined to times of famine (cf. Hos. viii. 7, ix. 1, and in vii. 14,
where the right reading [see the Sept.] is 'they cut themselves for
corn', instead of 'they assemble themselves for corn'). As G. A.
Smith has pointed out: 'from first to last, it is they (the olive, vine,
and fig) which have not only sustained her inhabitants, but by their
surplus supplied them with the means of exchange for goods in
which their own land was lacking' (*Jerusalem*, i. 298). Another important consideration in this connexion is dealt with by H. W. Hogg,
in the *Encycl. Bibl.*, i. 85: 'After making allowance for homiletic
colouring, we are bound to suppose that agricultural enterprise must
have suffered grievously from a sense of insecurity in regard to the
claims of property, and from the accumulation of debts, with their
attendant horrors. Civil disturbances (such as those abounding in
the later years of Hosea) and foreign wars would, in later times, take
the place of exposure to the inroads of nomadic tribes.' The custom
of the 'King's mowings', i. e. the right of the king to the first cutting
of the grass (and the right probably included that of the corn, see
Nowack, *Die kleinen Propheten*, on Am. i. 7), would have increased
the scarcity. There would, therefore, have been scope for the corn-
usurer in pre-exilic days, and it is not necessary to suppose, with Toy,
that 'the practice here denounced probably became familiar to the
Jews under Greek governments in great commercial and financial
centres'.

**27.** *He that diligently seeketh.* See note on i. 28.

**28.** *He that trusteth in* ... For the thought of wealth being a false
security, see Ecclus. vi. 2 (Hebr.):

　　　　*Trust not in thy wealth,*
　　　　*And say not, 'I have power',*

after which the explanatory gloss is added, *To walk after the desire of
thy soul.* Ben-Sira deprecates trust in riches because it panders to
self-indulgence.

**29.** The two lines of this verse seem to be independent proverbs.
The first says that the man who makes disturbances in his home will
bring confusion upon it, and be the chief sufferer. A similar proverb,
though of wider application, occurs in Hos. viii. 7: 'They sow the
wind, and they shall reap the whirlwind.' The second states the

30 The fruit of the righteous is a tree of life:
And he that is wise winneth souls.

31 Behold, the righteous shall be recompensed in the earth:
How much more the wicked and the sinner!

**XII.** 1 Whoso loveth [1]correction loveth knowledge:
But he that hateth reproof is brutish.

[1] Or, *instructions*

truth which the sage must often have observed in daily life, that many a man, through folly in one of its many forms, sinks in the social scale, and ends by becoming the slave of a better, and therefore a wiser man.

**30.** *The fruit of the righteous.* It is better to make a slight emendation in the Hebr. text, and read, following the Sept., 'righteousness' for 'righteous'; cf. Am. vi. 12.

*tree of life.* Cf. iii. 18, xiii. 12, xv. 4, a metaphorical expression for prosperity and well-being.

*And he that is wise . . .* The Hebr. text reads: 'But a wise man taketh souls'; the word translated 'winneth' cannot have this meaning according to O.T. usage, the root (*lāqach*), when used in connexion with 'life' or 'soul', always means to 'take away' in the sense of 'destroy', see e.g. i. 19; 1 Kgs. xix. 10, 14; Ps. xxxi. 13 (14 in Hebr.); Jon. iv. 3; so that as the text stands we must render: 'But the wise man taketh away (or destroyeth) souls', which must obviously be corrupt. The Sept. reads: 'But the lives of the lawless are taken away untimely'; on the basis of this the Hebr. text can be emended to read: 'But the souls (i.e. lives) of the violent are taken away', i.e. destroyed. This, it is true, is not an altogether satisfactory emendation, and the antithesis is not all that could be desired; but the general sense of the verse is clear enough, viz. that righteousness brings prosperity, and wickedness ends in death. Toy emends the text to read:

'The revenue of righteousness is a tree of life,
But rapine destroys men's lives.'

**31.** *in the earth.* Or 'in the land', cf. ii. 21, 22, i. e. during their lifetime; but it is not a contrast between this and the next world. The Sept. rendering (quoted in 1 Pet. iv. 18) is an adaptation of the Hebr., —to which it would easily have lent itself,—to the more developed doctrine of the future life in later times.

CHAPTER XII

**1.** *correction.* Hebr. *mūsār.* See note on i. 2. Read here, with R.V. marg., '*instruction*', though the underlying thought of discipline, or correction, or chastisement, must not be lost sight of.

2 A good man shall obtain favour of the LORD:
   But a man of wicked devices will he condemn.
3 A man shall not be established by wickedness:
   But the root of the righteous shall never be moved.
4 A virtuous woman is a crown to her husband:
   But she that [1] maketh ashamed is as rottenness in his bones.
5 The thoughts of the righteous are [2] just:
   *But* the counsels of the wicked are deceit.
6 The words of the wicked [3] are of lying in wait for blood:
   But the mouth of the upright shall deliver them.

[1] Or, *doeth shamefully*      [2] Heb. *judgement.*      [3] Or, *are a lying in wait*

Knowledge can only be attained by strenuous mental work, i.e. self-instruction and instruction given by teachers. If there is a real love of knowledge, there will also be a love of that by means of which knowledge is acquired.

*reproof.* Hebr. *tôkachath,* see note on i. 23. Cf. Ecclus. xxi. 6, 'He that hateth reproof (walketh) in the path of a sinner'.

*is brutish.* The word in Hebr. is, strictly speaking, a noun, 'is brutishness', though it is used as an adjective, as here and in xxx. 2. In Ps. xcii. 6 (7 in Hebr.), there is the phrase 'a brutish man', meaning one who is ignorant, where the word is paralleled by 'fool'; see also Ps. xlix. 10 (11 in Hebr.), and lxxiii. 22, where a 'brutish' man is likened to a 'beast' because of his stupidity.

A thought somewhat similar to this occurs in the *Proverbs of Achikar* ii. 40, quoted under ix. 9.

**2.** *shall obtain favour.* See note on iii. 13.

*wicked devices.* See note on i. 4.

*will he condemn.* Lit. 'will he cause to be wicked', i.e. will he pronounce or condemn as guilty, cf. xvii. 15; the term is a forensic one, see Exod. xxii. 9 (8 in Hebr.).

**3.** *the righteous shall* . . . Cf. x. 25.

**4.** *virtuous.* Lit. 'power', only here used in reference to women, and in xxxi. 10, 29, and Ruth iii. 11. Strength of character is what the expression connotes. Cf. Ecclus. xxvi. 1 (Hebr.), 26.

*a crown to her husband.* See Song of Songs, iii. 11[b].

*maketh ashamed.* Lit. 'causeth to be ashamed', in reference to her husband.

*rottenness.* Cf. xiv. 30; Job iii. 16.

**5.** *counsels.* Used in a good sense in i. 5, 'sound counsels', see note there, cf. xi. 14, xx. 18, xxiv. 6.

**6.** *lying in wait* . . . Cf. i. 11.

*them.* If retained in the text the reference is to the victims, implied but not expressed in the first line; but it is better omitted. It is expressed by one letter 'm' in Hebrew, which may easily have

7  ¹ The wicked are overthrown, and are not:
   But the house of the righteous shall stand.
8  A man shall be commended according to his wisdom:
   But he that is of a perverse heart shall be despised.
9  Better is he that is lightly esteemed, and hath a servant,
   Than he that honoureth himself, and lacketh bread.
10 A righteous man regardeth the life of his beast:
   But the tender mercies of the wicked are cruel.

   ¹ Or, *Overthrow the wicked, and they are not*

crept in as the preceding word ends with the same letter. The harm,
as well as the good wrought by words is a frequent theme in the
Wisdom Literature; cf. e.g. Ecclus. xxviii. 18:

> *Many have fallen by the edge of the sword,*
> *But not so many as have fallen by the tongue.*

**7.** *are overthrown.* The Hebr. word is in the infinitive absolute,
which is here best expressed by the passive. With the verse cf. x. 25,
xiv. 11.

**8.** *wisdom.* Hebr. *sekel*, see note on i. 3.
*perverse heart.* Lit. 'twisted' heart, i.e. mind; see Excursus IX.

**9.** *he that is lightly esteemed.* Toy interprets the Hebrew word as
referring to one who is socially in a humble grade, cf. 1 Sam. xviii. 23;
Isa. iii. 5; the fact of such a one having a slave is no difficulty; for,
according to Exod. xxi. 32, the value of either a manservant or a
maidservant was thirty shekels of silver (about £3 15s. in our money),
and the keep of a slave in those days would have cost very little.
But this interpretation demands that the second line should speak
of one who is of high grade, which is not the case. It seems upon the
whole best to make a slight emendation in the Hebrew text (following
the Sept.), and read 'and laboureth for himself' instead of 'and hath
a servant'. The contrast would then be between the humble-minded
man who works, and therefore gains sustenance for himself, and the
man who thinks highly of himself, but has not enough to eat. The
Hebr. of Ecclus. x. 27 has a couplet almost identical with this in
thought, though the wording of the first line is a little different:

> *Better is he that worketh and (therefore) hath wealth in abundance*
> *Than he who honoureth himself, and lacketh sustenance (māzôn).*

The last word is a synonym for 'bread' in Gen. xlv. 23. The context
of this passage suggests that Ben-Sira thinks of one 'that worketh'
as being humble-minded, for he goes on to say: *My son, esteem
thyself in humility,* i.e. do not be ashamed of being humble.

**10.** *regardeth the life.* Lit. 'knoweth', for the meaning of taking
into consideration, see Job ix. 21: 'I regard not myself', lit. my life,
i.e. I do not take myself into consideration.

*life.* Lit. 'soul' (*nephesh*), the principle of life, which every living

11 He that tilleth his land shall have plenty of bread:
 But he that followeth after [1] vain *persons* is void of understanding.
12 The wicked desireth [2] the net of evil men:
 But the root of the righteous yieldeth *fruit*.
13 In the transgression of the lips is [3] a snare to the evil man:
 But the righteous shall come out of trouble.

  [1] Or, *vain* things    [2] Or, *the prey*    [3] Or, *an evil snare*

creature possesses. With this line cf. xxvii. 23, and Ecclus. vii. 22
(Hebr.): *Art thou possessed of a beast of burden, look after (it) thyself.*
For the law on kindness to animals see Deut. xxv. 4.

**11.** With the exception of the words 'void of understanding' this
verse occurs again in xxviii. 19, see the notes there. With regard to
the presence of the couplet here, Toy says that it is probably an
editorial addition, or 'an extract from some current collection of
proverbs'. The probability of the truth of these last words will be
recognized in reading what is said on xxviii. 19ᵃ, where it will be
seen that there is every reason to believe that a couplet was borrowed
from the Egyptian Wisdom-book, the *Teaching of Amen-em-ope*, and
adapted to his Hebrew readers by the compiler of *Proverbs*.

**12.** The R.V. rendering of this verse is an attempt to make sense
of the Hebrew; but as the text stands this is not possible:

  *The wicked man hath desired the net of the wicked,*
  *But the root of the righteous giveth.*

The first line is meaningless, and the second is an incomplete sentence. Many emendations of the text are offered by commentators;
but their variety only shows how impossible it is to reach any
generally acceptable solution of the difficulty. The Sept. renders:
'The desires of the wicked are evil, but the roots of the righteous are
firm', lit. 'in strongholds'. This, at any rate, gives sense; but the
expected antithesis is lacking. It may be, as Toy suggests, that the
lines belong to different couplets. There are other instances of this
in our book. The second line may be made to give sense by reading
בְּאֵיתָן 'is in firmness' for יִתֵּן 'yieldeth'.

**13.** *In the* . . . Better, 'through' or 'by means of'.

*is a snare.* A slight change in the Hebr. enables us to read 'is
ensnared', see vi. 2 (cf. the Sept. 'falleth into snares'). The line
would then read: 'Through the transgression of (his) lips the wicked
is ensnared.' Cf. Ecclus. v. 13 (Hebr.):

  *Glory and dishonour come through speaking*
  *And the tongue of a man (bringeth) his fall.*

and xx. 18:

  *A slip on the pavement is better than (a slip of) the tongue,*
  *Thus the fall of the wicked cometh swiftly* (cf. also xxiii. 7, 8).

*trouble.* The reference implied is presumably to an unjust accusa-

14 A man shall be satisfied with good by the fruit of his mouth:
  And the doings of a man's hands shall be rendered unto him.
15 The way of the foolish is right in his own eyes:
  But he that is wise hearkeneth unto counsel.
16 A fool's vexation is ¹presently known:
  But a prudent man concealeth shame.
17 He that ²uttereth truth sheweth forth righteousness,
  But a false witness deceit.

¹ Or, *openly* Heb. *in the day.*        ² Heb. *breatheth out.*

tion of which the righteous man is the victim. With the verse cf. xxix. 6, which seems to be the same proverb in a slightly different form.

**14.** *A man shall be satisfied* . . . Hebr. lit. 'By the fruit of the mouth of a man he shall be satisfied (with) good'. Just as in the second line a general statement of fact is made to the effect that a man is requited according to his deeds, without specifying whether they are good or bad, so in this first line the same general statement is made regarding his words; it follows, therefore, that the word 'good' cannot have stood here in the original form of the proverb. It was probably added by a copyist who thought the line was intended to be a contrast with the first line of the preceding verse. Or else, as Volz suggests, we should read 'his belly' (בִּטְנוֹ) for 'good' (טוֹב): 'By the fruit of the mouth of a man his belly is satisfied.' Cf. xviii. 20ᵃ. The verse is not antithetical like xiii. 2.

*And the doings* . . . Hebr. lit. 'And the recompense of the hands of a man will return unto him'. This is better than the marginal reading of the Hebr., 'shall be requited unto him', or 'he (i. e. God) will requite unto him'. For the Hebr. usage of 'hand' in reference to acts see Exod. xiv. 31; Deut. xxxiv. 12; Job xxvii. 11; Ps. lxxviii. 42.

The content of the verse is best expressed by the words in Gal. vi. 7, 'Whatsoever a man soweth, that shall he also reap'.

**15.** *right in his* . . . Cf. iii. 7. As is shown in xxi. 2, the fool does not, in this respect, differ from the usual run of men; the real point of the saying, however, is in the implication that he will not listen to the advice of others, like the wise man in the second line.

**16.** *A fool's vexation* . . . Hebr. lit. 'A fool,—in the day his anger is made known', or 'exhibited'; 'in the day' means 'immediately' or 'on the spot'. The fool has no self-control; if anything annoys him he immediately gives vent to his feelings.

*prudent.* The noun is translated 'subtilty' in i. 4, see note there.
*concealeth shame.* The meaning is that he suppresses the resentment he feels when he has received an insult.

**17.** *uttereth.* Hebr. lit., as R.V. marg., 'breaketh out', cf. vi. 19, xiv. 5, 25, xix. 5, 9; the word is used to express intenseness.

*sheweth forth.* The Hebr. word will hardly bear this sense; it

18 There is that speaketh rashly like the piercings of a sword:
 But the tongue of the wise is health.
19 The lip of truth shall be established for ever:
 But a lying tongue is but for a moment.
20 Deceit is in the heart of them that devise evil:
 But to the counsellors of peace is joy.
21 There shall no mischief happen to the righteous:
 But the wicked shall be filled with evil.
22 Lying lips are an abomination to the LORD:
 But they that deal truly are his delight.

always means to declare something through utterance. The point of
the verse is that the man who speaks concerning what is righteous or
just is uttering what is true. As the second line shows, the reference
is to depositions in a court of justice.

*But a false witness* . . . i.e. he who says what is deceitful, untrue.

**18.** *that speaketh rashly.* Cf. Num. xxx. 7, 9; Ps. cvi. 33, 'spake
unadvisedly with his lips'.

*piercings of a sword.* Cf. Ecclus. xxviii. 18, quoted in the note on
verse 6 above.

*health.* Better 'healing', cf. iv. 22.

**19.** *but for a moment.* Lit. 'as long as I blink (my eye)', cf. Job
xx. 5; Jer. xlix. 19.

The sense of this verse is also contained in the *Proverbs of Achikar*
ii. 31, 32:

'My son, lie not in thy speech before thy lord, lest thou be convicted, and
he shall say to thee, "Away from my sight".

My son, let thy words be true, in order that thy lord may say to thee,
"Draw near me", and thou shalt live.'

**20.** *devise.* See note on iii. 29.

**21.** *happen.* The force of the Hebr. form of the word is 'shall be
allowed to happen'; the same form occurs in Ps. xci. 10, 'there shall
no evil (be permitted to) befall thee'.

*mischief.* The word in this connexion means rather 'trouble' or
'adversity'.

*But the wicked* . . . i.e. constant misfortune will be the lot of the
wicked. With the first line cf. Ecclus. xxxiii (xxxvi). 1 (Hebr.):
'No evil befalleth him that feareth the Lord'; and with the second
cf. Ps. xxxii. 10ᵃ: 'Many sorrows shall be to the wicked'.

**22.** A very similar proverb occurs in xi. 20, and cf. the following
quatrain in the *Teaching of Amen-em-ope* X. xiii. 15–18:

Speak not to a man in falsehood,
The abomination of God ;
Sever not thy heart from thy tongue,
That all thy ways may be successful (or, prosperous).

23 A prudent man concealeth knowledge:
   But the heart of fools proclaimeth foolishness.
24 The hand of the diligent shall bear rule:
   But ¹the slothful shall be put under taskwork.

¹ Heb. *slothfulness.*

The first two lines = the first line of the verse before us, the last
two = the second line. Having heart and tongue in accord is to 'deal
truly', and to the Hebrew thinker it is those who are Jahweh's
delight whose ways are prosperous. So that it looks as though we
had here either a Hebrew adaptation of the Egyptian passage, or
else Amen-em-ope's expansion of the Hebrew proverb. The identity
of thought between the two is so marked that the influence of one
on the other can scarcely be denied. See further Excursus I.

**23.** Here again a striking parallel occurs in Amen-em-ope XXI.
xxii. 15, 16:

> *He that concealeth his speech within himself*
> *Is better than he who uttereth it to his hurt.* Cf. Ecclus. xix. 4.

The sense is essentially the same in each, though the outward form
differs.

**24.** *The hand of the diligent.* See note on x. 4.

*shall bear rule.* This is not to be understood as referring to the
exercise of dominion, as though through diligence a man could attain
to the position of a ruler, whether as king, prince, or elder. While in
the O.T. generally the word (*māshāl*) has this meaning, in the first
two collections of *Proverbs* (i–ix, and x–xxii. 16), where the word
occurs fairly often, it never refers to a ruler in this sense (vi. 7 does
not properly come into consideration here); it is used of ruling the
spirit (xvi. 32), of a servant ruling over his master's son (xvii. 2),
of the incongruity of a servant ruling, i. e. being master over, a prince
(xix. 10); of the rich ruling over the poor (xxii. 7). In the case before
us the reference is simply to being placed in a position of authority
over others, work-people of one kind or another. In xxiii. 1, xxviii.
15, xxix. 2, 12, 26, on the other hand, the word has its ordinary
meaning.

*the slothful.* Lit. 'slothfulness' (R.V. marg.), cf. verse 27 and x. 4,
xix. 15; Jer. xlviii. 10; these are the only places in the O.T. where
the word occurs.

*taskwork.* The word (Hebr. *mas*) is of unknown origin; it means
properly a 'labour-gang'. There is some reason for believing that it
is an Egyptian loan-word (see McNeile's *Exodus* in this series, p. 3,
on Exod. i. 11). The line runs lit.: 'But slothfulness shall be for the
labour-gang'; i.e. he who is slothful shall be made to join a labour-
gang, he is then made to work by the lash of the whip.

25 [1]Heaviness in the heart of a man maketh it stoop;
　　But a good word maketh it glad.
26 The righteous is a guide to his neighbour:
　　But the way of the wicked causeth them to err.
27 [2]The slothful man [3]roasteth not that which he took in
　　　hunting:
　　But the precious substance of men [4]*is to* the diligent.

　　　[1] Or, *Care*　　[2] Heb. *slothfulness.*　　[3] Or, *catcheth not his prey*
　　　　　　　[4] Or, is to be *diligent*

**25.** *Heaviness.* Better 'anxiety', cf. Jer. xlix. 23; Ezek. xii. 18, or
with R.V. marg. 'care'.

*maketh it stoop.* This is the only example in the O.T. of the word
being used in a figurative sense; elsewhere it always means literal
bowing down or the like. For the thought cf. Ecclus. xxxviii. 18
(Hebr.): 'Sadness of heart bringeth down strength'; different words
from the corresponding ones in the verse before us are used for
'sadness', and for 'bringeth down'. With the second line of the
verse cf. xv. 13, xvii. 22, and the delightful section on good spirits
in Ecclus. xxx. 21–25 (Hebr.).

**26.** *The righteous . . .* We have here another instance (see verse 12)
of the Hebr. text being so corrupt as to be meaningless; lit. translated the first line runs: 'The righteous spieth out from his neighbour.'
The R.V. rendering is not justified. Toy's emendation, which does
not involve much change in the text ('The righteous departeth from
evil') is attractive; but so are some other suggestions; the Hebr.
letters so easily lend themselves to slight alterations which result in
an entire change of meaning. In the case of a passage like this,
where every emendation, however plausible, cannot be otherwise
than tentative, we must be content with the general sense, and that
is that the righteous man walks in the right way.

*causeth them to err.* The 'them' is a little doubtful.

**27.** *The slothful man.* Lit. 'slothfulness' as in verse 24.

*roasteth not.* The meaning of the Hebr. word (*charak*) is quite uncertain, it occurs nowhere else in the O.T.; in later Hebr. it means to
'char' and to 'burn' (Jastrow, *Talmud Dict.*, s.v.), hence the traditional Jewish explanation, to 'roast'. The cognate root in Arabic
means to 'set in motion', used of hunting; many commentators
adopt this meaning here (cf. R.V. marg. 'catcheth not his prey.).

*that which he took in hunting.* The Hebr. word for this (*zēydo*)
means 'his game', or 'venison' (cf. Gen. xxvii. 3, &c.). The meaning
of the line may, therefore, possibly be: 'The slothful man hunteth
not his own game', i. e. he is too lazy to use his opportunities.

*But the . . .* The order of the words in the Hebr. text seems to be
wrong, and the Sept. read them in a different order. By a slight

H

28 In the way of righteousness is life;
And in the pathway thereof there is no death.

**XIII.** 1 A wise son *heareth* his father's ¹instruction:
But a scorner heareth not rebuke.

2 A man shall eat good ²by the fruit of his mouth:
But ³the soul of the treacherous *shall eat* violence.

¹ Or, *correction*     ² Or, *from*
³ Or, *the desire of the treacherous* is for *violence*

transposition of the words a possible rendering would be: 'But the possession of the diligent man is precious', i.e. he values what he possesses, and therefore makes use of it. 'Diligent' would then be understood in the same sense as in x. 4 (see note there), 'discerning', or 'sharp', one who has his wits about him. If this interpretation be accepted the meaning of the verse is clear; it is the contrast between the dull sluggard who does not make use of his opportunities when offered, and the active, discerning man who makes the most of his opportunities; as an illustration we may perhaps think of Mark iv. 25: 'For he that hath, to him shall be given; and he that hath not, from him shall be taken away even that which he hath.'

**28.** *life.* i.e. temporal prosperity, see note on iii. 2.

*And in the pathway . . .* The R.V. does not represent the Hebrew, which is meaningless; lit. translated it runs: 'And the way of its pathway not death', the form of the negative being one which is only used with a verb. The text can be emended by reading instead of 'its pathway' *nĕthîbhah*) the word *nith'ābh*, 'abominable'; and, following a number of MSS., as well as the Versions, 'to' instead of 'not', which involves merely a vowel change. The line then runs: 'But an abominable way (leadeth) unto death' (cf. xv. 9: 'The way of the wicked is an abomination to Jahweh'). This gives an excellent antithesis between the two lines.

### CHAPTER XIII

**1.** 'heareth' of the R.V., added because there is no verb in the original as it now stands, is the more unfitting in that it occurs in the second line. Steuernagel makes the excellent emendation אהב ('loveth') for אב ('father'), the line thus running: 'A wise son loveth instruction.'

*heareth not rebuke.* i.e. giveth not heed to rebuke.

**2.** The first line of this verse is almost identical with xii. 14ᵃ, and, following this, we should probably read here: 'shall be satisfied', instead of 'shall eat', and omit 'good'.

*soul.* The meaning of the Hebr. *nephesh* means 'desire' in this connexion, cf. xxiii. 2; read the line as with the R.V. marg. With the verse cf. Ecclus. xvi. 13 (Hebr.).

3 He that guardeth his mouth keepeth his life:
  *But* he that openeth wide his lips shall have destruction.
4 The soul of the sluggard desireth, and hath nothing:
  But the soul of the diligent shall be made fat.
5 A righteous man hateth lying:
  But a wicked man [1]is loathsome, and cometh to shame.
6 Righteousness guardeth [2]him that is upright in the way:
  But wickedness overthroweth [3]the sinner.
7 There is that [4]maketh himself rich, yet hath nothing:
  There is that [4]maketh himself poor, yet hath great wealth.

[1] Or, *causeth shame and bringeth reproach*
[2] Heb. *uprightness of way.*    [3] Heb. *sin.*    [4] Or, *feigneth*

**3.** *openeth wide.* Cf. xx. 19, where, however, a different Hebr. word is used.

*shall have destruction.* Lit. '(it is) destruction to him'. The man who blurts out the first thing that comes into his mind brings ruin upon himself; 'destruction' is rather too strong in this connexion. With the verse cf. xxi. 23; Ecclus. ix. 18 (Hebr.), and the parallel thought in the *Teaching of Amen-em-ope*, III. v. 13, 14:

> Sleep a night before speaking,
> Lest the tempest arise as a flame in the straw.

See further note on xv. 1.

**4.** *The soul.* Hebr. 'his soul', rightly corrected by R.V. 'Soul' here means 'desire', as in verse 2.

*shall be made fat.* Cf. xi. 25ᵃ.

**5.** *hateth lying.* Lit. 'hateth a word of deceit'.

*is loathsome.* The Hebr. word is lit. 'causeth to shrink'; but excepting in 1 Sam. xvii. 12; 1 Chron. xix. 6 (= 2 Sam. x. 6), where a different form of the verb occurs, this word is not used in a figurative sense. The text should probably be amended to read, as in xix. 26, 'causeth shame' (יָבִישׁ).

*and cometh to shame.* Hebr. 'and causeth reproach' as R.V. marg. The two verbs in the second line must be understood as describing characteristics of the nature of the wicked man, in antithesis to the righteous man, who naturally hates deceit.

**6.** *upright.* The Hebr. word suggests rather that which is complete or perfect. The words, 'him that is upright in the way' can be rendered either concretely, as R.V. text, or abstractly, as R.V. marg.; the former, however, is to be preferred.

*sinner.* Here the Hebr. has the abstract, where we should expect the concrete, in contrast to the 'upright in the way', of the first line; a very slight correction in the Hebr. gives the word for 'sinner'.

**7.** This interesting verse admits of more than one interpretation. It can mean that one man makes a pretence of being rich, but in reality possesses nothing; while another affects poverty, though he is

H 2

8 The ransom of a man's life is his riches:
  But the poor heareth no ¹threatening.

9 The light of the righteous rejoiceth:
  But the lamp of the wicked shall be put out.

10 By pride cometh only contention:
  But with the well advised is wisdom.

           ¹ Or, *rebuke*

wealthy, i.e. a contrast between the spendthrift and the miser. A more likely interpretation, however, and one more in accordance with the mode of the Wisdom writers, is that one man, though poor, is really rich because he is content with a little and therefore has all that he wants; while another, who has plenty, is never satisfied and always wants more, and therefore from his own point of view he is a poor man.

**8.** *The ransom of* . . . One explanation of this line is that if a rich man's life is in danger for some cause or other he can ransom it by means of his wealth; e.g. if he is captured by robbers who threaten him with death, he can, by paying a ransom, get off with his life. The poor man, on the other hand, according to the second line, does not hear rebuke (cf. 1ᵇ) in the sense of 'threat', i.e. he is in no fear of such danger, because he is not worth molesting. So far as the second line is concerned this explanation will not do, because the Hebrew word for 'rebuke' never means 'threatening' (see R.V. marg.). Kittel suggests reading instead of 'heareth no rebuke', the words 'findeth not redemption'; the change is somewhat drastic; but if adopted the general sense of the verse might be held to be the advantages of wealth, and the parallel thought in Ecclus. xiii. 21 (Hebr.) could be adduced:

'When the rich is in difficulties (lit. shaken) he is supported by (his) friend.
But when a poor man is in difficulties he is thrust away by (his) friend.'

This, in another form, is the content of x. 15. If, on the other hand, we take the text of the second line as it stands,—and it must be recognized that it reads quite straightforwardly—there is no proper antithesis between the two lines of the verse, and we must assume that, as in some other instances in the book, the two lines stood originally in some other connexion, and have been erroneously joined together here.

**9.** *light*. For 'light' and 'lamp' cf. Job xviii. 6.

*rejoiceth*. This does not give the antithesis which one would expect as a contrast to 'shall be put out' in the second line. The emendation usually adopted is *yizrach*, 'shineth brightly' (cf. 2 Kgs. iii. 22; Job ix. 7; Isa. lviii. 10) for *yismach* ('rejoiceth').

**10.** *By pride* . . . The Hebr. text reads lit.: 'Only by pride one maketh strife'; the words for 'only by' (רַק־בְּ) should be omitted.

*the well advised*. The Hebr. word means 'those who take counsel

11 Wealth gotten [1] by vanity shall be diminished:
　　But he that gathereth by [2] labour shall have increase.
12 Hope deferred maketh the heart sick:
　　But when the desire cometh, it is a tree of life.
13 Whoso despiseth [3] the word [4] bringeth destruction on himself:
　　But he that feareth the commandment shall be rewarded.

[1] The Sept. and Vulg. have, *in haste*.　　　[2] Heb. *with the hand*.
[3] See ch. xvi. 20.　　　[4] Or, *maketh himself a debtor thereto*

together' (*no‘ātzīm*); but this does not give the required antithesis to 'pride' in the first line. It is better to read, as in xi. 2, to which this verse is similar, *tzĕnu‘īm*, 'the lowly'.

**11.** *by vanity.* There can be no doubt that the Hebr. *mēhebhel* ('by vanity') is a mistake for *mĕbhōhāl*, 'hastily' (cf. xx. 21), so the Sept. and Vulg.

*by labour.* The Hebr. expression *‘al-yad*, lit. 'on or, according to, hand' (see R.V. marg.) has a variety of meanings, according to the context in which it stands; but in later Hebrew, while it often means 'through', 'by means of', 'because', it has also the sense of 'slowly', 'gradually', or 'by degrees' (see Jastrow, *Talm. Dict.* s.v.); and this is the meaning it has here, as the contrast in the first line, 'hastily', shows.

In the *Proverbs of Achikar* ii. 51 it is said:

> *Better is the poverty that gathereth*
> *Than wealth that scattereth.*

It is, of course, not a parallel, but worth quoting in this connexion.

**12.** *But when the desire . . .* The Hebr. has: 'But a tree of life (is) a desire that has come'; the meaning is, of course, the same. But the emphasis is slightly different.

**13.** *the word.* Cf. xvi. 20ᵃ. As this is used as a parallel to 'commandment' in the next line it is evidently not used in the ordinary sense. In all probability Deut. xxx. 11–14 was in the mind of the writer; in this passage the 'commandment' is used as embracing all the divine precepts 'which are written in this book of the law', and the 'word' is used as synonymous with it: 'For this commandment which I command thee this day, it is not too hard for thee, neither is it far off . . . But the word is very nigh unto thee, in thy mouth, and in thy heart, that thou mayst do it.'

*bringeth destruction on himself.* The Hebr. means (1) 'becometh pledged to it' (cf. R.V. marg.), i.e. he becomes pledged to pay the penalty for his offence; and (2) 'shall be ruined', i.e. divine punishment will fall on him for despising God's word or law. The second meaning is clearly to be preferred in view of the antithesis in the second line; but in this case 'on himself' must be deleted.

*feareth.* In the sense of reverencing or honouring, as e.g. in Lev. xix. 3, 30.

14 The ¹law of the wise is a fountain of life,
    To depart from the snares of death.
15 Good understanding ²giveth favour:
    But the way of the treacherous is rugged.

¹ Or, *teaching*        ² Or, *getteth*

*shall be rewarded.* A better antithesis with 'shall be ruined' (according to the alternative rendering of the word) in the first line is, by changing the vowels only of the Hebr., and following the Sept., to read 'shall be safe', i.e. from the wrath of God.

The subject-matter of this verse and the way in which it is expressed suggests not so much the sage as the scribe; and the possibility must be recognized of its having originated in a different *milieu* from that of most of this collection.

**14.** *The law.* Read, as R.V. marg., 'the teaching'.
*fountain of life.* See note on x. 11.
*To depart from.* i.e. for, or as a means of, departing from. Cf. xv. 24ᵇ. The verse is almost the same as xiv. 27. It will be noticed that the form of this verse is different from the normal usage in this collection. Instead of the two lines being antithetic, the second continues the sentence of the first, though this is complete in itself. The verse stands isolated in this respect, while the following one (see notes on it) is probably composed of two originally independent lines; xiv. 27 follows a verse of similar structure. It is possible that in these cases, as well as in the few other occurrences of the same thing in this collection, the couplets do not owe their present position to the original compiler.

**15.** *Good understanding.* The two Hebr. words are joined by a hyphen, and are rendered 'culture' by some. Toy says the reference here 'is to that fine perception of propriety which makes a man discreet and courteous in his dealing with his fellows, whereby he wins favour'; he renders the Hebr. by 'fine intelligence', a rendering which could not be bettered.
*giveth.* The Hebr. word has various meanings, 'give', 'get', 'obtain', 'win', &c.
*rugged.* The Hebr. word (*'eythan*) means 'enduring', 'permanent', 'firm'. The R.V. rendering, which is quite impossible, is presumably based on Num. xxiv. 21: 'Strong (*'eythan*) is thy dwelling place, and thy nest is set in the rock'; here the word *'eythan* was regarded (so one must suppose) as descriptive of, or parallel to, 'rock', which was 'strong', and rocks are often, of course, rugged. While it must be granted that there is a certain connexion of ideas between what is strong, or firm, and what is enduring, yet it cannot be said that Hebrew usage permits the rendering 'strong' or 'rugged' for *'eythan*. There is a much simpler solution; it is clear from the Sept. that the

16  Every prudent man worketh with knowledge:
    But a fool spreadeth out folly.
17  A wicked messenger falleth into evil:
    But a faithful ambassador is health.


Hebr. text before it had 'their destruction' ('*eydham*), which in course of time became corrupted to '*eythan*.

The two lines are, however, not properly antithetic, and it is likely enough that they did not originally belong together.

**16.** *Every prudent man* ... According to the slight transposition of the Hebr. words, as suggested by the Syr. and Lat. Versions, we should read: 'Everything that the prudent man doeth (is done) with knowledge.'

*prudent.* Hebr. '*arūm*, see note on i. 4.

*spreadeth out.* In the sense of exhibiting.

**17.** *falleth.* The general sense of the verse justifies a slight change in the vowel-points of the Hebr. so as to read 'causeth to fail'; the reference is not to the messenger himself, but rather to him that sent him.

*a faithful ambassador.* The more general term 'envoy' is better than 'ambassador'; the Hebr. has lit.: 'an envoy of faithfulness', or 'trustworthiness', in xxv. 13 the adjective ('faithful') is used; this should probably be read here.

*health.* Lit. 'healing'; but the word has the sense here of 'profit' (iv. 22) or 'security' (xii. 18). In the Prologue to the *Teaching of Amen-em-ope* it is stated that one of the objects for which the book was written was that a man might learn 'how to return a report to one that has sent him', i. e. how to bring back the proper reply; and in the same book (V. iv. 8) the advice is given: 'Suffer not thyself to be sent on a wicked mission.' Both the Hebrew and the Egyptian sage are probably referring to the envoy who was sent on important missions to foreign courts, and who belonged to the class of scribes (in the earlier sense of the term), i. e. one who could write, and who would therefore occupy an important and responsible position (cf. Isa. xviii. 2; Jer. xlix. 14; Obad. 1, where the same word for 'envoy', *tzîr*, is used). In later days we have another instance of this in the scribe Ben-Sira, who is probably referring to himself primarily when he speaks of the scribe thus:

> He serveth among great men,
> And appeareth before a ruler ;
> He travelleth in the land of alien nations,
> And hath had experience of both good and evil things among men.

Ben-Sira was a representative of the scribe in both the earlier and later sense.

18 Poverty and shame *shall be to* him that refuseth [1]correction:
But he that regardeth reproof shall be honoured.

19 The desire accomplished is sweet to the soul:
But it is an abomination to fools to depart from evil.

20 [2]Walk with wise men, and thou shalt be wise:
But the companion of fools shall [3]smart for it.

21 Evil pursueth sinners:
But the righteous shall be recompensed with good.

22 A good man leaveth an inheritance to his children's children;
And the wealth of the sinner is laid up for the righteous.

---

[1] Or, *instruction*    [2] According to another reading, *He that walketh with wise men shall be wise.*    [3] Heb. *be broken.*

**18.** *that refuseth.* See note on i. 25.

*reproof.* The word in this context means 'reasoning' or 'argument'. The general thought of the verse is that if a man refuses to profit by the experience of others in business matters he will bring poverty, and therefore disgrace, upon himself (the mention of poverty points to failure in commercial undertakings); but if he listens to those who are experts in these things he will ensure respect for himself through attaining to a position of prosperity in business.

**19.** It is quite evident that we have here again a case of two independent lines which have been carelessly put together by a later scribe. There is no natural connexion of thought between the two lines, each of which constitutes a distinct proverb, and appears again in essence in a different connexion; thus the first line, though in slightly varying form, occurs in xiii. 12[b], and the second line, again a little differently expressed, in xxix. 27[b].

**20.** *Walk* . . . See R.V. marg.

*shall smart for it.* The Hebr. is lit. 'he will become evil' (cf. 'They that touch pitch will be defiled'). The R.V. marg. can be disregarded. In the *Proverbs of Achikar* ii. 12 it is said:

'My son, associate with the wise man, and thou shalt become wise like him; and associate not with a garrulous and talkative man, lest thou be numbered with him.'

**21.** *shall be recompensed.* It is perhaps better to follow the Sept. here, which has 'shall overtake them' (reading יַשִּׂגֵם), and make 'good' the subject: 'But (as for) the righteous, prosperity shall overtake them.' The verse again touches upon one of the favourite themes of the Wisdom writers, the adversity of the wicked and the prosperity of the righteous.

**22.** The doctrine of retribution here set forth is characteristic of the Wisdom literature, this being one of the ways in which it is illustrated. The fundamental thought is that God rewards obedience

23 Much food *is in* the ¹tillage of the poor:
  But there is that is destroyed by reason of injustice.
24 He that spareth his rod hateth his son:
  But he that loveth him chasteneth him ²betimes.

  ¹ Or, *tilled land*          ² Or, *diligently*

to His commands by prosperity, while the wicked, who disregard these, come to adversity, no matter what efforts they make. The teaching deals with the present life only (a good illustration is x. 3); after death nothing counts so far as the man himself is concerned; but when he is dead his children either benefit, or suffer, according as to whether he has been a good or a bad man, as in the verse before us. See further the notes on xxiii. 17, 18. For the way in which the Wisdom writers sought to explain the contradiction which the actual facts of life offered to their doctrine, see Excursus IV.

With the first line of the *v.* cf. the words in the *Proverbs of Achikar* ii. 13:

'My son, while thou hast shoes on thy feet, tread down the thorns and make a path for thy sons and for thy sons' sons.'

**23.** The Hebr. text, as it stands, yields no sense; to explain it, as some commentators do, by saying that the poor man fears God, and that therefore his land, however small, brings forth much food, is to read into the text what is not there. The variety of renderings in the Versions only shows the difficulty the verse presented. One Hebr. MS. reads 'the wicked' for 'the poor' (the two words in Hebr. are very similar, and this, taken with the second line, seems, at first sight, to give good sense, viz. 'Much food is in the tillage of the wicked, But there is that is destroyed because of injustice', i. e. Much though the fields of the wicked bring forth, it is of no good to them, because they (the wicked) having acquired the fields by injustice, will be destroyed. This, while a possible explanation as the text stands, is unsatisfactory, because it is forced, and involves reading into the text something which may or may not be implied; moreover, there is another difficulty in the first line; the word for 'tillage' (*nîr*) means 'untilled' or 'fallow' ground (it occurs elsewhere only in Jer. iv. 3; Hos. x. 12); and it is just the kind of ground which does *not* bring forth. It must be a corruption in the text. Indeed, the first line defies emendation, the text is too corrupt. The second line can either mean that a man is destroyed unjustly, or because he is guilty of injustice.

**24.** *He that spareth* . . . The great importance attached by Jews of all ages to the right upbringing of their sons accounts for the frequent reference to corporal punishment, see xix. 18, xxii. 15, xxiii. 13, 14, xxix. 15, 17; Ecclus. xxx. 1, 2, cf. Hebr. xii. 6–11, and see the quotation from *The Proverbs of Achikar*, in the note on xxiii. 13, 14.

*chasteneth him betimes.* Lit. 'seeketh him with chastisement'; the

25 The righteous eateth to the satisfying of his soul:
   But the belly of the wicked shall want.
**XIV.** 1 Every wise woman buildeth her house:
   But [1]the foolish plucketh it down with her own hands.
 2 He that walketh in his uprightness feareth the LORD:
   But he that is perverse in his ways despiseth him.

[1] Heb. folly.

addition of 'betimes' in the R.V., or 'diligently' (R.V. marg.), is not required; see note on i. 28.
**25.** Cf. x. 3 and the note on verse 22.

<h2 style="text-align:center">CHAPTER XIV</h2>

**1.** *Every wise woman . . .* House-building was not the concern of women; 'house' cannot be interpreted as 'household', which would require a different verb. Moreover, the Hebr. has 'women', with the verb in the singular. The R.V. does not represent the Hebrew text, which, moreover, is clearly corrupt. The word 'women' was put in because 'wise' (חַכְמוֹת) was taken as an adjective, fem. plur., but it should be חָכְמוֹת a noun, plur. abstract, 'Wisdom', as in i. 20 (see note there), and ix. 1. 'Women' should, therefore, be omitted, and we must read: 'Wisdom buildeth her house', cf. xxiv. 3.

*the foolish.* Read, with R.V. marg., 'folly'.

*plucketh it down.* Better 'overthroweth it' as in xxix. 4, where the same Hebr. word is used.

*with her own hands.* This was presumably inserted because of the mistaken addition of 'women', and should be omitted; it spoils the rhythm of the line. The couplet is a figurative way of describing the attributes of Wisdom and Folly as respectively constructive and destructive.

**2.** *in his uprightness.* 'his' is better omitted, as in x. 9.

*he that is perverse.* Cf. ii. 15, iii. 21, 32. The thought in this clause is strongly expressed; what is meant is that the man who is not straightforward and honest in his dealings ignores God, and in this way despises Him. It was of the essence of the sages' teaching regarding godliness that it involved dependence on the divine guidance; the ways of a man which are of his own choosing are, therefore, necessarily crooked and perverse, since this cardinal principle is not acted upon. It is important to recognize this tenet of the Wisdom teachers, because so very much of what they say seems to lay the main emphasis on human free will; but there is all through this underlying thought of divine grace, and therefore the need of dependence on God; to deny this, or to ignore it, is an insult to God. It is only he that 'feareth the Lord' who is able to walk rightly; see the striking passage in Ecclus. x. 19–24.

3 In the mouth of the foolish is a [1]rod [2]of pride:
    But the lips of the wise shall preserve them.
4 Where no oxen are, the crib is clean:
    But much increase is by the strength of the ox.
5 A faithful witness will not lie:
    But a false witness [3]uttereth lies.
6 A scorner seeketh wisdom, and *findeth it* not:
    But knowledge is easy unto him that hath understanding.
7 [4]Go into the presence of a foolish man,
    And thou shalt not perceive *in him* the lips of knowledge.

    [1] Or, *shoot*     [2] Or, *for* his *pride*     [3] Heb. *breatheth out.*
       [4] Or, *Go from . . . for thou wilt not &c.*

**3.** *a rod of pride.* This is the rendering of the Versions, but not of the Hebr., which, as R.V. marg. says, is 'shoot'; the word occurs elsewhere only in Isa. xi. 1, where it means a shoot from the stem of a tree. Here it is a figurative expression meaning that that which comes forth from the mouth of a fool, i.e. his words, is haughty; this denotes pride, which, as the Wisdom teachers so often declare, brings ruin; hence the antithesis in the second line.

    *shall preserve them.* i.e. the wise; the Hebr. תִּשְׁמוּרֵם is evidently an error, it should be תִּשְׁמְרֵם (so the Sept.).

**4.** *the crib is clean.* It is doubtful whether the Hebr. can bear this meaning, since the word for 'clean' is not used in a physical sense (not even in Cant. vi. 9), but always of moral purity (cf. Job xi. 4; Ps. xxiv. 4). It also has the meaning 'corn', and this is, no doubt, how it is to be understood here. The word for 'crib' (אֵבוּס) is a corruption of the negative particle אֶפֶס; so that the line should run: 'Where no oxen are there is no corn', a pregnant way of saying: 'no oxen, no ploughing; no ploughing, no sowing; no sowing, no corn.' It is an allegorical picture expressing the truth of cause and effect. The proverb is complete in itself, and sounds like a genuine popular proverb; but the sage thought well to add an antithetical line based, possibly, on xii. 11[a].

**5.** Cf. xii. 17; the second line occurs in vi. 19[a]; this is interesting as showing how isolated sayings were taken from various sources and a line added to make up a couplet, as in the preceding verse.

**6.** *A scorner seeketh wisdom.* The scorner is by no means a 'fool' in the sense of 'stupid', as a number of passages show; so that intellectually he would be quite capable of seeking wisdom; the reason why he cannot find it is because he lacks the prime condition for doing so, i.e. the fear of the Lord.

    *and* findeth it *not.* The terseness of the Hebr. lit. 'and not', i.e. there is none, is very effective. With the *v.* cf. Ecclus. xv. 8.

**7.** The Hebr. of this *v.* is unidiomatic, and cannot be right; the

8 The wisdom of the prudent is to understand his way:
  But the folly of fools is deceit.
9 ¹ The foolish make a mock at ² guilt:
  But among the upright there is ³ good will.
10 The heart knoweth its own bitterness;
  And a stranger doth not intermeddle with its joy.

¹ Or, *Guilt mocketh at the foolish*        ² Or, *the guilt offering*
³ Or, *the favour* of God

variety of renderings in the Versions show that difficulties in the text
were experienced. The general sense is, however, clear; the Hebr.
runs lit. 'Go from before a man that is a fool (*kĕsîl* 'stupid'), for (lit.
'and') thou wilt not know the lips of knowledge'; i. e. it is useless to
remain in the company of a silly person, since nothing sensible is
to be expected of him.

**8.** *The wisdom of* . . . In other words, foresight is characteristic
of the prudent man because he is possessed of wisdom.

*But the folly* . . . This does not form an antithesis to the first line;
and the saying is by no means always true. For 'deceit' (מִרְמָה) the
Sept. has ἐν πλάνῃ, 'in erring', which may well represent the Hebrew
מַתְעֶה, the participle *hiph'il* of a root meaning 'to err' (cf. x. 17ᵇ);
following this the line would read: 'But folly causeth fools to err';
this is both in accordance with fact, and offers a good antithesis to
the first line.

**9.** *The foolish make* . . . The Hebr. text is corrupt; as it stands it
says: 'a guilt-offering scorneth fools'; this is impossible as being
entirely foreign to Hebrew ideas; the same is true if we render 'guilt'
for 'guilt-offering'. With a slight emendation the Hebr. might be
rendered: 'Fools mock at guilt', or 'guilt-offering'; but as Toy
rightly says, 'it is not at *guilt*, but at *sin* (A.V.), that bad men may
be supposed to mock, but the Hebrew word is not a natural expression for sin'. The word *'āshām*, 'guilt', is the difficulty. The
Versions were evidently puzzled. Many emendations have been
suggested, but there is necessarily an element of uncertainty in them
all; what is expected is something antithetical to what is said in the
second line. A fairly obvious emendation would be to read אֱלֹהִים,
'God', for אֱוִלִים, 'the foolish'; for the word אָשָׁם, 'guilt' or 'guilt-
offering', which is foreign to *Proverbs*, we may possibly read רְשָׁעִים,
'the wicked', which would offer a kind of word-play to יְשָׁרִים,
'the upright', in the second line. The line might then be rendered:
'God mocketh at the wicked', cf. iii. 34; this would also support the,
no doubt correct, suggestion of R.V. marg. in the second line: 'But
among the upright there is the favour (of God).'

**10.** *The heart* . . . Lit. 'the heart knoweth the bitterness of its
soul'; here 'heart' stands for the inner man, cf. xv. 11, and 'soul',

11 The house of the wicked shall be overthrown:
    But the tent of the upright shall flourish.
12 There is a way which ¹seemeth right unto a man,
    But the end thereof are the ways of death.
13 Even in laughter the heart is sorrowful;
    And the end of mirth is heaviness.

¹ Or, *is straight before*

as so often, stands for individuality; so that the sentence means that sorrowful experiences can only be fully felt by a man himself.

*And a stranger* . . . Lit. 'And with its joy a stranger has no fellowship'; i.e. the joyful experiences are only fully felt by a man himself. The verse neither affirms nor denies that sorrows and joys are shared by others; that is not the point with which he is dealing; he is simply placing on record the common experience of mankind that one's innermost feelings cannot be shared with another in the same way in which he himself experiences them. The Wisdom writers had a very clear insight into human nature, and were fully cognizant of the intricacies of the mental and emotional ways and promptings of men. Following the Sept. some commentators read 'pride' instead of 'stranger', and render the clause: 'And with his joy pride is not mingled'; but this does not go nearly so well with the first clause; for the use of 'stranger' (זָר) here cf. Job xix. 27ᵇ.

**11.** *shall flourish.* The Hebr. word means to 'send out shoots', and in that sense 'to flourish'; and though used figuratively of righteous men (e.g. xi. 28), its use here in reference to a tent is curious, and it is perhaps better to follow the Sept. and read 'shall stand', see xii. 7ᵇ; cf. with the *v.* Ecclus. xxvii. 3.

**12.** The identical words occur again in xvi. 25.

*seemeth right unto.* This rendering, which follows the Sept., obscures the meaning of the Hebr., read: 'straight before'. As the proverb stands quite isolated it is impossible to say for certain whether its thought is that of 'the elusive character of an immoral life' (Toy); indeed, the word 'straight' applied to a way (יָשָׁר) could quite naturally be used in a non-ethical sense, see 1 Sam. vi. 12; Isa. xlv. 13 (on the other hand, see Prov. xi. 5, xxix. 27); so that possibly the reference here is simply to want of foresight in a general sense, cf. xxii. 3; Ecclus. v. 9, xxxvii. 16.

**13.** *Even in laughter* . . . As the text stands this can either mean that all joy is tinged with sorrow, a conception quite foreign to the Hebrew outlook on life; or, that outward joy is only a cloak of hidden sorrow; but to lay this down as a general truth is contrary to experience, as the Wisdom writers would know well enough. The Sept. seems to have read: 'With laughter sorrow is not mingled',

14 The backslider in heart shall be filled with his own ways:
    And a good man *shall be satisfied* from himself.
15 The simple believeth every word:
    But the prudent man looketh well to his going.
16 A wise man feareth, and departeth from evil:
    But the fool beareth himself insolently, and is confident.
17 He that is soon angry will deal foolishly:
    And a man of wicked devices is hated.

lit. 'with laughter sorrow doth not mingle itself' (reading: בִּשְׂחֹק
כַּעַם לֹא־יִתְעָרֵב); this, taken with the second clause, 'But the end of
mirth is grief', i. e. after mirth comes grief (cf. Sept.), gives a truth
of universal experience, viz. that joy alternates with sorrow. The
negative of the Sept. in the first clause undoubtedly makes the saying
accord better with the facts of ordinary life than the present form of
the Hebrew text.

**14.** *The backslider in heart.* 'Backslider' is quite misleading; the
Hebrew word means 'to move away', and is often used figuratively
of being faithless (e. g. Isa. i. 5, lix. 13; Jer. xxxviii. 22); as 'heart'
is used in Hebr. as the seat of the understanding, the expression
means one who is not using his senses, i. e. the stupid or senseless
man. Such a one is sated with the result of his ways, or manner of life.
    *And a good man* ... The Hebr. text is meaningless; read, following
the Sept., 'But a good man from his thoughts', i. e. he is sated or
satisfied through using his senses. The antithesis is between the un-
thinking and the thoughtful man; to the Wisdom writers all types
of fool were sinners, so that the 'good man' is in contrast to him who
does not use his brains, and who is, therefore, evil.

**15.** *looketh well to his going.* Hebr.: 'considereth his step'; the
latter word is always used of a man's mode of life (e. g. Job xxiii. 11,
xxxi. 7; Ps. xvii. 5, xl. 3, &c.); the antithesis is between the credulous
man, and one who walks warily.

**16.** *feareth.* Not in a religious sense; the meaning is that he exer-
cises caution.
    *beareth himself insolently.* Or 'is arrogant' (מִתְעַבֵּר), but it is
possible that the Sept. read מִתְעָרֵב, cf. *v.* 13, lit. 'mingles himself'
(μίγνυται), i. e. takes part; the clause would then read: 'But the fool
takes part (therein), confidently', i. e. as opposed to the caution of
the wise man.

**17.** *He that is soon angry.* The Hebr. expression is lit. 'he that is
short of face', the exact reverse of 'he that is long of face' in *v.* 29,
xv. 18, meaning respectively 'hasty-tempered' and 'forbearing'.
The root (אנף) from which the word for 'face' comes, means 'to be
angry'; the face expresses the feeling of anger.

18 The simple inherit folly:
  But the prudent are crowned with knowledge.
19 The evil bow before the good;
  And the wicked at the gates of the righteous.

*will deal foolishly*. Lit. 'doeth folly'.

*And a man of* . . . The Sept. must have had a better text before it in reading: 'But a wise man endureth much (lit. many things).' The word rendered 'wicked devices' is also used in a good sense, e. g. in i. 4, 'discretion'; a copyist who took the word to be used in a bad sense altered 'endureth (יִשָּׂא) to 'is hated' (יִשָּׂנֵא), hence the present R.V. rendering. It is an interesting illustration of the way in which the addition of a single letter in Hebr. will sometimes alter the entire meaning of a sentence. The Sept. rendering offers the proper antithesis between the foolish quick-tempered man and the wise one who weighs things before acting. Cf. xxix. 11.

**18.** *inherit*. The Hebr. word means equally 'to take as one's possession', see e.g. Exod. xxiii. 30; Isa. lvii. 13, and often; the clause does not mean that simple-minded people are endowed with folly whether they can help it or not, but that they actively take possession of folly, hence their stupidity.

*are crowned*. This rendering, again, represents the prudent as passive instruments, whereas the sense of the passage is that they actively achieve knowledge; the Hebr. word is difficult and might well be a corruption; the Sept. has 'take hold of' (κρατήσουσιν), representing perhaps יֹאחֲזוּ, which is used in Eccles. ii. 3 of taking hold of folly. The antithesis would then be between the foolish who take folly as their possession, and the prudent who grasp knowledge.

**19.** The thought expressed in this verse was in accordance with the Jewish doctrine of retributive justice, which was clung to in spite of many proofs of its fallibility; doubtless, individual cases would be pointed to as justifying the belief that the wicked come to grief and the righteous enjoy prosperity; as late as the time of Ben-Sira (*circa* 200 B.C.) historical events are cited as illustrating the truth of this belief (Ecclus. xvi. 6–14). But ultimately the logic of facts proved too strong, and the bankruptcy of the doctrine is witnessed to by many utterances of the psalmists. With the rise of the belief in immortality the doctrine assumed a new form, and it was taught that retribution on the wicked and the reward of the righteous took place in the world to come; this was especially the teaching of the apocalyptists, but the classical passage is Wisd. iii. 1–iv. 6.

*And the wicked* ... The Sept. supplies a verb, 'serve in attendance', but it is not needed.

20 The poor is hated even of his own neighbour:
   But the rich hath many friends.
21 He that despiseth his neighbour sinneth:
   But he that hath pity on the poor, happy is he.
22 ¹Do they not err that devise evil?
   But mercy and truth *shall be to* them that devise good.
23 In all labour there is profit:
   But the talk of the lips *tendeth* only to penury.

¹ Or, *Shall they not go astray*

**20.** This verse is a good illustration of the haphazard way in which the sayings in this collection are jumbled together; in the preceding verse the subject is one of the fundamental religious doctrines, the next verse touches on ethics, while the verse before us deals with the recognized fact of the power of wealth.

*But the rich* . . . Lit. 'But the lovers of the rich (man are) many'. Cf. with the *v.* xix. 4, 7; Ecclus. xii. 8, 9, and the *Proverbs of Achikar* ii. 44:

> 'My son, he whose hand is full is called wise and honourable; but he whose hand is scant is called abject and foolish.'

**21.** *He that despiseth* . . . See Lev. xix. 18.
*happy is he.* Or 'blessed is he', cf. xvi. 20, because he receives his reward from God.

**22.** *Do they not err* . . . This interrogative form is rare in *Proverbs*; none of the Versions have it; but as expressive of certainty it is a pointed form of speech. The Hebr. word for 'err' means wandering out of the way, and that for 'devise' is lit. 'to cut' or 'construct', cf. iii. 29, vi. 14.

*them that devise.* A preposition, 'to', ought probably to be added; but the Hebr. text is not altogether satisfactory; the Sept. seems to have found some difficulty with it, as two forms of the verse are given, though the general sense is the same in each.

**23.** *In all labour* . . . The Hebr. word for 'labour' connotes that which involves pain, cf. v. 10, x. 22, xv. 1, and also Gen. iii. 16 ('travail') and Ps. cxxvii. 2; these are the only occurrences of the word in the O.T., and it is not the usual one for 'labour'; in all probability it was used with the purpose of ennobling the idea of labour just because it did involve painful effort; for generally speaking, in the Old Testament labour is looked upon as a burdensome, if necessary, evil. The words in Gen. iii. 17–19 reflect this: 'Cursed is the ground for thy sake, in toil (the word is radically the same as that in the *v.* under consideration) shalt thou eat of it all the days of thy life . . .' The Wisdom writers were the first to teach that labour was to be regarded as something useful; and this is brought out in many

24 [1]The crown of the wise is their riches:
   *But* the folly of fools is *only* folly.
25 A true witness delivereth souls:
   But he that [2]uttereth lies *causeth* deceit.

[1] Or, *Their riches is a crown unto the wise*
[2] Heb. *breatheth out.*

passages (see e. g. in addition to those just referred to, xiii. 11; Ecclus. vii. 15, xxxviii. 27–30, and against sloth, Prov. vi. 6–11 ; Ecclus. xxii. 1, 2, and cf. *Pirqê 'Abôth* i. 17, 'Love work', the reference is to manual labour, ii. 2). On the other hand, it must be recognized that they did look upon labour as in itself noble and inspiring ; it is its practical advantage and profit upon which they lay stress, its value lies in its fruit, not in its intrinsic worth.

*But the talk* . . . One expects a rather more definite antithesis, and it is possible that the Sept., which speaks of the luxurious and easy-going man coming to be in want, reflects a different text in the Hebrew.

*penury.* Cf. vi. 11, xi. 24, xxi. 5, 17, xxii. 16, xxviii. 27.

**24.** *The crown* . . . While the phrase itself gives sense, the senti-ment can hardly be regarded as in harmony with what the Wisdom writers say about riches (see xi. 16, 28, xxii. 1, xxx. 8; Ecclus. xxxi. 1–4, 5–7); they have higher ideals, and though they recognize that wealth may be a gift of Wisdom (iii. 16, viii. 18), or the reward of godliness (xxii. 4), and that it has its uses (xiii. 8), the true ornament of a wise man is something better (cf. iv. 9, xii. 4, xvi. 31, xvii. 6). It is better to make a slight emendation in the Hebr. text (reading עָרְמָה, 'prudence', for עָשְׁרָם, 'their riches') and rendering with the Sept.: 'The crown of the wise is prudence.'

*the folly of* . . . On the face of it this jejune sentence cannot be right. For ' the folly of fools ' read : ' The chaplet (or "diadem") of fools ' (לִוְיַת i. 9, iv. 9 for אִוֶּלֶת). This gives an excellent antithesis to the first line.

**25.** *A true witness* . . . Sayings like this (cf. xii. 17, xiv. 5, xvii. 26, xviii. 5, xxiv. 23 ; Ecclus. viii. 14) are ultimately based on the teaching of the prophets. In times when an accused man was not represented by counsel everything depended on the witnesses, and a true witness might often be the means of averting the death penalty.

*delivereth souls.* i. e. saveth lives.

*who uttereth lies.* Lit. 'puffeth out lies', cf. *v.* 5, vi. 19, xix. 5, 9, used of bearing false witness, cf. *Pirqê 'Abôth* i. 9.

*causeth deceit.* A pointless truism ; read, on the basis of the Sept. (ἐκκαίει, 'consumes '), 'destroyeth ' (מְדֻמֶּה for מִרְמָה), i.e. souls, though, it is true, this form (מדמה) does not occur elsewhere in the Old Testament.

I

26 In the fear of the LORD is strong confidence:
   And [1] his children shall have a place of refuge.
27 The fear of the LORD is a fountain of life,
   To depart from the snares of death.
28 In the multitude of people is the king's glory:
   But in the want of people is the destruction of the
      prince.
29 He that is slow to anger is of great understanding:
   But he that is hasty of spirit [2] exalteth folly.

---

[1] Or, *the children of him* that hath it          [2] Or, *carrieth away*

**26.** *In the fear of the Lord.* If the first line of this verse stood alone
no exception could be taken to the Hebr. text as it stands; but 'his'
children in the second line assumes a person as subject in the first
line; the R.V. marg. is an unnatural rendering; it is, therefore,
better to emend the text so as to read 'he that feareth the Lord
hath . . .', lit. 'to him who . . . (there is) . . .'

*a place of refuge.* 'a place of' is not needed, as it is the Lord Who
is the refuge. A God-fearing father will have God-fearing children,
and therefore the Lord is the refuge of each. Cf. xiii. 22ᵃ, xx. 7;
Ecclus. iii. 1.

**27.** *The fear of the Lord.* For this xiii. 14 has 'the law (better
"teaching") of the wise', but with this exception the two verses are
identical. This verse evidently preserves the earlier form. With the
verse cf. Ecclus. i. 29.

**28.** This is the only instance in *Proverbs* of the king being mentioned in a purely secular connexion; the reference here is to a king's
safety if his people are numerous, but of his danger from enemies if
they are but few. Wherever else the king is mentioned a religious,
or at least an ethical, note is sounded in connexion with him, see
further xvi. 10, 12, xx. 8, 26, 28, xxi. 1, xxv. 2, 4, 5, xxix. 4, 12,
xxi. 1–9.

**29.** *He that is slow.* The root idea of the Hebr. word is that of
*being long,* of time, hence postponing, or putting off, cf. xix. 11.

*he that is hasty of spirit.* Here the root idea is that of shortness,
'short-tempered' as we should say.

*exalteth.* The Hebr. verb when used transitively has almost in-
variably a material object, so that in this connexion it raises suspicion
as to its genuineness, see note on iii. 35; it is probably best to read
'increaseth' (מַרְבֶּה for מֵרִים, so Toy), following the Targum (סְנֵי);
this affords an excellent parallel to 'great' in the first line, besides
giving a word-play in Hebrew.

30 A ¹sound heart is the life of the flesh:
   But ²envy is the rottenness of the bones.
31 He that oppresseth the poor reproacheth his Maker:
   But he that hath mercy on the needy honoureth him.

¹ Or, *tranquil*          ² Or, *jealousy*

**30.** *A sound heart.* Read, with R.V. marg., 'tranquil'; the phrase
means 'mental composure'.

*the life of the flesh.* This is the lit. rendering of the Hebr. which in
modern phraseology might be expressed by 'is advantageous to the
physical body'.

*envy.* This is the usual meaning of the Hebr. word, but it also has
the sense of zeal, ardour, passion (see, e.g. Job v. 2; Ps. cxix. 139;
Cant. viii. 6); it is the latter which is meant here, in antithesis to the
mental composure spoken of in the first line.

*the rottenness of the bones.* This is not a figurative expression, as
the framework of the human body and its most enduring part, the
bones, were thought of as synonymous with man in his material
capacity (see Job iv. 14, xx. 11; Ps. xxxv. 10; Jer. xxiii. 9). This
phrase therefore means simply bodily ill-health. Toy says that:
'*Body* (lit. *flesh*) and *bones* stand for the man's whole being (as often
elsewhere), and are not to be understood as referring to the close
relation between body and mind; this physiologico-psychological
observation is not found in O.T.' This is not correct; the ancient
Jewish sages fully recognized the influence of the mind on the body.
They knew well enough that the state of the mind directly affected
bodily health. As Volz rightly points out, the Jewish Wisdom writers
'recommend an equable cheerfulness of mind, which reminds one of
the "Epicuræan ideal". A man should take advantage of the enjoy-
ments of life, and have his pleasure in "ointment and perfume"
(xxvii. 9), i.e. those things which give delight to existence.' On the
other hand, he must not allow the sadder side of life to have an
exaggerated influence on him, mourning, grief, worry, and the like;
for, with their knowledge of human nature and their experience of
life, the Wisdom writers saw that to give unlimited rein to grief or
worry ultimately mastered a man's whole being, with the result that
his health became affected. That this is no imaginary estimate of the
Wisdom writers' insight will be realized by pondering the words and
implications of such passages as xiv. 13, xv. 13, 15, xvii. 22, xviii. 14;
Ecclus. xiii. 25, 26, xxx. 21–25, xxxviii. 18, 19.

**31.** With this verse compare xvii. 5, xix. 17, xxii. 2; Job xxxi. 15;
Ecclus. iv. 4. The influence of prophetical teaching is seen here
clearly.

*reproacheth.* i.e. insulteth.

*Maker.* For this name for God cf. Job iv. 17, xxxv. 10; Isa. li. 13,
liv. 5.

I 2

32 The wicked is thrust down in his ¹evil-doing:
  But the righteous ²hath hope in his death.

33 Wisdom resteth in the heart of him that hath understanding:
  ³ But *that which is* in the inward part of fools is made known.

34 Righteousness exalteth a nation:
  But sin is a reproach to ⁴any people.

¹ Or, *calamity*      ² Or, *hath a refuge*      ³ Or, *And in the midst of fools*
*it maketh itself known*      ⁴ Heb. *peoples.*

**32.** *in his evil-doing.* i. e. through his wickedness, or, as the result of it; the Hebr. word for 'is thrust down' is used of pushing down violently; but not in reference to death. The thought here is that of the wicked man having, by unscrupulous methods, raised himself to some important position, from which he is thrust down by over-reaching himself; so that his wrongdoing is the means of his downfall.

*hath hope.* Read with R.V. marg. 'hath a refuge', cf. Ps. xviii. 2, 30 (Hebr. 3, 31).

*in his death.* This cannot be right, as it would imply hope in a future life, and such a hope had not yet come into existence in Israel. The Sept. has 'in his piety', reading probably בְּתֻמּוֹ ('in his integrity', cf. x. 9, xx. 7, xxviii. 6) for בְּמוֹתוֹ. This gives a very pointed antithesis, since integrity as a means of safety is contrasted with evil-doing as the means of downfall.

**33.** *resteth.* Or 'abideth', i. e. uses it as a continuous place of abode.

*that which is.* There is no justification for this addition, which is an impossible rendering of the Hebr. The text has simply: 'But in the inward part of fools it is made known.' As Wisdom is the subject this could only mean (so far as the English is concerned) that to the inner consciousness of fools was revealed the fact that Wisdom rested in the heart of a man of understanding; apart from the futility of such a remark, it is not a meaning which the Hebrew could bear. It must be recognized that the text is corrupt. The Sept. reads for 'it is made known', the negative, 'it is not discerned'; this makes sense, but offers a somewhat jejune antithesis. It is best, with Toy, to read for 'it is made known' (תִּוָּדֵעַ), 'folly' (אִוֶּלֶת), for this is used several times in *Proverbs* in connexion with the type of 'fool' (כְּסִיל) here mentioned, see xii. 23, xv. 2, 14. The contrast is then between Wisdom and Folly being the permanent guests, respectively, of the wise man and of the fool.

**34.** *Righteousness* . . . Here again the influence of the prophets is to be seen. That the sage has in mind any other than the Israelite nation is highly improbable; even the Wisdom writers, with all their breadth of view, can hardly have contemplated the possibility of any nation being righteous if it was idolatrous, as every nation was, with the exception of Israel; they never divorce ethics from religion, so

35 The king's favour is toward a servant that dealeth wisely:
But his wrath shall be *against* him that [1]causeth shame.
**XV.** 1 A soft answer turneth away wrath:
But a grievous word stirreth up anger.

[1] Or, *doeth shamefully*

that a righteous nation could only be one which was religious; and
this meant 'the fear of the Lord'. The antithesis in this verse, therefore, implied, but not explicitly stated, is between the nation of
Israel and other peoples. Wisdom is righteousness, and folly is sin;
the Wisdom writers are never tired of reiterating this truth; but, as
Ben-Sira points out, Wisdom, in the ethical-religious sense—which
is the only sense in which it is understood by the Wisdom-writers—is
confined to Israel; he says:

'Then the Creator of all things gave me commandment,
And He that created me fixed my dwelling-place;
And He said, "In Jacob let thy dwelling-place be,
And in Israel take up thine inheritance" . . .
And I took root among an honoured people,
In the portion of the Lord, and of His inheritance.'
(Ecclus. xxiv. 8–12, from the Greek; the Hebrew is not extant.)

*exalteth.* In the sense of bringing it material prosperity.

*sin.* The Hebr. has 'loving-kindness' (חֶסֶד), which is evidently a
mistake for 'want' (חֶסֶר, cf. xxviii. 22), the Sept. reading; the line
should thus run: 'But sin (brings) want (or poverty) to peoples';
poverty is in contrast to the material prosperity of the first line.

**35.** *The king's favour* . . . On the mention of the king in *Prov.* see
Intr. § III, (iv).

*shall be.* The Sept. read 'slayeth' (תַּהֲרֹג) for תִּהְיֶה, 'shall be'), which
is perhaps to be preferred.

*causeth shame.* Read, with R.V. marg., 'doeth shamefully'. The
reference is to one employed upon the king's business.

## CHAPTER XV

**1.** *A soft answer.* Cf. *v.* 23, xxiv. 26, xxv. 15. This is the best
known of the many sayings in the Wisdom literature on the subject
of speech. The primary emphasis is naturally laid on moral *action*;
but the immense importance of forethought, control, and mode of
expression, where the tongue is concerned, was profoundly realized
by the Hebrew sages; hence their frequent exhortations to careful-
ness in speech, since this is the most potent means both of peace
and strife among men in ordinary life. One can discern, speaking
generally, four main directions in the treatment of this subject:
kindliness of speech, courtesy in reply, the wisdom of silence, and
caution in speaking; this last receives most attention. The fundamental guiding principles throughout are consideration for the feel-

2 The tongue of the wise uttereth knowledge aright:
   But the mouth of fools poureth out folly.

3 The eyes of the LORD are in every place,
   Keeping watch upon the evil and the good.

4 ¹ A wholesome tongue is a tree of life:
   But perverseness therein is a breaking of the spirit.

¹ Heb. *The healing of the tongue.*

ings of others, and self-respect in the speaker, though warnings lest
unadvised speech should get a man into trouble also play a part. As
the precepts on such a subject applied to all mankind, we naturally
look for parallels in the ancient literatures of other peoples, where
available; and we do not look in vain, see e.g. the notes on x. 19, xvi.
24. There is no need to postulate borrowing here; the interest of such
parallels lies in the fact that their existence illustrates the truth that
the Hebrew Wisdom Literature belongs to a World Literature, each
part of which, as represented by different nations, while exhibiting
its special individual characteristics, utilized material common to all.

*turneth away.* For the Hebr. word cf. the Isaianic refrain in Isa.
v. 25, ix. 12, 17, 21 (11, 16, 20 in Hebr.), x. 4.

*stirreth up.* Lit. 'causeth to go up', cf. Ps. lxxviii. 31, 'when the
anger of God went up against them'; cf. also Eccles. x. 4.

**2.** *uttereth aright.* The Hebr. word (תֵּיטִיב) will not bear this sense;
it means 'to do well', and cannot be original. Following the Sept.
we must read 'disperseth' (תָּפִיץ, lit. 'droppeth'), as in v. 13, where it
is said that the lips of the strange woman drop honey, figurative of
her sweet words. The same expression is used in Am. vii. 16; Mic.
ii. 6; Ezek. xx. 46 (xxi. 2 in Hebr.) of scattering words. It gives a
better parallel to 'poureth out' in the second line.

**3.** Cf. x. 29; Ps. xxxiii. 13–15; the thought of the all-seeing eye of
God occurs also in the *Teaching of Amen-em-ope* XV. xvii. 10. See
Excursus I.

**4.** *A wholesome tongue.* i.e. a tongue that soothes or heals (see R.V.
marg.); cf. xiv. 30, xvi. 24, and the *Wisdom of Anii*: 'If thy words are
soothing to the heart, then will the heart incline to receive them.'

*a tree of life.* See note on iii. 18.

*perverseness.* Lit. 'crooked dealing', cf. xi. 3ᵇ; the reference is to
lying, slander, or the like.

*a breaking of the spirit.* Cf. Isa. lxv. 14. Ben-Sira has such an
instructive comment on these words that the passage is worth
quoting in full; it is from the Greek, the Hebrew is not extant:

> Curse the whisperer and the double-tongued,
> For it hath destroyed many that were at peace.
> The third tongue hath shaken many,
> And hath dispersed them from nation to nation;
> Even strong cities hath it destroyed,

5 A fool despiseth his father's [1] correction:
　But he that regardeth reproof [2] getteth prudence.

6 In the house of the righteous is much treasure:
　But in the revenues of the wicked is trouble.

7 The lips of the wise disperse knowledge:
　But the heart of the foolish [3] *doeth* not so.

8 The sacrifice of the wicked is an abomination to the LORD:
　But the prayer of the upright is his delight.

9 The way of the wicked is an abomination to the LORD:
　But he loveth him that followeth after righteousness.

[1] Or, *instruction*　　　[2] Or, *dealeth prudently*　　　[3] Or, is *not stedfast* or *right*

　　And overturned the houses of the great.
　　The third tongue hath cast out brave women,
　　And deprived them of their labours.
　　He that giveth heed thereto shall not find rest,
　　Neither shall he dwell in quietude.
　　The stroke of a whip maketh a mark,
　　But the stroke of a tongue breaketh bones.
　　Many have fallen by the edge of the sword,
　　But not so many as have fallen by the tongue (Ecclus. xxviii. 13–18).

**5.** *correction.* Read, with R.V. marg., 'instruction', cf. xiii. 1.

*getteth prudence.* Read, with R.V. marg., 'dealeth prudently'; cf. xix. 25[a].

**6.** *In the house ...* The Hebr. has, 'The house of the righteous is a great treasure'.

*But in the revenues.* The sense of the verb (see next note) demands the omission of 'in'; it is omitted in a number of MSS.

*is trouble.* The form of the Hebr. word is a passive fem. participle and cannot be translated as an abstract noun; no doubt Frankenberg and Toy are right in emending the word so as to read 'is cut off'; in the Hebr. 'revenues' is a sing. noun.

**7.** *disperse.* This is the only occurrence in the O.T. of the Hebr. word being used in this figurative way; otherwise it is always used in a literal sense; many commentators, therefore, prefer to read 'preserve' (יִצְרוּ), as in xx. 28, instead of 'disperse' (יְזָרוּ).

*doeth not so.* This jejune antithesis is not in the style of the Wisdom writers; it is better to read 'discerneth not' (לֹא יָבֵן) instead of 'not so' (לֹא־כֵן).

**9.** This *v.* is the complement of the preceding; religion is a thing of everyday life; right living is at least as necessary as acts of sacrifice and prayer. The influence of prophetical teaching is again observable here.

*followeth after.* The form of the Hebr. verb is intensive, implying steadfast, continuous action.

10 There is grievous correction for him that forsaketh the way:
   *And* he that hateth reproof shall die.

11 ¹Sheol and ²Abaddon are before the LORD:
   How much more then the hearts of the children of men!

12 A scorner loveth not to be reproved:
   He will not go unto the wise.

13 A merry heart maketh a cheerful countenance:
   But by sorrow of heart the spirit is broken.

14 The heart of him that hath understanding seeketh know-
      ledge:
   But the mouth of fools feedeth on folly.

¹ Or, *The grave*          ² Or, *Destruction*

**10.** *grievous correction.* 'Stern chastisement' is closer to the meaning of the original; it is to be taken as a parallel to 'shall die' in the
second line.

**11.** *Sheol and Abaddon.* See Excursus: V. Cf. Job xxvi. 6. If the
hidden and mysterious abodes of the dead lie open before God, how
much more the thoughts and motives of men, invisible as these are.
Probably the reference is not only to evil thoughts, see Jer. xvii. 10;
Ps. xxxviii. 9 (10 in Hebr.), cxxxix. 1–5.

**12.** *to be reproved.* Lit. '(one) to reprove him'; the verb is in the
inf. absolute (cf. the Sept.).

*He will not go* . . . It is better to follow the Sept. and read: 'He
walketh not with the wise', in the sense of having communication
with them; see also xiii. 20.

**13.** *merry.* The Hebr. word connotes as a rule the emotion of being
pleased; a man can be cheerful and happy without being what is
meant by the modern sense of 'merry'; as Toy well says, 'the word
"merry" now implies more of movement and utterance than is contained in the Hebrew word'. At the same time there are three or four
passages in which the word has the sense of boisterous merriment:
1 Kings iv. 20, 'Judah and Israel were many . . . eating, and drinking,
and making merry'; Eccles. viii. 15, ' . . . because a man hath no
better thing under the sun than to eat and to drink and to be merry';
x. 19, 'A feast is made for laughter, and wine maketh life merry',
and Isa. xxiv. 7, 'the new wine mourneth, the vine languisheth, and
the merry of heart do sigh'. In the last passage the phrase is the
same as in the verse before us (לֶב שָׂמֵחַ).

*broken is spirit.* Cf. xvii. 22, xviii. 14. Ben-Sira says similarly:

'A cheerful face is the sign of a happy heart,
   But sad eyes the sign of worry' (Ecclus. xiii. 26, Smend's emendation;
                         the Hebr. text is corrupt).

**14.** With the first line cf. xviii. 15ᵃ.

15 All the days of the afflicted are evil:
  But he that is of a cheerful heart *hath* a continual feast.
16 Better is little with the fear of the LORD,
  Than great treasure and trouble therewith.
17 Better is a ¹dinner of herbs where love is,
  Than a stalled ox and hatred therewith.
18 A wrathful man stirreth up contention:
  But he that is slow to anger appeaseth strife.

¹ Or, *portion*

*the mouth.* So the Hebr. marg. followed by the Sept. and other ancient Versions; the text reads 'face'.

*feedeth on.* The fig. use of the Hebr. word is rare, but not without precedent in the O.T., see e.g. Hos. xii. 2; Isa. xliv. 20, but it can also mean 'associates with' (cf. xxix. 3ᵃ), in the sense of being concerned with. The Sept. has 'knoweth', but this may be merely a misreading of the Hebr. (the two words are very similar). The R.V. is to be preferred in view of the 'mouth'.

**15.** *the afflicted.* Lit. 'one who is bowed down', whether through misfortune or ill-treatment, cf. Am. viii. 4. But the word is also used of one who voluntarily afflicts himself, or humbles himself in the sight of God, hence the rendering 'meek' in Ps. ix. 12, 13 (13, 14 in Hebr.), xxii. 26 (27 in Hebr.), xxxvii. 11, and often elsewhere; he is also spoken of as 'pious'. It is probably the former sense in which the word is used in the *v.* before us, as the pious would rejoice in the conviction of being right in the sight of God, however much outward circumstances might be against them, cf. e.g. Ps. lxviii. 10 (11 in Hebr.).

*feast.* Lit. 'a drinking feast', used here, of course, figuratively.

**16.** This *v.* is almost identical with xvi. 8, cf. xvii. 1; Ps. xxxvii. 16; Eccles. iv. 6. On the striking parallel to this in the *Teaching of Amen-em-ope* VI. ix. 5–8 see note on xvi. 8.

**17.** *a dinner.* Better 'a portion', cf. 2 Kgs. xxv. 30; Jer. lii. 34.

*a stalled ox.* Lit. 'a fattened ox', cf. 1 Kgs. iv. 23 (v. 3 in Hebr.), where the same word is used in reference to fatted fowls. On this *v.* see further the note on xvi. 8, 9.

**18.** *A wrathful man.* Lit. 'a man of heat', i.e. one whose fiery temper is soon roused, cf. xxviii. 25, xxix. 22.

*slow to anger.* Cf. xiv. 29. With the whole *v.* cf. xv. 1, and see also Ecclus. viii. 16, xxviii. 8–12. A parallel to the thoughts here expressed occurs in Amen-em-ope XXII. xxii. 20–xxiii. 7, where a man is admonished not to irritate one who is inclined to be quarrelsome, but to be still in his presence and thus gain him; the passage is too long to quote.

19 The way of the sluggard is as an hedge of thorns:
　　But the path of the upright is made an high way.
20 A wise son maketh a glad father:
　　But a foolish man despiseth his mother.
21 Folly is joy to him that is void of [1] wisdom:
　　But a man of understanding maketh straight his going.
22 Where there is no counsel, purposes are disappointed:
　　But in the multitude of counsellors they are established.

[1] Heb. *heart*.

**19.** *the sluggard.* A favourite word in *Proverbs*, but very rarely used elsewhere in the O.T.

*as an hedge of thorns.* Following the Sept., read 'is hedged up with a briar-hedge', cf. Hos. ii. 8, omitting 'as' which is not required, and does not occur in the second line.

*the upright.* The Sept. undoubtedly represents a more pointed antithesis in reading 'diligent', cf. x. 4, xii. 24, 27, xiii. 4, xxi. 5.

*is made an high way.* Lit. 'is a high way cast up', a figurative expression meaning that a way has been constructed and everything is cleared out of his path; cf. Isa. lvii. 14; Jer. xviii. 15.

**20.** *A wise son* ... The identical sentence occurs in x. 1ᵃ.

*But a foolish* ... A number of MSS., as also the Sept., read, 'And a foolish son', which may, as Toy suggests, be 'assimilation of the expression here to the more familiar form of x. 1'; but it is also possible that the whole verse was originally the same as in x. 1; the word for 'despiseth' (בּוֹזֶה), and that for 'heaviness' (תּוּגַת) being not very dissimilar, the former may be a corruption of the latter. The idea of despising a mother would have been very repugnant, and it is noteworthy that in both the other passages where the idea occurs there is every reason to believe that the text is corrupt (see notes on xxiii. 22, xxx. 17). In x. 1, moreover, the words 'maketh glad', and 'is the heaviness (better "grief")' offer a better antithesis than is the case in this verse.

**21.** *void of wisdom.* Lit. 'of heart', see Excursus VI. The antithesis between this and 'maketh straight his going' shows that 'folly' has an ethical as well as an intellectual connotation, being equivalent to sinfulness, cf. vi. 32.

*maketh straight his going.* For the ethical sense of this expression see iii. 6, ix. 15.

**22.** This verse offers a good example of the sane worldly wisdom which the Wisdom writers constantly inculcate; its content appears wholly unreligious, and its main application would naturally be in

23  A man hath joy in the answer of his mouth:
    And a word in due season, how good is it!
24  To the wise the way of life *goeth* upward,
    That he may depart from [1] Sheol beneath.

             [1] Or, *the grave*

the domain of purely secular affairs; but it was not therefore thought
to be outside the religious sphere by the sages. One of the peculiar
merits of the Hebrew Wisdom writers was their broad conception of
the divine interest in the affairs of men; and their untiring efforts to
bring home to the minds of men that since every form of wisdom is
the gift of God, so every exercise of it, in whatsoever sphere, is in
accordance with His will, and therefore in the nature of a religious
act. In the verse before us the pregnant Hebrew is lit. 'A frustrating
of plans (it is) where (there is) no counsel'; the last word implies
discussion on the part of others; the meaning thus is that a design
or purpose is doomed to failure from the outset unless the views of
others besides the originator are brought to bear upon it. And,
generally speaking, this is true, though in exceptional cases a far-
seeing genius may have a clearer perception of things and thus be
independent of counsellors.

**23.** *A man hath joy* . . . i.e. A man's own utterance gives him
satisfaction; but this is conditioned by what is said in the second
line, i.e. it must be appropriate to the occasion. This verse, therefore, is complementary to what is said in the preceding verse;
and the whole is a good illustration of the sense of proportion
among the Wisdom writers. To take the advice of others is no
hindrance to self-reliance; an enlightened balance of the two is
true wisdom.

**24.** As this verse stands it is difficult to get away from the impression that 'upward' and 'beneath' imply a somewhat advanced
conception of the hereafter; but *Proverbs*, and especially this earlier
collection, nowhere contains a developed conception of this kind;
hence the efforts of commentators to explain away what these expressions seem to imply. The probability, however, is that these two
words do not belong to the original text, but were added later when
more developed ideas regarding the future life had arisen. The two
lines are each quite long enough without these words, which do not
occur in the Sept., they could thus be read:

      *A path of life (there is) for the wise,*
      *That he may depart from Sheol.*

Cf. x. 17[a] and xiii. 14[b]. The verse means, then, that for the wise
man there is a path of life, i.e. worldly prosperity and well-being,
which leads away from death.

25 The LORD will root up the house of the proud:
But he will establish the border of the widow.

26 Evil devices are an abomination to the LORD:
But ¹ pleasant words *are* pure.

27 He that is greedy of gain troubleth his own house:
But he that hateth gifts shall live.

¹ Or, *the pure* speak *pleasant words*

**25.** *the proud.* Cf. xvi. 19; Job xl. 11, 12; Isa. ii. 12; Jer. xlviii. 29;
Ps. xciv. 2, cxl. 6; they are always represented as the enemies of God,
pride being regarded as a crime against religion.

*establish.* i.e. keep free from encroachment. It is, at first sight, not
quite easy to see how the Wisdom writers would represent to their
minds the way in which these acts of the Almighty were carried out.
The 'house' of the proud must be taken in the literal sense, not as
referring to his family or posterity, in view of the 'border of the
widow' in the parallel clause. So that the 'rooting up' (the Hebr.
means lit. 'to tear down') of the house must refer to the effect of
lightning or earthquake, which would be looked upon as the direct
intervention of God. As this would not affect the widow's plot, the
preservation of her border would likewise be thought of as due to
the divine will.

*the border of the widow.* Cf. Ps. lxviii. 5 (6 in Hebr.). See notes on
xxii. 28, xxiii. 10, 11.

**26.** *Evil devices.* Cf. vi. 18. The word for 'device' is used in a
good as well as in a bad sense.

*But pleasant* . . . The Hebr. has, 'But pure (are) pleasant words',
for which the Sept. reads, 'But the sayings of the pure are holy (or
"honourable", σεμναί).' The Hebr. text is corrupt, and probably
does not belong here at all as it is neither parallel nor antithetic to
the preceding line.

**27.** *greedy of gain.* The Hebr. word is used of making gain unjustly or by violence; the second clause shows that the reference here
is to unjust judges and unscrupulous officials, cf. Exod. xviii. 21;
Deut. xvi. 19, and *Teaching of Amen-em-ope* XX. xx. 21:

'Bring no man into misfortune in a court of justice,
And disturb not the just man.'

*But he that hateth* . . . The idea that the judge who took no bribes
enjoyed prosperity, while he who made unjust gain by receiving
them brought calamity upon himself, must often have been falsified
by the facts of experience, but this did not deter the Wisdom writers
from affirming that things happened which ideally ought to have
happened, but in fact often did not. They would doubtless have had
their reply if taxed with the contradiction between what they said,
and actual fact; but in aphorisms we cannot look for arguments.

28 The heart of the righteous studieth to answer:
   But the mouth of the wicked poureth out evil things.
29 The LORD is far from the wicked:
   But he heareth the prayer of the righteous.
30 The light of the eyes rejoiceth the heart:
   *And* good tidings make the bones fat.
31 The ear that hearkeneth to the reproof of life
   Shall abide among the wise.

**28.** From this *v.* to xvi. 9, inclusive, there is considerable variation in the order of the verses between the Sept. and the Hebr. text. This fact is of interest as suggesting that in some parts the order of the proverbs was not at one time as it is at present in the Hebr. text. The many isolated sayings were doubtless gathered from a variety of sources, and probably added to by sages at different times. Attempts at co-ordination of subject-matter are to be discerned here and there; but generally speaking the proverbs are thrown together in a very haphazard fashion in this collection. This is not the only place where the order of the verses is different in the Sept., and it is possible that where this occurs we may see the results of an attempted recension of the Hebrew text.

*studieth.* Cf. xxiv. 2. The Hebr. word means 'to muse', or 'think over'; the righteous, and therefore, wise man weighs his words before giving an answer.

*poureth out.* Cf. xv. 2. With this verse cf. Ecclus. v. 11–13 (Hebr.):

> 'Be swift in hearing
> But slow in replying.
> If thou canst, answer thy neighbour,
> But if not—hand on mouth.
> Glory and dishonour come through speaking,
> And the tongue of a man is his fall.'

**29.** *far from the wicked.* Because they, unlike the righteous, do not pray.

**30.** *The light of the eyes.* The parallel to this in the second clause is 'good tidings', so the words must refer to a joyful look in the eyes of one who brings good tidings, cf. xvi. 15.

*make the bones fat.* i.e. give marrow to the bones, a figurative expression for physical well-being, cf. xvi. 24, xvii. 22.

**31.** This *v.* is omitted altogether in the Sept.; it is one of the very few in this collection which consist of a single sentence.

*the reproof of life.* i.e. the reproof, or better, admonition, which is the means of giving life, in the sense of prosperity; this is defined as abiding among the wise, which gives the assurance that things will go well.

32 He that refuseth ¹correction despiseth his own soul:
   But he that hearkeneth to reproof getteth ²understanding.
33 The fear of the LORD is the instruction of wisdom;
   And before honour *goeth* humility.
**XVI.** 1 The ³preparations of the heart belong to man:
   But the answer of the tongue is from the LORD.

---

¹ Or, *instruction*          ² Heb. *heart.*          ³ Or, *plans*

**32.** *He that refuseth* ... For the converse of this see xix. 8, 'Despiseth his own soul' means that he is showing contempt for himself; the 'fool' would not realize this unless it were pointed out to him; so that the words are, in effect, an exhortation to self-respect.

*getteth understanding.* Lit. 'acquireth heart', a good illustration of the connotation of the word 'heart' in Hebrew.

**33.** *of wisdom.* We should say 'in wisdom'; divine and human wisdom are thus declared to belong together.

*And before honour* ... At first sight the connexion between the two lines does not strike one; but the point is that the fear of the Lord which necessitates humility must precede the honour which accrues to one who is instructed in wisdom; without the former the latter is impossible.


## CHAPTER XVI

*Vv.* 1–3 do not occur in the Sept., which has an entirely different text.

**1.** *The preparations of the heart.* i.e. What the mind, or understanding, plans.

*belong to man.* While this is the natural way of rendering the Hebrew, it would, however, be equally permissible to translate simply 'unto man'. The verse is usually interpreted either as the contrast between thought and its expression, or as meaning that man makes his plans, but that God has a different purpose in regard to them; in other words, man proposes but God disposes (on this see verse 9). The objection to both these interpretations is that where there is a question of thought and its utterance it is a very strange thing that the less important (i.e. the utterance) should be imputed to God's action; that is not the way of the Wisdom writers. There is no contrast here; but, as in verse 3, it is continuous: 'To man (are given) the processes (lit. arrangements) of the mind, also from Jahweh the reply of the tongue.' Parallel to this is Isa. l. 4: 'The Lord God hath given me the tongue of disciples (i.e. those who are taught) ... he wakeneth mine ear to hear ...'; in this passage both thought and its utterance are from God, and that seems to be what the verse before us really means.

2  All the ways of a man are clean in his own eyes:
      But the LORD weigheth the spirits.
3  [1]Commit thy works unto the LORD,
      And thy [2]thoughts shall be established.
4  The LORD hath made every thing for [3]its own end:
      Yea, even the wicked for the day of evil.

> [1] Heb. *Roll*.          [2] Or, *purposes*          [3] Or, *his own purpose*

**2.** *clean.* Originally a ritual term; here one may translate it
'righteous', as in xx. 11, where it is parallel to 'right'. The verb
means 'to be justified' in Ps. li. 4 (6 in Hebr.); Mic. vi. 11. With the
*v.* cf. iii. 7, xxi. 2.

*weigheth.* Or estimates, cf. xxi. 2, xxiv. 12, and 1 Sam. ii. 3. The
only other place in which the spirit is spoken of in connexion with
this word is Isa. xl. 13, 'Who shall weigh the spirit of Jahweh'.

**3.** *Commit.* The curious Hebr. expression 'roll' (see Ps. xxxvii. 5),
which is used of rolling a stone in xxvi. 27, contains the same idea as
that in Ps. lv. 22 (23 in Hebr.), 'Cast thy burden upon the Lord . . .'
(cf. 1 Pet. v. 7), though the word used is different.

*thoughts.* Read, with R.V. marg., 'purposes', cf. xix. 21; Isa. lv. 7,
lix. 7, &c. There is clearly a thought-connexion between this verse
and verse 1; just as utterance, which is the result of thought, comes
from God, like the thought itself; so deeds, which are likewise the
outcome of thought, must be referred to God, so that they are accomplished through Him. This verse would come more appropriately
immediately after *v.* 1. It is worth recording that the exhortation to
commit oneself or one's doings to God is not confined to Hebrew
teachers; in the Egyptian Wisdom book Amen-em-ope several times
has the words:

'Place thyself in the arms of God' (XXI. xxii. 7 and elsewhere).

**4.** This *v.*, which gives in a nutshell, as it were, the normal O.T.
doctrine of the all-embracing and purposive character of God's
creative work is elaborated by Ben-Sira:

> 'The works of God are all good,
>   And for every need He provided in its time.
> None may say: This is worse than that,
>   For everything in its own time is excellent . . .
> None may say: wherefore is this?
>   For all hath been chosen according to its purpose . . .
> The paths of the perfect are straight;
>   Even so are there stumbling-blocks to the presumptuous.
> Good things for the good hath He allotted from the beginning;
>   Even so (evil things) for the evil.   Good and evil.'
>                               (Ecclus. xxxix. 16–25, Hebr.)

The implication here that God created evil as well as good occasioned much difficulty to Ben-Sira, and he tried hard, but in vain,

5 Every one that is proud in heart is an abomination to the
    LORD:
    [1] *Though* hand *join* in hand, he shall not be unpunished.
6 By mercy and truth iniquity is [2] purged:
    And by the fear of the LORD men depart from evil.

      [1] See ch. xi. 21.            [2] Or, *atoned for*

to solve the difficulty.[1] The writer of *Proverbs*, however, was troubled
with no such difficulty; he simply believed, like other O.T. writers,
that all things were created by God for a special purpose; and since
there were wicked men in the world they too must have been created
by God for a special purpose, just as the poor as well as the rich were
created (xxii. 2, xxix. 13) by Him. The incongruity of a good God
creating an evil man did not strike Hebrew thinkers until a somewhat later time.

    **5.** *Every one* ... This clause is the same as xi. 20[a] excepting that
'proud' is substituted for 'perverse'. And the second clause is the
same as xi. 21[a] (see note there) excepting for the omission of 'the
wicked'. It is another illustration of the varying use made of existing
material. This is further illustrated by the insertion here in the Sept.
of two couplets, evidently of Hebrew origin, which seem to be
variants of other verses in our book. The first runs:

    'The beginning of a good way is to do right things,
      They are more acceptable to God than to offer sacrifices.'

This is very similar to the Hebrew of xxi. 3.

    'To do justice and judgement
      Is more acceptable to the Lord than sacrifice.'

The second is:

    'He that seeketh the Lord shall find knowledge with righteousness,
      And they that seek Him rightly shall find peace.'

These are variants of some saying such as that in xxviii. 5[b]: 'They
that seek the Lord understand all things.'

    **6.** *mercy and truth.* Cf. iii. 3, xiv. 22, xx. 28; Ps. lxxxv. 10 (11 in
Hebr.). The placing of this as a parallel to 'the fear of the Lord'
illustrates the influence of the teaching of the prophets on the Wisdom writers.

    *iniquity is purged.* Lit. 'covered', i.e. atoned for. This is an
illustration of the beginnings of what in later times developed into
the Jewish doctrine of works with its attendant danger of justification through works. In Ben-Sira we have some notable marks of the
development. Means of atonement mentioned by him are almsgiving
('Water will quench a flaming fire, and almsgiving will make atonement for sins', iii. 30, xxix. 8–13); honouring a father (iii. 3, 14);

      [1] See the present writer's *Ecclesiasticus* (Camb. Bible), pp. lvi–lxiv (1912).

7 When a man's ways please the LORD,
  He maketh even his enemies to be at peace with him.
8 Better is a little with righteousness
  Than great revenues with injustice.
9 A man's heart deviseth his way:
  But the LORD directeth his steps.

forgiving, ('Forgive thy neighbour the hurt that he hath done thee,
and thy sins shall be pardoned when thou prayest', xxviii. 2);
fasting (xxxiv. 26); death (xviii. 22). The full development was
reached in later Judaism, when the fulfilling of the works of the Law,
oral as well as written, justified a man in the sight of God. In this
verse the danger involved in this doctrine is avoided by what is said
in the second clause.

**7.** Cf. Jer. xxxix. 12.

**8, 9.** In these two verses, which are quite independent, we have
some striking parallels in Amen-em-ope's Wisdom book, though
they do not run consecutively as here. Regarding *v.* 8 it will be seen
that the Egyptian sage expresses an almost identical thought in
writing as follows:

> 'Better is poverty (being) in the hand of God,
>   Than wealth in the storehouse (i.e. without God).
>   Better is bread with a happy heart,
>   Than wealth with trouble.' (VI. ix. 5–8.)

The second couplet, with which cf. xv. 17, occurs again in XIII.
xvi. 11–14 after the words:

> 'Better is it to be praised as one loved of men
>   Than to have wealth in the storehouse.'

Another couplet which is perhaps a still closer parallel to the verse
before us is:

> 'Better is one bushel given thee by God,
>   Than five thousand unjustly gained.' (VI. viii. 19, 20.)

With this compare also Prov. xv. 16, 17, xvii. 1, xxviii. 6, 20; Ecclus.
v. 8, xl. 13, 14; see also Eccles. iv. 6.

Then as to *v.* 9, Amen-em-ope says:

> 'God is in His perfection,
>   Man is in his imperfection;
>   Different are the words which men speak,
>   Different is that which God does.' (XVIII. xix. 14–17.)

Prof. Ll. Griffith renders the second couplet:

> 'The words which men say are one thing,
>   The things which God doeth are another.'

The Egyptians, as Prof. Sethe points out, are fond of using the expression 'speaking' as denoting 'thinking', so that the proverb

K

10 [1]A divine sentence is in the lips of the king:
His mouth shall not transgress in judgement.
11 A just balance and scales are the LORD'S:
All the weights of the bag are his work.

[1] Heb. *Divination.*

means that what God brings about is different from what man thinks
or plans; it is, in fact, an ancient Egyptian form of our proverb:
'Man proposes, God disposes', which is precisely what is meant by
the words of the verse before us. The thought must have been
common property among the sages of the ancient east who observed
the facts of life, so that as far as this proverb is concerned there is
no need to postulate borrowing here. On the other hand, the large
amount of community of thought between *Proverbs* and Amen-em-
ope suggests a relationship of some kind between the writers of the
two books; on this see Excursus I; with the *v.* in *Proverbs* cf. xvi. 33.

**10–15.** These *vv.*, with the exception of *v.* 11, deal with the attributes of kings. What the writer says leads to the supposition that
he is referring to a good Judaean king, rather than to sovereigns in
general. For the bearing of this on the date of this collection, see
Intro. § III. The Wisdom writers have much to say about kings;
both in pre- and in post-exilic times the monarchical is their ideal
form of government; an evil prince will, it is recognized, do great
harm (see xxviii. 15, xxix. 12; Ecclus. x. 3), but in general it is
taught that a monarchy is beneficial for a people; it makes for order.
The chief function of a king is to give right judgement (see xxix. 4),
to uphold righteousness (see *v.* 12), and to protect the weak (see
xxix. 14). It is in the exercise of such-like things that the divine
character of the kingly office is shown forth. Throughout the ancient
east the king was regarded as in some sense a divine person; among
the Babylonians and Egyptians the king was called 'the son of God';
in early Israel the king was called an 'angel of God' (see 1 Sam. xxix.
9; 2 Sam. xiv. 17, xix. 27), and as late as the time of Ben-Sira he is
looked upon as God's representative (Ecclus. x. 5, Hebr.).

**10.** *A divine sentence.* The Hebr. word means 'divination', used
only here in a good sense, 'divine oracle'. Elsewhere the practice of
divination was connected with false gods, hence its prohibition in the
Law (Deut. xviii. 10, cf. 1 Sam. xv. 23; 2 Kings xvii. 17), and the
prophetical utterances against it (see e.g. Isa. ii. 6; Ezek. xiii. 6, 9,
&c.). Here, where it is of course used in a figurative sense, it points
to the belief that a righteous decision uttered by the king is divinely
inspired.

*shall not transgress* . . . In the Hebr. the sentence expresses simply
a statement of fact: 'his mouth doth not deal treacherously against
justice'; that is the natural outcome of the Godlike oracle in his lips.

**11.** *A just balance and scales.* This rendering is grammatically

12 It is an abomination to kings to commit wickedness:
   For the throne is established by righteousness.

incorrect; as the text stands 'just' can only refer to 'scales'; that
the adjective should only be applied to the scales is unnatural (cf. xx.
23ᵇ). But it is quite clear that the word for 'just' did not belong to
the original text, but was added by a scribe who did not see the point
of the proverb; besides which it overloads the sentence. If balance
and scales are the Lord's it goes without saying that they are just;
the question of their being just or otherwise only arises with man's
use of them; but that is precisely what is *not* in question here. The
whole point of the proverb is that Jahweh is the author and giver of
balance and scales and weights; they belong to Him, and come from
Him. Toy remarks, with perfect justice, that 'as the text stands,
God is the ordainer of the machinery of commercial transactions, a
statement which is not elsewhere found in the O.T.; He is said (as in
Lev. xix. 36, and elsewhere) to demand just weights, he is not said to
make or establish them'. Hence Toy and others would read instead
of 'are the Lord's', the words 'are the king's', meaning that 'the
system of weights and measures is ordained by the king as supreme
authority and fountain of justice; this emendation brings the couplet
into formal accord with the context'. Now the discovery of Amen-
em-ope's *Teaching* shows that the Hebrew text (apart from the word
'just') is correct as it stands; for the compiler of this collection
borrowed the idea contained in this couplet from Amen-em-ope, and
adapted it, not too skilfully, to his Hebrew readers. The idea, as Toy
says, is wholly foreign to Hebrew religious thought, but quite in
accord with that of the Egyptians; a fact which proves that the
Hebrew sage borrowed the idea. And that the *Teaching of Amen-em-
ope* was the source from which he borrowed will be seen from the
words of the Egyptian sage:

'Move not the scales, and falsify not the weights,
    And diminish not the parts of the corn-measure.' (XVI. xvii. 18, 19.)

He then goes on to say:

'The Ape (the symbol of the god Thoth) sitteth by the balance,
    His heart being the plummet.[1]
    Where is a god so great as Thoth,
    Who discovered these things and made them?'

We have thus an interesting illustration of the influence of Egyptian
religious thought on the Hebrew sage.

*All the weights* . . . Cf. Deut. xxv. 13; Mic. vi. 11; and with the *v.*
as a whole cf. xi. 1, xx. 10, 23.
**12.** Cf. xx. 28, xxv. 5, xxix. 14.

---

[1] The plummet of Egyptian balances was often made in the form of a heart
(Ranke).

13 Righteous lips are the delight of kings;
   And they love him that speaketh right.
14 The wrath of a king is *as* messengers of death:
   But a wise man will pacify it.
15 In the light of the king's countenance is life;
   And his favour is as a cloud of the latter rain.
16 How much better is it to get wisdom than gold!
   Yea, to get understanding is rather to be chosen than silver.
17 The high way of the upright is to depart from evil:

**13.** *of kings.* Read, with some Hebr. MSS. and the Sept., 'of a king'. *they love.* The Hebr. text has 'he loveth'. The reference is to courtiers.

**14.** For the thought of this verse, the writer appears to have made use of another foreign Wisdom book, this time a Babylonian one, *The Wisdom of Achikar* (Elephantiné papyrus), it is said here:

> 'In presence of a king, if (a thing) is commanded thee, it is a burning fire; hasten, do it; let it not kindle upon thee and hide (?) thy hands; for also the word of a king is with wrath of heart; why should wood strive with fire, flesh with a knife, a man with a king?' (103, 104, Cowley, *Jewish Documents of the time of Ezra*, pp. 81 f. (1919).)

The Hebrew sage has compressed this into a more pointed and terse form; but the Babylonian makes quite clear what is otherwise a little ambiguous in the Hebrew; for the second clause of the latter may mean either that it is the wise man who is able to pacify the king's wrath, by foresight or the like, or else that he is a wise man who seeks to pacify it rather than show a bold front and brave the royal displeasure; it is evidently this latter that, in the light of the Babylonian saying, is meant here. With the *v.* cf. xix. 12, xx. 2; Eccles. viii. 2–4.

**15.** *In the light.* For this figurative use of the word in the sense of pleasurable expression see Job xxix. 24; Ps. iv. 6 (7 in Hebr.), xliv. 3, (4 in Hebr.), lxxxix. 15 (16 in Hebr.).

*a cloud of the latter rain.* A pointed simile; the 'latter rain' (*malkôsh*), which fell at the end of March or beginning of April, was necessary for the ripening of the corn; the king's favour heralded prosperity to the fortunate courtier just as the 'cloud' announcing the coming rain which would impart fruitfulness to the sprouting corn.

**16.** *How much . . .* The Hebr. of this clause is lit.: 'To acquire wisdom—how much better than gold'; the 'how much' (מה), which probably crept in through the preceding word, ending with the same letters, makes bad syntax in the Hebr., and should be deleted; read: 'The getting of Wisdom is better than (the getting of) gold.' With the *v.* cf. iii. 14, viii. 10, 19, see also Ecclus. xl. 25, 26.

**17.** Upright men are those who pursue a path in life which leads

He that keepeth his way preserveth his soul.

18 Pride *goeth* before destruction,
And an haughty spirit before a fall.

19 Better it is to be of a lowly spirit with the [1]poor,
Than to divide the spoil with the proud.

20 He that [2]giveth heed unto [3]the word shall find good:
And whoso trusteth in the LORD, happy is he.

[1] Or, *meek*    [2] Or, *handleth a matter wisely*    [3] See ch. xiii. 13.

away from evil, so that this path is a highway, i.e. one in which there are no stumbling-blocks; as long as this path is followed men are safe. The Sept. paraphrases this verse, and adds two couplets which were evidently translated from Hebrew, and may in all likelihood be regarded as having belonged to some earlier form of our text. They run:

'He who receiveth instruction shall enjoy prosperity (lit. "shall be in good things"),
And he who regardeth reproofs shall become wise.
He who keepeth his ways preserveth his own soul,
And he who loveth his life guardeth (lit. "spareth") his mouth.'

With these lines cf. respectively vi. 23[b], xv. 5[b], the third line = the second of the *v.* before us, cf. xiii. 3[a].

**18.** The Wisdom writers, following herein again the teaching of the prophets, regarded pride, whether in the nation or in the individual, as a religious offence; this was ultimately grounded upon the conviction of the dependence of all men upon higher powers; so that pride was the result of arrogating to oneself something for which a man was indebted not to his own effort or energy so much as to the benevolence of the higher power. Hence pride meant an offence against God, by whom it would inevitably be punished. For the prophets' teaching on this see, e.g. Am. vi. 8, 13, 14; Isa. ii. 11–17, v. 15, 16; Jer. xiii. 15, 16; Zeph. iii. 11.

**19.** *the poor.* This is the proper antithesis to those who 'divide the spoil', i.e. the rich; not 'the meek', as in R.V. marg.

*divide the spoil.* This military term is used here because the reference is to that which has been taken by violence, either in a literal sense (cf. i. 13), or through the violation of justice, cf. Luke iii. 14.

**20.** *He that giveth heed* . . . i.e. he that dealeth wisely in regard to the word, in the sense of obeying it. The R.V. marg. 'handleth a matter wisely', might well be adopted were it not that 'word' is, in all probability, used in a special sense here, as in xiii. 3 (see note there), and this is borne out by the second line.

*good.* i.e. temporal prosperity.

*happy is he.* In the sense that he enjoys the good things of life; cf. xiv. 21, xxix. 18.

21 The wise in heart shall be called prudent:
   And the sweetness of the lips increaseth learning.
22 Understanding is a wellspring of life unto him that
      hath it:
   But the correction of fools is *their* folly.
23 The heart of the wise instructeth his mouth,
   And addeth learning to his lips.

**21.** *shall be called prudent.* i.e. is recognized as a man of experience. *the sweetness of the lips.* i.e. kindly speech, cf. *v.* 24 and xxiv. 26. *increaseth learning.* Better 'persuasion', see note on i. 5. In a different connexion Ben-Sira says:

> 'Kindly speech maketh many friends,
> And gracious lips (multiply) those that give greeting.'
> (Ecclus. vi. 5, Hebr.)

In the verse before us, this friendly and persuasive way of speaking is urged as in other passages (e.g. xv. 23; Ecclus. xx. 5–8), for two reasons: first, in reference to teachers, in order that they may by courteous speech and cogent argument commend the pursuit of Wisdom to others. But, in addition to this, such exhortations applied also to pupils. There were, of course, various offices in the Jewish State, the holders of which had in some sense to be orators, e.g. preachers, spiritual teachers, among them the sages themselves, pleaders in the courts of justice, politicians, and the like. The Wisdom teachers laid themselves out to train young men for callings such as these; their teaching is wonderfully apt and sane; among other things they say, for example, that friendly speech is like a tree of life, i.e. edifying through the excellent fruit which it bears; they lay stress on the art of apt repartee, and of opportuneness in reply, of not answering excitedly, and of knowing when it is wisest not to answer at all, of saying the right thing at the right moment; on the other hand, they warn against modes of speech which offend and which rankle in the heart of the hearer; and they speak in strong terms against evil speaking of every kind, swearing, slandering, false imputation, &c. (See, among other passages, xv. 4, 23, xvii. 28, xxiv. 26; Ecclus. xx. 5–8, xxiii. 9, 11; and on caution in speaking see note on xviii. 21.)

**22.** *a wellspring of life.* Cf. x. 11, xiii. 14, xiv. 27, xviii. 4, and for the converse xxv. 26.

*correction.* Here *mūsār* has the sense of chastisement. The punishment of the fool lies in his folly, because it hinders him from walking in the path of Wisdom.

**23.** *The heart of* . . . Toy gives the free, but excellent rendering: 'The wise man's mind makes his speech judicious, and gives persuasiveness to his discourse'; see further note on *v.* 21.

24 Pleasant words are *as* an honeycomb,
Sweet to the soul, and health to the bones.
25 [1]There is a way which [2]seemeth right unto a man,
But the end thereof are the ways of death.
26 The appetite of the labouring man laboureth for him;
For his mouth [3]craveth it of him.
27 A worthless man [4]deviseth mischief:
And in his lips there is as a scorching fire.

[1] See ch. xiv. 12.          [2] Or, *is straight before*
[3] Or, *urgeth him* thereto   [4] Heb. *diggeth.*

**24.** *honeycomb.* Cf. Ps. xix. 10 (11 in Hebr.), of 'the judgements of the Lord'.
*bones.* See note on iii. 8, and cf. xv. 30.
**25.** This *v.* occurs in xiv. 12, see notes there, and cf. Ecclus. xxi. 10.
**26.** *appetite.* Lit. 'soul', here in the sense of 'hunger'.
*craveth it of him.* Read as R.V. marg. This rather poor conception regarding labour reflects that of the O.T. generally. Manual labour is thought of as a curse in Gen. iii. 17–19. But though the Wisdom writers never speak of the dignity of labour, or of its being an honourable and noble thing in itself, they by no means depreciate it. They regard it mainly from a utilitarian point of view, valuable because it is a means of gain, cf. x. 4, 5, xii. 24, xiv. 23, xxviii. 19; Ecclus. x. 27.
**27.** This verse, together with the three which follow, deals with the subject of mischief-making, especially by means of the tongue, libel, false imputation, innuendo, and the like. There is much in the various sayings concerning this which is in the same vein as numerous passages in the Psalms; and in each there is, in all probability, to be seen the reflection of the state of bitter antagonism which existed in Jerusalem between the 'saints', as they are called in the Psalms, i.e. those godly ones who were loyal to the Law, and those who, under the influence of Greek culture, looked with derision upon the homely piety of the God-fearing. The state of enmity thus engendered within the circumscribed area of a relatively small city like Jerusalem formed precisely the kind of *milieu* in which the rank growths of slander, misrepresentation, unscrupulous innuendo, underhand intrigue, and petty spite would flourish. It was against the minority of the pious observers of divine precepts that activity of this kind was directed; a minority which included the *Chakamim*, or Wise men; and the many sayings which are directed against the 'worthless', and 'froward', and 'scorner', &c. represent the sages' rejoinder, whereby they both fought the adversary, and heartened the victims of malign slander. That this type of 'proverb' belongs, in the main, to the Greek period, does not necessarily mean that the whole of this collection is of that date; additions to collections of

28  A froward man scattereth abroad strife:
    And a whisperer [1]separateth chief friends.
29  A man of violence enticeth his neighbour,
    And leadeth him in a way that is not good.
30  [2]He that shutteth his eyes, *it is* to devise froward things:
    He that compresseth his lips bringeth evil to pass.

[1] Or, *alienateth his friend*     [2] Or, *He that shutteth his eyes to devise froward things, that compresseth his lips, bringeth &c.*

proverbs were, without any doubt, constantly made. On the general subject of *vv.* 27–30 see further xvi. 30, xviii. 8, xxv. 23, xxvi. 20, xxix. 5; Ecclus. v. 14–vi. 1, xxi. 28, xxvii. 22–24, xxviii. 13–23.

**27.** *A worthless man.* Lit. 'a man of Belial'; the expression means more than merely worthless, it expresses the state of one thoroughly degraded.

*deviseth.* Lit. 'diggeth', used figuratively of plotting, the idea being that of digging a pit into which the victim falls, cf. xxvi. 27; Ps. vii. 15 (16 in Hebr.), xciv. 13. The Sept. read 'furnace' (כּוּר) for 'diggeth' (כֹּרֶה); it is, therefore, possible that the line ran originally: 'A worthless man is a furnace of mischief'; this would accord well with the second line. Against this, however, is the fact that the word is never used in such a connexion, see xvii. 3, xxvii. 21.

**28.** *A froward man.* Lit. 'a man of perversities'; the root suggests the idea of turning things upside down; an extremely apt word in this connexion.

*a whisperer.* i. e. a backbiter; in this sense the Hebr. word occurs only here and in xviii. 8, xxvi. 20, 22.

*separateth chief friends.* i. e. causes a division between a man and his most intimate friend, cf. xvii. 9[b], and the *Proverbs of Achikar* ii. 52:

'My son, restrain a word in thy heart, and it shall be well with thee; because when thou hast exchanged thy word, thou hast lost thy friend.'

**29.** *enticeth* . . . Cf. i. 10–19.

*in a way that is not good.* Lit. 'in a way not good', cf. Ps. xxxvi. 4 (5 in Hebr.); Isa. lxv. 2.

**30.** *He that shutteth* . . . The R.V. rendering is based upon an emendation, probably correct, of the Hebr. text.

*compresseth his lips.* The same word is used in reference to the eyes in vi. 13, x. 10. In each case it refers to a facial expression more eloquent than words; it is the method of conveying to an observer the imputation of a lie or a slander without uttering it, and therefore the more dangerous because it may imply so much more than the facts warrant.

31 The hoary head is a crown of [1]glory,
  [2]It shall be found in the way of righteousness.
32 He that is slow to anger is better than the mighty;
  And he that ruleth his spirit than he that taketh a city.
33 The lot is cast into the lap;
  But the whole disposing thereof is of the LORD.
**XVII.** 1 Better is a dry morsel and quietness therewith,
  Than an house full of [3]feasting with strife.

[1] Or, *beauty*          [2] Or, If *it be found*
[3] Heb. *the sacrifices of strife.*

**31.** *The hoary head* . . . Cf. iii. 16.
*It shall be found* . . . i.e. it is to be acquired in the way of righteousness; in other words, old age is only to be attained by righteous living, cf. Ecclus. xxv. 4–6. It is assumed that the wicked do not reach old age, cf. ii. 22, xii. 7, and elsewhere; but Ben-Sira sees that this is not necessarily the case, for among three types of men which his soul hates is 'an old man who is an adulterer' (Ecclus. xxv. 2, Hebr.).
**32.** *He that is slow to anger.* See note on xiv. 29. Ben Zoma (end of 1st century A.D.) says, in *Pirqê 'Abôth* iv. 1: 'Who is mighty? He that masters his nature (*yetzer*), as it is said', then he quotes this verse.
*he that ruleth* . . . Cf. xxv. 28; Ecclus. xxii. 16.
**33.** *The lot is cast* . . . For the casting of lots see Judg. i. 3; 1 Sam. xiv. 41, 42; Isa. xxxiv. 17; Jon. i. 7. The Hebrew word for 'cast' (lit. 'hurl') is never used elsewhere in this connexion.
*the lap.* See note on vi. 27. The reference is to the fold in the garment at the breast in which things were carried. The two lots ('Aye' and 'Nay') were thrown into this kind of pocket, and one was drawn out; the divine will was believed to be indicated by whichever was drawn out. Cf. also *Urim* and *Thummim*, Num. xxvii. 21.
*the whole disposing thereof.* i.e. the decision indicated is entirely Jahweh's doing.

## CHAPTER XVII

**1.** *feasting with strife.* Lit. 'sacrifices of strife'. The reference is to the feast which accompanied one of the private sacrifices. The verse is a variation of xv. 17, but the same in meaning. Originally the word here used (*zebach*) was the ordinary and most ancient form of sacrifice, the essential part of which was a feast at which the flesh of the victim was eaten by the worshippers. In later days (post-biblical) the word came to mean a feast in the ordinary sense. In the Talmud the verb is used of giving a feast (see Jastrow, *Talmud Dictionary*, s.v.). With this verse cf. the note on xvi. 8.

2 A servant that dealeth wisely shall have rule over a son that
   ¹ causeth shame,
   And shall have part in the inheritance among the brethren.
3 The fining pot is for silver, and the furnace for gold:
   But the LORD trieth the hearts.
4 An evil-doer giveth heed to wicked lips;
   *And* ² a liar giveth ear to a mischievous tongue.

   ¹ Or, *doeth shamefully*        ² Heb. *falsehood.*

**2.** *A servant that dealeth wisely* . . . The position here represented
is that of a household in which the master raises a slave to a position
of a son of the house; so that slave and son virtually change places;
the twofold reason being the wise dealing of the slave and the dis-
graceful behaviour of the son. In the house of a wealthy man, such
as is here contemplated, the service was carried out by different
classes of servants. There were free men who offered their labour of
various kinds, mostly on the land owned by the householder; then
there were slaves both men and women, who did duty within the
house; these were either bought by the householder, and were often
foreigners, or else Jewish men and women who in one way or another
had become indebted to the householder and had sold themselves to
him. Ben-Sira refers to these different kinds of servants in Ecclus.
vii. 20, 21 (Hebr.):

> 'Maltreat not a slave who serveth faithfully,
> Nor an hireling who spendeth himself (for thee).
> A wise slave love as thine own self,
> And deny him not his freedom.'

It is this last who is the subject of the verse before us. As a master
had absolute power over his children as well as over his slaves he
could raise one of the latter to the highest position in his house, give
him his freedom, and adopt him as his own son.

   *among the brethren.* As the wise slave has been raised to the status
of a son of the house the other sons are spoken of as his brethren.
With the verse in general cf. xxvii. 18; Eccles. x. 7; Ecclus. x. 25.

   **3.** *The fining pot* . . . This line occurs again in xxvii. 21ᵃ.
   *But the Lord* . . . Cf. xxi. 2ᵇ, xxiv. 12ᵇ. For the figurative use of
refining see Isa. xlviii. 10; Ps. lxvi. 10; Zech. xiii. 9.

   **4.** And *a liar.* Lit. 'falsehood' (שֶׁקֶר), but as the first line begins
with a participle (in the Hebr.), it is better, with a slight emendation,
to read a participle here too (מְשַׁקֵּר), as in the Sept., 'He that dealeth
falsely'.

   *mischievous.* The Hebr. word is stronger than this; it means lit.
'a chasm', and is used figuratively for 'destruction' or 'calamity', as
in xix. 13, cf. Job vi. 2. In other connexions the word means 'desire'
(cf. x. 3, xi. 6); here it is best rendered 'destructive'.

5 Whoso mocketh the poor reproacheth his Maker:
  *And* he that is glad at calamity shall not be unpunished.
6 Children's children are the crown of old men;
  And the glory of children are their fathers.
7 [1]Excellent speech becometh not a fool:
  Much less do lying lips a prince.

                    [1] Or, *Arrogant*

**5.** *Whoso mocketh . . .* This is a variation of xiv. 31ᵃ. For 'mocketh'
or 'derideth' cf. i. 26ᵇ.

*reproacheth . . .* According to the belief of the times, the poor
existed because this was God's will, so that to deride what was in
accordance with the divine purpose was to reproach God Himself;
cf. the quotation of Ben-Sira below.

*at calamity.* This is a parallel to 'the poor'; but it is not in accordance with the writer's usage to equate an abstract noun with a
concrete one; hence, it is better to emend the text, and for 'at
calamity' (לְאֵיד) to read 'at him that is perishing' (לְאֹבֵד), following
the Sept. (τῷ ἀπολλυμένῳ). With this *v.* cf. Ecclus. vii. 11 (Hebr.):

  'Mock not at him who is in bitterness of spirit;
    Remember there is One Who exalteth and humbleth.'

Amen-em-ope's words are also worth noting in this connexion:

  'Laugh not at a blind man, and mock not at a dwarf,
    And harm not him that is a cripple.
  Mock not at a man who is in the hand of God,
    And be not wrath (?) with him when he hath transgressed.'

                                        (XXV. xxiv. 9–12.)

The meaning of the last line is uncertain; Egyptologists differ in
their rendering of it.

**6.** Cf. xiii. 22, xx. 7; Ecclus. iii. 1–16, xxv. 7ᶜ.

*the glory.* The parallel 'crown', demands the rendering 'pride', or
'glorying', cf. xix. 11, xx. 29.

**7.** *Excellent speech.* The Hebr. reads lit. 'lip of excess', i.e. the
mouth that pours forth more words than is necessary; this is quite
inappropriate in the present context, and it offers neither a parallel
nor an antithesis to the next line; moreover, it is a most unusual
phrase and occurs nowhere else. It is better to emend the text so as
to read 'a lip of uprightness' (יֹשֶׁר instead of יֶתֶר, cf. Sept. πιστά),
i.e. upright or straightforward lips, in antithesis to 'lying lips' in the
next line. Cf. *v.* 26, xii. 22.

*a fool.* Hebr. *nabal*, rarely used for 'fool' (only elsewhere in Prov.
in xvii. 21, xxx. 22); the word means one who is churlish, ignoble,
and it is used of the man who is wanting in religious and ethical
perception, cf. 1 Sam. xxv. 25.

*prince.* As contrasted with *nabal*, the word must mean a man of

8 A gift is *as* a precious stone in the eyes of him that hath it:
    Whithersoever [1]it turneth, [1]it [2]prospereth.
9 He that covereth a transgression seeketh love:
    But he that harpeth on a matter [3]separateth chief friends.
10 A rebuke entereth deeper into one that hath understanding
    Than an hundred stripes into a fool.
11 [4]An evil man seeketh only rebellion;
    Therefore a cruel messenger shall be sent against him.
12 Let a bear robbed of her whelps meet a man,
    Rather than a fool in his folly.

[1] Or, *he*      [2] Or, *dealeth wisely*      [3] See ch. xvi. 28.
    [4] Or, *A rebellious man* (Heb. *Rebellion*) *seeketh only evil*

noble character, but the usual meaning is prince, cf. *v.* 26, viii. 16,
xxv. 7.

**8.** *gift.* i. e. bribe. The verse is somewhat ambiguous, but the
meaning seems to be that a bribe is, in the eyes of him who gives it,
a thing of great value, like a precious stone, because wherever he
turns, i. e. whatever he undertakes, he is able, by means of it, to gain
his end, i. e. prosper. Cf. xviii. 16.

**9.** *He that covereth* . . . i.e. He who takes no notice of wrong done
to him or said about him promotes an atmosphere of kindliness, cf.
1 Cor. xiii. 7, πάντα στέγει.

*harpeth.* Lit. 'repeateth', but 'harpeth' is precisely what is meant.
*separateth chief friends.* See note on xvi. 28. With the verse cf. x. 12.

**10.** This saying well illustrates how the efforts of the Wisdom
writers were concentrated on the appeal to the inner man, i.e. on the
formation of character, the most essential part of education. Here
the writer states the widely recognized fact of the sensitiveness, in
the best sense, of a refined and exalted character in contrast to the
thick-skinned unimpressionableness of a 'fool'. The 'hundred stripes'
are, of course, not meant to be taken literally; forty was the maxi-
mum, see Deut. xxv. 3.

**11.** *An evil man* . . . On the basis of the ancient versions read:
'A rebellious man (lit. a man of rebellion) seeketh evil.'

*Therefore a cruel* . . . Cf. xvi. 14. The Hebr. text reads: וּמַלְאָךְ
אַכְזָרִי יְשֻׁלַּח־בּוֹ, for which Dyserinck ingeniously suggests: וּמֶלֶךְ אַכְזָרִי
יְשַׁלַּח־בּוֹ, 'And the king will send a fierce one against him' (the Sept.
has the verb in the active); the emendation is very slight, and, upon
the whole, gives a better text.

*cruel.* Cf. v. 9, xi. 17, xii. 10; the word is used both as a noun and
as an adjective.

**12.** *Let a bear* . . . To avoid the ambiguity of the proverb owing
to its pregnant form it is better to say, 'Let a bear robbed of her

13 Whoso rewardeth evil for good,
    Evil shall not depart from his house.

14 The beginning of strife is *as* when one letteth out water:
    Therefore leave off contention, before there be quarrelling.

15 He that justifieth the wicked, and he that condemneth the
        righteous,
    Both of them alike are an abomination to the LORD.

whelps, rather than a fool in his folly, meet a man'. The quaintness
of the saying suggests antiquity. Cf. 2 Sam. xvii. 8; Hos. xiii. 8;
Am. v. 19.

**13.** Cf. 1 Sam. xxv. 21, and see note on xx. 22. On the doctrine of
retribution in the Wisdom Literature see Excursus IV.

**14.** *The beginning of strife* . . . Hebr. lit.: 'He that setteth free
(or letteth out) water, (it is) the beginning of strife'; with a little
reading-in sense can be made of this. But the Hebr. text is doubtful;
the word for 'when one letteth out' is never used in this sense either
in biblical or post-biblical Hebrew; Ben-Sira uses it once (Ecclus.
xxxii. (xxxv.) 11) of departing from a banquet. The Sept. has no
equivalent for it, but reads, lit., 'he that giveth authority'; the Sept.,
moreover, read 'words' for 'water' (מִלִּים for מַיִם), which certainly
gives better sense. It is very difficult to say what stood originally in
the text for the word 'he that letteth out' (פּוֹטֵר). If we read 'words',
then some such expression as 'in the multitude' (בְּרֹב, x. 19) might
have stood there, viz. 'in a multitude of words is the beginning of
strife'. This would offer a word-play with the word for 'quarrelling'
(רִיב) in the next line. In Ecclus. xx. 8 we have, 'he that is abundant
in word is abhorred', but unfortunately the Hebrew of this verse is
not extant.

*Therefore leave off* . . . The Hebr. permits the rendering: 'And
before quarrelling breaks out, cease (*sc.* words).' The verse would
then mean that since strife arises through much talking, stop arguing
before a quarrel begins. There is, in some respects, a parallel to this
in Amen-em-ope, he says in III. v. 10–12:

> 'Do not join wrangling with the hot-mouthed,
> Nor goad him with words;
> Pause before an intruder (or adversary),
> And give way unto him that attacketh.'

**15.** *justifieth . . . condemneth.* Both judicial terms; the reference
is to an unjust judge. There is a couplet in Amen-em-ope which is
at least reminiscent of this verse, but experts are a little uncertain
as to its exact meaning; it is in XX. xx. 21, 22:

> 'Do not pervert (?) a man in the law-court,
> Nor disturb the just man (?).'

This may quite conceivably represent the justifying of the wicked

16 Wherefore is there a price in the hand of a fool to buy wisdom,
   Seeing he hath no ¹understanding?
17 A friend loveth at all times,
   And ²a brother is born for adversity.

   ¹ Heb. *heart*.                    ² Or, *is born as a brother*

and condemning the righteous in the verse before us. A few lines
further on Amen-em-ope says:

> 'Justice is a great gift of God,
>   He will give it to whom He will.'

It is noticeable that both the Egyptian and the Hebrew sage recognize that God is not indifferent to the proceedings in a court of
justice. With the general sense of the verse before us cf. xv. 27,
xxiv. 24; Deut. xxv. 1; Isa. v. 23.

**16.** *a price*. This seems to imply that a fee was paid by those who
went to the sages for instruction; Ben-Sira, however, says he makes
no charge for attendance at his *Yeshibah*, i.e. academy of learning;
in the autobiographical conclusion to his book he says:

> 'My mouth I open and speak of her,
>   Get wisdom for yourselves without money.' (Ecclus. li. 25, Hebr.)

**17.** *A friend loveth* . . . The subject of friendship is often referred
to by the Wisdom writers; their insight and their sympathy with
young men caused them to see the intense importance of true friend-
ships being formed in youth. They estimate the possession of friendship as so precious that every right-minded youth should seek to
gain it and treasure it. They teach that the choice of a friend demands discernment and care if friendship is to be lasting and secure,
for it will be severely tested by many things in life, therefore he who
would seek a friend must not be carried away by any passing and
attractive acquaintance; he must make sure by testing and by proof
that his choice of a friend shall be justified. To place one's trust in
one who is only a friend in name brings disappointment and dis-
illusionment. He who is conversant with men and things will have
many acquaintances with whom he is on friendly footings, but few
to whom he will open his heart and in whom he will repose confidence; this must be reserved for the few who have the qualities for
forming true friendship. Old friends are better than new (Ecclus. ix.
10). The Wisdom writers sometimes raise the question as to whether
the tie of friendship or that of blood-relationship, i.e. a brother, is
the more steadfast; upon the whole, they regard the former as, at
any rate, the stronger. In *Proverbs*, e.g. the brotherly relationship
is not highly estimated in two passages (xviii. 19, xix. 7), and in
xviii. 24, xxvii. 10 a friend is thought to be more reliable than a
brother; on the other hand, Ben-Sira says:

> 'Change not a friend for money,
>   Nor a natural brother for gold of Ophir' (Ecclus. vii. 18);

18 A man void of [1]understanding striketh hands,
   And becometh surety in the presence of his neighbour.

19 [2]He loveth transgression that loveth strife:
   He that raiseth high his gate seeketh destruction.

20 He that hath a froward heart findeth no good:
   And he that hath a perverse tongue falleth into [3]mischief.

21 He that begetteth a fool *doeth it* to his sorrow:
   And the father of a fool hath no joy.

22 A merry heart [4]is a good medicine:
   But a broken spirit drieth up the bones.

---

[1] Heb. *heart.*     [2] Or, *He that loveth transgression loveth strife*
[3] Or, *calamity*     [4] Heb. *causeth good healing.*

so that he evidently thought of both as equally valuable. On the
subject in general see further xvii. 9, xx. 6, xxvii. 5, 6, 9, 10, 17, 19;
Ecclus. vi. 5–17, xii. 8–18, xix. 13–17, xxii. 19–26, xxxvii. 1–6.

**18.** See note on vi. 1–5.

*striketh hands.* Cf. vi. 1, xi. 15.

**19.** *transgression.* Some commentators would emend the Hebr. by
reading 'wounds' (פֶּצַע for פֶּשַׁע 'transgression'), the word occurs in
xx. 30, xxiii. 29, xxvii. 6. This is to be preferred as it gives more
point to the saying; a quarrelsome person soon comes to blows.

*his gate.* This does not offer the parallelism with the first line
which one is led to expect; nor is any such custom as raising high a
gate ever referred to or known of. Frankenberg would read 'mouth'
(פִּי) for the word which stands in the text (פִּתְחוֹ); but it is just
possible that this word itself may mean 'mouth'; for it is used of the
opening of the mouth in Ps. cxix. 130, and in the Targums, so that
by 'his opening' as the word here might be translated, one could
understand 'his mouth'. The meaning of the verse would then be
that just as he who is fond of quarrelling will get wounds, so he who
is proud or noisy in his speech will bring destruction upon himself.
With the verse cf. xi. 2, xvi. 18, xviii. 12, xx. 3, xxix. 22, 23.

**20.** A reiteration of the theme so often dealt with in *Proverbs* that
evil, whether of the inward thought or of the spoken word, results in
adverse conditions of life, cf. ii. 12, viii. 13, x. 31, xi. 20, xiii. 17,
xvi. 20.

**21.** *to his sorrow.* See note on x. 1. Cf. Ecclus. xxii. 3: 'Shame
(there is) to a father that begetteth an uninstructed (son).'

**22.** *A merry heart* . . . Cf. xv. 13[a]. The Hebr. word translated
'medicine' (גֵּהָה) never occurs elsewhere; some commentators would
emend it so as to read 'body' (גְּוִיָה), 'maketh a good (or sound)
body'; so the Syr. and Targum; this word, however, is used of a
corpse, though here and there of a living human body (Ezek. i. 11, 23).

*bones.* See note on iii. 8.

23 A wicked man taketh a gift out of the bosom,
   To pervert the ways of judgement.

24 Wisdom is before the face of him that hath understanding:
   But the eyes of a fool are in the ends of the earth.

25 A foolish son is a grief to his father,
   And bitterness to her that bare him.

26 Also to [1]punish the righteous is not good,
   *Nor* to smite the noble for *their* uprightness.

27 [2]He that spareth his words hath knowledge:
   And he that is of a cool spirit is a man of understanding.

[1] Or, *fine*    [2] Or, *He that hath knowledge spareth his words: and a man of understanding is of a cool spirit*

**23.** *taketh a gift.* i. e. accepts a bribe.

*out of the bosom.* i. e. from some one, cf. xxi. 14, and see notes on vi. 27, xvi. 33.

*the ways of judgement.* i. e. the course of justice, cf. xviii. 5.

**24.** *Wisdom is before* . . . i. e. the man of understanding concentrates his attention on wisdom, whereas the fool is incapable of fixing his mind on anything; his thoughts wander, he is for ever star-gazing.

**25.** See the similar sayings in verse 21, x. 1, xv. 20.

*bitterness.* The form of the Hebr. word is curious (מֶמֶר), it does not occur elsewhere.

**26.** *Also.* This reads as though the verse were the continuation of something which preceded, possibly verse 23, in which case 'moreover' would be a better rendering; but in the present position of the verse 'also' is better omitted.

*punish.* Read, with R.V. marg., 'fine'; the word occurs again in xxi. 11, xxii. 3, xxvii. 12; cf. Am. ii. 8.

*Nor to smite* . . . The Hebr. of this line is, lit.: 'To smite princes for uprightness'; the text is obviously out of order. The word for 'smite' is often used for 'chastise'; and 'noble', as parallel to 'the righteous' in the first line, must be understood in the sense of the morally noble (cf. the antithesis between 'fool' and 'noble' in verse 7); and finally, 'for their uprightness' (עַל־יֹשֶׁר) may, on the basis of the Sept., be emended to read '(is) not fitting' (בַּל יָשָׁר), so Grätz. The line would then run: 'To scourge the upright is not seemly'; this affords a proper parallel to the first line, fining and scourging were the two most common forms of punishment. Cf. xviii. 5.

**27.** *He that spareth* . . . Cf. xiii. 3, x. 19. Ben-Sira says: 'He that hateth talk hath the less malice' (Ecclus. xix. 6ᵇ).

*hath knowledge.* Lit. 'he that knoweth knowledge', he that is conversant with knowledge.

*of a cool spirit.* This is preferable to the other reading 'precious of

28 Even a fool, when he holdeth his peace, is counted wise:
   [1] When he shutteth his lips, he is *esteemed as* prudent.
**XVIII.** 1 He that separateth himself seeketh *his own* desire,
   And [2] rageth against all sound wisdom.
 2 A fool hath no delight in understanding,
   But only that his heart may reveal itself.

   [1] Or, *He that shutteth his lips is &c.*        [2] Or, *quarrelleth with*

spirit'; the word occurs again in reference to water in xxv. 25. The
verse can also be rendered as in R.V. marg.

**28.** *Even.* Omit, with the Sept. and Syr. With this *v.* compare
Ben-Sira:

> 'One keepeth silence and is accounted wise,
> And another is despised for his much talking;
> One keepeth silence, having nought to say,
> And another keepeth silence, for he seeth it is a time for silence.'
>
> (Ecclus. xix. 5, 6 Hebr.)

### Chapter XVIII

**1.** As the text of this difficult verse stands, the meaning would
seem to be that the morose, self-centred man, who shuns the company of his fellows, shows himself to be the enemy of sound wisdom.
But the Hebr. text is not above suspicion, and the Sept. differs from
it in some particulars.

*He that separateth himself.* The Hebr. word is not used in this way;
it takes the preposition 'from' after it, e.g. xix. 4, and Judg. iv. 11.
'Now Heber the Kenite had *severed himself* from the Kenites.' The
Sept. has: 'A man desiring to be separated from friends.'

*seeketh* his own *desire.* Hebr. simply 'seeketh desire' (תַּאֲוָה); the
Sept. has 'seeketh motives' (= תְּאֵנָה), i.e. for being separated.
Whether the Greek translator read a different text, or was merely
trying to make sense of the Hebrew, cannot be said with certainty;
but the Hebrew word for 'motive' only occurs twice in the O.T.
(Judg. xiv. 4; Jer. ii. 24), and in neither case does it mean 'motive'
or 'pretext' in the sense here required.

*And rageth against* . . . There is no 'and' in the Hebr., it has
'against all wisdom he breaketh out' (cf. xx. 3, where the same word
is rendered 'will be quarrelling', see also xvii. 14). The Sept. has,
'and he will at all times be reproached', which clearly presupposes a
different text. It will be seen that the text offers grave difficulties;
and one feels with Toy that 'it seems impossible to get a satisfactory
sense from the Hebrew, and no good emendation presents itself'.

**2.** *may reveal itself.* The fool is one who is never tired of displaying
his inanity; to him this is wisdom, cf. xii. 23[b], xv. 2[b]. With the first
line of this *v.* cf. the *Teaching of Ptah-hotep* (last section, Erman,
*op. cit.*, p. 97, where it is said of the ignorant man who will not

L

3 When the wicked cometh, there cometh also contempt,
  And with ignominy *cometh* reproach.
4 The words of a man's mouth are *as* deep waters;
  [1] The wellspring of wisdom is *as* a flowing brook.
5 To accept the person of the wicked is not good,
  [2] *Nor* to turn aside the righteous in judgement.

[1] Or, *A flowing brook, a wellspring of wisdom*      [2] Or, *So as to turn aside*

hearken that *he regardeth wisdom as ignorance, and what is excel-lent as evil. He doeth that which is blameworthy, and daily he is reproached* . . .

**3.** *When the wicked cometh.* An abstract noun would accord better with the second clause, and, on the pattern of xi. 2, some com-mentators would read 'wickedness', which involves only a vowel-change in the Hebrew; this is preferable, the meaning of the line being that the presence of wickedness brings with it contempt for him who is its advocate. The emendation does not alter the meaning, but it improves the form.

*ignominy.* i.e. a passive conception, the state in which a man is held in dishonour, while reproach, or scorn, is the active conception of the feeling which others have for him.

**4.** *The words of* . . . As Toy rightly says, 'this unrestricted state-ment does not accord with the thought of *Proverbs*, in which no such excellence is ascribed to men in general'; one expects the type of man to be specified of whom such a thing can be said; in xx. 5, where the phrase 'deep water' also occurs, the sense of the verse shows that the reference is to the wise man; and doubtless that is the type which is here intended; hence it is best to emend the text so as to read: 'The words of the wise are deep waters' (דִּבְרֵי חֲכָמִים as in i. 6, xxii. 17), in the sense that they are full of content; they contain deep thoughts, as we might say.

*The wellspring of wisdom* . . . The Hebrew does not begin a new sentence with this line, but makes it a continuation of the first line, as in the previous verse, and elsewhere, see R.V. marg. For 'wisdom' some Hebrew MSS. and the Sept. read 'life' (cf. x. 11[a], xiii. 14[a]), and this perhaps is to be preferred; the whole verse would then run: 'The words of the wise man are deep waters, a flowing brook, a well of life.' That 'words' is here used as synonymous with thoughts is interesting, for this is in all likelihood a mark of Egyptian influence; Sethe shows that the Egyptians were fond of using 'speaking' for 'thinking',[1] so that in this verse as in so many others in *Proverbs* Egyptian influence must be discerned; see further note on xvi. 9.

**5.** *To accept the person of the wicked.* Hebr. lit.: 'To lift up the face

---

[1] 'Der Mensch denkt, Gott lenkt bei den alten Ägyptern', in *Nachrichten der Gesellschaft der Wissenschaften zu Göttingen, Philologisch-historische Klasse*, pp. 141 ff. (1926).

6 A fool's lips [1]enter into contention,
  And his mouth calleth for stripes.
7 A fool's mouth is his destruction,
  And his lips are the snare of his soul.
8 The words of a whisperer are as dainty morsels,
  And they go down into the [2]innermost parts of the belly.

---

[1] Or, *bring contention*     [2] Heb. *chambers.*

---

of the wicked (man)'; the reference is, as in xvii. 26, to proceedings in
a law-court; for the phrase, see e.g. Lev. xix. 15; see note on xvii. 15.

Nor *to turn aside* . . . The Hebr. reads more naturally as rendered
in the R.V. marg.

*in judgement.* i.e. in the administration of justice.

**6.** *enter.* The emendation implied by the R.V. marg. should undoubtedly be adopted, 'bring', or 'lead' into contention. Cf. xvii.
14, 19, xix. 29, xx. 3.

**7.** Cf. xii. 13. Verses 6, 7, which belong together, are closely
paralleled in thought by Amen-em-ope's words in his *Teaching* (IX.
xii. 3–6), where the 'passionate man' is spoken of:

> 'He is ruined and he is built up by his tongue,[1]
> Yet he maketh an ugly (?)[2] speech;
> He maketh an answer worthy of stripes,
> For its burden[3] is of evil.'

A careful comparison between these words and the two *vv.* before us
will reveal a striking identity of thought.

**8.** This verse occurs again in xxvi. 22.

*whisperer.* See note on xvi. 28.

*dainty morsels.* Lit. 'things greedily swallowed', but the meaning
of the word is uncertain; it occurs only here and in xxvi. 22. In the
Midrash *Sifre*, where reference is made to this verse, the word is
explained as meaning 'hypocritical sympathizers' (Jastrow, *op. cit.*,
s.v.); in this case the verse would mean that the words of a slanderer
whispered into the ear of a man profess sympathy with him, as
though he were the victim of some evil-disposed person, while their
real object is to create mischief; such words sink into the heart of a
man because they are apparently spoken by one who has a fellow-
feeling for him. The sage intends it to be understood that this is the
vilest form of slander, because it purports to be prompted by a good
motive, whereas it is in reality the outcome of the worst.

*the innermost parts of the belly.* Hebr. 'the chambers of . . .'; the
word for 'chamber', though common enough, is never used in this
figurative sense excepting in this verse (= xxvi. 22), and in xx. 27, 30.
We have just seen in *vv.* 6, 7 a striking identity of thought with a

---

[1] So Griffith; others render: 'He destroyeth and buildeth up by his tongue.'
[2] The word for 'ugly' may mean 'slanderous' (Erman).
[3] Or 'result' (Lange).

9 He also that is slack in his work
  Is brother to him that is a destroyer.
10 The name of the LORD is a strong tower:
  The righteous runneth into it, and [1]is safe.
11 The rich man's wealth is his strong city,
  And as an high wall in his own imagination.

---

[1] Heb. *is set on high*.

passage from Amen-em-ope; this fact supports the belief that in this verse the un-Hebraic expression quoted came from him, for he uses the more or less identical phrase 'casket of thy belly'.

**9.** *also*. Omit with the Sept., the verse is in no way connected with what precedes; possibly this may have been so at one time, which would explain the presence of the copulative adverb; the word for 'also' begins the *v*. in the Hebrew.

*to him that is a destroyer*. Lit. 'master (or possessor) of destruction'. The sage teaches that he who leaves a work undone is next of kin to him who destroys it. With this strong condemnation of sloth cf. Ecclus. xxii. 1, 2; in our book cf. also vi. 6–11, x. 4, xii. 24, xv. 19, xx. 4, 13, xxi. 25, xxiv. 30–34, xxvi. 13–16.

**10.** *The name of the Lord*. This otherwise frequently used phrase in the O.T. occurs here only in *Proverbs*; but in xxx. 9 there is 'the name of my God.' This does not, however, mean that the Wisdom teachers were in any way wanting in religious fervour; over and over again to fear the Lord and rely upon Him is the burden of their exhortations; see, among other passages, iii. 5–8, xiv. 2, xvi. 9, 33, xxi. 31, xxii. 4, xxix. 25, 26; Ecclus. x. 19–24, &c.

*a strong tower*. Cf. Ps. lxi. 3 (4 in Hebr.).

*is safe*. See R.V. marg. The thought is that of a man fleeing from an enemy and taking refuge in a high tower, such as often existed in the vicinity of cities.

**11.** This verse is not intended to contrast the rich man's trust in his wealth with a man's trust in God; it is an isolated saying unconnected with the preceding one, and simply expresses the thought of x. 15[a] (see note on this).

*in his own imagination*. Read, on the basis of the Sept. and other Versions, 'is his hedge', in reference to his wealth which is his protection (reading מְשׂוּכָתוֹ, see Isa. v. 5, for בְּמַשְׂפִּיתוֹ, 'in his imagination'), meaning that that which is his security (*sc*. his wealth) is like a high wall. Frankenberg would read נְכָשִׁיו or נְכָסִיו, 'his property' or 'wealth', but this only occurs in post-biblical Hebrew. Toy thinks that the text as it stands, 'in his own imagination', i.e. in his estimation, is 'possibly the correction of an editor who took offence at the *rôle* ascribed to wealth'; this is likely enough.

12 Before destruction the heart of man is haughty,
 And before honour *goeth* humility.
13 He that giveth answer before he heareth,
 It is folly and shame unto him.
14 The spirit of a man will sustain his infirmity;
 But a broken spirit who can [1]bear?
15 The heart of the prudent getteth knowledge;
 And the ear of the wise seeketh knowledge.
16 A man's gift maketh room for him,
 And bringeth him before great men.

[1] Or, *raise up*

**12.** *Before destruction* . . . Cf. xvi. 18ᵃ.
*And before honour.* . . . This line occurs again in xv. 33ᵇ.

**13.** *He that giveth answer* . . . Cf. Ecclus. xi. 8: 'My son, answer nothing before thou hast heard, and in the midst of a discourse speak not.' Amen-em-ope, in giving advice as to how one should act towards an opponent in a debate, says:

'Leap not to go in and meet him,
 When thou hast not seen what he doeth' (XXII. xxii. 22—xxiii. 1).

The underlying thought here seems similar to that of the words before us.

**14.** *The spirit* . . . In the Hebr. each line of the verse begins with the same word, 'spirit', which is against the usage of *Proverbs*; it is better to delete 'spirit' here and to read: 'A man may endure his sickness', i.e. he may be able to overcome that, but a broken spirit who can bear! The contrast is between bodily and mental suffering.

*bear.* Hebr. lit. as R.V. marg., 'who will raise it up?' The Hebr. word for 'broken' is lit. 'cowed'.

**15.** *The heart of* . . . Cf. xv. 14ᵃ. The repetition of the word 'knowledge' in the second line is not in accordance with the usage of *Proverbs*; following the Sept. it is better to read 'discretion' (מְזִמָּה), cf. i. 4, v. 2, where knowledge and discretion occur together. The verse points to the fact that both the inner and outer organs of perception are used by the wise man in acquiring wisdom.

**16.** *A man's gift* . . . By 'gift' here is not meant a bribe; the verse is well illustrated by the words of the Preacher in Eccles. x. 19: 'Money answereth all things', i.e. money responds to all requirements, or as we might say money unlocks every door. Experience of life had taught the Wisdom writers the many uses of wealth, which could be employed quite justifiably in various circumstances of life for the furtherance of legitimate aims. Here the reference is to the custom, quite common in both public and private life of the times,

17 He that pleadeth his cause first *seemeth* just;
   But his neighbour cometh and searcheth him out.
18 The lot causeth contentions to cease,
   And parteth between the mighty.
19 A brother [1] offended *is harder to be won* than a strong city:
   And *such* contentions are like the bars of a castle.

[1] Or, *injured*

of making a present, by way of compliment, to men in influential positions whose favour and friendship were thereby gained. By this means a man widened the circle of acquaintance and was brought into contact with persons of rank and importance. Such utilization of wealth obviously brought advantages of various kinds, and helped a man towards the attainment of a position of dignity and respect among his fellows. The verse is an illustration, among many others, of how the sages deal with a subject of purely worldly wisdom; their many-sided interest in the affairs of men induced them to recognize and inculcate wisdom of every type.

**17.** This verse deals with procedure in a court of justice. The first to present his case, i. e. the plaintiff, naturally puts things in such a way as to appear in the right, whether he is actually so or not. Then comes the defendant, or a witness, and something in the shape of what we should call a cross-examination takes place, though, of course, in those days there was nothing corresponding to counsel. The verse says nothing about the function of the judge; it simply states the fact of general experience that he who has the first say always seems to be in the right; he may be; but another point of view may show that he is in the wrong.

*searcheth him out.* Cf. xxviii. 11.

**18.** This verse, too, deals with litigants. Where a case was difficult to decide recourse would sometimes be had to the lot, i. e. the decision was placed in the hands of God. This would especially be the case when a poor man was opposed to one in high position. The lot settled the matter and decided between the litigants.

*parteth . . .* i. e. decides even between litigants who are powerful.

**19.** *A brother offended . . .* This rendering is hardly justified by the Hebr. text, which is undoubtedly corrupt. The form of the word rendered 'offended' is not known elsewhere; on the basis of the Sept. we should read 'a helping brother', or 'a brother who helps', lit. saves (מוֹשִׁיעַ for נִפְשָׁע); and, again following the Sept., read 'like' (כְ) instead of 'than' (מְ); the line will then run: 'A helping brother is like a strong city' (brother is not necessarily used in a literal sense); cf. 'A friend in need is a friend in deed'.

*And such contentions.* Here again the Hebr. text is corrupt, and

20  A man's belly shall be filled with the fruit of his mouth;
    With the increase of his lips shall he be satisfied.
21  Death and life are in the power of the tongue;
    And they that love it shall eat the fruit thereof.

there is nothing corresponding to 'such'; the word for 'contentions' may have got in from the previous verse. Some word parallel to 'brother' is expected; the Sept. gives no help here, but evidently read a different text. Volz suggests with much probability 'friend' or 'close acquaintance' (reading instead of מִדְיָנִים, the word which occurs several times in the Psalms, מְיֻדָּע, cf. Ps. xxxi. 11 (12), lv. 13 (14), lxxxviii. 8 (9), and elsewhere); the line would then be rendered: 'And a friend is like the bar of a castle', i. e. he is a protection in time of trouble. Cf. xvii. 17, and Ecclus. vi. 14 (Hebr.):

> 'A faithful friend is a strong defence,
> And he that findeth such findeth a treasure.'

**20.** *A man's belly* ... Lit. 'From the fruit of the mouth of a man his belly is sated', or filled; the fruit of the mouth means, of course, the words of a man; so that to speak of these as filling the belly is to mix together abstract and concrete, a rare lapse on the part of the Wisdom writers. The possible misunderstanding is, however, avoided by the second line, which is synonymous.

*the increase.* Lit. that which comes out, the 'outcome', or 'product', i. e. a man must abide the consequences of his words; the proverb means, in effect, 'Whatsoever a man soweth that shall he also reap', applied to the tongue; cf. the similar thought in xii. 14, xiii. 2, 3.

**21.** Continuation of the preceding. The result of a man's words, either death or life, is to be understood literally; hasty and inconsiderate words make enemies, and the result might easily, in those days, be fatal. On the other hand, judicious and well-spoken words, by making a favourable impression, would gain friends through whom prosperity ('life') would be achieved. It was evidently this line upon which Ben-Sira enlarged (Ecclus. xxxvii. 17, 18, Hebr.):

> 'The roots of the deliberations of the heart
> Throw out four branches:
> Good and evil, life and death,
> But the tongue ruleth over them altogether.'

*And they that love it* ... As the reference here is obviously to the tongue, they that love it must be understood in the sense of those who love to use it, though, it must be allowed, this is stretching the meaning of the Hebr. word.

With the *v.* cf. the *Proverbs of Achikar* ii. 38:

> 'My son, sweeten thy tongue, and make savoury the opening of thy mouth;
> for the tail of a dog gives him bread, and his mouth gets him blows.'

22 Whoso findeth a wife findeth a good thing,
   And obtaineth favour of the LORD.
23 The poor useth intreaties:
   But the rich answereth roughly.
24 [1] He that maketh many friends *doeth it* to his own destruction:
   But there is a [2] friend that sticketh closer than a brother.

---

[1] Heb. *A man of friends.*　　　　　　[2] Heb. *lover.*

---

**22.** *a wife.* One Hebr. MS. and all the Versions add 'good'; but
this is unnecessary, as it is clearly a good wife that is understood, the
context implies it; cf. xii. 4, xix. 14; and Ben-Sira says:

> 'A good wife, blessed is her husband,
>   The number of his days is doubled.' (Ecclus. xxvi. 1, Hebr.)

> 'A good wife is a good portion,
>   She shall be given as a portion to them that fear the Lord.'
>                         (xxvi. 3, Grk.; the Hebr. is not extant.)

*a good thing.* The Hebr. has 'good', meaning prosperity, good for-
tune, the reference is not to the wife, but the result of possessing her.
*of the Lord.* See the quotation from Ben-Sira above.

**23.** *useth.* Lit. 'uttereth'.
*roughly.* Lit. 'fiercely'. Cf. Ecclus. xiii. 3, Hebr.:

> 'The rich man doeth wrong and boasteth thereof,
>   And the poor is wronged and hath none to entreat.'

**24.** *He that maketh* . . . The Hebr. text of this line is corrupt; it
reads: 'A man of friends (is) to be broken in pieces', i.e. destroyed.
The first word 'man' (אִישׁ) must be read, 'there is (יֵשׁ), or 'there
are' (see note on second line). The Hebr. word rendered in the R.V.
'doeth it to his own destruction' is a corruption of one which comes
from the root meaning 'to associate with' (see xxii. 24, R.V. 'make
no friendship with'). The line, which in Hebrew consists of only
three words, should therefore be rendered: 'There are friends for
keeping company' (so Syr., Targ.), i.e. friends who are only such
because they can enjoy the hospitality of others, the type of whom
Ben-Sira says:

> 'And there is a friend who is a table-friend,
>   Who is not to be found in the evil day.'
>                         (Ecclus. vi. 10, Hebr.; cf. xxxvii. 4.)

In contrast to this type of 'friend' the second clause speaks of the
friend (lit. 'lover', a different word from that used in the first clause)
who 'sticketh closer than a brother'; the reference is not to God, but
to the kind of friend mentioned in xvii. 17, cf. Ecclus. vi. 14–16,
Hebr.:

**XIX.** 1 Better is the poor that walketh in his integrity
 Than he that is perverse in his lips and is a fool.
 2 Also, [1]that the soul be without knowledge is not good;
 And he that hasteth with his feet [2]sinneth.

 [1] Or, *desire without knowledge is not good*   [2] Or, *misseth* his way

> 'A faithful friend is a strong defence,
> And he that findeth such findeth a treasure.
> A faithful friend is beyond price,
> And there is no weighing of his goodness.
> A bundle of life (see 1 Sam. xxv. 29) is a faithful friend;
> He that feareth God obtaineth him' (cf. also xxxvii. 5).

With the first line of our verse cf. the *Teaching of Ptah-hotep* 33,
where caution in making friends is enjoined, see Excursus I.

### CHAPTER XIX

**1.** *Better is the poor* . . . The identical line occurs again in xxviii. 6[a].
The Hebr. word for 'poor' is used of one who is in absolute want; the
same word is used in Ps. xxxiv. 10 (11 in Hebr.) of young lions in
want and suffering hunger. This verse does not appear in the Sept.
. . . *in his lips and is a fool.* For 'lips' the Syr. and Targ. have
'ways', and for 'fool' the Syr. and Lat. have 'rich'. The Versions
are clearly right, as 'rich' is required for the antithesis to 'poor' in
the first line, and this brings the whole verse into conformity with
xxviii. 6. We have thus another example of the same proverb occurring in two different collections; the difference in the form of this
verse shows that the collections of which our book is made up were
originally independent. The Versions evidently corrected this verse
from its form in xxviii. 6, which is no doubt the original form, but it
does not therefore follow that its form here is a textual corruption;
it points rather to the free way in which, on occasion, a collector
utilized his material. This throws light on the many parallels existing
between our book and Babylonian and Egyptian Wisdom books, for
while these parallels are often similar in essence they differ in detail,
showing that the Hebrew sage utilized foreign sources and adapted
them as he thought proper. Our verse must therefore be regarded
as an adaptation for a particular purpose, though in this case he has
spoiled the symmetry of the original.

**2.** This verse is wanting in the Sept.
*Also.* To begin a proverb thus is not in accordance with the usage
of our book (see note on xviii. 9); it might conceivably be used if in
close connexion with what precedes, but this is not the case here.
The word was probably added thoughtlessly by a scribe, but it does
not belong to the original text; none of the Versions have it. Possibly
it has displaced some other word, see next note.
*that the soul be without knowledge.* Neither this nor the R.V. marg.

3 The foolishness of man subverteth his way;
    And his heart fretteth against the LORD.

rendering is acceptable because the Hebrew expression for 'without
knowledge' must qualify a preceding noun, not 'soul' which follows
it.  Hence it is possible that instead of 'also' (גַּם) we should read 'a
heart' (= 'mind' לֵב) as in vi. 18, xv. 14, xviii. 15; 'soul' probably
does not belong to the original text.

*he that hasteth with his feet.*  It is more in accordance with what
appears to be the general sense of the verse to read 'with his words'
(cf. xxix. 20, 'he that is hasty with his words') for 'with his feet',
which refers to motion, and is inappropriate here.  It is the man
without knowledge, i.e. the fool, who is always ready to pour forth
words, cf. Ecclus. xxi. 26:

> 'The heart of fools is in their mouth,
>     But the mouth of the wise is in their heart.'

*sinneth.*  Lit. 'misseth the mark', cf. viii. 36.

**3.** *subverteth.*  Cf. xiii. 6, xxi. 12, xxii. 12.

*fretteth.*  According to the later, post-exilic, meaning of the Hebr.
word a stronger expression should be used, 'enraged', or the like, cf.
2 Chron. xxvi. 19.  The thought of this verse is enlarged upon in the
important passage Ecclus. xv. 11–20 (Hebr.), which is well worth
quoting in full in connexion with the verse before us:

> 'Say not, "From God is my transgression",
>     For that which He hateth made He not.
> Say not, "It is He that made me to stumble",
>     For there is no need of evil men.
> Evil and abomination doth the Lord hate,
>     And He will not let it come nigh them that fear Him.
> God created man from the beginning,
>     And placed him in the hand of his *Yetzer*.
> If thou desirest thou canst keep the commandment,
>     And it is wisdom to do His good pleasure.
> Poured out before thee are fire and water,
>     Stretch forth thine hand unto that which thou desirest.
> Life and death are before man,
>     That which he desireth shall be given him.
> Sufficient is the Wisdom of the Lord,
>     He is mighty in power, and seeth all things.
> And the eyes of God behold His works,
>     And He knoweth every deed of man.
> He commandeth no man to sin,
>     Nor gave He strength to men of lies.'

The teaching of this passage that no man can blame God for his sin,
and the insistence on man's free will, witnesses to the settlement
of a question which was an open one at the period during which
*Proverbs* was written.

4 Wealth addeth many friends:
   But [1]the poor is separated from his friend.
5 A false witness shall not be unpunished;
   And he that [2]uttereth lies shall not escape.
6 Many will intreat the favour of [3]the liberal man:
   And every man is a friend to him that giveth gifts.
7 All the brethren of the poor do hate him:
   How much more do his friends go far from him !
   [4]He pursueth *them with* words, *but* they are gone.

[1] Or, *the friend of the poor separateth himself from him*   [2] Heb. *breatheth out.*
[3] Or, *a prince*      [4] Or, *He pursueth after words,* which *are nought*

**4.** *Wealth addeth* . . . Cf. xiv. 20.
*But the poor* . . . This can be rendered both as in R.V. text and
marg. See further under *v.* 7.

**5.** This verse is almost identical with *v.* 9.
*unpunished.* Lit. 'shall not be held innocent', cf. vi. 29, xi. 21,
xvi. 5, xvii. 5, xxviii. 20.
*uttereth.* Lit. 'breatheth', or 'puffeth out'; used also of 'truth' in
xii. 17.

**6.** *will entreat the favour.* The interesting Hebrew expression of
which these words are a rendering has a long history behind it, and
is only used in reference to men here and in Job xi. 19; Ps. xlv. 12
(13 in Hebr.); otherwise it is a purely religious expression, the idea
of which arose originally during the stage of religious development
in which 'the deity is conceived as the king of his people and the
lord of the land, and as such was habitually approached with gifts
and tribute. It was the rule of antiquity, and still is the rule in the
East, that the inferior must not present himself before his superior
without a gift "to smooth his face" and make him gracious. The
same phrase is habitually applied in the Old Testament to acts of
sacrificial worship, and in Ex. xxiii. 15 the rule is formulated that no
one shall appear before Jehovah empty-handed', Robertson Smith,
*The Religion of the Semites,* pp. 346 f. (1927). The expression before
us is, therefore, a purely religious term adapted to secular life.
*the liberal man.* This rendering of the word ('noble' in viii. 16,
xvii. 26, 'prince' in xxv. 7) is presumably given to bring out the
parallelism with 'him that giveth gifts' in the second clause; at the
same time, the root idea of the word is that of voluntariness (cf. a
'free-will offering', from the same root, a 'willing spirit', Ps. li. 12,
14 in Hebr.), so that 'liberal' is fully justified.
*to him that giveth gifts.* Lit. 'to a man of gift.'

**7.** The Hebr. text of this verse, as the R.V. shows, has three lines,
unlike the usual form of proverbs in this collection; the third is in

8 He that getteth [1] wisdom loveth his own soul:
 He that keepeth understanding shall find good.
9 A false witness shall not be unpunished;
 And he that [2] uttereth lies shall perish.
10 Delicate living is not seemly for a fool;
 Much less for a servant to have rule over princes.

[1] Heb. *heart.*        [2] Heb. *breatheth out.*

all probability the remnant of a now lost couplet which perhaps told of how, in spite of his entreaties, the poor man's friends and relatives turned a deaf ear to him. The Sept. has two couplets in place of the third line, but of entirely different content; they read, however, as though translated from Hebrew.

*do hate him.* Because of his importunity. If his brethren, they of blood relationship, hate him, how much more will his friends, upon whom he has no claim, avoid him.

*He pursueth* . . . The R.V. is a paraphrase of something which is certainly not offered by the Hebrew text as it stands, and which is incomprehensible; it runs lit.: 'He that followeth after words, not they' (or 'they are his', as the Hebr. marg. reads). Various emendations of the text have been suggested, but as the words form only a fragment these are necessarily precarious. Cheyne, on the basis of the Versions, emends the text so as to mean: 'He that doeth much evil perfecteth mischief; he that provoketh with words shall not escape', (*Job and Solomon,* p. 134); this is one of the couplets which the Sept. has in place of this line. Cf. the *Teaching of Amenemhet* (§ 3 in Griffith's translation): 'Friends exist not for a man on the day of troubles'; and the Babylonian proverb: 'Friendship is of a day, but posterity is of eternity' (Langdon, *op. cit.,* p. 86).

**8.** *He that getteth wisdom.* Cf. xv. 32[b], 'getteth understanding'; in each case the word is lit. 'heart'; see further Excursus IX.

*loveth his own soul.* As often, 'soul' means personality. The man who acquires wisdom shows that he has due regard for himself; it is a mark of self-respect.

**9.** See notes on *v.* 5, with which this *v.* is almost identical.

**10.** Unlike most of the couplets in this book the connexion of ideas between the clauses is obscure; but probably the object of the writer was simply to enumerate two incongruous things; this is sometimes done by Ben-Sira, see e.g. Ecclus. xxv. 2.

*Delicate living.* i.e. luxurious living, the Hebr. word is used in both concrete and abstract senses.

*not seemly.* This is hardly the meaning of the original; 'incongruous' or 'inappropriate' would better express what is meant; cf. xvii. 7, xxvi. 1, where the same applies.

*for a servant to have rule* . . . That slaves sometimes rose to positions

11 The discretion of a man maketh him slow to anger;
   And it is his glory to pass over a transgression.
12 The king's wrath is as the roaring of a lion;
   But his favour is as dew upon the grass.

of great power is well known; and as men of outstanding ability, as
suchlike must in most cases have been, there would not necessarily
have been anything incongruous in this, more especially as slaves who
were prisoners of war were often far from being of low birth; but the
sages were men of aristocratic instinct, and the idea of one who had
been in a servile position to rise to that of a ruler was repellent to
them. With the second clause of the verse cf. xxx. 22; Eccles. x. 7;
Ecclus. xi. 5.

**11.** *maketh him slow to anger.* The Hebr. has 'his anger'; a slight
alteration in the vowel points of the verb turns it to an infin. (so the
Syr. and two of the Grk. Versions), and makes a better sentence: 'It
is discretion in a man to restrain his anger'; this is also in accord
with the form of the second clause. Cf. xiv. 17ᵃ, 29ᵃ.

*his glory.* The Hebr. word has the sense of both 'renown' or
'honour', and 'glorying' in the sense of 'boasting'.

*to pass over . . .* For this rare use of the Hebr. word, in the sense
of forgiving, see Am. vii. 8, viii. 2; Mic. vii. 18. Cf. the *Teaching for
King Meri-ka-re* (Erman, *op. cit.*, p. 111): 'Be not angry; to be
friendly is good. Let the memory of thee abide because of loving-
kindness.'

**12.** *The king's wrath . . .* Almost identical with xx. 2ᵃ; cf. xvi. 14ᵃ,
xxviii. 15.

*his favour.* Cf. xvi. 15ᵇ. The references to the king in *Proverbs*
belong to different periods, and whether pre- or post-exilic must be
decided by various considerations. In the present instance the reference is almost certainly to post-exilic times, and the writer probably
has in mind Jewish sages who served offices at the courts of the
Ptolemaic kings. Various names of prominent Jews who occupied
honourable positions under these Egyptian kings have come down
to us. What the sage here tells us of the variability of the king's
humours is borne out by what is said in historical sources which have
come down to us regarding the precariousness of life at the Egyptian
court. Ben-Sira speaks of the presence of the Jewish sage in foreign
courts in Ecclus. xxxix. 4:

> 'He serveth among great men,
> And appeareth before a ruler,
> He travelleth in the land of alien nations,
> And hath tried both good and evil things among men.'

Cf. Eccles. viii. 2–4.

13 A foolish son is the calamity of his father:
   And the contentions of a wife are a continual dropping.
14 House and riches are an inheritance from fathers:
   But a prudent wife is from the LORD.
15 Slothfulness casteth into a deep sleep;
   And the idle soul shall suffer hunger.
16 He that keepeth the commandment keepeth his soul:
   *But* he that ¹is careless of his ways shall die.

¹ Heb. *despiseth.*

**13.** Cf. verse 26, x. 1, xvii. 21, 25; Ecclus. xxii. 3.
*calamity.* See note on xvii. 4, where the R.V. renders the word a
'mischievous' tongue (the phrase is lit. 'a tongue of mischief').
*a continual dropping.* Both words in Hebr. occur only here and in
xxvii. 15 (though in Aramaic in Dan. iv. 25 (22), &c.), but as a verb
'to drop' is used in Job xvi. 20; Ps. cxix. 28; Eccles. x. 18. 'An Arab
proverb which Delitzsch heard from Wetzstein, says that three
things make a house intolerable: *tak* (the leaking through of rain),
*nak* (a wife's nagging), and *bak* (bugs)' (Toy, *op. cit.*, p. 373).

**14.** This is, from one point of view, an anomalous saying for a
Hebrew sage, both because prosperity, such as house and riches, were
believed to come from God, and also because it was the father who
chose a wife for his son. From this point of view, the sage, in his
anxiety to set forth the blessing of a 'good wife', ignored theology
and custom. On the other hand, however, the first line states what
was obviously the fact, while the second would be the conviction of
every pious mind. All depends upon the point of view.
*But a prudent wife* ... Cf. xviii. 22 and Ben-Sira's words in Ecclus.
xxvi. 3:

'A good wife is a good portion;
She shall be given as a portion to them that fear Jahweh.'

**15.** *Slothfulness casteth* ... The sage purposely exaggerates the
effect of idleness in order to impress his youthful hearers. He who
will not work ultimately reaches a state in which he cannot work,
and this is what he calls a 'deep sleep' (cf. Gen. ii. 21). He drives
home his lesson by touching on a sensitive point; hunger will rouse
the laziest.
*the idle soul* ... Cf. 2 Thes. iii. 10: 'If any will not work, neither
let him eat.' Cf. also x. 4ᵃ, xx. 13ᵃ.

**16.** *He that keepeth the commandment.* The form of the Hebr.
which has not the definite article, makes it probable that we have
here what had already become a technical term, and that 'commandment' connotes 'law' just as the plural of commandment (*mizwōth*)
came to mean works of the law. The same is found in the Hebr. of
Ecclus. xliv. 20, xlv. 5, xlvi. 14. The Wisdom writers, though not

17 He that hath pity upon the poor lendeth unto the LORD,
   And his good deed will he pay him again.

legalists in what we call the Pharisaic sense, had, nevertheless, a very
high regard for the Law, as this verse, among other passages, shows.
The second 'keepeth' is better translated 'preserveth', for although
it is the same word in Hebr. in both cases, the two objects 'commandment' and 'soul' alter its meaning; the first 'keepeth' should
be rendered 'observeth', the second 'preserveth'.

But *he that is careless.* There is no 'but' in the Hebr., though there
is in the Versions, and it is required because the line is antithetical.
'He that is careless' does not quite represent the Hebr., the word
never has this sense, a stronger term is required; 'despises' or 'has
contempt for', is what it means.

*his ways.* For a man to despise his ways does not give adequate
sense; it is better to read for 'his ways' (דְּרָכָיו), 'the word' (הַדָּבָר),
as in xiii. 13 (see note on that verse) where it is parallel to 'commandment', as here; cf. xv. 10; Eccles. viii. 5.

**17.** *He that hath pity . . .* Doubtless we must see here again one
of the marks of prophetic influence. In such passages as Am. ii. 6, 7,
iv. 1, v. 12; Isa. x. 1, 2, and many others, it is seen how the prophets
championed the cause of the poor and the helpless; in this they
established an ethical principle which has been a basic one in the
social life of the nation ever since. The Wisdom writers take up this
burden of the prophets and insist again and again on duty to the
poor which they regard as wisdom in one of its highest forms, because
well-pleasing in the sight of God (cf. e.g. xiv. 31). It is to be noted,
moreover, that this duty does not confine itself to refraining from
oppressing or taking an unfair advantage of the poor, but that it has
an active side; tangible help must be given both in a sympathetic
attitude towards them, as well as in definite almsgiving; herein, too,
the Wisdom writers are in the following of the prophets. He who
gives to the poor, who are of God's creation (cf. xxii. 2), are lending
to God, as it says in the verse before us; in doing this a man is, as it
were, depositing a treasure in the care of God, who will repay it in
due time. A danger lurked here, it is true; Ben-Sira, for example,
goes so far as to say that almsgiving makes atonement for sins
(Ecclus. iii. 30), and the inevitable consequence of such teaching was
seen in the doctrine of merit and of justification through the works
of the Law. But though the germ of such doctrines is to be discerned
in the passage before us, they did not assume a definite form until
later times. For the teaching of the Wisdom writers see further
iii. 27, 28, xvii. 5, xxii. 16, 22, 23, xxviii. 3, xxix. 7; Ecclus. iv. 1, 2, 5,
xx. 10, xxxi. 25–27, xxxii. 14–26. In view of some of these passages
it seems somewhat of an overstatement when Toy says that 'the
motive urged is not the obligation to do right, but the reward of

18 Chasten thy son, seeing there is hope;
    And set not thy heart on ¹his destruction.
19 A man of great wrath shall bear the penalty:
    For if thou deliver *him*, thou must do it yet again.

¹ Heb. *causing him to die.*

right doing'. If, as is maintained, the Wisdom writers were influenced
by the teaching of the prophets in this matter it is difficult to believe
that the motive was merely a selfish one.

**18.** *Chasten.* i.e. chastise; bodily scourging is meant.

*seeing there is hope.* i.e. when there is still hope of its having an
ameliorative effect. When the son grows older and is no longer under
his father's control, such remedial means cannot be employed; and
if he goes wrong then, the case is hopeless.

*And set not* . . . The Hebr., which is difficult, has lit.: 'But unto
the killing of him lift not up thy soul'; as the text stands the meaning
seems to be, 'But let it not be thy desire to cause him to die' (for the
phrase 'lift up the soul' in the sense of satisfying a desire, see Deut.
xxiv. 15). This, it must be granted, is unsatisfactory, for the sage
can hardly have contemplated such a deliberate breach of the Law
as this would have entailed (see Deut. xxi. 18–21); see, however, the
next verse. If he had this law in mind, it is more likely that his
words, in their original form, deprecated the idea of a father taking
the extreme course of delivering his son over to the elders to be
stoned; but as the text stands, this meaning cannot be got out of it,
and it is impossible to say what the original form was. See further
the notes on xxiii. 13, 14. Cf. the *Proverbs of Achikar* ii. 23:

'My son, subdue thy son while he is yet a boy, before he wax stronger than
    thee and rebel against thee, and thou be shamed in all his corrupt doing.'

**19.** *A man of great wrath.* This rendering is apparently a combination of what the Versions read, together with the Hebr. marginal
reading; the former have the equivalent of 'man' (נבר), while the
latter reads 'great' (גדל). The Hebr. text is clearly corrupt, it reads
'stony' or 'rough' (גרל), an adjective which does not occur elsewhere. We should, no doubt, read: 'He that is great in wrath', cf.
the analogous phrase, 'he that is great in counsel' in Jer. xxxii. 19
(see also 2 Kgs. xxii. 13).

*shall bear the penalty.* The word for 'penalty' occurs elsewhere only
in 2 Kgs. xxiii. 33, where it means an 'indemnity' or a 'fine' (for the
verb cf. xvii. 26, xxii. 3, xxvii. 12; Am. ii. 8). If we may be guided by
v. 14, it was the congregation who inflicted the fine; but as the mere
fact of exhibiting great anger would not involve the paying of a fine,
the verse before us must be understood as referring to what this
anger resulted in, viz. bodily injury to another. This throws light,
perhaps, on the second clause.

*if thou deliver him* . . . This is meaningless, and it is obvious that

20 Hear counsel, and receive ¹instruction,
   That thou mayest be wise in thy latter end.
21 There are many devices in a man's heart;
   But the counsel of the LORD, that shall stand.
22 ²The desire of a man is *the measure of* his kindness:
   And a poor man is better than a liar.

¹ Or, *correction*     ² Or, *That which maketh a man to be desired is his kindness*

the Hebr. text is corrupt. The various interpretations offered require
so much to be supplied in order to make sense that they are as
improbable as they are unsatisfactory. It is likely that *vv.* 18, 19
deal with the same subject and belong together. Verse 18 bids a
man chasten his son, yet not to such an extent as to cause his death;
it then goes on in verse 19 to say that if a man, meaning the father,
is of such a violent temper as to do this, he will have to bear the
penalty, 'for surely he that slayeth shall also add his own life',
emending the words: 'for if thou deliver him' (אִם־תַּצֵּל) to: 'for
surely he that slayeth' (כִּי אִם־יַהֲרֹג), and adding 'his life' as in the
Sept. (נַפְשׁוֹ, see the last word of the preceding line); cf. Exod. xxi. 14.
These two verses, therefore, deal with the subject of a father
punishing a son; it is best that this should take place, but it must be
done in moderation; above all, let a hot-tempered man be careful,
for in the event of his inflicting a fatal injury on his son, the result
will be the loss of his own life in addition to that of his son.

**20.** *Hear counsel* . . . Cf. viii. 10, xii. 15.
*in thy latter end.* This word (אַחֲרִיתֶךְ), when used in reference to
time, often means the end of life, as e.g. in v. 4, 11; but in such
passages as xiv. 12, xxiii. 32, xxiv. 14, xxv. 8, the meaning is the
result or the issue of a course of action; this is the sense in which it
must be understood here. But it is possible that the Syr. is right
in reading 'in thy ways' (אָרְחֹתֶיךָ), which certainly gives a more
natural sense. In xxiii. 18, xxiv. 20 the idea of a posterity is suggested by the word.

**21.** See the notes on xvi. 9, and cf. xx. 24.
*devices.* Better 'plans' or 'purposes'. By 'heart' we must, as so
often in *Proverbs*, understand 'mind'.
*counsel.* As e.g. in Ps. xxxiii. 11, when this word (עֵצָה) is used in
reference to God, it means 'design', or 'plan'. Elsewhere it occurs as
a parallel to 'sound knowledge' (viii. 14), 'wisdom and understanding', (xxi. 30), 'wise guidance' (xx. 18), 'instruction' (xix. 20).

**22.** *The desire of a man* . . . Neither this rendering nor the R.V.
marg. can be got naturally out of the Hebr. which has simply: 'The
desire of a man is his kindness'; and this does not give sense without
reading in what is not there. The Sept. (καρπός, 'fruit') presumably
read a word meaning 'product', 'revenue', or 'possession' (תְּבוּאַת

M

23 The fear of the LORD *tendeth* to life:
   And he *that hath it* shall abide satisfied;
   He shall not be visited with evil.

24 The sluggard burieth his hand in the dish,
   And will not so much as bring it to his mouth again.

for תְּאַוַת), which occurs in x. 16, xiv. 4, xv. 6, xvi. 8 in this sense;
if this reading is correct the line will mean that a man's possession
is his kindness; but this does not commend itself because this would
be more naturally expressed by saying that a man's kindness is 'his'
possession, or capital, or revenue, i.e. the possessive pronoun is
attached to the wrong word; and even so the sentence would not be
satisfactory. The probability is that the Hebr. text is corrupt; but
the material for emendation is wanting, especially as the clause as
it now stands has no connexion with what follows, though the conjunction suggests that there was such originally.

*And a poor man* . . . Following the Sept. we may read: 'Better is
a poor man (who is) honest than a rich man (who is) a liar'; but it is
probably best to omit 'honest', and to read simply: 'Better (to be)
a poor man than a rich one (who is) a liar' (טוֹב רָשׁ מֵעָשִׁיר כָּזָב); the
word for a 'poor man' (רָשׁ) never takes an adjective after it; the
Sept. added 'honest' under the impression that it would give better
sense; but it is not wanted, the point is simply that poverty is
better than wealth with wickedness.

**23.** *The fear of* . . . Cf. xiv. 27ᵃ. The text of the second clause is
clearly out of order; it runs lit.: 'And satisfied he dwells, he will not
be visited (by) evil', but there is no subject to the verb, and in other
ways the Hebrew is unacceptable. Instead of 'satisfied he dwells
. . .' (שָׂבֵעַ יָלִין) Toy suggests the emendation '(he) who hopeth in
Him, shall not be visited (with) evil' (שֹׂבֵר עָלָיו . . . . . .); this verb,
however, is only used in the *pi'el*, and never takes this preposition
after it; moreover, the verb for 'visit' should have a preposition
after it; x. 27 might suggest 'but the years of scorners shall be
shortened' (וּשְׁנוֹת לֵצִים תִּקְצֹרְנָה), though this would be a rather drastic emendation; but the condition of the text is so bad that a large
variety of emendations could be suggested without there being any
feeling of security as to their correctness.

**24.** *burieth*. The Hebr. word is lit. 'hide' or 'conceal'; this is a
perfectly appropriate word to use; neither spoon, knife, nor fork
were used in those days, and if the contents of the dish happened to
be a broth (see e.g. Judg. vi. 19), it would be necessary to bury the
whole hand in the broth, making it cup-shape. The suggested emendation of the Hebr. word, so as to read 'dippeth' (Toy), is therefore
unnecessary. What is here said about the sluggard is doubtless a
deliberate over-statement with the object of ridiculing lazy people;
in xxvi. 15 the statement is a little modified.

25 Smite a scorner, and the simple will learn prudence:
   And reprove one that hath understanding, *and* he will under-
      stand knowledge.
26 He that [1] spoileth his father, and chaseth away his mother,
   Is a son that causeth shame and bringeth reproach.

[1] Or, *violently entreateth*

**25.** The verse sets in contrast the ways in which the foolish and
the sensible man, respectively, acquire knowledge. The former requires something in the shape of a warning; there must be some
tragic object-lesson before he will be deterred from following his evil
course. To a sensible man the appeal of wisdom suffices. This is one
of a number of passages which show that though the Wisdom
writers have a profound contempt for 'fools' in general they recognize that there are many such whose case is not hopeless. The
remedy may require to be severe, whether by way of warning in
seeing the plight of others, as in this verse, or by some dire personal
experience, as in v. 11 ff.; but, except in some extreme cases, the
possibility of amelioration is always contemplated. This is a point
in the Wisdom Literature which is sometimes apt to be overlooked
because of the great frequency of passages in which the sages pour
scorn on 'fools'. In spite of the preponderance of the foolish in the
world the Wisdom writers were not pessimists regarding mankind.

**26.** The conditions contemplated in this verse are those of a man
whose aged parents are dependent on him. There was no law to
force a son to provide for his parents if in penury; there was only the
appeal to filial duty and the dictates of humanity. It is likely enough
that Ben-Sira wrote the fine passage in Ecclus. iii. 1–16 on the basis
of this verse; among other things he says:

'Exult not in the dishonour of thy father,
For it is no glory to thee.
A man's glory is his father's glory,
And he that dishonoureth his mother multiplieth sin.
My son, help thy father in his old age,[1]
And grieve him not all the days of his life;
Yea, if his mind fail be considerate with him,
And dishonour him not all the days of his life.
Alms to a father shall not be blotted out,
And it shall stand firm as a substitute for sins.
In the day of affliction it shall be remembered to thy credit,
Obliterating thine iniquities as heat the hoar-frost.
As one that is arrogant is he that despiseth his father,
And as one that provoketh his Creator is he that curseth his mother.'
                                    (Ecclus. iii. 10–16, Hebr.)

[1] This line is from the Greek, which, as the context shows, has preserved the better
text.

M 2

27 Cease, my son, to hear instruction
   *Only* to err from the words of knowledge.
28 A worthless witness mocketh at judgement:
   And the mouth of the wicked swalloweth iniquity.
29 Judgements are prepared for scorners,
   And stripes for the back of fools.

**XX.** 1 Wine is a mocker, strong drink a brawler;
   And whosoever [1]erreth thereby is not wise.
  2 The terror of a king is as the roaring of a lion:
   He that [2]provoketh him to anger sinneth *against* his own
      [3]life.

[1] Or, *reeleth*    [2] Or, *angereth himself against him*    [3] Heb. *soul.*

**27.** The Hebr. text of this verse is, on the face of it, corrupt. The address 'my son' is alien to this collection, and when it occurs elsewhere its place is at the opening of a sentence; we are justified, therefore, in deleting it here. For 'cease' we must read 'he that ceaseth', which involves only a change in the vowel-points, not in the letters. The word 'only' does not in any case belong to the text. For 'to err' the finite verb must be read, 'erreth'; this involves but a slight change in the text (יִשְׁגֶּה for לִשְׁגוֹת). The verse then runs smoothly: 'He that ceaseth to hear instruction erreth from the words of knowledge.'

**28.** *A worthless witness.* Lit. 'a witness of Belial' (the word means more than 'worthlessness', something rather stronger, 'depraved' or the like (cf. vi. 12, xvi. 27).

*judgement.* It is better to render 'justice'.

*swalloweth.* This hardly gives sense; a slight change in the Hebr. enables us to read 'poureth forth' (reading יַבִּיעַ, cf. xv. 28, 'The mouth of the wicked poureth out evil things', for יְבַלַּע).

**29.** *Judgements.* The Hebr. (שְׁפָטִים) is evidently a textual error for 'strokes' (שְׁבָטִים), which offers a better parallel to 'stripes' in the next clause, and is what the Sept. read; see also xxvi. 3[b].

### CHAPTER XX

**1.** *erreth.* Read with R.V. marg. 'reeleth', cf. Isa. xxviii. 7.

**2.** *The terror of a king.* i.e. the terror inspired by the words of a king. Some commentators would read 'wrath' (חֵמַת as in xvi. 14, cf. xix. 12, but the Hebr. word there is different) for 'terror' (אֵימַת), others suggest 'word' (אִמְרַת) or 'words' (אִמְרֵי); but the text as it stands is preferable, pregnant sentences are characteristic of the Wisdom writers.

*He that provoketh him to anger.* The Hebr. word means 'he that

3 It is an honour for a man to ¹keep aloof from strife:
　　But every fool will be quarrelling.
4 The slothful will not plow by reason of the winter;
　　²Therefore he shall beg in harvest, and have nothing.
5 Counsel in the heart of man is *like* deep water;
　　But a man of understanding will draw it out.

¹ Or, *cease*　　² Or, *Therefore when he seeketh in harvest, there shall be nothing*

angers himself against him' (R.V. marg.), but the word is probably corrupt. The R.V. paraphrase no doubt represents the original text.

*sinneth* against *his own life*. The Hebr. text is again corrupt, though R.V. expresses the general sense; for 'sinneth' (חוֹטֵא) we should perhaps read 'wrongeth' or 'harmeth' (חֹמֵס) as in viii. 36. As the king has the power of life and death in his hands it is foolish for a man to cause him anger because he is only damaging himself thereby.　　Cf. Ben-Sira's words:

> 'Affect not wisdom in the presence of a king.
> Seek not to be a ruler,
> Lest thou be not able to suppress presumption,
> And thou be afraid in the presence of the mighty,
> And put a stumbling-block in (the way of) thine integrity.'

> (Ecclus. vii. 5, 6.)

**3.** *It is an honour . . .* With this cf. *The Proverbs of Achikar* ii. 8:

> 'My son, stand not in the house of those that are at strife, because from a word there comes a quarrel, and from a quarrel there is stirred up vexation; and from vexedness springs murder.'

*to keep aloof*. Lit. 'to sit', or 'abide'.
*will be quarrelling*. Cf. xvii. 14, and the note there.

**4.** *by reason of the winter*. Properly 'autumn'; the word is the general one for the colder part of the year; but we must read 'in the autumn'. It is not on account of the cold, but because of his laziness that the slothful does not plough; the autumn was the time for ploughing.

*Therefore he shall beg . . .* This is not the meaning of the Hebr. which has lit.: 'he asketh (or seeketh) in the harvest, and (there is) nought', i.e. he looks for the yield, but it is not there. Cf. xxiv. 30–32.

**5.** *Counsel in the heart . . .* i.e. the purpose which is in the mind of a man; this is like deep waters because it is hard to fathom, cf. xviii. 4. The verse is one of many which illustrate the observation and knowledge of men which was one of the outstanding endeavours of the Wisdom writers. Sayings such as this were intended to be an incentive to men to cultivate deep thinking, and at the same time to encourage others to profit by weighing the products of the minds of the sages.

6 [1]Most men will proclaim every one his own kindness:
But a faithful man who can find?

7 A just man that walketh in his integrity,
Blessed are his children after him.

8 A king that sitteth on the throne of judgement
[2]Scattereth away all evil with his eyes.

[1] Or, *Many a man will meet one that is kind to him*     [2] Or, *Winnoweth*

**6.** *Most men ... kindness.* This line in Hebr. permits of more than one translation and interpretation; (1) 'Many a man (lit. a multitude of men) proclaimeth each one his (own) kindness', meaning that many people love to vaunt any act of kindness they happen to show; this may or may not imply insincerity. (2) As the R.V. marg., 'Many a man meeteth a man who is kind to him'; here the kindness would be of a purely superficial character. (3) By a slight change in the Hebr. vowels we get the meaning: 'Many a man is called a kind man', the implication being that he is not so in reality. This last seems the best, and the most pointed antithesis is afforded to it by the second line, though, it is true, it offers a good antithesis to (1) and (2) as well.

*But a faithful man ...* Here, as always, the sage bases his words on that knowledge of men which can only be gained by one who is not only much in the world, but is above all an observer of men in the world. The Wisdom writers show that the shortcomings of humanity in their day were extraordinarily similar to those of to-day. It is this fact which makes the Wisdom Literature so exceedingly instructive to men in every age. The words before us are, of course, not intended to imply that there is no such thing as a faithful man, the contrary is to be understood in every case where a man's wisdom is extolled; the writer obviously means that a really faithful man, i.e. one who is to be relied upon in all circumstances, is, comparatively speaking, a rarity; and that, melancholy as the fact is, must be acknowledged to be true.

**7.** *in his integrity.* The Hebr. word connotes perfectness in the sense of completeness; to the Wisdom writers this means a man who is wise in his relationship to God, to his fellows, and to himself. This perfect example of upright living re-acts upon a man's children. For the converse cf. Ecclus. xli. 7:

'A wicked father do the children curse,
For because of him do they suffer reproach.'

**8.** *A king that sitteth ...* Although on occasion the Wisdom writers are not afraid to pillory an evil ruler (see e.g. xxix. 12; Ecclus. x. 3), the monarchical principle is regarded by them as essentially beneficial. They represent the king's chief function not so much as that of wielding power, but rather as that of administering justice (cf. xvi. 10, xxix. 14).

9  Who can say, I have made my heart clean,
   I am pure from my sin?

*Scattereth away.*  The meaning is that he sifts the evil from the
good; as king he is not like an ordinary judge who is open to bribery.
   *with his eyes.*  His discernment is greater than that of ordinary
men; Ben-Sira, uttering the general belief, says the king is placed in
his position by God (Ecclus. **x.** 4).
   **9.**  *I have made my heart clean* ...  The Hebr. word comes from the
root *zākhah* which is always used in a moral sense.  'The distinct recognition of sinfulness as an element in human nature begins to appear
in Ezekiel (xviii. 23, 24), and the formulation of the view is found in
philosophical or reflective writings (1 Kgs. viii. 46; Job iv. 17–19,
xiv. 4, apparently an interpolation; Ps. li. 5 (7), cxxx. 3; Eccles. vii.
20) ... The two conceptions, universal sinfulness (*v.* 9) and the possibility of practical perfectness (*v.* 7) were held together, without attempt to harmonize them logically ...' (Toy).  In the *v.* before us the
words, 'Who can say', imply, of course, that no one can do so, in spite
of *v.* 7; but it was not long before a development of doctrine began in
Jewish teaching, according to which a man, through the accumulation of good works, could reach a state of *zākhūth*; this word, which
comes from the root *zākhah*, mentioned above, means primarily 'pure-
ness' or 'cleanness', in an ethical sense, and later, 'satisfaction', i.e.
a man who has kept all the commandments of God has *zākhūth*; he has
attained that state of righteousness which is reached by having
satisfied all the divine demands made upon him.  He is thus justified
in the sight of God and therefore in a state of moral perfection.
   That this doctrine was held in comparatively early times is seen
from Ecclus. iii. 14 (Hebr.), where it is said that:

> *Alms (given) to a father shall not be blotted out,*
> *But it shall stand firm as a substitute for sin.*

That is to say, the righteous deeds done by a man in succouring his
father will be put down to his credit and thus counterbalance his sins;
cf. the words in T.B. *Qiddushin*, 40[b], where it is said that a man is
judged 'according to that which balances', i.e. according as to
whether the weight of sins or of good deeds is the heavier.  In the
latter case the divine requirements were of course satisfied, and man
had reached a state of *zākhūth*, and was therefore morally and re-
ligiously perfect.
   But in the *Proverbs* passage before us this dangerous development,
though in the making, had not yet taken place; the sense of sin was
still too strong.  It is very striking that a quite similar thought to
that here expressed should occur in the *Teaching of Amen-em-ope*,
but in XVIII. xix. 18, 19 we have this couplet:

> *Say not, 'I have no sin',*
> *And be not at pains to seek to (conceal it) (?).*

10 [1]Divers weights, and divers measures,
    Both of them alike are an abomination to the LORD.
11 Even a child maketh himself known by his doings,
    Whether his work be pure, and whether it be right.
12 The hearing ear, and the seeing eye,
    The LORD hath made even both of them.
13 Love not sleep, lest thou come to poverty;
    Open thine eyes, *and* thou shalt be satisfied with bread.
14 It is naught, it is naught, saith the buyer:
    But when he is gone his way, then he boasteth.

---

[1] Heb. *A stone and a stone, an ephah and an ephah.*

There is some doubt as to the meaning of the last word; Prof. Ll.
Griffith renders, '. . . to seek strife', possibly in reference to God; the
meaning would then be that a man must not seek to justify himself in
the sight of God. In any case the thought is strikingly similar to that
in *Proverbs*, and it is difficult to resist the conclusion that we have
here an instance of Hebrew influence on the Egyptian sage, rather
than the borrowing of the compiler of *Proverbs* from Amen-em-ope.

**10.** See R.V. marg. In the Sept. *vv.* 10–13 are placed after *v.* 22.
Cf. *v.* 23, xvi. 11. For the practice condemned see Lev. xix. 36; Deut.
xxv. 13–16; Am. viii. 5; Mic. vi. 11; Ezek. xlv. 10, and cf. Ecclus.
xxvi. 29. Amen-em-ope offers a parallel to this *v.* in XVI. xvii. 18,
19 of his book:

> *Move not the scales and falsify not the weights,*
> *And diminish not the parts of the corn-measure.*

**11.** *Even a child* . . . The Hebr. reads: 'Even in his doings a
child . . .', but the R.V. is, no doubt, right in emending the text by
transposing 'even'. The meaning is that even while yet a child the
character of an individual is portrayed by the kind of things he does.
Toy rightly points out that in i–ix 'child' is used of mature young
manhood, while in x–xxxi it means one living under the care of
parents.

**12.** *The hearing ear* . . . i.e. not only the organs of hearing and
sight, but their functioning is the work of God, cf. xvi. 4. The implication is that what the ear listens to, and what the eye rests upon,
should be right and pleasing to God.

**13.** *Love not sleep* . . . Cf. vi. 9–11, xxiv. 30–32.
*Open thine eyes.* This phrase, in the sense of keeping awake, occurs
here only.

**14.** *It is naught* . . . The Hebr. is more expressive: 'Bad, bad,
saith the buyer', in reference to what is offered him for sale.
*But when he is gone his way.* It is perhaps better to render: 'and
going his way.'

15 There is gold, and abundance of ¹rubies:
  But the lips of knowledge are a precious jewel.
16 Take his garment that is surety for a stranger;
  And ²hold him in pledge *that is surety* for ³strangers.

  ¹ See Job. xxviii. 18.                    ² Or, *take a pledge of him*
          ³ Another reading is, *a strange woman*.

*he boasteth.* i.e. he brags about having made a good bargain. Although the text does not directly say so, it is implied that he buys
what is offered. The writer merely records what in the east was a
normal procedure; it may occasion surprise that he has no word of
reproach for what was, after all, an unworthy trick; the reason no
doubt was that he meant to give a warning to his inexperienced
pupils, the moral being that the wise man will discount a buyer's
depreciatory exclamation. On the subject of buying and selling Ben-
Sira remarks:

  'As a nail sticketh fast between the joinings of stones,
    So doth sin thrust itself in between buying and selling.'
                          (Ecclus. xxvii. 2, emended text.)

**15.** *There is.* The Hebr. word for this (שׁ) can be translated in
a variety of ways according to the context. As the second line of
this verse is antithetical, it is best to translate, 'though there be gold
&c.', or 'A man may have gold &c.', and to begin the second line
with 'Nevertheless'. The word translated 'rubies' should probably
be 'corals', cf. Job xxviii. 18, and see iii. 15, viii. 11.

*lips of knowledge.* i.e. lips which utter wise things; the same expression occurs in xiv. 7.

*a precious jewel.* The Hebr. word for 'jewel' (כְּלִי) is used in a wide
sense; one could quite justifiably render, 'a precious thing', cf. Hos.
xiii. 15; Nah. ii. 9 (10 in Hebr.); Jer. xxv. 34. It is worth noting how
often the Wisdom writers speak of the acquirement of wisdom, discernment, &c., as the true riches, or as jewels (see e. g. xvi. 16, xxii. 1,
xxviii. 11; Ecclus. x. 30, 31, xxxi. 8). They had a special purpose in
doing so, for the young men in whose welfare they were particularly
interested were, naturally enough, dazzled with the thought of acquiring wealth. The mention of the subject would, therefore, be efficacious
in enlisting their attention, and, having gained this, the Sages were
able to place before their hearers the truths about the higher forms of
wealth to be obtained through the possession of Wisdom.

**16.** *Take his garment* . . . The meaning is that if a man has been
foolish enough to go surety for a stranger, do not spare him if, as a
natural consequence, he has to bear the penalty. According to Deut.
xxiv. 10–13, a man's garment could be taken as security (cf. Am. ii. 8).

*hold him in pledge.* i.e. hold him responsible.

*stranger.* Read, with the Syr., 'strangers'; the Hebr. marg. (cf.

17 Bread of falsehood is sweet to a man;
   But afterwards his mouth shall be filled with gravel.
18 Every purpose is established by counsel:
   And by wise guidance make thou war.
19 He that goeth about as a talebearer revealeth secrets:
   Therefore meddle not with him that openeth wide his lips.

R.V. marg.) can be ignored, it is merely an error. This verse occurs
again almost word for word in xxvii. 13. See further the notes on
vi. 1–5, xi. 15, xvii. 18.

**17.** *Bread of falsehood*. i.e. food obtained by dishonest dealing.
The man who fraudulently acquires anything will often be rather
pleased with himself at first for what he conceives to be his clever-
ness; ultimately, however, he is found out, with disagreeable consequences to himself.

*gravel*. The word occurs elsewhere only in Lam. iii. 16: 'He hath
also broken my teeth with gravel stones.'

**18.** *is established*. 'concerted'; the idea is that care should be
taken to make the carrying out of a plan certain, the context shows
that the reference is to military plans.

*counsel*. i.e. 'forethought', 'consultation', with others.

*make thou war*. It is very unlikely that in a precept of a general
kind an individual would be addressed and bidden to make war. In
xxiv. 6, where the same sentence occurs again, it says, 'thou shalt
make war' (future, not imperat. as here); but, as there, we ought
certainly to read 'war is made' (תֵּעָשֶׂה), instead of 'thou shalt make
war' (תַּעֲשֶׂה), a change in vowel-points only, so here we must emend
the text and read the passive and not the active imperative; 'war
is made', or waged. Cf. Luke xiv. 31.

**19.** *He that goeth* . . . An almost identical line occurs in xi. 13ª
(Hebr.).

*meddle not*. The form of the Hebr. verb is found almost exclusively
in late books; the root meaning is to 'give in pledge', i.e. 'exchange';
here it means to 'share' company or to 'have fellowship'; the best
rendering is perhaps, 'have thou nothing to do with'.

*that openeth wide*. Cf. xiii. 3ᵇ, and for this use of the Hebr. word
(*pāthah*) cf. Gen. ix. 27. But the word can equally well mean 'he that
is foolish' as to his lips. There is a parallel to this verse in the *Teaching of Amen-em-ope*, XXI. xxii. 13, 14:

> Let not thy words be spread abroad among others,
> And have thou nothing to do with the chatterbox.

Griffith renders the second line: 'Nor associate thyself with one who
lays bare his heart', but the meaning is, in essence, the same. In

20  Whoso curseth his father or his mother,
   His lamp shall be put out in the blackest darkness.
21  An inheritance *may be* gotten hastily at the beginning;
   But the end thereof shall not be blessed.

another Egyptian Wisdom-book, *The Teaching of Duauf*, the command is given:

> Utter no secret words, nor speak insolent words.

So, too, in *The Wisdom of Anii*:

> Utter not what is in thine heart to ... man. A wrong word, having issued
> from thy mouth will, if he repeateth it, make thee enemies. A man perisheth
> because of his tongue.

In the *Proverbs of Achikar* ii. 2, it is said:

> My son, if thou hast heard a word,
> Let it die in thy heart, and reveal it to no man.

In the corresponding passage to this in the Elephantiné pap. the
words are somewhat expanded:

> My son, do not chatter overmuch till thou reveal every word which cometh into
> thy mind ; for in every place are their eyes and their ears ; but keep watch over
> thy mouth, and let it not be thy destruction (96, 97).

See further Prov. xxv. 9, 10.

**20.** *Whoso curseth* ... Cf. Exod. xxi. 17; Lev. xx. 9; Deut. xxvii.
16, and see Prov. xxiii. 25, xxx. 17; Ecclus. iii. 1–15, vii. 27, 28. Duty
to parents is also enjoined both in Babylonian and Egyptian Wisdom-books. Thus, in *The Babylonian Book of Proverbs*, § 1, it is said:

> Give food to eat and wine to drink ;
> Seek justice, feed and honour (parents).
> In such an one will (his) god have pleasure.
> It is pleasing unto Shamash who will reward him with good.

In the *Wisdom of Anii* the father bids his son:

> Give a double portion of bread to thy mother who bore thee ...

In the *Proverbs of Achikar* ii. 26, it is said:

> My son, bring not upon thee the curses of thy father and of thy mother,
> Lest thou rejoice not in the blessings of thy children.

Cf. also the Elephantiné Version 138, the words:

> ' He who is not proud of the name of his father and the name of his mother,
> let not the sun shine upon him, for he is an evil man.'

*His lamp shall be put out.* 'Lamp' is a figurative expression for
worldly prosperity.

*in blackest darkness.* Lit. 'the (eye-) pupil of darkness', i.e. the
centre of darkness, which is thought of as radiating darkness, just as
light radiates light ; so that the centre is the darkest point.

**21.** This verse belongs to the preceding one and refers to a son
obtaining his father's inheritance before it is due ('gotten hastily'),

22 Say not thou, I will recompense evil:
   Wait on the LORD, and he shall save thee.

23 Divers weights are an abomination to the LORD;
   And [1] a false balance is not good.

24 A man's goings are of the LORD;
   How then can man understand his way?

---

[1] Heb. *a balance of deceit.*

cf. Luke xv. 11; this brings no blessing. The Hebr. text is evidently
not in order, but the general sense is clear. Unfortunately, the verse
does not occur in the Sept.

**22.** *Say not thou.* There is no need for 'thou', it is not expressed
in this emphatic way in the original.

*I will recompense evil.* The thought is perhaps better expressed
by, 'I will take vengeance for wrong'. Cf. Rom. xii. 19.

*Wait.* Better, 'trust'.

This couplet, which is one of the finest in the book, should be read
together with xxiv. 29, thus:

> Say not, '*I will take vengeance for wrong*';
> *Trust in Jahweh, and he will save thee.*
> Say not, '*As he did to me, so will I do to him,*
> *I will repay a man according to his deed.*'

> (cf. xvii. 13, xxv. 21, 22.)

And with this cf. the following quatrain from the *Teaching of Amen-
em-ope*:

> Say not, '*Find me a strong chief,*
> *For a man in thy city hath injured me*'.
> Say not, '*Find me a redeemer,*
> *For a man who hateth me* (*or whom I hate*) *hath injured me*'.

> (XXI. xxii. 1–4.)

In both these passages vengeance for wrong done is thus deprecated;
'redeemer' in the Egyptian (a hitherto unknown word, according to
Egyptologists) must be understood in the same sense as the Hebr.
*gō'ēl*, 'vindicator', or 'avenger'. To find this teaching, so far in advance of the ordinary conceptions on the subject at the time, in both
these books is a remarkable fact, however it be accounted for.

**23.** That this verse, too, has a parallel in the Egyptian Wisdom-
book is interesting; see note on xvi. 11.

**24.** *A man's goings* . . . Cf. Jer. x. 23; Ps. xxxvii. 23, 24. This is
a striking passage in view of the fact that man's free will and initiative receives much more emphasis in *Proverbs* than divine grace. It
is not that the latter is forgotten, but human responsibility is that
upon which most stress is laid. A verse like this, however, shows the
deep piety which lies at the back of the mind of the Wisdom writers
with all their interest in and teaching on worldly wisdom. This com-

25 It is a snare to a man [1]rashly to say, *It is* holy,
   And after vows to make inquiry.
26 A wise king winnoweth the wicked,
   And bringeth the *threshing* wheel over them.

  [1] Or, *rashly to utter holy* words   Or, *to devour* that which is *holy*

bination reflects one of the finest *traits* in the mental and religious
outlook of the Sages; and it is to be discerned in all the collections in
our book. It issues in the inculcation of the twin virtues of a due
sense of humility and a courageous trust in God; and stands a man
in good stead when perplexed by what appear to him as the incongruities of life.

*how then can* . . . It is interesting to find a similar thought to this
in Babylonian wisdom:

> *The counsel of God is full of knowledge.*
> *Who understandeth it?*

(*Babylonian Wisdom*, p. 41); see further Excursus I.

**25.** The Hebr. of the first line of this difficult verse runs lit.: 'A
snare to man (it is) that he cry rashly "Holy" ', i.e. consecrated. The
Sept. has: 'It is a snare to a man to sanctify any of his possessions
hastily.' The word for 'to cry rashly' occurs elsewhere only in Job
vi. 3. The reference is to the making of a vow in a moment of either
sudden religious exaltation, or of angry passion, to dedicate something to a good purpose, or, in the second case, with evil intent. Cp.
Eccles. v. 2, 4, 5. To pronounce the word *Qōdesh* ('Holy') in regard
to the thing consecrated, constituted the vow. Cf. the formula
*Qorbān* in Matt. xv. 5; Mark vii. 11. Such hasty action might often
result in regrets afterwards.

*to make inquiry.* The Hebr. word has a variety of meanings; the
context would suggest the rendering 'to consider' or 'think over'.
The construction of the original of this verse is uncertain, but the
general sense is clear:

'It is a snare to a man if he cry rashly, "Holy",
  And after vows (have been made) to think over (the matter);' i.e. to repent of it.

Cf. the words of Ben-Sira:

> *Before thou vowest, prepare thy vows,*
> *And be not as one that tempteth God* (Ecclus. xviii. 23).

The evil results of rash vows must in course of time have become
considerable if one may judge of the numerous ways to avoid fulfilling them which are recorded in the Mishnah tractate *Nedarim*.

**26.** *winnoweth.* The Hebr. word can also be translated 'scattereth',
cf. 1 Kings xiv. 15; Ps. xliv. 12; Jer. xxxi. 10, &c., and see note on
*v.* 8 of this chapter; it is in his judicial capacity that the wise king
eliminates the wicked.

*And bringeth* . . . While there is not necessarily any reason to

27 The spirit of man is the lamp of the LORD,
    Searching all the innermost parts of the belly.
28 Mercy and truth preserve the king:
    And [1]his throne is upholden by mercy.

           [1] Or, *he upholdeth his throne*

suppose that this punishment would not have been inflicted by an
Israelite king (on the assumption that such is here referred to), the
mention of it is hardly to be expected in a writing like this, especially
as, with the exception of 2 Sam. xii. 31 (where non-Israelites are the
victims), it is not elsewhere referred to in the O.T.; note also what is
said in *v.* 28. Slight emendations in the Hebrew text suggested by
Steuernagel (reading וְיָשִׁיב עֲלֵיהֶם עוֹנָם, a sentence which occurs in
Ps. xciv. 23), give the text: 'And bringeth upon them their own
iniquity.' This is certainly more in the style of the Wisdom
writers.

**27.** This verse seems to have got in here by mistake as *vv.* 26, 28
clearly belong together.

*The spirit of man.* The Hebr. has 'breath' of man (נְשָׁמָה), which
is not elsewhere used as synonymous with 'spirit'; it is, therefore,
possible that the emendation 'Jahweh preserveth the breath of man'
(נֹצֵר 'preserveth' for נֵר 'lamp') suggested by some commentators
is justified. On the other hand, the second line supports the text as
it stands; and in this case we must understand 'breath' as equivalent
to 'spirit'. The meaning then presumably is that man's spirit is
utilized by God as a means for discerning his innermost thoughts;
but, if so, the thought is unparalleled in the O.T., and quite out of
harmony with such a passage as xxiv. 12. It is, however, worth
considering whether the Hebrew sage had not been influenced here
by an Egyptian conception; the idea that some part of the human
body is identical with part of a god and must therefore be used in
accordance with the will of the deity occurs in the *Teaching of Amen-
em-ope*, XV. xvii. 7:

    *The beak of Ibis is the finger of the scribe.*

It is possible that the Hebr. sage made use of this idea and adapted
it in a more spiritual direction.

*the innermost parts of the belly.* 'Belly' is used in precisely the
same way several times in the *Teaching of Amen-em-ope*.

**28.** *Mercy and truth.* Cf. iii. 3, xi. 17, xiv. 22, xvi. 6.

*And his throne is . . . mercy.* Read 'And he upholdeth his throne
by equity'; the repetition of 'mercy' is not in the style of the Wisdom writers; the Sept. has 'equity', which probably represents the
original text.

29 The glory of young men is their strength:
　And the beauty of old men is the hoary head.
30 Stripes that wound cleanse away evil:
　And strokes *reach* the innermost parts of the belly.
**XXI.** 1 The king's heart is in the hand of the LORD as the
　　　watercourses:
　He turneth it whithersoever he will.

**29.** *And the beauty* ... Cf. xvi. 31. Ben-Sira says:

> How beautiful to grey hairs is judgement ...
> How beautiful is the wisdom of old men ... (Ecclus. xxv. 4, 5).

**30.** The Hebr. text of this verse is corrupt; various emendations
have been proposed. The first line is, as compared with the second,
somewhat overloaded; if we read: 'Stripes purify the wicked (man)'
(חַבֻּרוֹת תַּמְרִיק רַע), we get three words, the number which so often
makes up the line in this collection, and which correspond with the
three words of the second line: 'And strokes the innermost parts of
the belly'; the meaning being that chastisement is good for an evil
man because it deters him from further wrong-doing by affecting
both his body and his spirit.

## CHAPTER XXI

**1.** *The king's heart* ... i.e. the kindly acts of a king are of divine
prompting.
　*watercourses.* The reference is to artificially constructed channels
from a river for the purposes of irrigation; Steuernagel explains them
as small pits which were filled with water from a stream in order to
give plenty of moisture to plants; as neither were in any case used in
Palestine the idea was taken from elsewhere, quite possibly from
Egypt (see Deut. xi. 10–12, where Egypt is referred to). In the
*Teaching of Amen-em-ope* reference is made to one who 'is like a tree
grown in a plot' (IV. vi. 8); Egyptologists confess that the rendering
'plot' is a guess as the original word for it is unknown. Griffith says
that 'in Egypt the pit in which a tree has been planted in a garden
is surrounded by a raised rim to retain water; possibly the new word
in line 8 designates such a pit'. The context leads one to expect the
mention of water, it says that 'it grows green, it doubles its yield'. It
is, therefore, quite possible that this passage suggested the simile of
which the Hebrew sage makes use here.
　*He turneth it* ... Just as the water was directed wherever required
by the irrigator, so God inclines the heart of a king to deeds of mercy
in accordance with His will.

2 Every way of a man is right in his own eyes:
  But the LORD weigheth the hearts.
3 To do justice and judgement
  Is more acceptable to the LORD than sacrifice.
4 An high look, and a proud heart,
  ¹ *Even* the lamp of the wicked, is sin.

¹ Or, And *the tillage*

**2.** *Every way* . . . See xvi. 2, where a similar thought occurs; cf.
also xiv. 12, xvi. 25.

**3.** *To do justice* . . . Here again is to be seen the influence of the
teaching of the prophets, cf. e. g. Am. v. 22–24; Hos. vi. 6; Isa. i. 11–
14; Mic. vi. 6–8, and Ben-Sira illustrates this prophetical influence
more fully in Ecclus. xxxiv. 14–31, xxv. 1–26. Cf. Matth. ix. 13.

*Is more acceptable* . . . The attitude of the Wisdom writers towards
the sacrificial system and ceremonial worship was, briefly, that while
these should be observed they were to be regarded as subordinate to
ethical demands. The Law commanded the offering of sacrifices,
therefore they must be retained; this seems in the eyes of the Sages
to be the only justification for their retention. But everything depends upon the spirit in which offerings are made (iii. 9); the sacrifices of the wicked are unacceptable to God (xv. 8, cf. Ecclus. xxxiv.
21–23). Ben-Sira contemplates the abrogation of material sacrifices
in favour of spiritual ones in these striking words:

> He that keepeth the Law multiplieth offerings,
> And he that giveth heed to the commandments sacrificeth a peace-offering.
> He that rendereth kindness offereth fine flour,
> And he that giveth alms sacrificeth a thank-offering . . . (xxxv. 1–5).

On the other hand, he recognizes that they have their uses provided
the God-ward attitude is observed in regard to them (xxxv. 6–13).
In the *Midrash* on Deuteronomy v. 3, there is an interesting comment on this verse, referred to by Schechter; he says: 'It is pointed
out that the superiority of practising the works of charity and justice
over sacrifices consists in this, that while the atoning effect of the
former extends also to the sins committed wilfully, that of the latter
is confined only to sins committed unintentionally' (*Some Aspects
of Rabbinic Theology*, p. 296 [1909]).

**4.** It is only by means of artificially constructed mental links that
any connexion between the two lines of this verse can be made to
exist. There can be no doubt that they are fragments, the other line
belonging to each couplet having accidentally fallen out of the text.
Emendation, therefore, would be futile. The first line runs, lit.:
'Lifting-up of the eyes and largeness of heart,' i. e. overbearing eyes
and a puffed-up mind,—the rest of the sentence is wanting. The
second line has: 'The fallow-ground (or, the lamp) of the wicked is

5 The thoughts of the diligent *tend* only to plenteousness:
  But every one that is hasty *hasteth* only to want.
6 The getting of treasures by a lying tongue
  Is a vapour driven to and fro; [1]they *that seek them* seek
  death.

[1] Or, according to some ancient authorities, they are *snares of death* or, into *the snares of death*

sin'; in this fragment the text is out of order, for whether we read 'fallow-ground' (R.V. 'tillage') or 'lamp',—according as it is pointed, the Hebr. word can mean either,—it is not easy to get sense out of the words; if we read 'fallow-ground' and assume that the ploughing of it is implied, then the meaning might be that even when the wicked begin a new life it will still be sinful (Steuernagel), though this seems a little far-fetched. If, on the other hand, we read 'lamp', with all the Versions, the passage is still more wanting in sense. This is a case in which we must give up the attempt to extract any meaning from the verse; all that can be said is that of the two couplets of which we have the remnants here, the first line of one, and the last line of the other, seem to have been preserved.

**5.** This verse is omitted in the Sept.
*the diligent.* Cf. x. 4, where the acquisition of wealth is also referred to.
*only.* Better 'of a surety', or the like.
*every one that is hasty.* We are no doubt intended to understand 'hasty to become (rich)', as in xxviii. 20, where it is more fully expressed; otherwise the word is used of being hasty with his feet (xix. 2), or hasty in word (xxix. 20).

**6.** *The getting of treasures.* It is more in the style of the writer to read, with the change of one vowel-point, 'He that getteth'; so the Sept., i.e. a participle in place of a noun.
*Is a vapour* . . . The Hebr. text is corrupt; it reads, lit.: '(Is) a driven vapour, seekers of death', which is meaningless. Based partly on the Sept., Steuernagel emends the text so as to read: 'Pursueth after a vapour and the snares of death' (הֶבֶל רֹדֵף וּמוֹקְשֵׁי־מָוֶת) which gives excellent sense. Cf. Ecclus. xl. 13, 14:

> *Ill-gotten wealth is like a winter torrent,*
> *And like a water-course swollen by a thunderstorm ;*
> *When it riseth rocks are rolled down ;*
> *So doth it* (or, *he*) *suddenly come to an end for ever.*

See also Jer. xvii. 11.
  With the first line of this *v.* cf. the *Proverbs of Achikar* ii. 67:

'My son, if thy will is to be wise, refrain thy tongue from lying, and thy hand from theft, and thou shalt become wise.'

N

7 The violence of the wicked shall sweep them away;
  Because they refuse to do judgement.
8 The way of him that is laden with guilt is exceeding crooked:
  But as for the pure, his work is [1]right.
9 It is better to dwell in the corner of the housetop,
  Than with a contentious woman in [2]a wide house.
10 The soul of the wicked desireth evil:
   His neighbour findeth no favour in his eyes.
11 When the scorner is punished, the simple is made wise:
   And [3]when the wise is instructed, he receiveth knowledge.

[1] Or, *straight.*     [2] Or, *a house in common* Heb. *a house of society.*
[3] Or, *when one considereth the wise.*

**7.** *shall sweep them away.* The same word is used fig. of dragging fish away in Hab. i. 15; for a similar thought as that of this verse see i. 18, 19.

*to do judgement.* i.e. to act justly. The meaning of the verse seems to be that the wicked become so entangled in the net of their own wrong-doing that they lose the faculty of discerning what is upright and just.

**8.** *him that is laden with guilt.* The Hebr. word, (וָזֵר) if correct, does not occur elsewhere, and its meaning is taken to be that of the cognate Arabic word. Steuernagel believes it to have arisen through dittography, the following word being very similar (וְזַךְ), and that it is a corruption which has ousted whatever stood there originally.

*But as for the pure* . . . Cf. xx. 11[b].

**9.** This *v.* occurs again in xxv. 24.

*Than with a contentious woman.* The Hebr. suggests rather the rendering: 'Than (to have) a contentious wife.'

*in a wide house.* This assumes an emendation of the text, which as it stands has 'and the house of a companion'; we should, no doubt, read 'and a wide house' (וּבֵית רָחָב instead of וּבֵית חָבֵר). Cf. xix. 13, xxvii. 15, and Ecclus. xxv. 16:

> *I would rather dwell with a lion and a dragon,*
> *Than keep house with a wicked wife.*

**10.** *findeth no favour.* i.e. does not receive any consideration. The force of the Hebr. is brought out better by rendering: 'Even his neighbour (or companion) receives no consideration in his eyes', or, as we should say, 'at his hands'. With the verse cf. iv. 16 and Ecclus. xii. 13, 14:

> *Who pitieth a charmer bitten (by a serpent),*
> *Or any that approacheth a savage beast?*
> *So is he that is companion to a godless man.*

**11.** *is punished.* Lit. 'is fined', cf. xvii. 26, xxii. 3, xxvii. 12.

12 [1]The righteous man considereth the house of the wicked;
   *How* the wicked are overthrown to *their* ruin.
13 Whoso stoppeth his ears at the cry of the poor,
   He also shall cry, but shall not be heard.
14 A gift in secret [2]pacifieth anger,
   And a present in the bosom strong wrath.

[1] Or, *One that is righteous . . . he overthroweth the wicked &c.*
[2] Heb. *bendeth.*

Through the warning given by the fine laid upon a scorner for his wrongdoing, even a simple-minded fool (*pethī*) is brought to see wisdom.

*And when the wise . . .* It is perhaps better to take the Hebr. word for 'is instructed' in the sense of 'is prosperous', as in xvii. 8, and to delete the preposition 'to' (not expressed in English); this gives a smoother rendering. The simple-minded man learns both from the adversity of the scorner, by taking warning from him, and by the prosperity of the wise, by encouragement ('he receiveth knowledge').

**12.** The R.V. rendering of the second line of this verse is not justified by the Hebr. as it stands, but the text is quite obviously out of order. Taking the verse as a whole the subject of it is 'the righteous man'; but the words 'overthroweth the wicked to ruin' (lit. 'evil') necessitate our understanding 'the righteous' as referring to God; but this term, isolated as it is here, is never used for God. We must, probably, regard the two halves of the verse as being independent of one another originally, and as having been mistakenly joined together by a scribe who had in mind such a passage as Ps. xxxvii. 35, 36; the same word being used for 'wicked' in each line is sufficient to show that they do not belong together, the Wisdom writers do not do this. The first line can be translated as in the R.V. (the marg. may be ignored); but the second is: 'He overthroweth the wicked to ruin', i.e. he plungeth the wicked into misfortune. Each line in its original context gave, no doubt, excellent sense.

**13.** *at the cry of the poor.* Here again is to be seen the influence of the prophets.

*shall not be heard.* Hebr. 'shall not be answered'. With the verse cf. Ecclus. iv. 4, 5:

> *Despise not the supplication of the poor,*
> *And turn thyself not from the broken in spirit,*
> *From him that asketh turn not away thine eye,*
> *And give him no cause to curse thee.*

**14.** *A gift.* The reference is, as in xvii. 23, to a bribe.

*pacifieth.* The R.V. rightly assumes an emendation in the Hebr. text (יְכַפֶּר for יִכְפֶּה); to have one verb governing both lines occurs elsewhere in *Proverbs*, but it is unusual.

N 2

15 It is joy to the righteous to do judgement;
   [1] But it is a destruction to the workers of iniquity.
16 The man that wandereth out of the way of understanding
   Shall rest in the congregation of [2] the dead.
17 He that loveth pleasure shall be a poor man:
   He that loveth wine and oil shall not be rich.

[1] Or, *But destruction* shall be *to* &c.
[2] Or, *the shades* Heb. *Rephaim*.

**15.** *to do judgement.* i.e. the doing of justice; the words do not mean here that it is the righteous man who does justice; what they mean is that he rejoices at the doing of justice; when he sees justice carried out. In contrast to this it is said that this is a terror to evil-doers; they are naturally dismayed at seeing justice done because they fear the result for themselves. The Hebr. word means both 'destruction' and 'dismay'; the latter is the meaning here. The antithesis between 'joy' and 'dismay' is a more pointed antithesis; moreover, in antitheses of this kind the Wisdom writers usually place two abstract nouns or two concrete nouns in contrast. By his words the Sage is implicitly inculcating respect for constituted authority; the wise man is he who loves law and order, which the administration of justice ensures. In thus teaching the young what are the bases of a civilized community the Wisdom writers were patriots in the best sense of the word. See further xi. 11, 14, xxix. 2; Ecclus. xxxvii. 22–26.

**16.** The verse simply means foolish people die prematurely; the same is often said about the wicked in spite of the fact that the experience of life shows that the idea was erroneous; but a rooted conviction, however mistaken, takes long to eradicate.

**17.** *pleasure.* As the second line shows, what is referred to is feasting. Wine to make one merry and oil to give a 'cheerful countenance' were indispensable at feasts. Too much indulgence in the pleasures of the table, as the Sage says, brings poverty. While a very sane and human view is taken by the Wisdom writers on the subject of social life, they were fully alive to the dangers of luxury and self-indulgence to young men belonging to the wealthier classes; and it is to these, more especially, that such words as those of this verse would be addressed. That such warnings were applicable in pre-exilic as well as in post-exilic times is clear from such passages as Am. iv. 1, vi. 3–6. In later times, when the danger was still greater owing to the influence of the Greeks, Ben-Sira wrote:

> *Delight not thyself in overmuch luxury,*
> *For double is the poverty thereof.*
> *Be not a squanderer and a drunkard,*
> *Else will there be nothing in thy purse* (Ecclus. xviii. 32, 33).

18 The wicked is a ransom for the righteous;
   And the treacherous *cometh* in the stead of the upright.
19 It is better to dwell in a desert land,
   Than with [1] a contentious and fretful woman.
20 There is precious treasure and oil in the dwelling of the wise;
   But a foolish man swalloweth it up.
21 He that followeth after righteousness and mercy
   Findeth life, righteousness, and honour.
22 A wise man scaleth the city of the mighty,

     [1] Or, *a contentious woman and vexation*

**18.** This verse might almost be called a comment on Ps. lxxiii. 1–14; it is the bitter cry of one of the 'pious ones', often mentioned in the Psalms, who cannot understand why the godly should be in adversity while the wicked prosper. The words are an exaggerated utterance such as would be cried out by one in bitterness of spirit; they are meant to say that the righteous man suffers in order that the wicked may be in prosperity; he is, as it were, a ransom for the wicked; he takes his place. It is a sarcasm spoken by the victim of adverse circumstances in order to give vent to his feelings. That it is quite out of place here goes without saying; but it only shows how this collection of 'proverbs' was put together from all kinds of sources.

**19.** Cf. verse 9, xxv. 24.
*Than with* . . . Or, as in verse 9: 'Than (to have) a wife of contentions and vexation', i.e. than a quarrelsome and aggravating wife.

**20.** *precious treasure*. Lit. a 'desirable treasure'; clearly not wealth in the ordinary sense; it is used figuratively of wise words (see below).
*and oil*. This is meaningless and has got into the text by mistake; the Sept. omits it.
*in the dwelling*. Read with the Sept., 'in the mouth'. The meaning of the verse seems to be that the wise man utters wisdom, this 'treasure' is constantly on his lips, whereas the fool, instead of talking sense, suppresses ('swallows') any sensible utterance that suggests itself to him. It must be remembered that the word for fool used here is '*kĕsil*', i.e. the type which is capable of 'apprehending understanding' (viii. 5); see on this, Excursus XI.

**21.** *righteousness*. This includes all pious works in the sight of God and towards man. In the second line the repetition of 'righteousness' is no doubt a clerical error, and should be omitted, with the Sept.
*life and honour*. Cf. iii. 16, xxii. 4.

**22.** *scaleth*. i.e. conquers (lit. ascends); cf. Jos. ii. 7; the idea is that the spiritual power of wisdom is greater than that of material things.

And bringeth down the strength of the confidence thereof.
23 Whoso keepeth his mouth and his tongue
Keepeth his soul from troubles.
24 The proud and haughty man, scorner is his name,
He worketh in the arrogance of pride.
25 The desire of the slothful killeth him;
For his hands refuse to labour.
26 There is that coveteth greedily all the day long:
But the righteous giveth and withholdeth not.
27 The sacrifice of the wicked is an abomination:
How much more, when he bringeth it [1] with a wicked mind!

[1] Or, to atone *for wickedness*

*the strength of the confidence.* What is meant is the city walls, or bulwarks. With the thought of the verse cf. Eccles. ix. 13–18.

**23.** Cf. xiii. 3, xviii. 21.

*troubles.* As in xii. 13, the reference is to the difficulties into which a man may get himself through incautious speech. With the verse cf. the quotation from the *Teaching of Amen-em-ope*, given in the note on xiii. 3.

**24.** The verse forms a single sentence in Hebr.; it might be rendered: 'The proud and haughty man, working in the arrogance of pride,—"Scorner" is his name.' Toy remarks that the couplet 'must be taken as a definition of the term *scoffer*; in that case it and xxiv. 8 are the only examples of formal definition in the book. If this interpretation be correct, it appears to point to the existence of a precise, philosophical form of instruction in the schools, and to the distinct recognition of a class of arrogant disregarders of moral Law . . .' The latter point is borne out by certain passages in the book of Job.

*scorner.* See Excursus XI.

**25.** *killeth him.* The form of the Hebr. verb means 'causeth him to die'; this brings out the sense better, for it is slothfulness—the sluggard's desire is to do nothing—which really kills him. Cf. xix. 24.

**26.** *There is that coveteth* . . . The Hebr. of this line is lit.: 'all day he desires desire'; that is meaningless, and the want of a subject also points to a corruption in the text. The Sept. has 'the wicked' as the subject, and as 'desire' might very easily have arisen through dittography—but for one letter it is the same as 'desireth'—the probability is that 'the wicked' (רָשָׁע) originally stood in the place of 'desire' (תַּאֲוָה). The line would thus mean that the wicked are for ever wanting something. As against this the righteous man, so far from desiring what others have, is generous and is always ready to give. Cf. xx. 9.

**27.** *an abomination.* In xv. 8ᵃ, where this line also occurs, 'to the

28 A false witness shall perish:
   But the man that heareth shall speak [1]unchallenged.
29 A wicked man hardeneth his face:
   But as for the upright, [2]he ordereth his ways.
30 There is no wisdom nor understanding
   Nor counsel against the LORD.
31 The horse is prepared against the day of battle:
   But [3]victory is of the LORD.

[1] Or, *so as to endure*       [2] Another reading is, *he considereth his way.*
[3] Or, *deliverance*

Lord' is added; as the Sept. has this here as well, it should, no doubt,
be read.

   *with a wicked mind.* Better 'for wickedness', see R.V. marg. Evidently there were men who believed that sacrifices absolved from sin;
see further, Excursus VI. Ben-Sira says:

*The sacrifice of an unrighteous man is a mocking sacrifice,*
*And the oblations* (so the Syriac; the Grk. has 'mockeries') *of the wicked are*
   *not acceptable.*
*The Most High hath no pleasure in the offerings of the ungodly,*
*Neither is He pacified for sins by the multitude of sacrifices.*
                    (Ecclus. xxxiv. [xxxi] 21–23.)

That a similar idea obtained in later days is seen from the words of
the Targum to Eccles. iv. 27 (Hebr. v. 11): 'Be not like the fools who
bring a sacrifice for their offences, but turn not from the evil deeds
which they have in their hands, and are not accepted in grace' (quoted
by Schechter, *op. cit.*, p. 296).

   **28.** *A false witness.* Lit. 'a witness of lies', cf. xix. 5, 9, but the
Hebr. word is different.

   *But the man . . .* The Hebr. has: 'But a man that heareth talketh
continually'; the text is corrupt. For 'heareth' (שׁוֹמֵעַ) read, with
the Sept., 'guardeth' (שֹׁמֵר); and for 'continually' (לָנֶצַח), read 'his
tongue' (לְשׁוֹנוֹ), cf. *v.* 23; the line will then run: 'But he that guardeth
his tongue will speak.' The writer is thinking of a court of justice,
and the contrast is between the false witness and him that is careful
in his evidence; it is the latter who will have the right to speak while
the former will perish.

   **29.** *hardeneth his face.* Cf. the modern expression 'brazen-faced',
i.e. impudent.

   *he ordereth his ways.* See R.V. marg.; either reading gives good
sense; the two words are very similar in Hebr.: 'he ordereth' יָכִין,
'he considereth' יָבִין; the Sept. reads the latter, which, upon the
whole, is to be preferred as it contrasts better with 'hardeneth'.

   **30.** *against.* i.e. which is in opposition to, *all* wisdom being from
God.

   **31.** With the verse cf. Ps. xx. 7 (8 in Hebr.).

**XXII. 1** A *good* name is rather to be chosen than great riches,
And [1]loving favour rather than silver and gold.
2 The rich and the poor meet together:
The LORD is the maker of them all.
3 A prudent man seeth the evil, and hideth himself:
But the simple pass on, and [2]suffer for it.
4 The reward of humility *and* the fear of the LORD
*Is* riches, and honour, and life.

[1] Or, *favour is better than &c.*    [2] Heb. *are mulcted.*

## CHAPTER XXII

**1.** *A* good *name* ... 'Good' is not expressed in the Hebr. though the Versions insert it; but it is not required. Ben-Sira enlarged on this line, thus:

> *Be in fear of thy name, for that abideth longer for thee*
> *Than thousands of precious treasures.*
> *Life's goods (last) for limited days,*
> *But the reward of a name for days without number.*

> (Ecclus. xli. 12, 13, Hebr.)

A somewhat similar thought in which, however, 'beauty' takes the place of riches, occurs in *The Proverbs of Achikar* ii. 49:

> *Better is a good name than much beauty,*
> *Because a good name standeth for aye,*
> *But beauty waneth and wasteth away.*

*is rather to be chosen.* So the Hebr. lit.; but the form of the verb permits of rendering the words: 'More precious (or "choice") a name than great riches', cf. xvi. 16, xxi. 3.

*loving favour.* Read as R.V. marg.; by favour is meant to be loved of men.

**2.** The Wisdom writers, while fully recognizing differences in social rank, desire that all men should recognize their common humanity, and should also remember their common origin. With the verse cf. xxix. 13, and Ecclus. xi. 14 (Hebr.):

> *Good and evil, life and death,*
> *Poverty and wealth, are from the Lord.*

**3.** This verse occurs again in xxvii. 12.

*prudent.* The Hebr. word would be better translated 'shrewd'; in *Proverbs* the word is always used in a good sense. It is the same word which is applied to the serpent in Gen. iii. 1.

*hideth himself.* i.e. keeps out of the way.

*suffer for it.* R.V. marg. expresses the Hebr., cf. xvii. 26, xxi. 11.

**4.** With this verse, which expresses one of the fundamental themes of the Wisdom writers, dependence on God, cf. iii. 5–8, xxix. 25, 26; Ecclus. xl. 26, 27.

5 Thorns *and* snares are in the way of the froward:
　He that keepeth his soul shall be far from them.
6 Train up a child [1] in the way he should go,
　And even when he is old he will not depart from it.
7 The rich ruleth over the poor,
　And the borrower is servant to the lender.
8 He that soweth iniquity shall reap [2] calamity:
　And the rod of his wrath shall fail.
9 He that hath a [3] bountiful eye shall be blessed;
　For he giveth of his bread to the poor.

　　　[1] Heb. *according to his way.*　　　[2] Or, *vanity*　　　[3] Heb. *good.*

**5.** *Thorns.* Though the Hebrew word is very rare, occurring elsewhere only in Job v. 5, and of uncertain meaning, it is appropriate enough here as it implies a hedge, a good figure of the kind of obstacle that bars the way of the 'froward', i.e. one whose path in life is devious; he is the opposite to the upright or 'straight' man.

*He that keepeth his soul.* i.e. he that looks after himself, cf. xvi. 17.

**6.** This verse does not occur in the Sept. As Wildeboer points out, it contains a word, the meaning and construction of which is late Hebr. (חֲנֹךְ לְ); it is, therefore, probable that this verse was one of the latest additions to the book, and did not stand in its present place when the Greek translation was made.

*in the way he should go.* i.e. according to the way in which he is intended to go.

**7.** *ruleth over.* i.e. in the sense of 'lords it over'.

*servant.* The Hebr. word means lit. 'slave'; but this is not to be taken literally here.

**8.** Cf. xii. 14; Gal. vi. 7.

*calamity.* Here the Hebr. word has the sense of 'trouble' or 'sorrow', as in xii. 21, cf. Deut. xxvi. 14; Hos. ix. 4 (plur. form); Am. v. 5; Jer. iv. 15; Hab. iii. 7.

*And the rod . . .* It is difficult to get any sense out of the Hebr. as it stands; the text is evidently corrupt. One expects some thought-connexion between the two lines. Following the Sept. we may read, instead of 'the rod of his wrath' (שֵׁבֶט עֶבְרָתוֹ), 'the rod of his labour' (שֵׁבֶט עֲבֹדָתוֹ), i.e. the rod he uses for his labour of threshing. The word is used in Isa. xxviii. 27 of the rod for beating cummin; this continues the agricultural figure of the first line. Then, in place of 'shall fail' (יִכְלֶה), Steuernagel suggests the reading 'will smite him' (יַכֵּהוּ). According to this emended text the line would then run: 'And the rod of his labour will smite him', i.e. the rod which he used for threshing will be applied to his back. This gives an excellent connexion with the first line to which it offers an illustrative parallel, couched similarly in figurative form.

10 Cast out the scorner, and contention shall go out;
   Yea, strife and ignominy shall cease.

11 He that loveth [1]pureness of heart,
   [2]*For* the grace of his lips the king shall be his friend.

12 The eyes of the LORD preserve *him that hath* knowledge,
   But he overthroweth the words of the treacherous man.

13 The sluggard saith, There is a lion without:
   I shall be [3]murdered in the streets.

14 The mouth of strange women is a deep pit:
   He [4]that is abhorred of the LORD shall fall therein.

[1] Another reading is, *the pure of heart.*   [2] Or, *Hath grace in his lips* Or, *That hath grace in his lips*   [3] Or, *slain*   [4] Or, *against whom the Lord hath indignation*

**9.** *a bountiful eye.* Lit. 'a good eye', i.e. one of generous disposition. Contrast the envious man of 'evil eye', in xxiii. 6, xxviii. 22. With the thought of the line cf. xi. 25, and Ecclus vii. 32 (Hebr.):

> Also to the poor stretch forth thine hand,
> That thy blessing may be full.

In the *Wisdom of Anii* it is said: 'Eat no bread if another suffereth want, and thou hast not offered him bread in thine hand.'

**10.** *Scorner.* See Excursus XI.

**11.** The Hebr. text of this verse is corrupt as the syntax is at fault. On the basis of the Versions, the first line may be rendered: 'The Lord loveth the pure in heart.' The second line may be emended so as to read: 'He maketh gracious (cf. xxvi. 25) his lips, a king is his friend' (וְיֵחַנֵּ שְׂפָתָיו רֵעֵהוּ מֶלֶךְ); it is better to retain 'king' (against some commentators) because it is supported by the Sept.

**12.** Here again the Hebr. text of the first line can hardly be in order. As Toy points out, the verb can here 'mean only *guard*, and cannot be followed by the abstract term *knowledge*, nor does O.T. usage permit the interpretation of this term as equivalent to *him who has knowledge*; and the verb is not an appropriate predicate of *the eyes of Jahweh*, which are said elsewhere to "rest upon, be directed toward", but never to "guard, protect"'. He suggests the emendation: 'The eyes of the Lord are on the righteous' (עֵינֵי יְהֹוָה בַּצַּדִּיקִים), cf. Ps. xxxiv. 15 (16 in Hebr.), ci. 6.

*he overthroweth.* Cf. xix. 3, xxi. 12.

**13.** *The sluggard saith* ... The line occurs again with slight variation in xxvi. 13.

*There is a lion* ... Any excuse suffices for the sluggard to remain at ease. Cf. vi. 9, xix. 24, xx. 4, xxi. 25; Ecclus. xxii. 1, 2.

**14.** *the mouth.* Cf. ii. 16[b], 'which flattereth with her words'.

*strange women.* i.e. adulteresses, cf. ii. 16, v. 3 ff., vii. 5 ff., xxiii. 27.

*a deep pit.* In xxiii. 27[b] it is the strange woman herself who is spoken of as 'a narrow pit'.

15 Foolishness is bound up in the heart of a child;
   *But* the rod of correction shall drive it far from him.
16 He that oppresseth the poor to increase his *gain*,
   *And* he that giveth to the rich, *cometh* only to want.

*He that is abhorred.* The Hebr. word always has the sense of indignation; the form of the verb here (passive partic.) means one who
is the object of indignation.

*fall therein.* i.e. because he has aroused the Lord's wrath by
consorting with the adulteress. The falling into a deep pit is the
figurative way of expressing the trouble in which a man involves
himself by his action; he is unable to get himself out of it.

**15.** On the treatment of children see xiii. 24, xxii. 6, xxix. 15, 21;
Ecclus. xxx. 7–13.

**16.** There are few verses in the book to which such various interpretations have been given as to this one. The Hebr. is ambiguous.
The first line runs: 'He that oppresseth the poor to cause increase to
him'; the words 'to him' can refer either to him that oppresseth, or
to the poor man; the former would be the more natural. The second
line continues the sentence: 'giveth to a rich man only to cause
want'; the rich man is presumably he who oppressed the poor,
whereby he became rich. In this case the words would mean that he
who enriches himself by oppressing the poor will only come to want.
Excellent as the sense of this would be, it must be confessed that it
is not in the style of the writer, and also involves a rather forced
interpretation of the second line. Steuernagel renders: 'He that
oppresseth the poor (it tends) to increase his (goods)', i.e. those of
the poor man; 'he that giveth to the rich (it turns) only to want',
i.e. of the rich man. This he explains to mean that the poor man
works all the harder on account of his being oppressed, but the rich
man carelessly spends all the more, and thus comes to want. This
also gives good sense, but appears even more forced than the former
interpretation. Toy would alter the text, and, following xxviii. 8,
27 (cf. xi. 24), change 'oppresseth' to 'giveth to', reading: 'He who
giveth to the poor it is gain to him, he who giveth to the rich it is
only loss'; we should then, he says, 'have a double contrast, between
*poor* and *rich*, and between *gain* and *loss*, and the couplet would be a
commendation of benevolence and a condemnation of bribery and
servility'. The objection to this is that the alteration of the text is
quite arbitrary, and the use of the identical verb, 'giveth', in each
line is not in the style of the writer.

This is a case in which a wholly satisfactory solution is perhaps
not to be looked for.

# THE THIRD COLLECTION OF PROVERBS

## XXII. 17—XXIV. 34. *The Sayings of the Wise*

THIS section of *Proverbs* comprises three short collections: (*a*) xxii. 17–xxiii. 14; (*b*) xxiii. 15–xxiv. 22; (*c*) xxiv. 23–34. Most commentators regard (*a*) and (*b*) as one collection, and call (*c*) an Appendix. We believe that (*a*) xxii. 17–xxiii. 14 is in itself a separate collection because it is almost wholly paralleled by sayings in the *Teaching of Amen-em-ope*, whereas in (*b*) xxiii. 15–xxiv. 22, with one exception, there is no affinity with the Egyptian Wisdom book. Moreover (*b*) begins with a special address to 'My son', which marks it off from the preceding collection. These two collections were, however, combined and made into one before they were incorporated in our book, see note on xxii. 20. Why (*c*) xxiv. 23–34 should be called an Appendix is not clear; it is a distinct collection with a separate title: 'These also are sayings of the Wise.' While in content these three collections follow, in the main, the line of the preceding collections, in form they differ; though this difference is more marked in comparison with x–xxii. 16 than with i–ix. The completed couplets of the former are rare here, instead of which a strophic arrangement is adopted, four lines to a strophe, and we get something more in the nature of a miniature essay. The same strophic form occurs, with some exceptions, in the *Teaching of Amen-em-ope*. While in x–xxii. 16 the sayings are simply recorded, here the sage directly addresses his hearer.

17 Incline thine ear, and hear the words of the wise,
    And apply thine heart unto my knowledge.

## XXII. 17–21. *Introduction, adapted from the 'Teaching of Amen-em-ope'*.

**17, 18.** The Sept. is doubtless right in prefacing this collection with the title: 'Sayings of the Wise.' Originally this must have stood in the Hebr., but a scribe mistakenly put it into the text ('the words of the wise'); in place of this, following the Sept. again, we must read 'my words'; so that the line should run: 'Incline thine ear, and hear my words.'

*apply thine heart*. The Hebr. phrase occurs often of setting one's mind to something, to pay attention to, give heed to, cf. xxvii. 23.

*unto my knowledge*. Following the Sept. it is better to read 'to know' (לָדַעַת), or, as Erman suggests, 'to know them' (לְדָעְתָּם). By 'know' here is meant 'apprehend'.

18 For it is a pleasant thing if thou keep them within thee,
   If they be established together upon thy lips.

The parallel to this in A[1] runs:

> *Give thine ear, and hear what I say,*
> *And apply thine heart to apprehend.*

It may be pointed out that the expression 'Give, or incline, thine
ear' is one common in Hebrew; but, as a rule, it is used in a different
connexion, mostly as an appeal from man to God (e.g. Ps. xvii. 6,
xxxi. 2 (3 in Hebr.), lxxi. 2, lxxxvi. 1), and even when, as here, it is
addressed by a teacher to his pupil (Prov. iv. 20, v. 1), there is not
the addition, 'and apply thine heart . . .', which our text has in
common with the Egyptian sage, and which, therefore, points to
indebtedness on the part of the Hebrew writer.

**18.** *For it is a pleasant thing.* Hebr. simply 'for it is a pleasant'
used for qualifying words; it is used in xv. 26, xvi. 24. It is hardly
the word one would expect here; 'profitable' (יִתְרוֹן, Eccles. x. 10)
would have been more appropriate.

*within thee.* Lit. 'in thy belly'.

*If they be established.* Hebr. 'they will be established', or 'ready',
i.e. for use, cf. xix. 29.

*together.* This word is meaningless here; instead of it Gressmann
suggests 'peg' (יָתֵד), Sellin, 'as a peg'; it would be a very unusual
use of the word, as it never occurs in this sense, though it is used
figuratively, e.g. in Zech. x. 4; Ezra ix. 8; the meaning of the line
would then be that the fixed habit of uttering wise words would act
as a check if anything arose which might ruffle the serenity proper
to a wise man. In favour of the adoption of this suggestion is the
fact that it would correspond with the word which occurs in the
parallel line in A, as well as implying here the same content as
the passage there. In this latter the corresponding passage consists
of six short lines, not all of which, of course, offer a parallel to this
verse; but they are worth quoting in full, because they illustrate how
the Hebrew sage seems to have condensed the words of his Egyptian
*confrère*, but to have extracted the essence of the passage:

> *It is good to place them in thine heart,*
> *—Woe to him who refuseth them—*
> *Let them rest in the casket of thy belly,*
> *That they may be a threshold in thine heart;*
> *That if a hurricane of words arise,*
> *They may act as a peg upon thy tongue.*

Experts differ as to the precise meaning of one or two words; in the

---

[1] Abbreviation for the *Teaching of Amen-em-ope*: for chapter and line see
Excursus I, pp. xlvi ff. Wherever permissible the same English word in the parallels
is used in order to bring out the close relation between the Hebrew and Egyptian
books.

19 That thy trust may be in the LORD,
  I have made *them* known to thee this day, even to thee.

fourth line 'threshold' is uncertain; 'lock' (Lange), 'key' (Ranke),
are suggested; and in the last line 'peg' is rendered 'mooring-post'
by Griffith, though he queries it. In any case, the idea is that the
wise man's sayings should be something to hold on to when tempers
rise, a check upon the tongue. The expression 'hurricane of words'
recalls Job viii. 2:

> 'How long wilt thou speak these things,
>   And the words of thy mouth be a mighty wind?'

With the passage in A, Griffith compares the following words in the
introduction to the *Teaching of Ptah-hotep* (Prisse Pap., 5, 7–8):

> *Instructing the ignorant to knowledge*
> *And to the rules of good speech ;*
> *A profitable thing to him who shall obey,*
> *(But) baneful to him that shall transgress it.*

In comparing the passages in *Proverbs* and A it will be noticed that
each line of the former represents three lines of the latter. One
would be equally justified in arguing that the Egyptian is an expansion of the Hebrew as that the Hebrew is a condensed form of the
Egyptian, so far as this passage is concerned. But what is certain is
that there is a close relationship of some kind between the two; such
a close parallelism cannot be fortuitous.

**19.** *this day, even to thee.* 'This day' is a curious expression in
this connexion; and 'even to thee' is pleonastic; it is not required
after 'I have made known to thee', there is no point in emphasizing
'thee' in this way. The Sept. reads simply 'thy way', on the basis of
which Gressmann emends the text so as to read: 'I have made
known to thee this day thy ways' (אָרְחֹתֶיךָ). But it is perhaps better
to read, as in ii. 19, 'the ways of life', thus getting rid of 'this day'
(reading אָרְחוֹת חַיִּים for הַיּוֹם אַף־אַתָּה). The 'ways of life', as generally
in *Proverbs*, means prosperity; the verse would then run: 'That thy
trust may be in Jahweh, I have made known to thee the ways of life.'
To be in prosperity was, according to the belief of the times, to be in
God's favour, which would therefore strengthen trust in Him.

As in the preceding verse, the Hebrew puts in a much shorter form
the thoughts expressed in A; this has:

> *If thou spend thy life-time with these things in thy heart,*
> *Thou wilt find that it brings prosperity ;*
> *Thou wilt find my words a storehouse of life,*
> *And thy body will prosper upon the earth.*

These two couplets express, in effect, the same thought; one is in
the nature of a repetition of the other. The Hebrew sage seems, in
this case, to have adapted the Egyptian thought of the passage to

20 Have not I written unto thee [1]excellent things
    [2]Of counsels and knowledge;

[1] The word is doubtful. Another reading is, *heretofore*.     [2] Or, *In*

his readers with their belief in Jahweh. In Prov. iii. 21, 22, wisdom
is said to give life, and there is no reference to God; this is, in essence,
what the Egyptian sage says here. The mention of Jahweh in the
Hebr. form may, however, possibly be due to the wish on the part
of the Hebrew sage to give a religious tone to his adapted saying, the
original of which was purely secular.

But there is another passage in A which offers a parallel to this verse;
the writer says that, among other things, he undertook his work

> To direct (a man) upon the ways of life,
> And to make him prosper upon earth.

So that in the case of the verse before us it seems clear that the
Hebrew writer utilized A.

**20.** *Have not I written.* Toy says, naturally enough, 'the verb
*write* is suspicious, since elsewhere in the book the instruction given
by the sage is oral; but cf. Eccles. xii. 10. The verb suggests a very
late date for the final recension of our passage'. The recently published Egyptian Wisdom book was, of course, unknown when these
words were written. The reference to writing is an indication that
the Hebrew sage was utilizing A; and it does not, of course, point to
a late date.

*excellent things.* The Hebrew word of which this is the rendering
is שִׁלְשׁוֹם, which lit. means 'three days ago', i.e. the day before
yesterday; it might conceivably be rendered 'formerly', though this
would be a very unusual way of expressing it, as it always occurs in
combination with another word (תְּמוֹל); on the assumption that this
word has accidentally fallen out of the text, and should be supplied,
the passage would refer to some former writing. But one has only to
read the preceding verses to see how inappropriate this would be.
The Hebrew margin gives 'officers' (שָׁלִישִׁים), which is meaningless
here. Some commentators and the R.V., on quite insufficient grounds,
render this word 'excellent things', i.e. excellent precepts, or the like;
the R.V. adds the marginal note to the effect that 'the word is doubtful'. The difficulty is not helped by the Versions. In the light,
however, of A the solution is simple; his book had been arranged in
thirty chapters; a very trifling alteration in the word under consideration gives the meaning 'thirty' (שְׁלִשִׁים); and the Hebrew compiler of this collection of sayings adopted the number thirty as the
basis of his collection 'which he proceeded to make up of thirty
maxims, and thus quite appropriately refers to them in a phrase

21 To make thee know ¹the certainty of the words of truth,

¹ Or, *of a certainty the words &c.*

similar to that used by Amen-em-ope in referring to his own composition' (Griffith), viz.:

> *Consider these thirty chapters ; they delight, they instruct ;*
> *They are the chief among all books,*
> *They make the unlearned wise.*

Gressmann has shown[1] that the collection comprised in xxii. 17–xxiv. 22 (see above, p. xviii), apart from the introductory verses, 17–21, make up exactly thirty sayings. The line before us must, therefore, run: 'Have I not written unto (or, for) thee thirty (sayings)'; the addition of 'sayings' is not necessary in Hebrew, for, as Gressmann has pointed out, where indications of measures, weights, and time are concerned, the noun is usually omitted because there is no doubt as to what is meant (cf. Gesenius-Kautzsch, § 134, iii. 3).

From what has been said, two important facts emerge (it is Gressmann who draws attention to them); it is seen, first, that in the Wisdom literature, just as in the prophetical books, the various literary pieces incorporated in the books as we now have them were originally independent and comparatively short ; and, secondly, that the collections of proverbs or sayings now gathered together in one book originally circulated independently. It may be added that this fact shows how easily corruptions in the text could occur ; if different copies of a collection were in circulation any owner might add marginal notes—probably badly written as extant examples show[2]; these would be often put into the text by a copyist who might well have misread them. It will have been noticed how often corruptions in the Hebrew have been pointed to above ; the circumstances being what they were, the wonder is that these corruptions are not more numerous.

**21.** The Hebr. text of this verse is corrupt, as a literal translation will show: 'For thee to make known truth, words of truth, to carry back words, truth to him that sendeth thee.' There is clearly something wrong here.

*To make thee know.* This should be: 'that thou mayest make known.'

*the certainty.* The original here is an Aramaic word (קְשְׁט) which occurs elsewhere only in Daniel ii. 47, iv. 34. It was probably the marginal note of an Aramaic-speaking scribe to 'words of truth', which has got into the text by mistake, and should be omitted.

*the words of truth.* For 'words of' (אִמְרֵי) Gressmann reads 'him that speaketh' (אֹמֵר), which, in view of the parallel passage in A, strongly commends itself. The line thus emended would read: 'That

---

[1] *Zeitschrift für die alttestamentliche Wissenschaft,* xlii, p. 285 (1924).
[2] e. g. the recently found Hebrew MSS. of *Ecclesiasticus.*

That thou mayest carry back words of truth to them that
  send thee?
22 Rob not the poor, [1]because he is poor,

  [1] Or, *for*

thou mayest make known truth to him that speaketh'; for the
meaning see below.

*That thou mayest carry back . . .* The line in Hebr. is overloaded;
'truth' has been inadvertently repeated from the first line and should
be deleted.

*to them . . .* The Hebr. has 'to him'. The line should therefore be
read: 'That thou mayest carry back words to him that sent thee.' As
it stands the verse, even as emended, is quite unintelligible; it can
only be understood in the light of A. In the introduction to his book
Amen-em-ope describes the purposes for which he wrote it, among
them are these two; to give

> Knowledge how to answer him that speaketh,
> And (how) to carry back a report to one that hath sent him.

The first of these lines, Griffith says, means knowledge how to 'rebut
a charge to the accuser'; the second refers to the proper delivery of
a message. This shows quite clearly what is meant by the words of
the verse before us; and it is no less obvious that the Hebrew writer
made use of A here. Regarding the second line we may compare a
saying in the *Proverbs of Achikar*, ii. 41:

> My son, send a wise man, and give him no orders;
> But if thou wilt send a fool, go rather thyself, and send him not.

The meaning evidently is that if a message is to be sent, let it be by
the hand of a wise man, and let it be in writing, not by word of
mouth; but if the messenger is not a reliable person, then do not send
him, but carry your own message. Another instructive passage on
this subject occurs in the *Teaching of Ptah-hotep*, viii:

> If thou art one of those trusted ones sent from one noble to another, do thy
> duty conscientiously if thou art sent. Thou must carry out thy commission as
> it is commanded thee. Of what he tells thee keep nothing secret, and beware of
> forgetting anything. Keep to the truth, and transgress it not, even though what
> thou hast to tell be unpleasant. Beware of making bad blood which would cause
> one noble to despise the other through the talk of people.

## XXII. 22—XXIII. 14. *Maxims adapted from the 'Teaching of Amen-em-ope'.*

**22, 23.** *Rob not the poor, because . . .* This can mean either, because,
being poor, he is unable to invoke the law and get restitution; or
else, because he is poor it is doubly reprehensible to take the little
he possesses; or, finally, as a poor man he is not worth robbing. The
second is, in all probability, the meaning here.

o

Neither [1] oppress the afflicted in the gate:

23 For the LORD will plead their cause,
And despoil of life those that despoil them.

24 Make no friendship with a man that is given to anger;
And with a wrathful man thou shalt not go:

25 Lest thou learn his ways,
And get a snare to thy soul.

[1] Or, *crush*

*oppress.* Lit. 'crush', always used in a figurative sense.

*afflicted.* Better 'lowly', as in iii. 34.

*in the gate.* The place where the court of law was held, at the city entrance, cf. i. 21, xxiv. 7. The parallel in A runs:

> Beware of robbing the poor,
> And of being valorous against the afflicted.

The 'afflicted' is lit. a man with a broken arm (Griffith); to be valorous against such is to oppress him. So that there is practical identity between the two here.

**23.** *the Lord will plead their cause.* Cf. xxiii. 11[b].

*despoil.* The Hebr. word occurs elsewhere only in Mal. iii. 8, 9; the meaning of the word is uncertain. There is no parallel to this verse in A, nor is it to be expected; it is a comment of the Hebrew sage based on such a passage as Exod. xxii. 21-24 (Hebr. 20-23).

**24, 25.** *Make no friendship.* This expresses more than the Hebr. word connotes, it is better to render, 'make not a companion of', or 'do not associate with', see xiii. 20, xxviii. 7, xxix. 3.

*given to anger.* Lit. 'owner of anger', 'passionate'.

*a wrathful man.* Lit. 'a man of wraths'; the plur. in this expression does not occur elsewhere, and is used to denote intensity of wrath; for 'a man of wrath' cf. xvi. 4, xix. 19. Simpson is no doubt right in saying that this plural form is 'apparently chosen for the express purpose of best representing the "passionate man" of the Egyptian original'. The parallel in A is:

> Associate not with a passionate man,
> Nor approach him for conversation.

The two are again almost identical, for in the second line of the Hebr. to 'go with' a wrathful man is to converse with him.

**25.** *Lest thou learn.* The Hebr. word is a rare one and occurs elsewhere only in Job xv. 5, xxxiii. 33, xxxv. 11.

*And get a snare . . .* By following the example of a man of violent temper there will be the danger of falling out with others, the consequence of which might be easily fatal. In A we have what certainly looks like a parallel; it comes at the end of the long chapter of which the last quotation (above) was the opening sentence; it is, therefore, in reference to the passionate man:

26 Be thou not one of them that strike hands,
　　*Or* of them that are sureties for debts:
27 If thou hast not wherewith to pay,
　　Why should he take away thy bed from under thee?
28 Remove not the ancient landmark,
　　Which thy fathers have set.

> *Leap not to cleave to such an one,*
> *That the terror carry thee not away.*

A thought-connexion is evidently to be discerned here, though the mode of expression is different. And it is possible that this is also the case with another couplet in the same chapter:

> *For he is able to ensnare thee with his words,*
> *(Therefore) give not free rein to thine answer.*

The reference here is also to the passionate man.

With the two verses in *Proverbs* (*vv.* 24, 25) cf. Ecclus. viii. 15:

> *Go not with a fierce man* (equivalent to 'passionate', cf. Job xli. 2, E.V. 10),
> *Lest evils overwhelm thee ;*
> *For he will do according to his will,*
> *And thou wilt perish through his* (we should expect thy) *foolishness.*

It is to be observed how greatly the Wisdom writers are concerned with the formation of character in adolescents, for it is these that they have primarily in mind. The kind of companionship sought by young men, in most instances, affects them permanently; it was, therefore, of the highest importance that the choice of companions should be watched, lest through thoughtlessness this should be of the wrong kind, and an evil example and influence should pervert a youth in his path in life from the start. Ben-Sira teaches:

> *In the midst of fools watch closely the time,*
> *But with a man that is thoughtful abide continually*
> 　　　　　　　　　(Ecclus. xxvii. 12, see further xiii. 13–18).

And in the *Proverbs of Achikar* ii. 11, 12 it is said:

*My son, with a wise man thou wilt not be depraved,*
*And with a depraved man thou wilt not become wise.*
*My son, associate with the wise man, and thou wilt become wise like him ;*
*And associate not with a garrulous and talkative man, lest thou be numbered*
　　*with him.*

**26, 27.** *that strike hands.* See vi. 1, xi. 15, xvii. 18, xx. 16, and notes. There is no parallel in A to this or the next verse.

**27.** *Why should he take away.* Read, with the Versions, 'they will take away' (יִקְּחוּ for לָמָּה יִקַּח), the word for 'why' overloads the line, it got in through dittography; the preceding word ends with the same letters.

**28.** *Remove not the ancient landmark* ... Cf. Deut. xix. 14, 'Thou shalt not remove thy neighbour's landmark, which they of old time have set', and xxvii. 17; Hos. v. 10; Isa. v. 8; Job xxiv. 2. The first

o 2

29 Seest thou a man [1] diligent in his business ? he shall stand
        before kings ;
    He shall not stand before [2] mean men.

                    [1] Or, *skilful*                    [2] Heb. *obscure.*

line occurs again in xxiii. 10. The verse consists of a simple couplet,
a form which occurs only four times in this collection, otherwise the
usual form is a strophe of four lines, two verses belonging together.
It is possible that this verse did not belong here originally (especially
as part of it is repeated) and was added by the final redactor of the
book ; why it should have been put in here one does not see. But as
the other collections and *Ecclesiasticus* show, the sayings are often
put together in a somewhat haphazard manner. There is a parallel
to this in A for which see the notes on xxiii. 10, 11.

**29.** *Seest thou.* There is no interrogative in the Hebr. ; indeed, this
word overloads the line, and is better omitted ; it is more in the style
of the writer to read simply 'A man (that is) diligent in his business
(or office) shall stand before kings .

*diligent . . . he shall stand before kings.* The Hebr. word (מָהִיר) is
properly 'skilful' (cf. R.V. marg.), and shows that the reference is to
a scribe, for it is used in Ps. xlv. 1 (2 in Hebr.) and Ezra vii. 6 of a
scribe (it only occurs elsewhere in Isa. xvi. 5 in reference to one
zealous in righteousness). The connexion between scribes and Wisdom writing in the ancient east may be seen, e.g. in the opening
sentence of *The Words of Achikar*: 'These are the words of one named
Achikar, a wise and ready (*māhīr*) scribe . . .' (Cowley) ; and in the
Egyptian Wisdom book, *The Teaching of Duauf*, a saying is quoted
from an earlier work, 'The scribe, every post at court is open to
him . . .', which evidently held good in later days too, for Ben-Sira
says of the scribe :

> He serveth among great men,
> And appeareth before a ruler (Ecclus. xxxix. 4).

The parallel passage to this verse in A runs :

> A scribe who is skilful in his business,
> Findeth himself worthy to be a courtier.

That the same was true of the Babylonian scribe is seen from *The
Words of Achikar* 55, where Achikar is spoken of as the 'father of all
Assyria, by whose counsel king Sennacherib and all the army of As-
syria were guided'. So that we have here Egyptian, Babylonian, and
Jewish evidence regarding the important position which a scribe
could hold.

In the verse before us it will be noticed that we have three lines :

> 'A man that is skilful in his office
> Shall stand before kings ;
> He shall not stand before obscure men.'

This is not in accordance with the usage in this collection, which, as

**XXIII.** 1 When thou sittest to eat with a ruler,
  Consider diligently [1]him that is before thee;
2 [2]And put a knife to thy throat,
  If thou be a man given to appetite.

  [1] Or, *what*          [2] Or, *For thou wilt put*

already pointed out, consists of four-lined strophes. So that we must either suppose that the third line is a later addition (Gressmann), and that the two other lines should be joined to the two of the preceding verse, or, what seems more probable, that the third line of this strophe has fallen out, and that it ran approximately, according to Steuernagel:

> 'But he who is slow at his work
> (Shall not even stand before obscure men).'

*stand before.* i.e. to be in the presence of some one, cf. Job i. 6, ii. 1.
*mean.* R.V. 'obscure'; the Hebr. word occurs nowhere else; it comes from the root meaning 'to be dark'.


CHAPTER XXIII

**1–3.** These verses, which deal with the subject of good manners at table, offer a striking illustration of the way in which the Wisdom writers brought religion into the affairs of everyday life. For to eat in a well-bred way, and to have consideration for one's fellow-guests was, fittingly enough, regarded as a form of wisdom; and since wisdom of every sort and kind comes from God, good behaviour at a feast was also in the nature of a religious act. It is interesting to observe that directions on this subject occur in the Wisdom literatures of other oriental peoples. While in this particular instance the Hebrew writer seems to have been indebted to Amen-em-ope (see below), it is probable enough that precepts of conduct for festal occasions of this kind were general among the wealthier classes.

*him that is before thee.* The Hebr. can mean either 'him', or 'what' (R.V. marg.); the Sept., followed by the other Versions, had 'the things that are set before thee'; the context shows that we should render 'what is before thee', and this is borne out by the parallel passage in A.

*And put a knife . . .* This is a figurative expression meaning that self-restraint in eating is to be observed. The word for 'knife' (שַׂכִּין) does not occur elsewhere in the O.T.; on its use at meals, however, see Krauss, *Talmudische Archäologie*, iii. 53, 264, in reference, it is true, to later times.

*If thou be . . .* Lit. 'if thou be the owner of desire'; the word for 'desire' (*nephesh*, 'soul') is used in this sense in xiii. 4, xxi. 10.

3 Be not desirous of his dainties;

**3.** *Be not desirous* . . . This line is repeated in verse 6ᵇ, and probably does not belong here; and the second line of this verse is either an added explanatory comment (Steuernagel), or should come after verse 8ᵃ (Kittel). But most likely the whole verse is out of place. It will be noted that the subject is taken up again in verses 6–8; it certainly looks as though some disorder of the whole passage had taken place. The parallel passage in A is as follows:

> *Eat not bread in the presence of a ruler,*
> *And do not lunge forward (?) with thy mouth before a governor (?).*
> *When thou art replenished with that to which thou hast no right,*
> *It is only a delight to thy spittle.*
> *Look upon the dish that is before thee,*
> *And let that (alone) supply thy need.*

The second and third lines offer difficulties to the experts; Griffith renders them:

> *Nor apply thy mouth at the beginning.*
> *If thou art satisfied (with) false munchings . . .*

Although there are considerable differences between this and the passage in *Proverbs*, one can see that there is a real connexion between the two. Ben-Sira has a passage which comes somewhat closer to A:

> *My son, if thou sittest at the table of the great one,*
> *Open not thy mouth (lit. throat) upon it.*
> *Say not, "There is plenty upon it !"*
> *Remember that an envious eye is an evil thing . . .*[1]
> *Stretch not out thine hand at that which he (i.e. thy neighbour) looketh,*
> *And reach not thy hand with his into the dish.*
> *Eat like a man that which is set before thee,*
> *And eat not greedily lest thou be despised*
>
> (Ecclus. xxxi [xxxiv]. 12–16, Hebr.).

There is an interesting passage in the *Teaching of Ptah-hotep* vii, which is worth quoting here:

> *If thou art one who sitteth where the table of a greater man than thou stands,*
> *Take what is set before thee when he gives it. Do not dart many glances at him . . .*
> *Look downwards till he greets thee, and only speak after he has greeted thee.*
> *Laugh when he laughs. That will greatly cheer his heart ; and what thou doest*
> *Will be pleasant to him. One knows not what is in his mind.*

The last sentences, as Erman explains, mean that one never knows what humour he may be in, therefore one must always be cautious.

---

[1] The rest of this verse (13) is parenthetical, and not part of the original text; the verse which follows has got out of place.

Seeing they are deceitful meat.

4 Weary not thyself to be rich;
Cease [1]from thine own wisdom.

5 [2]Wilt thou set thine eyes upon that which is not?
For *riches* certainly make themselves wings,
Like an eagle that flieth toward heaven.

Or, *by reason of thine own understanding*       [2] Or, *Wilt thou set thine eyes
upon it? it is gone:*   Heb. *Shall thine eyes fly upon it and it is not?*

Advice is also given on the subject in another Egyptian Wisdom
book, *The Teaching for Ka-Gemni* ii, where it is said:

*When thou sittest (at table) with many others, refuse the food, even when thou
likest it. It only meaneth self-control for a moment; and it is horrid to appear
greedy.*

Finally, in the Babylonian *Proverbs of Achikar* ii. 15, this short
precept is given:

*My son, eat thy portion, and despise not thy neighbours.*

*deceitful meat.* The hospitality offered by a ruler is so called because a man cannot trust a ruler; the act of hospitality may be
merely to cloak some ulterior purpose. A saying of Gamaliel (the
third of the name), son of Judah the Prince, is preserved in *Pirqê
'Abôth* ii. 3, which runs: 'Be ye cautious regarding those in authority,
for they permit not a man to draw nigh unto them but for their own
purpose. They appear to be friends when it suits them, but do not
help a man in time of his need.' Wildeboer quotes from Fleischer,
*Ali's Hundert Sprüche*, pp. 71, 104: 'The dainties of a king burn
the lips.'

**4–5.** *Weary not thyself.* Better, 'Toil not', which is the primary
meaning of the Hebr. root.

*Cease from . . .* This line gives no proper sense; the Hebr. is evidently corrupt; Gressmann suggests the good emendation: 'And
cease from thy dishonest gain' (מִבִּצְעֶךָ חֲדָל); the shortness of the line
is no objection to this (Simpson), as the preceding line also consists
of only two words, with the negative joined to the verb.

*Wilt thou set thine . . .* The Hebr. has: 'shall thine eyes fly to it,
and it is not?' The word for 'fly' cannot be used in this sense; the
line is evidently a marginal gloss which has got into the text by
mistake, it should be deleted, thus making the form of *vv.* 4, 5 the
usual four-lined strophe.

*For riches certainly make . . .* The insertion of 'riches', though
not in the text as it stands, should without doubt be expressed according to an obvious emendation of the text (reading עֹשֶׁר 'riches'
for עָשֹׂה which is the inf. absol. added to the finite verb in Hebrew
for emphasis, so that 'certainly' in the R.V. should go out).

6 Eat thou not the bread of him that hath an evil eye,
   Neither desire thou his dainties:

These two verses should, therefore, run:

> 'Toil not to become rich,
> And cease from thy dishonest gain;
> For wealth maketh to itself wings,
> Like an eagle that flieth heavenwards.'

The passage in A which seems to have suggested this strophe is much longer and goes into more detail; but the Hebrew sage appears to have taken the two opening and two closing lines, and to have constructed his four lines from them. The passage in question is the following:

> *Toil not after riches*
> *When thy needs are made sure to thee.*[1]
> *If stolen goods are brought to thee,*
> *They remain not over the night with thee;*
> *At daybreak they are no more in thy house.*
> *One seeth where they were, but they are not (there).*
> *The earth has opened its mouth and swallowed them;*[2]
> *They are drowned in the underworld;*[3]
> *(Or) they have made them a great hole which fitteth them;*
> *They are sunk in the treasure house;*
> *(Or) they have made for themselves wings like geese,*[4]
> *And have flown into the heavens.*

The uncertainty of riches was, of course, a theme often dwelt upon, e. g. in the *Teaching of Ptah-hotep* it is said: 'Riches pass away, but a right spirit abideth.' But in this case the resemblance of thought in the main subject between *Proverbs* and A is too striking to be fortuitous. With the verse cf. xxviii. 22.

**6–8.** These three verses belong together; in all probability they consisted originally of two strophes of four lines each, the last line of the first strophe appears to have fallen out of the text. With them cf. Ecclus. xxxii (xxxv). 1–13, xxxvii. 27–31.

**6.** *an evil eye.* As in xxviii. 22, the only other occurrence of the expression in the O.T., the reference is to the niggardly man who grudges others everything.

*dainties.* Cf. verse 3[a].

---

[1] i. e. when thou hast all thou needest.

[2] Griffiths renders: 'It adjusts it and swallows it', as a quotation inserted in the text.

[3] Griffith has: 'And has sunk them in Tei' (i. e. the underworld).

[4] Geese were common in Egypt; sometimes a goose was kept as a pet (Erman, *Aegypten* (2nd ed., pp. 271, 531).

7 For [1] as he reckoneth within himself so is he:
   Eat and drink, saith he to thee;
   But his heart is not with thee.
8 The morsel which thou hast eaten shalt thou vomit up,
   And lose thy sweet words.

            [1] Or, *as one that reckoneth*

**7.** *For as he reckoneth* . . . There is no satisfactory sense to be got out of this line; the meaning of the word rendered 'reckoneth' is quite uncertain. We expect a line to follow which has some connexion with what precedes; but the next two lines now in the text belong together, so that it is after this line (7[a]) that something has fallen out of the text. Both the emendation of the line before us, as well as what the content of the missing line may have been, is too problematical to suggest a solution. The proposals made by various commentators are all more or less plausible, but there is absolutely no certainty about them; and there is nothing to go upon to substantiate them. The one exception is Gressmann, who has a line in A to support what he conceives to have been the missing line ('And as one who has choking (lit. who is bitter) in his throat'); but the rendering of A itself here is uncertain (see below), so that it is precarious to build upon it.

*But his heart* . . . i.e. He does not mean honestly by thee.

**8.** *thy sweet words.* 'Words' must be omitted, for, as Gressmann rightly maintains, the reference is to what has been 'eaten', though the sense is figurative, as the parallel passage in A shows. Owing to the corrupt state of the Hebrew text of these verses it is difficult to say what the meaning of them is. And what has apparently increased the difficulty is that, on the assumption (assuredly justified) that the Hebrew sage utilized A, he does not appear to have realized that two different kinds of people were spoken of in the Egyptian writing, and he has used two independent strophes in this latter and joined them together as though they both referred to the same subject. This will come out more clearly in reading A; but it may be pointed out that in the one strophe the Egyptian sage is directing his hearer how to treat a dependant, in the other he is telling him how to behave as a dependant in the presence of his chief. In both cases the reference to food is figurative. The following is the passage in question, but it is more instructive to read it side by side with the *Proverbs* verses, as on pp. xlix f.

*Covet not the goods of a dependant,*
*And hunger not after his bread.*
*The property of a dependant is a storm* [1] *for the throat,*
*And as a vomiting for the gullet.*
    (Four lines follow)

----

            [1] Griffith: 'choking'.

9 Speak not in the hearing of a fool;
  For he will despise the wisdom of thy words.

10 [1] Remove not the ancient landmark;
  And enter not into the fields of the fatherless:

[1] See ch. xxii. 28.

*When thou failest before thy chief,*
*And art embarrassed [1] in thine utterances,*
*Thy flatteries [2] are answered by curses,*
*And thy obeisances by beating.*
*Thou swallowest (indeed) thy too great mouthful, and must vomit it forth again,*
*And thus art emptied of thy good.*

Both Lange and Griffith say that the text offers great difficulties; but the general sense of the first passage seems to be that if the property of a dependant is appropriated it will have to be given up again; that of the second that by taking too much upon oneself in the presence of a chief (by flattery and servility), one loses whatever advantage one might otherwise have gained. The references to food are to be understood figuratively. If this is even approximately what is meant, it is clear that the Hebrew sage entirely misapprehended the meaning of the passages.

**9.** *in the hearing.* Hebr. 'in the ears', so as to give him every chance of understanding. In A the parallel to this verse runs:

*Empty not thine inmost soul to everybody,*
*Nor spoil (thereby) thine influence.*

All the experts are agreed on this rendering. Ben-Sira has a still closer parallel:

*Reveal not thy heart to all flesh,*
*And drive not away (thereby) prosperity from thee*
(Ecclus. xix. 7); cf. xxvii. 16 ff. and Prov. xxv. 10.

There is also an interesting illustration in the *Proverbs of Achikar* ii. 62:

*My son, If the waters should stand up without earth,*
*And the sparrow fly without wings,*
*And the raven become white as snow,*
*And the bitter become sweet as honey,—*
*Then may the fool become wise.*

**10–11.** *Remove not* . . . Cf. xxii. 28. Some commentators would alter 'ancient' to 'widows' because of the frequent collocation of the terms 'widows and orphans', Deut. x. 18, xiv. 29; Jer. vii. 6; Job xxii. 9, xxiv. 2, 3; Ps. cxlvi. 9, and elsewhere; in view of the expression in the parallel passage in A it is probable that 'widow' should be read here, see also Prov. xv. 25[b].

---

[1] Griffith: 'And art feeble'.        [2] Griffith: 'entreaties'.

11  For their redeemer is strong;
    He shall plead their cause against thee.
12  Apply thine heart unto ¹instruction,
    And thine ears to the words of knowledge.
13  Withhold not correction from the child:
    *For* ²if thou beat him with the rod, he shall not die.

¹ Or, *correction*                    ² Or, *though*

*redeemer.* The Hebr. word *gō'ēl* is the technical one for the next of
kin who was bound by the law to redeem his kinsman's land, cf.
Lev. xxv. 25 ; Num. v. 8 ; for Jahweh taking the place of *gō'ēl*, as here,
see Exod. xxii. 21–23; Job xix. 25.

*He shall plead* . . . Cf. xxii. 23ª.

The parallel to these verses in A again offers some difficulties to the
experts, but the general similarity of thought is unmistakable:

> *Remove not the landmark from the bounds of the field,*¹
> *Nor shift the position of the measuring-cord.*²
> *Covet not* (*even*) *a cubit of land,*
> *And violate not the widow's boundary.*
> *A furrow* . . . *worn by time,*³
> *He who wrongfully seizeth it in a field,*
> *Though he claim it with false oaths,*
> *Will be taken captive by the might of the Moon*(-*god*).⁴

Possibly the similar thought is to be discerned in another Egyptian
Wisdom writing, the *Teaching for Meri-ka-re*:

> *Comfort the mourners. Do despite to no widow, drive no man from the
> possession of his father* . . .

**12.** Cf. i. 2, xxii. 17. A passage in A, quoted above (see note on
xxii. 17), offers a parallel to this verse:

> *Give thine ears, hear* (*the words*) *that are said,*
> *Give thine heart to interpret them.*

For the last two verses of this section there is no parallel in A.

**13, 14.** Cf. xiii. 24, xix. 18. In arresting phrases such as 'he shall
not die', and 'thou shalt deliver his soul from Sheol', Volz discerns
the influence of the mode of prophetical utterances; this is undoubtedly true, and in this particular instance it is instructive to

---

¹ Griffith: 'on the boundaries of the sown.'
² Griffith's rendering.
³ Griffith: 'The rut of trampling (?), the wear of time', or 'which time has diminished'. Lange also thinks that this may perhaps refer to a foot-path; 'in Egypt',
he says, 'owing to the general coveting of land the foot-paths between the plots
became ever narrower because every one tried to grab for himself part of his neighbour's land'.
⁴ Griffith renders the last two lines:
    '(If) he snare by false oaths,
        Is lassoed by the power of the Moon' (i. e. Thôth).

14 Thou shalt beat him with the rod,
    And shalt deliver his soul from ¹Sheol.
15 My son, if thine heart be wise,
    My heart shall be glad, even mine:
16 Yea, my reins shall rejoice,
    When thy lips speak right things.
17 Let not thine heart envy sinners:
    But *be thou* in the fear of the LORD all the day long:

¹ Or, *the grave*

observe how the Hebrew sage seems to have adapted two sayings in *The Proverbs of Achikar* ii. 22, 23:

    '*My son, withhold not thy son from stripes; for the beating of a boy is like manure to the garden, and like rope to an ass, and like tether on the foot of an ass. My son, subdue thy son while he is yet a boy, before he wax stronger than thee and rebel against thee, and thou be shamed in all his corrupt doing.*'

In what is presumably the corresponding passage to this in the Aramaic version, 81, 82 (Elephantiné pap.), the parallel with *vv.* 13, 14 is much closer:

    '*Withhold not thy son from the rod if thou canst not keep him from wickedness. If I smite thee, my son, thou wilt not die, but if I leave thee to thine own heart thou wilt not live.*'

Here we have an interesting point; for it looks as though the Aramaic form of the Babylonian original had been made to approximate to the Hebrew of the passage before us, and there are other instances of this. If this is so, it throws an instructive light on the question of the date of this collection of *Proverbs*; for the Elephantiné papyri, which are nearly all dated, 'cover practically the whole of the fifth century B.C., 494–404' (Cowley). This collection must, therefore, belong, at the latest, to the sixth century B.C., and not to the middle of the third, to which Toy (*op. cit.*, p. xxx) and others assign it.

## XXIII. 15—XXIV. 22. *Further maxims of the Hebrew sage addressed to 'My son'.*

**15, 16.** *reins.* Lit. kidneys, the seat of the emotions according to the ancient Hebrew idea; cf. Ps. xvi. 7; Job xix. 27. For the joy of the teacher at his pupil's progress cf. xxvii. 11ᵃ, and for the pleasure of the pupil see Ecclus. iii. 29: *The ear that listeneth to wisdom rejoiceth.*

**17, 18.** *But* be thou *in* . . . The Hebr. has: 'But in the fear of the Lord all the day', where it is clear that the verb has fallen out. Toy emends the text so as to read, 'But fear the . . .' (יְרָא אֶת for בְּיִרְאַת); this occurs in xxiv. 21ᵃ, and is to be preferred here.

18 For surely there is a ¹reward;
    And thy hope shall not be cut off.
19 Hear thou, my son, and be wise,
    And guide thine heart in the way.
20 Be not among winebibbers;
    Among gluttonous eaters of flesh:
21 For the drunkard and the glutton shall come to poverty:
    And drowsiness shall clothe *a man* with rags.
22 Hearken unto thy father that begat thee,
    And despise not thy mother when she is old.

¹ Or, *sequel*   Or, *future* Heb. *latter end.*

*For surely.* The Hebrew means 'for if'; we can either omit the
'if' (אִם), or follow the Sept. and insert the verb: 'For if thou
keepest (it)' (כִּי אִם־תִּשְׁמְרֶנָּה), i.e. the fear of the Lord; this is better,
as the shortness of the Hebr. line points to a word having fallen out.

*reward.* Read, with the R.V. marg., 'sequel', or 'future', cf. xxiv.
14, though of course reward is implied.

*And thy hope* . . . The same words in xxiv. 14ᵇ.

**19.** *the way.* The word is never used in this undefined manner
when it occurs in this sense, hence Kittel alters the text so as to read
'and walk in the paths of prudence' (וְאַשֵּׁר בְּדֶרֶךְ בִּינָה instead of וְאַשֵּׁר
בְּדֶרֶךְ לְבֶּךָ); this offers also a better parallel with the preceding line;
the phrase occurs in ix. 6, cf. also iv. 14.

**20, 21.** *winebibbers.* The Hebr. word implies drinking to excess,
cf. Deut. xxi. 20; Isa. lvi. 12.

*gluttonous eaters.* Lit. 'those who are lavish with flesh', cf. xxviii. 7.

*drowsiness.* The Hebr. word comes from a root meaning to be
'drowsy', or to 'slumber', e.g. 2 Sam. iv. 6 (emended text); Isa. lvi.
10; its meaning here as the effect of too much wine is not found elsewhere in the O.T., nor in post-biblical Hebrew. It is to be observed
that gluttony is regarded as equally vicious as drunkenness; a point
of view not always held in modern days. With the passage cf. xxi.
17. Ben-Sira says:

> *Delight not thyself in overmuch luxury,*
> *For double is the poverty thereof.*
> *Be not a glutton and a drunkard,*
> *Else will there be nothing in thy purse.*
> (Ecclus. xviii. 32, 33, Hebr.)

The word for 'glutton' and 'squanderer' is the same as in *Proverbs.*

**22-25.** With *v.* 22 cf. i. 8, xxx. 17, and the words of Ben-Sira:

> *My son, help thy father in his old age,*
> *And grieve him not all the days of his life ;*
> *Yea, and if his mind fail, be considerate with him,*
> *And dishonour him not all the days of his life.*
> (Ecclus. iii. 12, 13, the last three lines are from the Hebrew.)

23 Buy the truth, and sell it not;
　　*Yea*, wisdom, and instruction, and understanding.
24 The father of the righteous shall greatly rejoice:
　　And he that begetteth a wise child shall have joy of him.
25 Let thy father and thy mother be glad,
　　And let her that bare thee rejoice.
26 My son, give me thine heart,
　　And let thine eyes [1] delight in my ways.
27 For a whore is a deep ditch;
　　And a strange woman is a narrow pit.

[1] Another reading is, *observe*.

The words of Achikar are also worth quoting as showing that parental respect was also taught in Babylon:

> *My son, bring not upon thee the curses of thy father and thy mother*
> *Lest thou rejoice not in the blessings of thy children.*
>
> (*Prov. of Achikar* ii. 26.)

**23.** This verse, which does not appear in the Sept., is clearly out of place here as it breaks the connexion between *vv.* 22 and 24; it belongs in all probability to *v.* 19, which is isolated and requires another couplet to make up the four-lined strophe; the content of the two belong together.

**24.** Cf. *v.* 15, x. 1ᵃ, xxix. 3ᵃ.
*he that begetteth.* As both father and mother are mentioned in *vv.* 22, 25, it seems better to read here 'and she that beareth', which involves but a slight change in the Hebrew (יֹלַרְת for יוֹלִר).

**25.** *and thy mother.* This has been apparently added thoughtlessly, as the mother is referred to in the next line.

**26.** *give me thine heart.* i.e. pay attention to me; as the Sage is about to speak of temptations by which, as he knew, the young men of his day were particularly affected, he takes up the address again.
　*delight.* Read, with the Hebr. marg., 'observe', cf. iii. 1, iv. 13, vi. 20, xxii. 12.

**27, 28.** *a whore.* The Sept. read, apparently, 'a strange woman' (זָרָה) as in ii. 16, in place of 'whore' (זוֹנָה); in the second line 'strange woman' is an 'alien woman'. Toy may be right in supposing that two classes of unchaste women are meant, the unmarried and married respectively. The two expressions 'deep ditch' (better 'pit') and 'narrow pit' (but *bĕ'er* means a 'well') point perhaps to the different kinds of difficulty into which a man gets himself by intercourse with these two types of woman. In any case, he is involved in trouble, but the 'narrow well' is a more difficult thing to get out of than a 'deep pit'.

28 Yea, she lieth in wait [1]as a robber,
   And increaseth the treacherous among men.
29 Who hath [2]woe? who hath [3]sorrow? who hath contentions?
   Who hath complaining? who hath wounds without cause?
   Who hath [4]redness of eyes?
30 They that tarry long at the wine;
   They that go to [5]seek out mixed wine.
31 Look not thou upon the wine when it is red,
   When it giveth its colour in the cup,
   When it [6]goeth down smoothly:
32 At the last it biteth like a serpent,
   And stingeth like [7]an adder.

[1] Or, *as* for *a prey*     [2] Heb. *Oh!*     [3] Heb. *Alas!*     [4] Or, *darkness*
[5] Or, *try*       [6] Or, *moveth itself aright*       [7] Or, *a basilisk*

**28.** *as a robber.* The Hebr. word does not occur elsewhere in the O.T., but the verb is used in Job ix. 12, its only occurrence. The R.V. marg. can be ignored.

**29–35.** This passage, an exhortation against inebriety, reminds one of the miniature essay style of Ben-Sira.

**29.** *Who hath woe* ... As the R.V. marg. shows, the Hebr. for the words 'woe' and 'sorrow' are interjections. These are very expressive.

*redness.* More probably, in view of the context, it is the dull glassiness of the eye that is meant; 'dullness of eyes'; the word is only used here and in Gen. xlix. 12, though in this latter passage the idea seems to be that of inflamed eyes.

**30.** *to seek out.* The R.V. marg. 'try' is, no doubt, better, cf. xviii. 17, xxviii. 11, of testing.

*mixed wine.* i.e. wine mixed with spices, *Song of songs* viii. 2, cf. Prov. ix. 2, 5; Isa. v. 22; Ps. lxxv. 8 (9 in Hebr.). With the *v.* cf. Isa. v. 11.

**31.** *When it giveth* ... Lit. 'when it giveth its eye in the cup', i.e. when it gleams in the cup; the same word is used in reference to sparkling gems and the gleaming of metal in Ezek. i. 4, 7 &c., viii. 2, x. 9; Dan. x. 6.

*When it goeth down* ... These (in the Hebr.) two words overload the line, and cannot well have belonged to the original text; a similar phrase occurs in *Song of songs* vii. 9 (10 in Hebr.), whence it may have been taken and inserted here by a later scribe.

**32.** *At the last.* Or, as we should say, 'Ultimately'.

*stingeth.* The meaning of the Hebr. word is uncertain; it may mean 'to sting', or 'to spurt out', i.e. poison; this is the sense Steuernagel gives it here.

*adder.* What kind of snake is uncertain, cf. Isa. xi. 8, lix. 5; Jer. viii. 17; it is described as a small but particularly poisonous snake,

33 Thine eyes shall behold [1]strange things,
    And thine heart shall utter froward things.

34 Yea, thou shalt be as he that lieth down in the midst of the
       sea,
    Or as he that lieth upon the top of a mast.

35 They have stricken me, *shalt thou say*, and I was not hurt;
    They have beaten me, and I felt it not:
    When shall I awake? I will seek it yet again.

**XXIV.** 1 Be not thou envious against evil men,
    Neither desire to be with them:

           [1] Or, *strange women*

having a small white spot on its head; the word is mostly translated
'basilisk' (Nowack, *Hebr. Arch.* i. 80).

**33.** *strange things.* R.V. marg. can be disregarded; as there is no
neuter in Hebr. the fem. plur. (as here) is used, so too in the next
line, 'wonderful things' in Exod. xxxiv. 10, also fem. plur.

*froward things.* i.e. perverted, distorted, cf. ii. 12.

**34.** *that lieth down in the* . . . i.e. the ground seems to rise and fall
as though he were on board a ship in a rough sea; he is pictured as
lying down, since in the circumstances standing is out of the
question.

*as he that lieth.* The repetition of the same verb in two consecutive
lines is not in accordance with usage, probably a different word stood
here originally, see next note.

*upon the top of a mast.* A difficult proceeding. But the meaning of
the word rendered 'mast' is quite uncertain; it occurs nowhere else.
It is best to follow the Sept. and read: 'And like a pilot in a great
storm' (וּכְחֹבֵל בְּסַעַר גָּדוֹל). This, it is true, involves a somewhat drastic
change in the text; but as it now stands this line almost looks as
though it were a corrupt copy of the first line.

**35.** *They have stricken me* . . . i.e. he had a fight while in his
drunken state, but does not remember anything about it.

*When shall I awake?* But as he has just been speaking he must
already be awake. On the basis of the Sept. one may suggest that
the text read originally: 'Would God it were morning' (מִי־יִתֵּן בֹּקֶר)
for (מָתַי אָרִיץ).

With the first two lines of the *v.* cf. the *Proverbs of Achikar* ii. 43:

> 'My son, withdraw at the first cup, and tarry not for lickerish draughts
> lest there be to thee wounds in thy head.'

### Chapter XXIV

**1, 2.** *Be not thou envious* . . . Cf. *v.* 19[b], iii. 31, xxiii. 17.

*Neither desire to be* . . . In *The Wisdom of Anii* it is said: *Keep far
from an unfriendly man, and take him not as a companion.*

2 For their heart studieth oppression,
  And their lips talk of mischief.
3 Through wisdom is an house builded;
  And by understanding it is established:
4 And by knowledge are the chambers filled
  With all precious and pleasant riches.
5 A wise man ¹is strong;
  Yea, a man of knowledge ²increaseth might.
6 For by wise guidance thou shalt make thy war:
  And in the multitude of counsellors there is ³safety.
7 Wisdom is too high for a fool:
  He openeth not his mouth in the gate.
8 He that deviseth to do evil,
  Men shall call him a mischievous person.

¹ Heb. *is in strength.*     ² Heb. *strengtheneth might.*     ³ Or, *victory.*

**2.** *their lips talk mischief.* Cf. Ps. cxl. 9 (10 in Hebr.).

**3, 4.** *Through wisdom* . . . Cf. ix. 1; Ecclus. i. 17, xiv. 20–27; as Wisdom has built her own house men will do well to consult her in building their own houses; the same is true whether these words are meant literally or figuratively.

**4.** Cf. viii. 21; Ecclus. xxiv. 15 ff.

**5, 6.** The Hebr. text of *v.* 5 does not read smoothly; the first line is too short, a word has evidently fallen out; and the Sept. shows that the verse was in the form of a comparison. The text must be emended so as to read: 'Better is a wise man than one that is strong; and a man of knowledge than one mighty in strength' (גְּבָר־חָכָם טוֹב מֵעָז וְאִישׁ דַּעַת מֵאַמֶּץ כֹּחַ).

**6.** *thy war.* Omit 'thy', with the Sept., see xx. 18ᵇ.

*And in the multitude* . . . Cf. xi. 14ᵇ and xx. 18ᵃ; the Hebr. word for 'safety' can mean also 'victory' (see R.V. marg.), but the general sense of security is probably what is meant.

**7.** *Wisdom.* In Hebr. this is in the plur., as in i. 20, ix. 1, an emphatic form.

*too high.* The Hebr. has 'corals', cf. Job xxviii. 18; Ezek. xxvii. 16, where the same word occurs; if the text is correct we must understand the line to mean that wisdom is too beautiful a thing for a fool to appreciate; but possibly 'corals' (רָאמוֹת) should be 'terrors' (אֵימוֹת), see xx. 2 and Ps. lv. 4 (5 in Hebr.), though this is never used in reference to Wisdom.

*He openeth not* . . . i.e. he cannot, therefore, be one of those to whom the multitude listen when they assemble in the public meeting-place. The verse stands by itself.

**8.** *shall call him* . . . 'mischievous person', lit. 'owner of mis-

P

9 The thought of ¹the foolish is sin:
And the scorner is an abomination to men.
10 If thou faint in the day of adversity,
Thy strength is small.
11 Deliver them that are carried away unto death,
And those that are ²ready to be slain ³see that thou hold
back.

---

¹ Heb. *foolishness*.          ² Heb. *tottering to the slaughter*.
³ Or, *forbear thou not to deliver*

---

chiefs', would thus seem to be a well-known term applied to a certain
type of man, cf. our 'chatterbox'.

**9.** *the foolish.* As the R.V. marg. says, the Hebr. has 'foolishness'
which is evidently a mistake; the Versions have 'the foolish man',
as we must doubtless read here.

**10.** Part of this verse has fallen out; all that is left of the first line
is the verb, 'thou hast shown thyself slack' (R.V. 'If thou faint' does
not bring out the force of the Hebr.). As the second line speaks of
what will happen in the day of adversity and reads like an antithesis,
it is likely enough that Steuernagel is right in reading for the first
line: 'If thou hast shown thyself slack in the day of prosperity'
(בְּיוֹם טוֹבָה). The second line will then run: 'In the day of adversity
thy strength will be small.' The Hebr. word rendered 'small' means
narrow, restricted, or limited; although this word is never used in
reference to 'strength', it may well have been purposely chosen here
in order to make a word-play, for in Hebr. the words for 'narrow'
and 'adversity' are respectively *tzar* and *tzārah*.

**11.** On this *v.* Toy says: 'The expressions *taken* and *tottering* appear to describe the gait of persons who are condemned, by the
political or judicial authorities, to death. The reference may be to
the ransom of prisoners of war, or to the rescue, by legal means, of
innocent men who have been condemned by the tribunals . . . The
vigorous character of the expressions (*death, slaughter*) makes it improbable that the reference is merely to the ordinary oppression of
the poor by the rich, who deprive them of wealth, and thus of liveli-
hood (i.e. life).' Nevertheless, it is probable that this latter view is
correct, for it is more in accordance with the usual counsel of the
Wisdom writers. If the former interpretation were the correct one
it would rightly be expected that some definite allusion to the circumstances presupposed should be made. One may also ask what
means the sage's disciple—almost always assumed to be a young
man, as the address 'my son' implies—could have whereby to deliver any one from the judicial or political authorities, which would
require not only money, but also interest and position such as would
be extremely unlikely for a young man to possess.

12 If thou sayest, Behold, we knew not ¹this:
　　Doth not he that weigheth the hearts consider it?
　　And he that keepeth thy soul, doth not he know it?
　　And shall not he render to every man according to his work?

¹ Or, *this man*

As to the objection that the expressions *death* and *slaughter* are
too vigorous to be applied to the ordinary oppression of the poor by
the rich, this will hardly stand in view of such passages as Am. ii. 7;
Hos. iv. 2; Ps. lxiv. 3–5 (Hebr. 4–6), xciv. 3–6, a specially instructive
passage, cix. 16, cxliii. 3, and others. It is more natural to interpret
the *v.* in the light of such passages as Isa. lviii. 6, 7; Ps. lxxxii. 4.
There is in the *Teaching of Amen-em-ope* a couplet which may well
have suggested the *v.* under consideration; this runs:

　　*Cry not 'Crime' at a man,*
　　*Hide the manner of (a fugitive's) flight* (VIII. xi. 6, 7).

Pregnant as the first line is, its meaning is not doubtful when read
in the light of the second, viz. one must not assume that because a
man is a fugitive he is therefore a criminal; rather, as the second
goes on to say, do the merciful thing, and assist him in his flight by
keeping it secret. There is no question here of helping a criminal to
escape from justice; the reference is to one fleeing from oppression.
In the light of the large number of parallel passages between these
two books which are demonstrably dependent the one on the other,
we are fully justified in regarding our verse as an adaptation of the
Egyptian sage's precept. To deliver from death, as in the *Proverbs*
form, is a parallel thought to that of not condemning a man as a
criminal; and in the second line both forms urge that protection
should be given to any menaced by destruction. In the second line
the Hebr. word for 'hold back' (תַּחְשׂוֹךְ) is a rare use of the word, and
a slight change gives the reading 'hide' (תַּחְשִׁיךְ as in Ps. cxxxix. 12,
and for the construction see Ps. cxxxix. 10), which is supported by
the Egyptian parallel. If, then, as seems probable, we have here a
thought parallel between the two books, the verse before us must be
understood as referring to the victims of oppression by the wicked
so often spoken of in the Psalms and in the prophetical books.

**12.** This verse has caused much trouble to commentators; upon
the whole it seems most likely to be a comment on the preceding
verse, but not by the original writer of the collection, for the verse
is not in the writer's style. Verse 11 has laid down a general precept;
in this verse the thought seems to be of a particular case in regard to
which some action ought to have been taken, in accordance with the
foregoing precept, but which had been neglected owing to ignorance
of the circumstances. The writer says that this excuse is not valid;
and implies, presumably, that the required help ought to have been

13 My son, eat thou honey, for it is good;
   And the honeycomb, which is sweet to thy taste:
14 So shalt thou know wisdom to be unto thy soul:
   If thou hast found it, then shall there be a [1]reward,
   And thy hope shall not be cut off.

<hr>

[1] See ch. xxiii. 18.

<hr>

given to one in distress, whatever the circumstances. This offers
perhaps the most natural explanation of what is admittedly a difficult passage.

*we knew not this.* This should, no doubt, be read 'I knew not', with
the Sept.; moreover, it is demanded by 'if thou sayest', and by 'he
that keepeth thy soul' in the third line. 'This' is most naturally
understood as in the R.V. marg. 'this man' (the neuter would be
more likely to be expressed by זאת, see Gesenius-Kautzsch, § 34), the
reference being to some particular case. The meaning of the line will,
therefore, be: 'It is no use saying, I know nothing about this man who
was a fugitive, nor about the reason of his flight, so how could I be
expected to help him?' The reply to this is contained in the three
queries of the following lines.

*he that weigheth the hearts.* In reference to the heart or spirit the
Hebr. word (תכן) is never used outside of *Proverbs* (xvi. 2, of spirits,
xxi. 2 and here, of hearts); in all probability this points to the influence of Egyptian thought, for in A it is Thôth who weighs hearts
(XVI. xvii. 22–xviii. 3, XXIV. xxiv. 4, 5, and cf. II. iv. 19).

*he that keepeth thy soul.* The Sept. has 'he that formed' (יֹצֵר instead
of (נֹצֵר); if this was the original reading it might also (though not
necessarily) point to Egyptian influence; in A it is Khnum who is the
moulder of men, and who also moulds hearts (IX. xii. 15–17); in
Hebr. the word is never used in reference to the heart or the soul.

*shall not he render . . .* Cf. xii. 14, xxiv. 29.

**13, 14.** *My son.* This does not stand at the beginning of the sentence in Hebr., and somewhat overloads the line; it is probably a
later addition and is better omitted.

*honey . . . honeycomb.* Cf. v. 3, xvi. 24, xxv. 16, 27, xxvii. 7.

*thy taste.* Properly 'thy palate'.

**14.** This verse is hopelessly corrupt. Although verse 13 makes it
clear enough what the general sense of this verse must have been—
just as honey is sweet to the mouth, so is wisdom sweet to the mind—
there are no means of saying what the actual form was. Steuernagel,
with much probability, regards the first line, as it now stands, as
representing the beginning of the first line and end of the second.
The words 'so shalt thou know wisdom' must, following the Sept.,
be read: 'So knowledge' (דֵּעָה for דְּעָה); this was the beginning of the

15  Lay not wait, [1]O wicked man, against the [2]habitation of the
       righteous;
    Spoil not his [3]resting place:

16  For a righteous man falleth seven times, and riseth up again:
    But the wicked are overthrown by calamity.

17  Rejoice not when thine enemy falleth,
    And let not thine heart be glad when he is overthrown:

18  Lest the LORD see it, and it displease him,
    And he turn away his wrath from him.

    [1] Or, *as a wicked man*          [2] Or, *pasture*          [3] Or, *fold*

first line; all that follows has fallen out, with the exception of the
last two words of the second line, thus:

> 'So knowledge . . . . . .
> . . . . . . Wisdom to thy soul.'

Toy, following ii. 10, xvi. 24, surmises the original form of the couplet
to have been:

> 'So knowledge will be pleasant to thee,
> And sweet (will be) wisdom to thy soul.'

*If thou hast found* . . . This couplet may well have been added
from xxiii. 18.

**15, 16.** *O wicked man.* Most commentators omit this as a late
gloss; it is the Sage's pupil who is being addressed in this collection;
and the word overloads the line in Hebrew.

*habitation.* Cf. iii. 33, xxi. 20; the same Hebr. word in each case.

*resting place.* As indicated in the R.V. marg., both this word and
that for 'habitation' are pastoral expressions in Hebrew. This is
an interesting point as showing that the reference is not to city life.

**16.** As Toy rightly says, the reference here is 'not to the natural
inspiriting power of integrity and the depressing effect of moral evil,
but to divine retribution', see further, Excursus IV.

**17, 18.** The precept of the first verse would be beautiful if it stood
alone, but it is deplorably marred by what is said in the second. It
is useless to ignore the plain sense of the Hebrew. For example, Toy
says that the words, 'And he turn away his wrath from him', i.e.
from the enemy, are 'not to be understood as affirming that God will
cease punishing a wicked man because another man is pleased at the
punishment; the full form of the expression is "turn from him to
thee", and the stress is to be laid on the "to thee"'. But this is
reading into the text what is not there; to say that the full form of
the expression is 'turn from him to thee' is pure imagination and
based on nothing in the text. The same must be said when Toy
writes further: 'Thou', says the sage, 'wilt then become the greater
sinner, and Jahweh will be more concerned to punish thee than to
punish him.' The sage says nothing of the kind either directly or by

19 Fret not thyself because of evil-doers;
   Neither be thou envious at the wicked:
20 For there will be no [1]reward to the evil man;
   The lamp of the wicked shall be put out.
21 My son, fear thou the LORD and the king:
   *And* meddle not with them that are given to change:

               [1] See ch. xxiii. 18.

implication. What *v.* 18 means is something quite different. As is
pointed out, for example, by Volz, in some of the older utterances in
the Wisdom Literature regarding a man's attitude towards a fallen
enemy a remnant of old-world ideas is to be discerned. Delight at
calamity overtaking an enemy would cause God to rehabilitate him;
so that if it is hoped that the enemy may continue in misfortune, one
must not gloat over his fall. In reference to *v.* 18 he says: 'This
curious passage is a counterpart of the envy of the gods, and is connected with the antique conception, according to which, a curse
pronounced against one in misfortune will bring him good luck.' For
illustrations of this see Frazer, *The Golden Bough*, 'The Magic Art',
i. 279 ff.

That an echo of this old-world idea should be contained in our book
need not cause heart-searchings; that it exists at the present day,
even though it works subconsciously, would not be denied by any one
in close touch with humanity. The Wisdom writers had an astonish-
ing insight into man and his many-sidedness; and these two verses
reflect what the writer knew to be no uncommon phenomena among
the men of his day. Higher teaching on the subject is not lacking in
our book, see e.g. xxv. 21, 22. With *v.* 17 taken alone cf. the *Proverbs
of Achikar* ii. 17:

      *My son, envy not thou the prosperity of thine enemy,*
      *And rejoice not at his adversity.*

In a similar spirit it is said in ii. 20:

      *My son, if thine enemy meet thee with evil,*
      *Meet thou him with wisdom.*

**19, 20.** *Fret not thyself* . . . Cf. xxiii. 17[a]; Ps. xxxvii. 1, 7.

*reward.* Cf. xxiii. 18; it has almost the sense of 'future'. We have
again here the doctrine that the wicked will not continue to live, in
spite of the fact that experience taught that this was by no means
the case always.

*The lamp of the wicked* . . . Cf. xiii. 9[b].

**21, 22.** *My son.* As in verse 13, this does not come at the opening
of the sentence in the Hebr.; its presence makes the line too long; it
was clearly a later addition, and should be omitted. The mention of
the king proves a pre-exilic date here.

*meddle not with.* The word occurs also in xx. 19[b], 'have no fellowship with', or 'have nothing to do with'.

22 For their calamity shall rise suddenly;
   And who knoweth the destruction of ¹them both?

23     These also are *sayings* of the wise.

   To have respect of persons in judgement is not good.
24 He that saith unto the wicked, Thou art righteous;
   Peoples shall curse him, nations shall abhor him:
25 But to them that rebuke *him* shall be delight,
   And a good blessing shall come upon them.

¹ Or, *of their years*

*them that are given to change.* As this stands it is in reference to
Jahweh as well as to the king; was the sage thinking of the evil conditions in the northern kingdom during the years 743–735 B.C., when
five kings followed each other in quick succession; and of the southern
kingdom a little later, during the reign of Manasseh, when alien cults
were introduced? It is not impossible. On the other hand, it may be
that the text is at fault (see next note), and that the Sept. has preserved the right reading: 'Against both of them (i.e. Jahweh and the
king) be not disobedient.'

*of them both.* It is difficult to see to whom 'both' can refer, as
the first line must be in reference to those who are given to change;
to make 'their calamity' refer to Jahweh and the king, i.e. the
calamity they bring, is unnatural; divine and human action are not
coupled together in this way by the writer. It seems best to read
instead of 'them both' (שְׁנֵיהֶם), 'those who are given to change' (שׁוֹנִים)
as in *v.* 21. The R.V. marg. 'of their years' is highly improbable.
After this verse the Sept. inserts xxx. 1–14.

## XXIV. 23–34. *Further sayings of the Wise men.*

**23–26.** *These also* . . . This title shows that the sayings were
gathered from different sources.

*To have respect of persons* . . . Cf. Deut. i. 17, xvi. 19. Lit. 'to
have regard for faces'. The line, with the exception of 'in judgement',
occurs again in xxviii. 21ᵃ, cf. also xviii. 5ᵃ.

*judgement.* i.e. in giving a judicial decision.

In xxviii. 21 the line is followed by a parallel one; as the following
verses have two lines each it is probable that originally the same
was the case with the verse before us, and that the second line has
accidently fallen out.

**24.** *Peoples* . . . *nations.* Cf. xi. 26, xxix. 2; a general statement,
not meant to be taken in a literal sense.

**25.** *them that rebuke.* The force of the Hebrew word in this connexion is rather 'they that convict', as in xxx. 6. The contrast is

26 He [1]kisseth the lips

    That giveth a right answer.

27 Prepare thy work without,

    And make it ready for thee in the field;

    And afterwards build thine house.

28 Be not a witness against thy neighbour without cause;

                   [1] Or, *kisseth with the lips*

between declaring innocent ('thou art righteous' in *v.* 24) and therefore not deserving punishment, and convicting, and therefore fixing a penalty. It is a court of justice that is pictured in these verses.

*a good blessing.* Cf. Ps. xxi. 3 (4 in Hebr.).

**26.** *He kisseth the lips.* This is an exceedingly strange expression; the kissing of the lips is nowhere mentioned in the O.T.; possibly for superstitious reasons it was not practised. Neither of the two emotions connected with kissing, i.e. reverence and affection, would be appropriate here, since it is a question of uttering a just sentence in a court of law. In three passages (Ps. lxxviii. 9; 1 Chron. xii. 2; 2 Chron. xvii. 17) the Hebr. word means 'to equip', or 'arm'; a sense which it has also in post-biblical Hebr.; but in this latter the word is also used in a figurative sense of equipping the lips with words for a verbal contest; e. g. Jastrow (*op. cit.*) s.v. quotes the Midrash, *Cant. R.* i. 2: 'If thou studiest the words of the Law so that thy lips be equipped (ready for contest) . . .' It is, therefore, conceivable that the word is to be understood in this sense here, viz.: 'He that equippeth the lips' (we should expect the addition of 'with knowledge', or the like, which may have dropped out). It is true this figurative meaning of the word is unknown in the O.T., but there are other cases, as we have seen, of words being used in this book which have no parallel in the O.T.

*a right answer.* Lit. 'upright words', the reference is to a just decision.

**27.** *Prepare thy work . . .* Another reference to country life, showing that the Wisdom writers were concerned with all classes of the community.

*afterwards.* In the Hebr. the 'and' comes before 'build', showing that between 'afterwards' and 'and build . . .' some words have fallen out; the obvious suggestion of most commentators is to supply 'take thee a wife'.

*build thine house.* i.e. build up thine household, cf. Ruth iv. 11. The general sense of the verse is that a young man should secure an adequate means of living before setting up as a family man.

**28, 29.** *Be not a witness . . . without a cause.* As the next line shows, we must read, with the Sept., 'be not a false witness against thy neighbour' (reading עֵד־חָמָם 'a witness of violence' for עֵד־חִנָּם 'a witness without a cause'), Exod. xxiii. 1; Ps. xxxv. 11.

[1] And deceive not with thy lips.

29  Say not, I will do so to him as he hath done to me;
I will render to the man according to his work.

30  I went by the field of the slothful,
And by the vineyard of the man void of understanding;

31  And, lo, it was all grown over with thorns,
The face thereof was covered with [2] nettles,
And the stone wall thereof was broken down.

32  Then I beheld, and considered well:
I saw, and received instruction.

> [1] Heb. *And wouldest thou deceive with thy lips?*
> [2] Or, *wild vetches*

*And deceive not.* The Hebr. as in the R.V. marg.; but it is clearly better to follow the Sept. and read: 'And mislead not', i. e. the course of justice by false witness. Cf. the words in the *Bilingual Book of Proverbs*, § 20:

> *Words thou shalt not employ falsely* . . .  (*Babylonian Wisdom*, p. 83).

**29.** Although this verse is appropriately added here it is independent of the preceding words. 'This regulation, it is true, was, in the later legislation, not a matter of private revenge, but a legal right, controlled by judges; it was, however, based on the old principle of retaliation, and breathed its spirit. It was gradually modified by the advance of moral and refined feeling, and would be substantially set aside by the principle announced . . .; the sage here expresses the higher moral idea of his time' (Toy). In this he was, of course, influenced by the Deuteronomic legislation based, in its turn, on the prophetical teaching. For the remarkable parallel to this in the *Teaching of Amen-em-ope* see note on xx. 22; and cf. xvii. 13, xxv. 21, 22. In the Babylonian Proverb it is said:

> *Unto him that doeth thee evil shalt thou return good,*
> *Unto thine enemy justice shalt thou mete out* (the last word is uncertain)
> (Langdon, *op. cit.*, § G).

**30-34.** With these verses cf. vi. 6-11; the two passages are very similar, and *vv.* 33, 34 are practically identical with vi. 10, 11.

**31.** *grown over with thorns.* A very rare word occurring elsewhere only in Hos. ix. 6 as a sign of desolation.

*nettles.* This is likewise a rare word occurring elsewhere only in Zeph. ii. 9; Job xxx. 7.

*And the stone wall* . . . This third line is either a later addition or, as Steuernagel thinks, it is the second line of a couplet the first of which has fallen out of the text.

**32.** *received instruction.* i. e. took warning.

33 [1]*Yet* a little sleep, a little slumber,
    A little folding of the hands to sleep:
34 So shall thy poverty come as a robber;
    And thy want as an armed man.

        [1] See ch. vi. 10, 11.

**33, 34.** As these two verses are a direct address to the sluggard, differing therein in form from the rest of the passage, it is probable that they were added here later from vi. 10, 11 as an appropriate conclusion.

**34.** *shall come as a robber.* The Hebr. has 'as one walking' (מִתְהַלֵּךְ); the R.V. emendation from vi. 11 (כִּמְהַלֵּךְ), 'as a robber', is no doubt right.

# THE FOURTH COLLECTION OF PROVERBS

## XXV. 1—XXIX. 27.  *The Proverbs of Solomon*

THIS collection consists, in the main, though not exclusively, of short, independent sayings, and in so far partakes of the character of the second collection (x–xxii. 16) rather than of that of the others. But it differs from that collection, which includes only single verse proverbs, in having a certain number of sayings comprising two or more verses (e.g. xxv. 6, 7; 9, 10; 21, 22; xxvi. 18, 19; 24–26; xxvii. 23–27). In xxviii, xxix only single verse proverbs occur, and it is noticeable that in these two chapters the observance of the Law receives an emphasis which is not found in xxv–xxvii (see xxviii. 4, 7, 9, xxix. 18). It is also to be noted that in xxv–xxvii it is almost wholly purely worldly wisdom which finds expression; religious thought is much more pronounced in xxviii, xxix than in the other three chapters. This difference of standpoint suggests that the collections xxv–xxvii and xxviii, xxix were not the work of the same collector, but were subsequently joined together and made into one collection by a later scribe who added the title.

The subject-matter of these chapters is very varied, and the repetition of sayings which occur in the other collections shows that the collectors of each must have had access to some common source which was utilized by each independently.

The collection, as Budde has pointed out,[1] consists of a hundred and thirty-seven proverbs, which very nearly corresponds with the numerical value of the Hebrew letters forming the name of Hezekiah. The full form of this name, which was probably the form in which it originally stood in xxv. 1, is equal to a hundred and thirty-six; the extra proverb might have got in by mistake. In any case, the close correspondence between the numerical value of the name of Hezekiah and the number of proverbs in the collection can hardly be fortuitous, especially as something similar occurs in other collections, see Introd. § IV.

The choice of the name of Hezekiah in the title is quite comprehensible. It is said of him in 2 Kgs. xviii. 7 that 'whithersoever he went forth he prospered'; but this last word means 'to have understanding' or 'insight'; the noun is used in Prov. i. 3 of 'wise dealing'. It is also worth noting that in 2 Chron. xxx. 26 Hezekiah is placed side by side with Solomon. Proverbial sayings are also imputed to him (see note on xxv. 1). Among the traditions concerning Hezekiah in the Talmud he is said to have been a great champion of the study of the Law (*Sanh.*, 94 b); he is also said to have redacted the Wisdom books of *Proverbs* and *Ecclesiastes* (*Baba Bathra*, 15a).

---

[1] *Geschichte der alt-hebräischen Literatur*, p. 292 (1906).

**XXV.** 1  These also are proverbs of Solomon, which the men
of Hezekiah king of Judah copied out.

CHAPTER XXV

**1.** *These also ... Solomon.* Cf. the superscription in x. 1. The word
'also' seems to imply that there were in existence other collections
of Solomonic proverbs, or what were believed to be such. x–xxii. 16
would, of course, be one of these.

*the men of Hezekiah.* While there is no evidence which would justify
Hezekiah being described as 'the Jewish Pisistratus' (Delitzsch) or
'the Jewish Asshurbanipal' (Sellin), there is, on the other hand, no
reason to deny the possibility that he may have been a patron of
literature. But it is more likely that the tradition to which this title
owed its origin arose from one or two details contained in the account
of Hezekiah's reign in 2 Kgs. xviii, xix; thus, in xviii. 18, 37, xix. 2
(cf. Isa. xxxvii. 2) it is clear that Shebna the *Sōphēr* ('Scribe') occupied an important post at the court; in xix. 3 Hezekiah is credited
with the utterance of the proverb: 'The children are come to the
birth, and there is not strength to bring forth'; and there is a point
of attachment between the emphasis laid on the observance of the
Law in xxviii, xxix, and Hezekiah's observance of the Mosaic commandments and other pious acts mentioned, e.g. in 2 Kgs. xviii. 6,
xx. 3. These points would have been sufficient to give rise to the
tradition that Hezekiah gathered round him men of the *Chakham*
type.

*copied out.* The root meaning of the Hebr. word is 'to remove',
cf. Job ix. 5; the use of it here in the sense of 'removing' from one
roll to another, i.e. transcribing, is very late, and is not found elsewhere in the O.T. It occurs in this sense, as well as in that of 'trans-
lating', in later Rabbinical literature (for examples see Jastrow,
*Talmud Dictionary*, s.v.). The occurrence of this word stamps this
title as belonging to a much later time.

**2–7.** These verses have as their subject the king, see also xxviii.
2, 15, 16, xxix. 4, 12, 14, 26. These comparatively frequent references, in a book of this kind, to the king ('ruler' and 'prince' cannot
be understood in a different sense) point indubitably to the pre-
exilic date of the collection. Such references to the king in post-
exilic times would be pointless; in the first collection (i–ix), which is
confessedly post-exilic, there are no references to the king. The
passages in *Ecclesiasticus* which speak of a king are of a different
character; Ben-Sira has in mind foreign courts which were visited
by Jewish envoys, or he lays down some general principle (vii. 4–6,
viii. 2, x. 1–18, xxxix. 4).

2 It is the glory of God to conceal a thing:
   But the glory of kings is to search out a matter.
3 The heaven for height, and the earth for depth,
   And the heart of kings is unsearchable.
4 Take away the dross from the silver,
   And there cometh forth a vessel for the finer:
5 Take away the wicked *from* before the king,
   And his throne shall be established in righteousness.
6 ¹Put not thyself forward in the presence of the king,
   And stand not in the place of great men:

¹ Heb. *Glorify not thyself.*

**2.** An antithetic couplet; the inscrutability of the acts of God, on the one hand, are contrasted with the kingly duty of making his acts clear and comprehensible to all, on the other. In each case the action reflects glory on the doer.

*to conceal a thing.* Cf. one of Pascal's favourite themes in his *Pensées*: *Vere tu es Deus absconditus* (Isa. xlv. 15); see also Job xi. 7, 8. It is possible that this verse, read in conjunction with the episode recorded in 2 Kgs. xx. 1–11, may have been a contributory cause for connecting this collection with the name of Hezekiah.

*to search out.* i.e. to examine thoroughly, and thus to be able to place a matter in the clear light of day.

**3.** Just as the height of heaven is unattainable and the depth of the earth unapproachable, so the purpose of the king is inscrutable. The king is in some sense compared with God here, cf. xvi. 10. It is hardly conceivable that the sage should have been thinking of any Gentile king in writing thus; the words are strong evidence of this collection belonging to pre-exilic times.

**4, 5.** These two verses form a quatrain.
*the dross from the silver.* Cf. xxvi. 23.
*And there cometh forth* . . . The Hebr. text as it stands is lacking in sense; the mere fact of eliminating the dross is not sufficient to produce a vessel. The Sept. has a reading which presupposes the Hebr.: נִצְרָף כֻּלּוֹ, 'wholly purified'; evidently, therefore, we must read: 'And it cometh forth wholly purified.'
*the wicked.* Possibly Shebna may have been meant, see Isa. xxii. 15–25.
*And his throne* . . . Cf. xvi. 12.

**6, 7.** These two verses also form a quatrain, the third line of verse 7 belongs to verse 8.
*Put not thyself forward.* Hebr. as R.V. marg. The second line shows that the prohibition is against arrogating to oneself a more

7 For better is it that it be said unto thee, Come up hither;
  Than that thou shouldest be put lower in the presence of the
      prince,
  Whom thine eyes have seen.
8 Go not forth hastily to strive,
  [1] Lest *thou know not* what to do in the end thereof,
  When thy neighbour hath put thee to shame.
9 Debate thy cause with thy neighbour *himself*,
  [2] And disclose not the secret of another:
10 Lest he that heareth it revile thee,

[1] Or, *Lest* it be said *in the end thereof, What wilt thou do? when &c.*     [2] Or, *But*

honourable place at a royal feast than is justified by the rank of the
aspirant. With the verse cf. Ecclus. vii. 4, 5 (Hebr.):

> *Seek not dominion from God,*
> *Nor from a king a seat of honour.*
> *Justify thyself not in the sight of God,*
> *And affect not wisdom in the presence of a king.*

**7.** The verse reminds one irresistibly of Lk. xiv. 8–11 ; it may have
been in our Lord's mind.

*Whom thine eyes* . . . This line belongs to the following verse. For
'whom' we must put 'what'; in Hebr. the word is the same for both.

**8.** *Go not forth* . . . Read: 'Bring not forth' (תֹּצֵא for תֵּצֵא). 'Strive'
refers to action in a court of justice. Paraphrased the two lines (7[c]
and 8[a]) mean: Do not rashly bring a matter before a judge regarding
something that you have seen somebody do. It is a warning against
precipitate action on the part of one who by a hasty conclusion mis-
judges the nature of another's act.

*Lest* . . . For 'lest' (פֶּן) read 'for' (כִּי). This line, to which the
following one belongs, is a question: 'For what wilt thou do in the
end thereof when thy neighbour doth put thee to shame?' i. e. What
is he going to do when, having realized that he had made a mistake,
he looks foolish before the man he had wrongly accused?

**9, 10.** These two verses form a quatrain and belong together; they
continue the subject of the preceding quatrain, and give the advice
that the matter in dispute is better settled by discussing it privately
than by bringing it into a court of justice. Cf. Matth. xviii. 15.

*of another.* It gives better sense if we follow the Latin and read
'to another'.

**10.** *he that heareth it.* The Sept. reads 'thy neighbour', which is
perhaps to be preferred.

*revile thee.* The Hebr. word (an Aramaism) occurs nowhere else in
the O.T., though the noun, 'reproach', is used in xiv. 34 (see Robertson Smith, *The Prophets of Israel*, p. 408 [1897], where an interesting
note on the word will be found).

And thine infamy turn not away.

11 A word ¹fitly spoken
 Is *like* apples of gold in ²baskets of silver.

   ¹ Or, *in due season*   ² Or, *filigree work*

*infamy.* 'Ill-repute' is a better word; it is translated 'slander' in
x. 18; he gets a bad name for what he has said.

With the thought of this quatrain cf. the quotations under xi. 13.

As showing a general community of thought with verses 8–10 the
following passage from the *Proverbs of Achikar* ii. 53–55, is worth
quoting:

> *My son, let not a word go forth from thy mouth,*
> *Until thou hast taken counsel within thine heart;*
> *Better it is for a man to stumble in his heart*
> *Than to stumble with his tongue.*
> *My son, if thou hear an evil matter,*
> *Put it seven fathoms deep underground.*
> *My son, tarry not where there is contention,*
> *For from strife ariseth murder.*

There is, of course, no question of borrowing here, but the essential
identity of thought in all is worth drawing attention to.

**11.** The R.V. has transposed the two lines of this verse; the Hebr.,
which contains some difficult words the meaning of which is uncertain, runs:

> 'Apples of gold in silver carvings
> Is a word appropriately uttered.'

*fitly.* The Hebr. word occurs here only in the O.T.; the point of
the comparison with the ornament spoken of in the first line would
suggest the idea of appropriateness, cf. xv. 23; the Version of Sym-
machus and the Vulgate have 'in its season'.

*apples of gold.* It is somewhat uncertain what fruit is meant by the
Hebr. word; 'gold' is presumably intended to be taken literally in
such close juxtaposition with 'silver', so that it would not necessarily
indicate the colour of the fruit referred to. 'Apple' in any case is
out of the question, for, as Tristram says: 'Though the apple is
cultivated with success in the higher parts of Lebanon, out of the
boundaries of the Holy Land, yet it barely exists in the country
itself. There are, indeed, a few trees in the gardens of Jaffa; but they
do not thrive, and have a wretched, woody fruit. Perhaps there may
be some at Iskalān. What English and American writers have called
the "apple", however, is really the quince. The climate is far too
hot for our apple tree' (*The Natural History of the Bible*, pp. 334 f.
[1889]). If, as is probable, the Hebr. word is derived from the root
meaning 'to breathe' (נפח), it may be taken that this is because of
the perfume exhaled by the fruit in question; this would also point
to the quince as being the fruit meant, for this gives forth a much
stronger aroma than the apple. The orange cannot come into con-

12 *As* [1]an earring of gold, and an ornament of fine gold,
   *So is* a wise reprover upon an obedient ear.
13 As the cold of snow in the time of harvest,
   *So is* a faithful messenger to them that send him;
   For he refresheth the soul of his masters.

   [1] Or, *a nose-ring*

sideration since it is known that this was only introduced into Medi-
terranean countries in the ninth century, by the Arabs (see *Encycl.
Bibl.* i. 269).

*baskets.* The precise meaning of the Hebr. word is uncertain; the
sing. is rendered 'imagination' in xviii. 11, but there it is joined to
'heart', cf. Ps. lxxiii. 7. It is used of carved (idolatrous) images in
Lev. xxvi. 1; Num. xxxiii. 52, so that 'carvings' is perhaps the best
rendering here; the only difficulty is as to what kind of carvings are
meant, and where they would be set up. From what is said in the
next verse it is permissible to suppose that the writer had in mind
some costly ornament in the house of some wealthy person.

**12.** As *an earring.* Omit 'as'. The Hebr. word for 'earring' means
simply 'ring', e.g. Gen. xxiv. 30; Hos. ii. 15 (Hebr.); Job xlii. 11; when
used of an ear- or nose-ring this is specifically mentioned, see e.g.
Gen. xxxv. 4; Exod. xxxii. 2, 3 for the former, and Gen. xxiv. 47; Isa.
iii. 21; Prov. xi. 22, for the latter.

*an ornament.* The Hebr. word occurs elsewhere in the O.T. only
in *Song of songs* vii. 2.

*fine gold.* The Hebr. word (*kethem*) is used in the *Teaching of
Amen-em-ope* XVI. xviii. 12: . . . *it is a perversion before God if gold-
bases* (?) *be overlaid* (?) *to appear as pure gold* (Griffith's rendering).

So is *a wise reprover.* Omit 'So'. For 'reprover' (מוֹכִיחַ) Toy suggests the emendation 'reproof' (תּוֹכַחַת), which is certainly preferable.

*an obedient ear.* The Hebr. can mean this, but it can also be rendered 'a hearing ear', which is better. With the thought of the verse
cf. Ecclus. xxii. 17:

   *A heart fixed on thoughtful understanding
   Is as an ornament graven on a polished wall.*

**13.** *snow.* As the time of harvest varied, according to the crops,
from March to September, snow might fall during the barley harvest
in March; for recorded instances of snowfalls during this month see
Nowack, *op. cit.*, i. 49.

*in the time of harvest.* The Sept. has 'heat', and apparently read
בְּחֹם (instead of בְּיוֹם); if it represents the original reading the reference is possibly to the heat occasioned by the strenuous labour of
harvesting.

So is. Omit 'So'.

*For he refresheth* . . . This line must be regarded as a later gloss

14 *As* clouds and wind without rain,
   *So is* he that boasteth himself ¹of his gifts falsely.
15 By long forbearing is a ²ruler persuaded,
   And a soft tongue breaketh the bone.

¹ Heb. *in a gift of falsehood.*        ² Or, *judge*

as three-lined sayings do not occur in this collection; moreover, it is
not in the style of the writer to explain the obvious.

On the importance attached to the sending of a reliable messenger,
see the quotations from the *Proverbs of Achikar* on p. li, the *Teaching of Amen-em-ope* on p. 193, and the *Teaching of Ptah-hotep* on p.193.

**14.** As. The comparison is not expressed in the original.

*clouds.* The Hebr. word, which is a plural one and occurs elsewhere
only in Ps. cxxxv. 7; Jer. x. 13, li. 16, means rather 'mists' or
'vapours'; the root-idea is that of rising. The mist rises through
the wind blowing and the cloud-like appearance suggests that rain
may come, but it does not. The thought is that of expecting something which does not come, though the expectation is justified by
appearances.

*that boasteth himself* . . . i.e. who brags about what he gives, but as
a matter of fact gives nothing at all. The reference is to the type of
man who promises things, but fails to keep his promise. Somewhat
similar is Ben-Sira's saying:

> *Be not boastful with thy tongue,*
> *And careless or negligent in thy work* (Ecclus. iv. 29, Hebr.).

**15.** *ruler.* The Hebr. word (קָצִין) means both one who decides,
i.e. a judge, e.g. Dan. xi. 18, and more generally one in authority,
e.g. Isa. i. 10; Mic. iii. 1, cf. Prov. vi. 7. If 'long forbearing' is understood in the sense of patience, then the line could mean that by
patient pleading of one's cause a judge can be persuaded to decide
in one's favour. But patience is not the natural meaning of the
Hebrew word, which means rather forbearance; but forbearance is
for a judge or ruler to exercise, not the pleader; it is, therefore, better
by a slight emendation to read 'he that is wrathful' (קֶצֶף) for
'ruler' (קָצִין).

*is . . . persuaded.* This sense of the Hebr. word is found elsewhere
in i. 10, xvi. 29, though in both cases the meaning is rather to entice
through deception; and the word is mostly used of deceiving, e.g.
xxiv. 28; 2 Sam. iii. 25; Jer. xx. 10; Ezek. xiv. 9; hence there is justification for Toy's emendation 'is appeased' or 'pacified' (יִשְׁקִים, cf. xv.
18). The line would then run: 'By forbearance a wrathful man is
appeased.'

*soft.* Cf. xv. 1, where the word is used

With the line cf. the proverb: 'Continual dropping wears the
stone.' Though of entirely different content, there is a saying in the

16 Hast thou found honey? eat so much as is sufficient for thee;
   Lest thou be filled therewith, and vomit it.

17 Let thy foot be seldom in thy neighbour's house;
   Lest he be [1] weary of thee, and hate thee.

18 A man that beareth false witness against his neighbour
   Is a maul, and a sword, and a sharp arrow.

[1] Heb. *full of thee.*

Elephantiné version of the *Proverbs of Achikar* which, so far as words are concerned, recalls this verse:

> Soft is the tongue of a king,
> But it breaketh the ribs of a dragon (Cowley 105).

**16.** *Hast thou . . . ?* In the original this is not in interrogative form. Cf. verse 27[a], and xxiv. 13. Cf. Ecclus. xxxvii. 29, 30 (Hebr.):

> *Be not insatiable in every luxury,*
> *And give not thyself unrestrainedly to every dainty;*
> *For in much eating lurketh sickness,*
> *And he that is surfeited draweth nigh unto loathing.*

Self-control and moderation in all things was a cardinal precept among the sages.

**17.** Just as the Wisdom writers so often enjoin right living because of reward, and warn against evil living because of its untoward consequences, so here bad manners are deprecated because they entail drawbacks. It must be recognized that we have here that which is a real blemish in the teaching of the sages, and in this they represent a lower moral level than the prophets by whom in many other respects they were profoundly influenced. To do good for good's sake, to avoid evil because it is evil,—these are ideals which the Wisdom writers failed to envisage, at any rate as a general rule.

*Let . . . be seldom.* The Hebr. word is lit. 'Make precious', in the sense of rare; 'let thy foot be rarely in thy neighbour's house'. An almost identical saying occurs in the *Proverbs of Achikar* ii. 74:

> *My son, let not thy foot run after thy friend,*
> *Lest he be surfeited with thee and hate thee.*

Cf. also Ben-Sira's saying:

> *If a noble draw near, keep away (from him),*
> *The more will he (then) desire thee to approach* (Ecclus. xiii. 9, Hebr.).

**18.** The R.V. has transposed the lines of this verse; it is with the purpose of *emphasizing* the injurious elements in false witness that the Hebrew has these, in metaphorical language, in the first line.

*a maul.* The Hebr. has 'a scatterer' (מֵפִיץ), for which, following the Sept., we must read 'hammer' or 'maul' (מַפֵּץ), cf. Jer. li. 20. The words employed for describing what is brought about by a false witness are meant to express crushing, dividing, and piercing. The sage

19 Confidence in an unfaithful man in time of trouble
  Is *like* a broken tooth, and a foot out of joint.
20 *As* one that taketh off a garment in cold weather, *and as*
    vinegar upon [1]nitre,
  So is he that singeth songs to an heavy heart.

  [1] Or, *soda*

uses these strong metaphors in order to show what terrible consequences may follow false witness, and intends thereby to urge
caution upon his hearers should they have to appear as witnesses in
a court of law. With the verse cf. the Elephantiné version of the
*Proverbs of Achikar* (Cowley 140):

> There was a cruel witness against me,
> And who then has justified me?

**19.** R.V. has again transposed the lines of this verse.

*Confidence.* On both syntactical and rhythmical grounds this word
should, with the Sept., be deleted. Moreover, as Toy rightly points
out, with this word inserted a statement is made which is not quite
correct; 'it is not confidence, but the ground or basis of confidence
that is as unreliable as a broken tooth &c.'

*in.* This does not represent anything in the Hebr.

*broken.* This is an emendation of the Hebr. word (נִרְעָה for רֹעָה),
which means 'a grazing', or 'feeding' tooth; the Hebr. is obviously
wrong; but a better emendation is to follow the Versions and read
'a bad' tooth, this involves only a change in the vowel-points (רָעָה).

*out of joint.* Read 'a tottering' foot; the Hebr. is wrongly pointed
and means 'that which is witnessed to' (read מֹעֶדֶת for מוּעֶדֶת).

One cannot bite on a bad tooth, and one cannot walk steadily on a
tottering foot, both are unreliable; in the same way an unfaithful
man cannot be relied upon in time of trouble. The verse should
be read:

> 'A bad tooth and a tottering foot
> Is (as) an unfaithful man in the day of trouble.'

**20.** *As one that . . . cold weather.* Even without any knowledge of
Hebrew, it is easy to see how very similar this is to the last four
words of verse 19 (omitting that for 'confidence', see above):

19ᵇ   מועדת . . . בוגד ביום צרה

20ᵃ   מעדה בגר ביום קרה

It is evident that 20ᵃ is due in the first instance to the mistake of a
scribe who inadvertently copied the line twice over; then a later
scribe tried to improve upon it by making one or two slight changes,
but its pointlessness in the context shows that the attempt was not
a success. This must have taken place at a relatively late period, for
20ᵃ is wanting in the Sept. We must therefore delete this line here as
not belonging to the original text. But it is probable that it is the

Q 2

21 If [1] thine enemy be hungry, give him bread to eat;
   And if he be thirsty, give him water to drink:
22 For thou shalt heap coals of fire upon his head,
   And the LORD shall reward thee.

[1] Heb. *he that hateth thee.*

remnant of a couplet which may have stood originally after this
verse, for the Sept. has, after verse 20:

'As a moth in a garment and a worm in wood,
   So doth a man's sorrow hurt his heart.'

It should also be pointed out that the verse has two lines without
this added one; three-lined verses do not occur in this collection in
its original form. These two lines offer considerable difficulties; as
they stand they run lit.:

'Vinegar on soda,
   And he singeth with songs on an evil (i.e. heavy, or downcast) heart.'

That there is something wrong here is evident. In the first place, a
verb is wanting in the first line. Steuernagel accepts the line as it
stands, but its extreme brevity makes it probable that the verb has
fallen out, though it is difficult to say what this verb may have been.
The second line is corrupt; the simplest emendation is to delete
'songs' which is not required, and to read: 'So is a song to a heavy
heart.' The lines will then run:

'(As) vinegar . . . on soda,
   So is a song to a heavy heart.'

But what does this mean? As Steuernagel points out, when vinegar
is poured on soda, the carbonic acid in it makes it bubble up [1]; in like
manner, this is what, metaphorically speaking, happens when one
who is down in the mouth hears a song; it cheers him up. If the
suggested emendation is correct, this is an attractive explanation of
the couplet. On the other hand, Toy, following the Sept., emends the
text so as to read:

'Vinegar to a wound and . . .
   So is a song to a troubled heart.'

And he suggests that in the first line the words 'smoke to the eyes'
(see x. 26) have dropped out. In this case the couplet will mean that
just as a wound is made more painful if vinegar is poured on it, so
a man in low spirits is aggravated by hearing a song. This, too, gives
good sense. But the corrupt state of the text makes it very difficult
to feel certain about the correctness of either of these explanations.

**21, 22.** These two verses belong together and form a quatrain.
The words 'bread' and 'water' are omitted by the Versions (cf. also
Rom. xii. 20); they are, therefore, in all probability later additions.
*For thou shalt heap* . . . i.e. this is the form that vengeance on an

[1] See further, Nowack, *Hebr. Arch.* i. 245.

23 The north wind bringeth forth rain:
   So doth a backbiting tongue an angry countenance.
24 [1]It is better to dwell in the corner of the housetop,
   Than with a contentious woman in a wide house.
25 *As* cold waters to a [2]thirsty soul,
   So is good news from a far country.
26 *As* a [3]troubled fountain, and a corrupted spring,
   *So is* a righteous man that [4]giveth way before the wicked.
27 It is not good to eat much honey:
   [5]So *for men* to search out their own glory is *not* glory.

[1] See ch. xxi. 9.        [2] Or, *weary*        [3] Heb. *trampled*.        [4] Or, *is moved*
[5] Or, *But* for men *to search out their own glory is glory*  The Hebrew text is obscure.

enemy is to take. This fine precept is a little marred by the last line ;
as so often with the Wisdom writers, a good action is enjoined not
for good's sake, but because it brings its reward. Cf. xx. 22, xxiv. 29,
and the quotations there given ; cf. also Ecclus. xxviii. 1–7.

**23.** *an angry countenance.* Plur. in Hebr. With the verse cf. xxvi.
20 ; Ecclus. xxi. 28, xxviii. 13 ff.

**24.** See xxi. 9.

**25.** *good news from . . .* Friends would be journeying to distant
countries as traders, soldiers, or on missions to foreign courts ; news
from them in those days would be rare, so that the pleasure of
hearing about them would be the greater. The reference may include
exiles.

**26.** The meaning of this verse is not quite certain, but it seems to
be that when a righteous man falls from his high moral level it is
like a muddy fountain and a polluted spring.

*troubled.* Lit. 'trampled', cf. Ps. lxviii. 30[c] (31 in Hebr.) ; Ezek.
xxxii. 2, xxxiv. 18 ; in Prov. vi. 3 the word is used of humbling oneself, but the text there is probably corrupt.

*giveth way.* Lit. 'moved' ; in Ps. xvii. 5 the word occurs in the
phrase : 'My feet have not slipped', where the context shows that
moral slipping is meant. This, however, is not the usual way in which
the word is used ; more often it means being moved in the sense of
falling into adversity. But in this verse the comparison with the
fountain and spring points to the meaning as in the psalm.

*before the wicked.* This aggravates the case because the wicked will
point the finger of scorn, and gloat over the fall of the righteous.

**27.** One has but to read this verse to see that the two lines do not
belong together.

*to eat much honey.* The R.V. rightly follows the Versions in place
of the Hebrew, which has : 'To multiply the eating of honey' (read
הַרְבֵּה, as an adjective, for הַרְבּוֹת). With the line cf. verse 16.

*So* for men *to search . . .* The Hebr. has : 'And the searching of their

28 ¹He whose spirit is without restraint
    Is *like* a city that is broken down and hath no wall.

**XXVI.** 1 As snow in summer, and as rain in harvest,
    So honour is not seemly for a fool.

 2 As the sparrow in her wandering, as the swallow in her flying,
    So the curse that is causeless ²lighteth not.

---

¹ Or, *He that hath no rule over his spirit*          ² Heb. *cometh not.*

---

glory is glory'; without drastic textual changes it is impossible to
make anything of this. The Sept. reads: 'And to honour noble words
is fitting.' The isolated line had already got astray before the Sept.
version was made; its companion is lost; and the same applies to the
first line of the verse.

**28.** The R.V. has transposed the lines of the verse; Hebr. has:

> 'A breached city without wall
> (Is as) a man without self-control.'

Such a man is easily assailed and conquered by any and every attack.

## Chapter XXVI

The first twelve verses of this chapter, with the exception of verse
2, which probably did not originally stand in its present position,
deal with the type of fool called the *kĕsīl* (see further Excursus XI);
the word occurs in every verse of the section.

**1.** *snow in summer.* Cf., on the other hand, xxv. 13.

*honour.* The reference is, of course, not to the sense of honour,
but to an honourable position.

**2.** *the curse that is causeless* . . . i.e. a curse that is not justified.
The old-world belief that a curse had an inherent power is what
called forth this denial. 'Both blessings and curses, in some of their
characteristic forms at least, imply a process which either may be
styled an inherent one, or is operated by powers who, however, are
not necessarily specified. The process or mechanism is such that the
blessing once uttered cannot be taken back (Gen. xxvii. 33, 38), and
the curse of the wise will be effective even against the innocent
(Talm. Bab. *Makkōth*, 11 a)' (S. A. Cook, in his edition of Robertson
Smith's *Religion of the Semites*, p. 555 [1927]). See further, Gen.
xxvii. 33; Num. v. 11 ff.; Deut. xxi. 7; Judg. xvii. 2; Zech. v. 1–4.
The Hebr. marg. reads: 'cometh to him' instead of 'cometh not';
the idea, according to this, is that the curse rebounds upon the
utterer of it. There is, however, no doubt that the text, not the
margin, is the right reading because the negative is demanded by
the context.

In the Elephantiné version of the *Proverbs of Achikar* (Cowley

3 A whip for the horse, a bridle for the ass,
  And a rod for the back of fools.
4 Answer not a fool according to his folly,
  Lest thou also be like unto him.
5 Answer a fool according to his folly,
  Lest he be wise in ¹his own conceit.
6 He that sendeth a message by the hand of a fool
  Cutteth off *his own* feet, *and* drinketh in damage.

¹ Heb. *his own eyes.*

223 f.) the traditional belief, combated by the Hebrew sage, finds
expression:

> *If there goes forth good from the mouth of men, it is well; and if a curse*
> *shall go forth from their mouth, the gods will curse them;*

i. e. those against whom the curse is uttered.

**3.** *a bridle for the ass.* The Hebr. word is *ḥămōr*, which was used
mostly for carrying burdens and for agriculture; the she-ass (*'āthōn*)
was used generally for riding.

*And a rod . . .* Cf. x. 13ᵇ, xix. 29ᵇ.

**4, 5.** These are independent sayings, but the two verse belong
together.

*Lest thou.* In the original this is emphatic, 'Lest thou, even thou'.

**5.** *Answer a fool.* The apparent contradiction between this and
verse 4 is not such in reality; it is a question of different circumstances. As a rule, arguing with a fool is to descend to his level; but
on occasion it is well to answer him lest reason go by default. With
verse 4 cf. Ecclus. xxii. 13:

> *Talk not much with a fool,*
> *And consort not with a man without understanding . . .*
> *Turn from him, and thou shalt find rest,*
> *And thou wilt be wearied with his folly.*

*in his own conceit.* Read as R.V. marg.

**6.** The R.V. has transposed the lines of this verse.

*message.* Lit. 'words'; therefore the more likely to be wrongly
delivered by a fool.

*Cutteth off . . .* This line is difficult, the text seems to be corrupt.
Lit. the Hebr. runs: 'He cutteth off feet, violence he drinketh.' The
first phrase may be purposely exaggerated in order to express the
uselessness of sending such a messenger; in the second phrase we
may perhaps read חֶרְפָּה, 'reproach', with the Sept., for 'violence'
(חָמָס); 'drinking wrath' is a phrase which occurs in Job xxi. 20ᵇ. The
meaning would then be that the sender would be laying up trouble
for himself through sending an unreliable messenger who through his
foolishness made mischief.

7 The legs of the lame hang loose:
  So is a parable in the mouth of fools.

8 [1]As a bag of gems in a heap of stones,
  So is he that giveth honour to a fool.

9 *As* a thorn that goeth up into the hand of a drunkard,
  So is a parable in the mouth of fools.

  [1] Or, *As one that bindeth fast a stone in a sling*

Cf. the *Proverbs of Achikar* ii. 41:

> *My son, send a wise man, and give him no orders;*
> *But if thou wilt send a fool, go rather thyself, and send him not.*

On the importance attached to the proper delivery of a message see the quotation from the *Teaching of Amen-em-ope* in the note on xxii. 21.

**7.** *legs.* The Hebr. word means the lower part of the leg, i. e. the calf, as distinct from the thigh, see Judg. xv. 8.

*hang loose.* This word is difficult; as it stands in the Hebr. it comes from a root meaning 'to draw' (cf. e.g. xx. 5); with a very slight emendation, however (דַּלְיוּ for דָּלְיוּ), it can be taken as coming from a root meaning to 'hang loose'. The picture will then be that of a cripple on two crutches who has lost the use of both legs. This is represented as a parallel to a fool uttering a parable, the word for which is *māshāl* (see Excursus IV); as the normal form of a *māshāl* in this book is a two-lined saying, it is possible that the writer was thinking of two such lines, as composed by a fool, being as feeble and useless as the two lame legs of a cripple. Another explanation is that just as a lame man can make no use of his legs, so a fool is unable to profit by a wise saying (Wildeboer).

**8.** *As a bag of gems.* There is no justification for the rendering 'gems'; the Hebr. word is the ordinary one for 'stone', and is never used of precious stones unless some qualifying word is added (e.g. xvii. 8; 2 Sam. xii. 30; Ezek. xxviii. 14, 16). 'As a bag' (כִּצְרוֹר) was read 'as one that bindeth' (כִּצוֹרֵר) by the Sept., probably correctly.

*a heap of stones.* The Hebr. word occurs here only; it comes from the root meaning 'to stone', i. e. to kill by stoning. The rendering 'heap of stones' is quite uncertain; it is better to follow the Sept. and render the word 'sling'. The line will then run: 'As one that bindeth a stone in a sling', i. e. an act of folly since the stone is intended to be slung out. Equally foolish is it to give honour to a fool; in each case the act is lacking in sense.

*honour to a fool.* Cf. verse 1[b].

**9.** The Hebr. of the first line of this verse runs: 'A thorn goeth up in the hand of a drunkard'; this is said to be like a parable (*māshāl*), i. e. a wise saying, in the mouth of fools. At first sight the point of the parallel is not clear; but the word for 'goeth up' means also in late

10 ¹*As* an archer that woundeth all,
> So is he that hireth the fool and he that hireth them that
> pass by.

11 As a dog that returneth to his vomit,
> *So is* a fool that repeateth his folly.

12 Seest thou a man wise in ²his own conceit?
> There is more hope of a fool than of him.

13 ³The sluggard saith, There is a lion in the way ;
> A lion is in the streets.

---

¹ Or, *A master worker formeth all things; but he that hireth the fool is as one that hireth them that pass by*   The Hebrew text is obscure.        ² Heb. *his own eyes.*
³ See ch. xxii. 13.

Hebr. 'to come into', and the very phrase here used occurs in the Mishnah in the sense of 'coming into the hand' (Wildeboer), i. e. being taken hold of; so that the meaning here is that a thorn, by which of course is meant a stick from a thorn-bush, in the hand of a drunkard is like a parable in the mouth of fools, i. e. the stick is as useless in a drunkard's hand as the parable in a fool's mouth. The verse is, in effect, a variation of what is said in verse 7, the second line being identical in each.

**10.** This verse is a case of the Hebr. text being so corrupt that it is difficult to make anything of it. 'Many combinations and modifications of the words may be made', says Toy, 'but the text is in too bad a condition to permit a translation, and no satisfactory emendation has been suggested.' Steuernagel's emendation, however, which does not involve much alteration of text, is worth noting: 'Oft times doth a fool and a drunkard wound the passers-by' (רַב מְחוֹלֵל כִּסִיל וְשִׁכּוֹר עֹבְרִים) ; this he regards as an explanatory gloss to verse 9 which has inadvertently found its way into the text.

**11.** With this verse cf. 2 Pet. ii. 22. The Sept. quotes the following couplet from Ecclus. iv. 21 after it:
> *There is a shame that bringeth iniquity,*
> *And there is a shame (that bringeth) glory and grace.*

The Greek is identical with the Hebr.

**12.** *Seest thou* . . . In the Hebr. the clause is not in the interrogative. Some Hebr. MSS. and the Sept. read 'I saw'.

*in his own conceit.* Hebr. 'in his own eyes'

*There is more hope* . . . The same line occurs in xxix. 20, otherwise this type of fool is regarded as hopeless (see further Excursus XI).

**13–16.** These four verses, which treat of the sluggard, form a small section.

**13.** The first line of this verse is almost identical with xxii. 13ª. See note there.

14  *As* the door turneth upon its hinges,
      So doth the sluggard upon his bed.
15  ¹The sluggard burieth his hand in the dish;
      It wearieth him to bring it again to his mouth.
16  The sluggard is wiser in ²his own conceit
      Than seven men that can ³render a reason.
17  ⁴He that passeth by, *and* vexeth himself with strife belong-
      ing not to him,
      Is *like* one that taketh a dog by the ears.

¹ See ch. xix. 24.          ² Heb. *his own eyes.*          ³ Or, *answer discreetly*
      ⁴ Or, *He that vexeth himself . . . is* like *one that taketh a passing dog &c.*

**14.** *upon its hinges.* The 'hinges' took the form of bronze pivots
fixed above and below in the wooden door which were let into holes
in the stone framework. The point of the comparison is that just as
the door turns on its hinges but cannot otherwise be moved, so the
sluggard only turns over in bed, but is otherwise a fixture. Volz
quotes a present-day proverb in Palestine: 'While Hannah turns
over, the gate of Paradise is closed', i. e. a lazy person is so slow in
his actions that in the meantime the opportunity is lost.

**15.** This verse is almost identical with xix. 24; cf. also vi. 9, 10,
xv. 19ᵃ.

**16.** *in his own conceit.* Hebr. 'in his own eyes'.

*that can render a reason.* The Hebr. word for 'reason' is properly
'judgement', or 'discernment' (cf. xi. 22, 'without discretion'); the
R.V. marg. represents the Hebr. better. To be able to answer discreetly, to show right judgement, can only be acquired by being
trained in wisdom. The sluggard, who is of course reckoned among
the fools, does not go to the trouble of learning wisdom; he has,
therefore, not reached the stage of being able to form a rational
opinion on things, and in his crass stupidity always thinks he knows
best. This somewhat common type of person in all ages is very con-
temptible in the sight of the Wisdom writers; mental sloth is even
worse in their view than physical laziness. And, of course, worst of
all is the type here dealt with because his stupidity is aggravated by
an assumption of knowledge. In the *Proverbs of Achikar* ii. 30 it
is said:

> *My son, count not thyself to be wise,*
> *When others count thee not to be wise.*

**17.** The R.V. has transposed the lines of this verse. The first line is:

> *(As) one that taketh a dog by the ears;*

in the Hebr. the word which follows is 'that passeth by', and though,
according to the punctuation, this word should belong to the next
line, it is possible to take it as referring to the dog, 'a dog that
passeth by'; the Sept. and some Hebr. MSS., however, omit it

18 As a madman who casteth firebrands,
   Arrows, and death;
19 So is the man that deceiveth his neighbour,
   And saith, Am not I in sport?
20 For lack of wood the fire goeth out:
   And where there is no whisperer, contention ceaseth.
21 *As* coals are to hot embers, and wood to fire;
   So is a contentious man to inflame strife.

altogether, which is more likely to be correct, for the word seems to
have got in through its similarity with the one which follows. Its
omission improves the rhythm.

*vexeth himself.* So the Hebr. as it stands (מִתְעַבֵּר); but it is possible
that the Syr. and Vulg. are right in reading 'mixeth himself' (מִתְעָרֵב);
the two words are very similar in Hebr., the latter gives the better
sense. The meaning is that a man is inviting trouble if he interferes
in other men's quarrels, just as one is likely to get bitten if one takes
hold of a dog by the ears. The parallel was more pointed in those
days in Palestine where dogs were generally in a more or less wild
state, and therefore savage.

**18, 19.** These two verses belong together.

*a madman.* The R.V., in rendering the Hebr. thus, emends the
text, probably rightly; as the text stands it means 'one who is faint',
the word occurs elsewhere in Gen. xlvii. 13; a slight alteration gives a
word meaning 'one who is mad', as in 1 Sam. xxi. 14; Jer. li. 7.

*Am not I in sport?* As a practical joke the act seems somewhat
overdone.

**20.** *whisperer.* i.e. backbiter, cf. xvi. 28, xviii. 8; Ecclus. xxviii.
13–23.

**21.** *coals.* The exact meaning of the Hebr. word *pechām* (פֶּחָם) is
uncertain; the cognate Arabic word means 'charcoal', which would
offer a better parallel to 'wood' in the same line. In Isa. xliv. 12,
liv. 16 the Hebr. word is used of glowing coals, but probably glowing
charcoal is meant. Wildeboer's suggestion that in place of this we
should read 'bellows', *mappūach* (מַפֵּחַ) has much to commend it, see
Jer. vi. 29. The Sept. has 'brasier', Syr. and Targ. 'gridiron', which
shows that the word caused difficulties.

The figurative use of 'fire' applied to the tongue occurs in the
*Teaching of Amen-em-ope* IX. xiii. 6, 7, where, in speaking of a fiery-
mouthed man, who is also a backbiter, it is said:

> *His lips are sweet, his tongue bitter,*
> *But flame burns in his belly.*

With the verse before cf. also Ben-Sira's words:

> *Quarrel not with a loud-mouthed man,*
> *And put not wood in fire* (Ecclus. viii. 3, Hebr., cf. xxviii. 8–12).

22 [1]The words of a whisperer are as dainty morsels,
   And they go down into the innermost parts of the belly.
23 Fervent lips and a wicked heart
   Are *like* an earthen vessel overlaid with silver dross.
24 He that hateth dissembleth with his lips,
   But he layeth up deceit within him:
25 When he speaketh fair, believe him not;
   For there are seven abominations in his heart:
26 Though *his* hatred cover itself with guile,
   His wickedness shall be openly shewed before the congregation.

                                    [1] See ch. xviii. 8.

In the *Psalms of Solomon* xii. 2, the tongue of a malicious man is
compared with 'fire in a threshing-floor that burneth up the straw';
see also James iii. 5–6.

**22.** This verse occurs also in xviii. 8, see notes there.

**23.** The R.V. has transposed the lines of this verse.

*Fervent lips*. The Hebr. word for 'fervent' is never used figuratively as here; it is better to read, following the Sept., 'flattering',
lit. 'smooth' (חֲלָקִים for וְלֹקִים), with most commentators.

*dross*. This word spoils the sense of the line and overloads it; it is
better omitted. The verse will then run:

        'Silver laid over an earthen vessel,
        (So are) flattering lips and a wicked heart.'

**24–26.** These verses belong together.

*He that hateth* . . . Cf. x. 18.

*layeth up deceit*. Cf. Ps. xiii. 2 (Hebr. 3) for the use of the verb.

**25.** *speaketh fair*. Hebr. lit. 'shows favour, or is gracious, with his
voice'; the phrase occurs here only.

*seven abominations*. A forcible way of expressing the evil har-
boured in his heart.

**26.** *Though* his *hatred cover itself*. The Hebr. has: 'Hatred concealeth itself', where 'though' has to be supplied; but it is better to
follow the Sept., and to read: '(though) a man conceal . . .' (reading
מְכַסֶּה for תִּכַּסֶּה).

*the congregation*. i.e. the public assembly, cf. v. 14.

The point of the couplet seems to be that even though a man may
conceal his feelings towards one whom he hates, sooner or later his
hatred finds expression in some vicious act; the matter is then
brought before the public assembly acting in a judicial capacity, and
the true disposition of the hater is then made plain.

27 Whoso diggeth a pit shall fall therein:
  And he that rolleth a stone, it shall return upon him.
28 A lying tongue hateth those whom it hath [1]wounded;
  And a flattering mouth worketh ruin.

**XXVII.** 1 Boast not thyself of to-morrow;
  For thou knowest not what a day may bring forth.

¹ Heb. *crushed.*

**27.** *diggeth a pit.* i.e. for others; it is, of course, metaphorically meant, as in the next line.

*that rolleth a stone.* i.e. on another person; elsewhere this phrase always has a literal sense. Ben-Sira elaborates this verse in these words:

> He that casteth a stone on high casteth it upon his own head,
> And a deceitful blow apportions wounds to the deceiver.
> He that diggeth a pit will fall into it,
> And he that setteth a snare shall be taken therein.
> He that doeth evil things,—they shall roll back upon him,
> And he will not know whence they came unto him (Ecclus. xxvii. 25–27).

With the exception of the second line, which is from the Latin, this is from the Greek; the Hebrew is not extant.

**28.** *those whom it hath wounded.* As Toy points out, the form of this in the Hebr. is improbable, and in any case the R.V. rendering is incorrect. The word for 'those whom it hath wounded' (דַּכָּיו) is a simple adjective, 'the oppressed' or 'unfortunate'; and further, the tongue is never used in the Old Testament of hating or crushing a person. He proposes, therefore, the emendation 'brings destruction' (יָבִיא שֶׁבֶר), which would correspond with 'worketh ruin' in the next line.

## CHAPTER XXVII

**1.** *of to-morrow.* Hebr. 'the day of the morrow'; 'day' is probably intentionally inserted in each line to emphasize the day present with that of the morrow; if one does not know even what will happen to-day, much less can one boast oneself of what one will do to-morrow. There are two parallels to this verse in the *Teaching of Amen-em-ope*:

> Of a truth thou knowest not the design of God,
> Thou can'st not realize the morrow (XXI. xxii. 5, 6).

The lines occur again in XXII. xxiii. 8, 9. The other is:

> Man knoweth not how the morrow will be,
> The events of the morrow are in the hands of God (XVIII. xix. 12, 13).

In the *Babylonian Book of Job* it is said:

> 'He who was alive yester-eve died on the morrow;
> In a moment was he troubled, quickly was he crushed.'

2 Let another man praise thee, and not thine own mouth;
   A stranger, and not thine own lips.
3 A stone is heavy, and the sand weighty;
   But a fool's vexation is heavier than them both.

Cf. also Prov. xvi. 9, xix. 2. Similarly Ben-Sira says of the rich man:

> He knoweth not what the day will bring forth,
> He leaveth (his goods) to another, and dieth (xi. 19, Hebr.).

One is also irresistibly reminded of James iv. 13–16, esp. verse 14.

Doubtless, human experience had taught this truth to many, so that one must not necessarily assume the influence of one writer on the other in this case; nevertheless when it is remembered how numerous the parallels are between the Egyptian wisdom-book and *Proverbs*, the possibility of such influence must be allowed.

**2.** With the thought of this verse cf. the *Proverbs of Achikar* ii. 30:

> My son, count not thyself to be wise,
> When others count thee not to be wise.

And for the general sense cf. Ecclus. x. 26 (Hebr.):

> Play not the wise man in doing thy work,
> And esteem not thyself in the time of thy need.

**3.** *a fool's vexation.* One may also render the word 'provocation', the meaning being that the provocation offered by a fool is heavier than them both.

The comparison of something that is heavy in the literal sense with something that is metaphorically heavy is not generally characteristic of the Wisdom writers; so that it is not improbable that the construction of this couplet is due to extraneous influence. We have in the *Proverbs of Achikar* (Elephantiné Version, Cowley 111) these words:

> I have lifted sand, and carried salt,
> And there is nothing which is heavier than debt.

The more ancient form is fuller, there we have (ii. 45):

> My son, I have carried salt and removed lead ;
> And I have not seen anything heavier than that a man should pay back a debt when he did not borrow.

In the verse which follows there is a similar type of comparison:

> My son, I have carried iron and removed stones,
> And they were not heavier on me than a man who settles in the house of his father-in-law.

This mixing-up of literal and figurative occurs elsewhere in Achikar; but as a rule the Hebrew sage is more particular.

With the verse before us we must compare a couplet of Ben-Sira

4 Wrath is cruel, and anger is [1]outrageous;
  But who is able to stand before jealousy?

5 Better is open rebuke
  Than love that is hidden.

6 Faithful are the wounds of a friend:
  But the kisses of an enemy are profuse.

[1] Heb. *a flood.*

in which the same irregularity occurs, but verbally it is closer to the Elephantiné form:

> Sand and salt, and a weight of iron,
> Are easier to bear than a senseless man (Ecclus. xxii. 15).

**4.** *Wrath is cruel* ... This line is tersely but graphically expressed in the original, lit. 'Fierceness of wrath, overflowing of anger!' The form of the word for 'fierceness' occurs here only in the O.T., but the adjective is used in xii. 10, xvii. 11, and another form of the noun is found in v. 9, xi. 17.

*outrageous.* See R.V. marg.

*jealousy.* As in vi. 34, the reference is probably to the jealousy of a husband. Cf. Ecclus. ix. 1 (Hebr.):

> Be not jealous of the wife of thy bosom,
> That she learn not bitterness against thee.

**5.** *open.* Lit. 'revealed'.

*love that is hidden.* The Hebr. word for 'hidden' can also mean 'closed up' in the sense of being withdrawn; but even so the couplet does not give very good sense; on the analogy of the next verse which is somewhat parallel to this, one would expect the love to be spoken of as deceitful or feigned; possibly for 'hidden' (מְסֻתָּרֶת) we should read 'deceitful' (תַּרְמִית), cf. Zeph. iii. 13. Toy thinks that perhaps 'hate' should be substituted for 'love', which may have been induced from the similar word in Hebr. ('friend') in the next verse.

A somewhat similar thought to that of this as well as the next verse occurs in the *Proverbs of Achikar* ii. 73:

> My son, let the wise man strike thee with many blows,
> And let not the fool salve thee with sweet salve.

Cf. Ps. cxli. 5.

**6.** *friend.* Lit. 'lover'.

*kisses.* The Hebr. word occurs elsewhere only in *Song of songs* i. 2.

*enemy.* Lit. 'hater'.

*profuse.* This does not give the proper antithesis to 'faithful' in the first line; the meaning of the Hebr. word is also doubtful; one expects, as in the previous verse, 'deceitful' or 'false', possibly עִקְּשׁוֹת 'perverted', a word often used in *Proverbs*; it also gives a word-play in Hebr.

7 The full soul ¹loatheth an honeycomb:
   But to the hungry soul every bitter thing is sweet.
8 As a bird that wandereth from her nest,
   So is a man that wandereth from his place.
9 Ointment and perfume rejoice the heart:
   So doth the sweetness of a man's friend *that cometh* of hearty
      counsel.

¹ Heb. *trampleth upon*.

**7.** *loatheth.* Lit. 'trampleth upon', i. e. rejecteth; the Hebr. word
is only used in a figurative sense here and in Jer. xii. 10.

With the second line cf. the mutilated line in the *Proverbs of
Achikar* (Elephantiné version):

> *Hunger sweetens what is bitter,*
> *And thirst . . .* (Cowley 188).

**8.** *a man that wandereth.* It is highly probable that the sage was
writing from his own experience; that it was customary for the
Scribes, who were also sages, to travel into foreign lands we know
from what Ben-Sira says (Ecclus. xxxix. 4):

> *He serveth among great men,*
> *And appeareth before a ruler ;*
> *He travelleth in the land of alien nations,*
> *And hath tried both good and evil things among men.*

He tells us of his own travels in the words:

> *I was a youth before I wandered abroad* (li. 13);

and the dangers which were sometimes encountered during these
wanderings are graphically described in li. 1–7. Quite possibly an
allusion to such dangers is contained in the following saying from
the *Proverbs of Achikar* ii. 36:

> *My son, the flock that makes many tracks*
> *Becomes the portion of the wolves.*

There is every reason to believe that in earlier days the sages had
been travellers; this is also borne out by their knowledge of the
wisdom of other lands of which the collections in *Proverbs* bear such
ample witness.

**9.** *Ointment and perfume . . .* More exactly, 'oil and incense'. We
have here another illustration of the view of the Wisdom writers that
the pleasant things of life are not to be despised. A due sense of
proportion is strongly characteristic of their teaching; so that while
self-control and moderation in all things is constantly inculcated,
life's pleasures are always regarded not only as legitimate, but as fit
and proper, provided that they do not degenerate into a mere pan-
dering to self-indulgence. See, e. g., xiv. 13, xv. 15, xvii. 22, xxv. 16;
Ecclus. xxix. 21, xxxi (xxxiv). 25, xxxii (xxxv). 5, 6, xxxvii. 29–31.

*So doth the sweetness . . .* No sense is to be got out of the Hebr. as it

10 Thine own friend, and thy father's friend, forsake not ;
  And go not to thy brother's house in the day of thy calamity :
  Better is a neighbour that is near than a brother far off.

11 My son, be wise, and make my heart glad,
  That I may answer him that reproacheth me.

12 [1]A prudent man seeth the evil, *and* hideth himself :
  *But* the simple pass on, *and* suffer for it.

[1] See ch. xxii. 3.

stands ; it runs : 'But the sweetness of his friend from the counsel of the soul.' A number of emendations have been suggested, but they are necessarily problematical since it is uncertain whether the couplet is to be regarded as synonymous or antithetic. Toy holds to the former, and reads : 'And sweetness of counsel strengtheneth the soul' (וּמֶתֶק עֵצָה מֵאַמֵּץ נֶפֶשׁ). Steuernagel, on the other hand, thinks it is antithetical, and, though unable to make anything of the first word, emends the text, on the basis of the Sept., so as to read : 'But evil . . . grieveth the soul' (וְ . . . רָעָה מְעַצֶּבֶת נֶפֶשׁ). There is a good deal to be said for each ; but a final conclusion seems impossible in view of the corruptness of the text.

**10.** *Thine own friend* . . . The meaning of this line is clearly that a tried friend of the family is not to be spurned. But the second line does not give good sense because to go to a brother in time of trouble is a natural thing to do. The explanation of this is that the writer either misunderstood or misread the text of the source he was utilizing (see below), and constructed it on the basis of xxv. 17 ; then he added the third line from the same source because he thought it appropriate. That this source was the *Proverbs of Achikar* can hardly be doubted, for in ii. 57 occurs the following :

  *My son, remove not from thy father's friend,*
  *Lest perchance thy friend come not near to thee ;*

and in ii. 49 :

  *My son, better is a friend that is at hand,*
  *Than a brother who is far away.*

**11.** *My son.* In the Hebr. this does not open the sentence as is normally the case when this form of address is used.

*make my heart glad.* The personal interest shows the sage's solicitude for each individual pupil, cf. xxiii. 15 ; Ecclus. iii. 29.

*That I may answer* . . . This sense of responsibility further emphasizes the close interest that the sage has in each pupil. The reproach refers to the sage being accused of not having taught his pupil properly.

**12.** This verse is almost verbally the same as xxii. 3.

R

13 [1]Take his garment that is surety for a stranger;
　　And hold him in pledge *that is surety* for a strange woman.
14 He that blesseth his friend with a loud voice, rising early in
　　　　the morning,
　　It shall be counted a curse to him.
15 A continual dropping in a very rainy day
　　And a contentious woman are alike:

　　　　　　　　　　　[1] See ch. xx. 16.

**13.** With the exception of 'a strange woman', which should be
emended to 'strangers' or 'a stranger', this verse is identical with xx. 16.

**14.** *He that blesseth.* Better 'he that greeteth', cf. e. g. 1 Sam. xiii.
10 and elsewhere.

*rising early in the morning.* These words are evidently a gloss;
they overload the line, and should be omitted.

*It shall be counted* . . . This is an ambiguous phrase; the 'to him'
can refer either to the saluter or to the saluted, according as to how
one interprets the first line. Now, in the *Teaching of Amen-em-ope*
(X. xiii. 11–14) we have the following quatrain:

> *Salute not thy passionate (opponent), forcing thyself,*
> *Nor grieve thine own heart (thereby);*
> *Say not to him, 'Hail to thee', in falsehood,*
> *When there is terror in thy belly.*

This passage has a particular interest in this connexion because each
of these two couplets is a parallel to the verse before us, which can
be interpreted in two ways, each being illustrated by these two couplets respectively; thus, when a man salutes another ostentatiously,
not really meaning what he says, forcing himself, as it were, to do so,
it is a curse to him, i. e. he is grieving, or damaging himself by doing
so because he is guilty of a hypocritical act. This is the interpretation
represented by the first couplet of Amen-em-ope. Or our passage
may be interpreted in this way: If a man greets another ostentatiously, as a blind, because he fears him, and therefore meditates
harm against him, it is a 'curse' to him who is thus saluted. This is
the interpretation represented by the second couplet of Amen-em-ope.
The fact of these interpretations in this Egyptian Wisdom-book is
interesting, whatever deduction be drawn from it; but in this case it
rather looks as though Amen-em-ope had had some form of *Proverbs*
before him, though in most of the other parallels it must be recognized that the compiler of *Proverbs* is indebted to the Egyptian sage.

**15.** This verse is evidently a variation of xix. 13[b], see notes there.

*A continual dropping.* The reference must be to the dropping rain
from a roof.

*woman.* i. e. wife.

16 He that would ¹restrain her ²restraineth the wind,
   And ³his right hand encountereth oil.
17 Iron sharpeneth iron;
   So a man sharpeneth the countenance of his friend.

¹ Heb. *hide*.                          ² Heb. *hideth*.
³ Or, *the ointment of his right hand bewrayeth itself*

**16.** The Hebr. of this unintelligible verse runs lit.: 'They who hide
her, he hath hidden wind, and oil his right hand calleth', or 'oil
meeteth his right hand'. It is quite obvious that the text is in too
hopeless a condition to do anything with it. The attempts which
have been made to reconstruct the Hebrew text Toy rightly calls
'desperate expedients'.

**17.** *Iron sharpeneth iron.* The Hebr. has, 'iron sharpeneth with
(or by) iron', but the verb has the wrong vowel-points; read, 'iron
is sharpened by iron' (יֵחַד, so the Targ. and the Vulgate read,
instead of יַחַד).

*So a man sharpeneth.* The vowel-points of the verb again require
altering (יָחֵד, so all the Versions, instead of יַחַד).

*the countenance of.* It is not easy to see how a man can sharpen the
face of another; Wildeboer would understand the word in the sense
of 'person', which is possible (cf. 2 Sam. xvii. 11), but improbable;
usually when the word has this sense it is in reference to Jahweh,
e.g. Exod. xxxiii. 14, 15; Deut. iv. 37. Toy deletes the word; the
sentence reads more naturally without it.

In this saying the sage touches upon one of the most important
and far-reaching factors of education (in the highest sense) of a
young man, viz. the effect that intercourse with his fellows has upon
the formation of character. Just as iron is made fit for use by drastic
contact with its like, so a man is shaped for a profitable walk in life
by his intercourse with others. That a young man should realize this
and profit by the not always pleasant means of becoming 'polished',
(see xxvii. 6ᵃ), which the rough and tumble of life affords, is implicity
emphasized again and again by the Wisdom writers. But in this
verse the fact is explicitly stated. Hence the frequent insistence upon
the importance of choosing the right kind of men as companions,
see e.g. xiii. 20, xxii. 24, 25; Ecclus. ix. 16, xiii. 1, 13, xxvii. 12. The
Hebrew sages, while pre-eminent in urging this (so far as can be
judged by the available evidence), were not the only ones to do so;
quite in the same spirit it is said in the *Proverbs of Achikar* iii. 11, 12:

*My son, with a wise man thou wilt not be depraved,*
*And with a depraved man thou wilt not become wise.*
*My son, associate with the wise man, and thou wilt become wise like him;*
*And associate not with a garrulous and talkative man, lest thou be numbered*
   *with him.*

R 2

18 Whoso keepeth the fig tree shall eat the fruit thereof;
And he that waiteth on his master shall be honoured.

19 [1]As in water face *answereth* to face,
So the heart of man to man.

20 [2]Sheol and Abaddon are never satisfied;
And the eyes of man are never satisfied.

[1] Or, *As water* sheweth *face to face, so the heart* sheweth *man to man*
[2] See ch. xv. 11.

**18.** In the words of this verse the sage has the slave in mind, showing that all social grades were included in the purview of the *Chăkāmim*. With the verse cf. Ecclus. vii. 20, 21.

**19.** The very brief, but pregnant form of the Hebr. saying makes the interpretation somewhat uncertain. Lit. the Hebr. runs: 'As the water faces to faces, so the heart of a man to a man.' The first word, 'as the water' (כַּמַּיִם) should no doubt be read, with the Sept., simply 'as' (כְּמוֹ), and the meaning seems to be that just as one man looking at another recognizes him so far as his exterior is concerned, so also the spiritual vision of the one recognizes the character or disposition of the other. There is probably some thought-connexion between this and verse 17. Steuernagel, however, believes that there must originally have been in the first line some word corresponding to 'heart' in the second: 'As . . . of face in regard to face, so the heart of man in regard to man'; but he is not prepared to supply the missing word which, as he says, makes it impossible to say what the verse really means. Toy likewise thinks that a word has fallen out before 'face'; he renders:

'As [ . . . ] face answers to face,
So men's minds one to another,'

but he feels uncertain about the meaning. The explanation offered above seems to give an adequate sense to the words.

**20.** *Sheol and Abaddon.* See xv. 11 and Excursus VIII. The verse offers a striking saying on the insatiability of men's desires. The abode of the departed is never filled, the desires of man are never stilled. One is much tempted to believe that this verse belongs to a later period than the bulk of this collection; it reflects so strikingly the mental attitude of so many during the Hellenistic period that it seems likely that one of the later *Chăkāmim* felt impelled to insert it. That attitude has been so graphically described by Mr. Edwyn Bevan that some of his words may appropriately be quoted: 'Mankind seemed to be driven hither and thither in a sea of contrary desires; one impulse overrode and frustrated another; the things which men took for good brought them no satisfaction when they were gained, human life was a chaos, in which blind Desire was the propelling force, and action was spasmodic, furious, vain,—a misery

25 The ¹hay is carried, and the tender grass sheweth itself,
   And the herbs of the mountains are gathered in.
26 The lambs are for thy clothing,
   And the goats are the price of the field:
27 And *there will be* goats' milk enough for thy food, for the food
      of thy household;
   And maintenance for thy maidens.
**XXVIII.** 1 The wicked flee when no man pursueth:
   But the righteous are bold as a lion.

---

¹ Heb. *grass.*

error it was written in place of the word for 'wealth', corresponding
with 'riches' in the first line (read אֹצָר for נֵזֶר). The line should,
therefore, run: 'And wealth is not [i. e. endureth not] from generation
to generation.'

**25.** *is carried.* i. e. is removed, which is the lit. sense of the Hebr.
word. It is certainly better, and intended in the original, that this
verse should be regarded as belonging to the two which follow; this
verse says that 'when the hay has been carried in' &c., and verses
26, 27 say: 'then the lambs . . .'

**26.** *The lambs are for* . . . Read: '(Then wilt thou have) lambs for
thy clothing.'

*And the goats* . . . Read: 'And goats for the price of a field'; i.e.
he will be able to increase his property in land by selling his goats.
There can be no doubt that there is an underlying implication here
contrasting the settled and lasting nature of wealth produced by
agriculture with the uncertainty of that gained by trade and commerce.

**27.** *And* there will be . . . Read: 'And sufficiency of goats' milk
for thy food.' The words 'for the food of thy household' overload
the line and do not occur in the Sept.; they are a later gloss and
should be omitted.

*maintenance.* Lit. 'life'.

A fragmentary saying in the Elephantiné version of the *Proverbs
of Achikar* is reminiscent of these verses, and is worth quoting:

*. . . do thou, oh my son, gather every harvest and do every work, then shalt
thou eat and be filled and give to thy children.*

## Chapter XXVIII

**1.** *the righteous are.* As 'the wicked' in the first line is in the sing.,
it is better to read the sing. here too, as in the Sept.; the verb is
in the sing.

*bold.* The Hebr. root means 'to trust', so that 'confident' is the
better word to use.

*lion.* The word means properly a 'young lion', cf. Gen. xlix. 9.

2 For the transgression of a land many are the princes thereof :
But by [1]men of understanding *and* knowledge the state
*thereof* shall be prolonged.

3 A needy man that oppresseth the poor
Is *like* a sweeping rain [2]which leaveth no food.

---

[1] Or, *a man*     [2] Heb. *without food.*

**2.** *For the transgression . . . the princes thereof.* If the Hebr. text
is correct the reference may be to specific examples in the history
of the northern kingdom (and cf. Hos. vii. 16, viii. 4) of the quick
succession of kings, though one might expect that in that case they
would be spoken of as kings rather than as princes. But it by no
means follows that such succession should necessarily be due to the
transgression of a land; court intrigue, political unrest, or foreign
interference would be equally likely to bring about rapid changes of
rulers in a country. The sentiment expressed would be more natural
in the mouth of the Chronicler than in that of one of the Wisdom
writers. The Sept. apparently had a Hebr. text before it which
looked very similar to the present one, but which gave a very
different meaning; how much alike the two are can be seen by placing
them side by side; the present Hebr. text is: בְּפֶשַׁע אֶרֶץ רַבִּים שָׂרֶיהָ;
that underlying the Sept. translation is: בְּפֶשַׁע אָרִיץ רִיבָם יֵעֹרוּ, meaning: 'Through the transgression of the violent quarrels arise', lit.
'are aroused'. 'Violent' is in the singular.

*But by men of understanding* . . . As in the first line so here the
Sept. read a different text, but which was very similar so far as the
letters were concerned. There is no difficulty about the first two
words, which should be read: 'But by a man of understanding'; the
remaining words of the line in the present Hebr. text are: יֹדֵעַ כֵּן יַאֲרִיךְ,
lit. 'he that knoweth the right prolongeth'; the text underlying
the Sept. is: יְדֹעְכָן (Isa. xliii. 17, Steuernagel): 'they are quenched',
lit. 'they quench', i.e. they disappear; the last word has no equivalent in the Greek. The Sept., therefore, offers here a distinctly
superior text; the Hebr. as it stands is not altogether intelligible.
The text, thus emended, will read:

> 'Through the transgression of the violent quarrels arise,
> But by a man of understanding they are settled.'

**3.** *A needy man* . . . For a poor man to oppress the poor is an
unnatural idea, utterly improbable in the times, and never contemplated by the Wisdom writers. The text is obviously corrupt. The
Hebr. word for 'rich' (עָשִׁיר) contains the two letters which compose
the word for 'poor' (רָשׁ); the two might easily be confused, especially as the letter ע is the first one of the word which follows. The
text must, therefore, be emended so as to read: 'A rich man that

4 They that forsake the law praise the wicked:
  But such as keep the law contend with them.

oppresseth the poor' (the word for 'poor' is a different one from that
given above).

*a sweeping rain.* The Hebr. word for 'sweeping' means 'beating
down', the reference being to the torrential rain which lays the
standing corn flat; hence the following words 'which leaveth no
food', or according to the graphic but pregnant Hebrew expression,
'no bread'. The couplet may thus be rendered:

> 'A rich man who oppresseth the poor,
> Is (like) a torrential rain,—(there is) no bread.'

The simile is extraordinarily apt, for the grinding down of the poor by
the rich in those days often meant literal starvation for the former.

**4.** *the law.* See also verses 7, 9. It is not easy to say with certainty
what precisely is meant here by 'law' (*Tôrah*); in *Proverbs* it is
always used in the sense of 'instruction' or 'guidance' given either
by parents or by the sages (i. 8, iii. 1, iv. 2, vi. 20, 23, vii. 2, xiii. 14,
cf. also xxxi. 26); but here and in verse 9 as well as in xxix. 18 it
seems to have a wider sense, and in verse 5, though the word 'law'
is not used, the expression 'judgement' occurs, which in Isa. lvi. 1
(Trito-Isaiah) means 'the Law' in the technical sense of later Judaism
('Keep judgement and do righteousness'); in verse 7, on the other
hand, it has the sense which is the usual one in *Proverbs*. Further, the
word 'forsake' used in reference to 'law' certainly points to this as
meaning 'Law' in the later, technical, sense. This being so, one
would be led to infer that this collection belonged to a late post-
exilic period; but there are various points in it, especially the frequent mention of the king, which compel the belief that, as a whole,
it is pre-exilic. The conclusion to which one is, therefore, driven is
that those verses (4, 9, xxix. 18, to which verse 5 of this chapter must
be added) in which 'law' in the sense of 'the Law' is used, are later
insertions. It has been more than once pointed out that all the
collections in *Proverbs* are compilations; traditional proverbs, and
sayings borrowed from different sources, were from time to time
added to those which the sages composed; and it would be the most
natural thing in the world for later generations of sages to add
their quota. No book of the Bible lends itself better to later insertions of this kind than the book of *Proverbs*. The idea of a 'Canon'
did not arise until later times, so that there was nothing to prevent
a sage, say during the Greek period, from augmenting the body of
wise sayings which had been handed down, and whereby his people
were edified, by sayings of his own; on the contrary, there was every
reason why he should do so, since he followed in the line of those
whose duty it was to teach Wisdom, in the widest sense, to their
fellow-creatures.

5 Evil men understand not judgement:
   But they that seek the LORD understand all things.

6 [1]Better is the poor that walketh in his integrity,
   Than he that is [2]perverse in *his* ways, though he be rich.

7 Whoso keepeth the law is a wise son:
   But he that is a companion of gluttonous men shameth his
      father.

8 He that augmenteth his substance by usury and increase,
   Gathereth it for him that hath pity on the poor.

[1] See ch. xix. 1.                    [2] Heb. *perverse of two ways.*

This verse, then, as well as verse 5, must be understood as a
polemic against the tendency during the Greek period of a certain
section of the Jews to forsake the Law and its ordinances, and, under
the influence of Hellenic thought and culture, to order their lives in
accordance with these.

*the wicked.* i. e. the Hellenizers among the Jews.

**5.** *judgement.* i. e. the Law; see note on prec. verse.

*that seek the Lord.* Not, of course, in the earlier sense of consulting
the oracle (e. g. 2 Sam. xxi. 1), but of inquiring as to what is His will
as revealed in the Law.

*all things.* Here the reference is to all things contained in the Law.
With the verse cf. the *Proverbs of Achikar* ii. 56:

   *My son, every one who doth not judge right judgement angereth God.*

**6.** The first line of this verse is identical with that of xix. 1; the
second line varies.

his *ways.* The 'two ways' of the Hebr. is merely a mistake in the
vowel-points; 'his way' is the rendering of the Syr. and Targ., 'ways'
that of the Vulg.; the Sept. does not express the word. In Ecclus. ii.
12 (the Hebr. of which, however, is not extant), where the expression
'two ways' occurs, it is used in a different sense, viz. in that of
James i. 8, 'a double-minded man, unstable in all his ways'; in the
verse before us the expression refers to one who does not go straight,
i. e. a dishonest man. With the verse cf. xvi. 8; Ecclus. v. 8.

**7.** *keepeth the law.* Here 'law' means instruction, i. e. of a father
to a son; the Hebr. word for 'keepeth' is not that used for keeping
the Law in the later technical sense; here the root is *nāzar* (נצר), the
other is *shāmar* (שׁמר).

*But he that is . . .* Cf. xxiii. 20. The antithesis between one who
keeps the law and a companion of gluttons is far from apt; the two
lines seem to have been placed together by mistake.

**8.** *usury.* i. e. interest on money lent; the taking of interest was
forbidden except from non-Hebrews, cf. Exod. xxii. 25; Lev. xxv.
35–37; Deut. xxiii. 19, 20.

*and increase.* Some commentators would delete this, and perhaps

9  He that turneth away his ear from hearing the law,
   Even his prayer is an abomination.

10  Whoso causeth the upright to go astray in an evil way,
   He shall fall himself into his own pit:
   But the perfect shall inherit good.

11  The rich man is wise in [1]his own conceit;
   But the poor that hath understanding searcheth him out.

12  When the righteous triumph, there is great glory:
   But when the wicked rise, men [2]hide themselves.

---

[1] Heb. *his own eyes.*       [2] Heb. *must be searched for.*

---

rightly; it is not clear what it refers to, the interest having already been mentioned; moreover, the verse-balance is better preserved without it.

*Gathereth it for* . . . Cf. xiii. 22^b. The thought is that God will take it from him and give it to a better man.

**9.** *the law.* See note on verse 4.

*Even his prayer* . . . Or, as we might say, 'his very prayer'. There is a ring of the later Judaism in these words.

**10.** On the doctrine of Retribution taught by the Wisdom writers see Excursus IV.

*in an evil way.* i. e. into a vicious course of life; 'evil way' is used in this sense in viii. 13. The expression can also mean getting a man into trouble, especially in view of the second line (cf. xxvi. 27), but the use of the word 'causeth to go astray' points to the other interpretation, see v. 23, xix. 27, xx. 1, where this word is used.

*But the perfect* . . . The sayings in this collection are two-lined; either this is the second line of a saying the first of which has fallen out, or it is a marginal gloss which has erroneously been incorporated in the text; judging from the couplet from the Sept. which is added to this verse, the former supposition seems more likely.

**11.** Cf. xviii. 11.

*in his own conceit.* Hebr. 'in his own eyes'.

*But the poor* . . . The meaning is that the poor man who has discernment is able to see through him.

**12.** The meaning of this verse is not clear; but the Hebr. text is not in order.

*triumph.* The Hebr. word never has this sense, it means 'to rejoice'; but this is inappropriate here as it is not clear what is referred to. On the basis of the Sept. it is possible to emend the text so as to read 'give help', or 'succour', or 'come to the rescue' (reading בַּעֲזוֹר for בַּעֲלֹץ). Toy would read 'are exalted' (בְּהֵעָלֹת), which is likewise possible.

13 He that covereth his transgressions shall not prosper:
　　But whoso confesseth and forsaketh them shall obtain mercy.

*glory.* This word is also inappropriate here; Toy suggests the
emendation 'hope' or 'confidence' (תִּקְוָה); this would give excellent
sense, and the line thus emended would run:

'When the righteous come to the rescue there is great confidence.'

*But when the wicked rise.* i. e. when the wicked assert their power.
*men hide themselves.* Hebr. lit. 'are searched for', i. e. because of
the fear of the wicked in power, men hide themselves; the very converse of the general feeling of security when the righteous can be
relied upon. Cf. verse 28, and with the verse as a whole cf. xi. 11, 14,
xxi. 15, xxix. 2.

**13.** *covereth.* i. e. is silent about, as in xvii. 9, though in a very
different connexion; the Hebr. word is the same in each passage;
cf. also x. 18.

*whoso confesseth and forsaketh.* Nowhere else in *Proverbs* is confession of sin dealt with; and the particular form of the word here
used for 'confess', never (with the exception of Ps. xxxii. 5) has this
meaning elsewhere in the O.T.; it usually means 'to praise' or 'to
give thanks'; in the two or three passages (1 Kgs. viii. 33, 35 =
2 Chron. vi. 24, 26) where it means to 'confess', it is in the sense of
confessing the name of God. Otherwise when confession of sins is
spoken of it is a reflexive form of the verb that is used; and these
are all late post-exilic passages. This leads to the presumption that
the verse before us must belong to those which, like verses 4, 5, 9,
a later sage inserted. This is, moreover, borne out by the fact that
from early post-exilic times onwards the need and value of confession
became increasingly emphasized, see e.g. Ezra ix. 5 ff., x. 1. Among
the pre-Christian elements in the Jewish Liturgy congregational
confession is a marked feature; it occurs not only in the service for
the Day of Atonement, but also in the daily services. The forms of
confession are based on biblical passages (see the present writer's
*The Jewish Background of the Christian Liturgy,* pp. 52 f., 76 ff.
[1925]).

The addition of 'and forsaketh' is noteworthy, for there can be
little doubt that among some the belief obtained that confession
effected, as it were, forgiveness, and was, therefore, *per se,* sufficient
to obliterate sin, and with such an easy means of getting rid of the
weight of sins the repetition of them was not a very serious matter.
Hence the stress laid on forsaking sin. Ben-Sira deals more fully with
the subject; he says:

*Do not wickedly repeat a sin,*
*For of the first thou art (still) guilty* (Ecclus. vii. 8, Hebr.).

14 Happy is the man that feareth alway:
> But he that hardeneth his heart shall fall into ¹mischief.

15 *As* a roaring lion, and a ranging bear;
> *So is* a wicked ruler over a poor people.

16 ²The prince that lacketh understanding is also a great
>> oppressor:
> *But* he that hateth covetousness shall prolong his days.

¹ Or, *calamity*     ² Or, *O prince that lackest understanding and art a great oppressor, he &c.*

And again in xxi. 1, 2 (the Hebr. is not extant):

> *My son, hast thou sinned ? Add not thereto;*
> *And make supplication concerning thy former sins.*
> *Flee from sin as from the face of a serpent,*
> *For if thou come near it, it will bite thee;*
> *The teeth of a lion are the teeth thereof,*
> *Slaying the souls of men.*

And once more, in v. 4, 5 (Hebr.):

> *Say not, 'I sinned, and what happened unto me!'*
> *For the Lord is longsuffering.*
> *Count not upon forgiveness,*
> *By adding sin to sin.*

**14.** *that feareth.* The word here used is not that ordinarily used for fearing God (cf. iii. 7, xxiv. 21), in the sense of reverencing Him, so that probably those commentators are right who hold that fear of *sin* is here meant because sin brings calamity. At the same time, it must be remembered that this verb (פחד) *is* sometimes used in reference to God, viz. in Isa. lx. 5; Hos. iii. 5; Mic. vii. 17.

*hardeneth his heart.* Cf. xxix. 1.

*mischief.* Lit. 'evil', i. e. calamity, or misfortune.

**15.** *a roaring lion.* Cf. xix. 12; what is implied here is that the wicked ruler has the victims of his greed and tyranny in his power; cf. Am. iii. 4, 'Will a lion roar in the forest, when he hath no prey?'

*a ranging bear.* More appropriate would be the rendering 'longing', i. e. for food, as in Isa. xxix. 8; Toy suggests the emendation 'robbed of her whelps' (שַׁכּוּל for שׁוֹקֵק) as in xvii. 12, but that can hardly be the idea in this connexion.

*a poor people.* The only other occurrence of this adj. (דָּל) applied to people is in Zeph. iii. 12. For the pre-exilic date of the section Zeph. iii. 1–13 see Sellin, *Introd. to the O.T.*, p. 185 (1923).

**16.** *The prince that* . . . It is difficult to say with certainty what the original form of this verse was; the Versions read a slightly different text, but both the Hebr. and the Versions give good sense. On the basis of the Sept. one could read: 'A prince who lacketh wealth (reading תְּבוּאוֹת for תְּבוּנוֹת, but see below) is great in oppressions', i. e. is a great oppressor. Other commentators, with a slight emendation in

17 A man that is laden with the blood of any person
　　Shall flee unto the pit; let no man stay him.

the Hebr., read: 'A prince who lacketh understanding increaseth
(reading יָרֵב for וְרַב) oppression', or 'A prince who increaseth oppression lacketh understanding'. The word for 'prince', however,
overloads the line, and is never used elsewhere in *Proverbs*, and there
is nothing in the next line corresponding to it; there is, therefore,
justification for omitting it as a gloss induced by 'ruler' in the preceding verse. The line would then read: 'He that increaseth oppression lacketh understanding.'

But *he that hateth* ... The Hebr. has 'haters of'; the 'but' should,
however, be added, and the sing. read instead of the plural. The
reading 'wealth' of the Sept. in the first line may have been suggested by 'covetousness' here.

Now, it will be noticed that these two lines as they stand, and
even as emended, do not belong together, they are neither antithetical nor synonymous, nor have they anything in common. It
is possible that, as in other cases noticed, the lines stood originally
in some other context, and that their present position is due to
carelessness of redaction. But there is also another possibility. The
word for 'understanding' was not read, as we have seen, by the
Sept., so there was clearly some uncertainty about the Hebr. text,
of which there are also other signs. The words 'shall prolong his
days' in the second line demand, according to the general usage in
*Proverbs*, something corresponding to them in the first line; it is,
therefore, suggested that we should read instead of 'understanding' (תְּבוּנוֹת), 'years of life' (שְׁנוֹת חַיִּים), a not infrequent expression in *Proverbs* (see iii. 2, iv. 10, ix. 11; in the first of these we
have 'length of days and years of life'). When Hebr. words were
written without division they were often misread, and this would
happen very easily on account of their similarity; two letters were
often misread as one, and copied out wrongly in consequence, thereby
giving an entirely different meaning to a sentence. That may have
happened here. Then, as to the word rendered 'oppressor', this can
equally well mean 'extortion'; it is used in this sense in Lev. vi. 4
(v. 23 in R.V.); Hos. xii. 8; Mal. iii. 5; Ezek. xviii. 18, xxii. 29. Thus
the line would read: 'Lacking in years of life (shall he be) that increaseth, or "multiplieth", extortion' (חֲסַר שְׁנוֹת חַיִּים יָרֶב מַעֲשַׁקּוֹת); this
gives us the antithesis, 'lacking in years of life' and 'prolonging
days', as well as 'multiplying extortion' and 'hating covetousness'.

**17.** Both content and form as well as the style of this verse make
it very questionable whether it belongs at all to our book, though it
is difficult, perhaps impossible, to account for its presence here.
Moreover, it is not possible to get any real sense out of the verse, so
that there can be no doubt that the text has suffered corruption.
Literally translated the Hebr. has: 'A man oppressed by the blood

18 Whoso walketh uprightly shall be delivered:
  But [1]he that is perverse in *his* ways shall fall at once.
19 [2]He that tilleth his land shall have plenty of bread:
  But he that followeth after vain *persons* shall have poverty
    enough.

[1] Or, *he that walketh perversely in two ways*        [2] See ch. xii. 11.

of a soul (i. e. a person), unto a pit he fleeth, lay ye not hold of him.'
Of the various emendations suggested, not one of which is really convincing, Steuernagel's is perhaps that against which fewest objections
can be urged; he takes the first word, 'man' (אָדָם), to have been
originally 'if' (אִם); there is, in any case, something wrong with the
word because the Massoretic text has the middle letter, 'd', written
small. The next word, 'that is laden', cannot have this meaning;
Steuernagel renders it 'oppressed', but in the sense of one who is
being pursued. 'With the blood of any person' clearly refers to
murder, and can be rendered 'because of murder'. 'Shall flee unto
the pit' (עַד־בּוֹר יָנוּס) he emends so as to read: 'passes by as he flees'
(reading יַעֲבוֹר for עַד־בּוֹר). The last word, 'let no man stay him', has
the meaning both of to 'seize' or 'stop', and also to 'uphold' or
'assist'; Steuernagel takes it in the latter sense. The verse, according
to this interpretation, will run: 'If one, who is being pursued on
account of murder, passes by as he flees, do not assist him (i. e. in
escaping)'.

It is probable that the verse, which is in prose, and not in the more
or less poetical form of the rest of the book, is a comment on the
subject dealt with in Num. xxxv. 26 ff.; but where it came from and
how it got in here passes the wit of man to say.

**18.** *Whoso walketh uprightly.* The same Hebr. phrase occurs in
Ps. xv. 2.

*shall be delivered.* i. e. from the calamity which is the lot of the
wicked. In spite of the facts of life often pointing to the contrary,
the old traditional belief in the prosperity of the righteous and the
adversity of the wicked still persisted.

*But he that is . . .* The Hebr. has lit.: 'But he that is perverse (or
"crooked") in two ways shall fall in one.' As in verse 6 'two ways'
in the Hebr. is wrongly pointed, and should be simply 'ways', as in
the Sept. The 'at once' of R.V. does not represent the Hebr.; but
in all probability the text is corrupt, and we should read with the
Syr. 'into a pit', cf. verse 10 (בְּשַׁחַת for בְּאֶחָת); the Sept. omits it and
reads 'shall become entangled' for 'shall fall at once'; this suggests
that the 'at once' (or, if emended, 'into a pit') did not originally
form part of the text and may have been added from verse 10; the
rhythm of the verse is certainly improved by its omission, and the
general sense does not require it.

**19.** *He that tilleth . . .* Cf. xii. 11[a].

20 A faithful man shall abound with blessings:
   But he that maketh haste to be rich shall not be unpunished.
21 To have respect of persons is not good:
   [1] Neither that a man should transgress for a piece of
   bread.

   [1] Or, *For for a piece of bread a man will transgress*

*vain* persons. The word to be supplied may equally well be 'things'
or 'pursuits'. While the antithesis between 'plenty of bread' and
'poverty enough' is perfect, this is not so pronounced in the rest of
the verse; the antithesis to 'he that tilleth his land' is not entirely
satisfied by 'he that followeth after vain persons (or things)'; one
might rather expect 'he that letteth his land lie fallow', or the like.
The point would perhaps not demand attention were it not that in
the *Teaching of Amen-em-ope* the following lines occur:

> *Plough thine own fields, then wilt thou find what is needful,*
> *And wilt obtain bread from thine own threshing-floor* (VI. viii. 17, 18).

Here the first line is such an obvious parallel to the first line of the
*Proverbs* couplet that the borrowing of one writer from the other
must be assumed. For reasons already given (see p. liv), it was in
all probability the compiler of *Proverbs* who was the borrower. His
love of antithesis (even when not perfect) induced him, presumably,
to alter the form of the couplet. It is interesting to note that Ben-
Sira, too, seems to have known the Egyptian book, for he condenses
Amen-em-ope's couplet into one line, and writes:

> *He that tilleth his land raiseth high his heap* (Ecclus. xx. 28[a]).

The mention of the 'heap' (i.e. of corn) is certainly reminiscent of
Amen-em-ope's 'threshing-floor'. This is not the only instance in
which Ben-Sira apparently drew upon the Egyptian book rather than
*Proverbs*, which, again, points to the former as having been in existence in Palestine in some form.

**20.** *shall not be unpunished.* Lit. 'shall not be held innocent'.
With this verse cf. Ecclus. xxxi (xxxiv). 5-8 (Hebr.):

> *He that runneth after gold will not be guiltless,*
> *And he that loveth gain will go astray thereby . . .*
> *Blessed is the man that is found perfect,*
> *That hath not gone astray after Mammon* (cf. xi. 10, 11).

See also the quotation under xiii. 11 from the *Proverbs of Achikar*.

**21.** *To have respect . . .* Cf. xviii. 5, xxiv. 23, and notes there. The
reference is to partiality in a court of law.

*Neither that . . .* Hebr. 'Even for a piece of bread a man will transgress', meaning that even for the smallest bribe a man will sin
through partiality.

*a piece of bread.* Cf. vi. 26.

22 He that hath an evil eye hasteth after riches,
   And knoweth not that want shall come upon him.
23 He that rebuketh a man shall afterward find more favour
   Than he that flattereth with the tongue.
24 Whoso robbeth his father or his mother, and saith, It is no
      transgression ;
   The same is the companion of a destroyer.

**22.** *an evil eye.* The expression means one who is envious, it occurs elsewhere only in xxiii. 6 in the O.T., but more than once in Ecclus. ; in xxxi (xxxiv). 13 (Hebr.) it is said:

> *Remember that an evil eye is an evil thing ;*
> *God hateth an evil eye.*

Cf. also xiv. 10 (Hebr.): *the evil eye hasteth after food.*

*knoweth not.* i. e. doth not realize. It is implied that God will bring him to want.

**23.** This verse, quite unlike the usage in *Proverbs*, is divided into two unequal parts, the first part containing (in Hebr.) five words, the second only two. The word translated 'afterward' does not represent the Hebr., which has 'after me'; this is probably an explanatory marginal note which has crept into the text; it is omitted in the Syriac. 'Man' seems likewise to be a later addition; the line runs more smoothly if read: 'A rebuker findeth favour rather than a flatterer', lit. one that smootheth the tongue ; the thought is similar to that of xxvii. 6, and cf. xxvi. 28, xxix. 5.

**24.** The first line of this verse is too long; most commentators rightly regard 'and his mother' as a gloss; the 'and' before 'saith' is also unnecessary ; the line reads better if rendered: 'He that robbeth his father, saying (it is) no sin.'

*The same is . . .* The Hebr. has: 'A companion (is) he to the man destroyer.' As Steuernagel says, 'destroyer' appears to be used in a technical sense which is, however, otherwise unknown to us. As to what the verse is referring to, Toy's excellent note is worth quoting ; it is aimed, he says, 'at attempts (legal or other) by children to get control of the property of parents, and thus diminish their resources (cf. Mk. vii. 11, 12). For ordinary theft, or for simple unkindness, no such form of condemnation would have been used. The practice in question was evidently not uncommon, and (as appears from the second line) was sometimes defended as morally proper, probably on the ground that the family was a unit, that what belonged to the parents belonged legally to the children. The O.T. legislation, in fact, contains no provision bearing on this point; the declaration of the proverb is based on general ethical grounds'.

s

25 He that is of a greedy spirit stirreth up strife:
   But he that putteth his trust in the LORD shall be made fat.
26 He that trusteth in his own heart is a fool:
   But whoso walketh wisely, he shall be delivered.
27 He that giveth unto the poor shall not lack:
   But he that hideth his eyes shall have many a curse.
28 When the wicked rise, men hide themselves:
   But when they perish, the righteous increase.

**25.** *He that is of a greedy spirit.* Lit. 'He that maketh wide his soul'; a similar expression occurs in Isa. v. 14 ('Hell hath enlarged her soul'), cf. Hab. ii. 5. In xxi. 4 we have the expression, 'he that maketh wide the heart', meaning one who is proud.

*shall be made fat.* i. e. shall prosper, cf. xi. 25, xiii. 4, xv. 30.

The verse means that the avaricious man arouses antagonism against himself, and is thus brought to ruin, but that he who trusts in God instead of in his own wealth will be made to prosper. The next verse is in essence parallel to this. Somewhat similar to the thought of the first line is that in Ecclus. v. 8 (Hebr.):

> *Trust not in unrighteous gains,*
> *For they profit nothing in the day of wrath.*

**26.** *He that trusteth . . .* i. e. he that relieth on his own understanding, cf. xiv. 16b.

*wisely.* Lit. 'in wisdom'.

*shall be delivered . . .* i. e. from misfortune.

**27.** *He that giveth . . .* Cf. xi. 24, 25, xiv. 21b, xix. 17, xxii. 9; in Ecclus. vii. 32 (Hebr.) it is said:

> *And also to the poor stretch forth thine hand,*
> *That thy blessing may be full.*

It will be noticed that again, as so often in the Wisdom Literature, good deeds are enjoined because of reward.

*he that hideth his eyes.* The same expression occurs in Isa. i. 15, meaning, to take no notice.

*many a curse.* The man who turned his back on the poor would have curses hurled at him; in such cases it was, no doubt, held that the curse might be effective; cf. xxvi. 2, and note.

**28.** This verse is a variation of verse 12, cf. also xxix. 2. The reference is to those who occupy positions in the public administration of affairs. As the pupils of the sages were largely drawn from the families of the upper classes, many of whom would in due course be called to fill administrative offices, the words of this and similar verses were very much to the point. It is interesting to note how wide the scope was of the interests and concerns of the Wisdom writers.

**XXIX.** 1 He that being often reproved hardeneth his neck
Shall suddenly be broken, and that without remedy.

2 When the righteous [1]are increased, the people rejoice:
But when a wicked man beareth rule, the people sigh.

3 Whoso loveth wisdom rejoiceth his father:
But he that keepeth company with harlots wasteth *his* substance.

4 The king by judgement establisheth the land:
But [2]he that exacteth gifts overthroweth it.

[1] Or, *are in authority*   [2] Or, *he that imposeth tribute* Heb. *a man of offerings.*

## CHAPTER XXIX

**1.** *He that being often reproved.* Hebr. 'a man of reproofs'; cf.
xxviii. 20, 'a man of faithfulnesses', and verse 4, 'a man of exactions'.
Some commentators would read 'he that hateth reproofs' (שׂוֹנֵא for
אִישׁ), cf. xii. 1, xv. 10; but this hardly seems necessary.

*hardeneth his neck.* The implication seems to be, 'and yet hardeneth his neck'; the word 'reproof' includes the idea of exhortation for the purpose of amelioration, so that the type of man here
thought of is one who obstinately refuses to profit by the efforts
which are made for his improvement, cf. xiii. 18, xv. 10.

*Shall suddenly be broken.* For the thought cf. i. 27, vi. 15.

*remedy.* Lit. 'healing'; translated 'health' in xii. 18, xiii. 17, xvi. 24.

**2.** *are increased.* Read, with R.V. marg., 'are in authority', or
'rule'; the emendation of the Hebr. text is very slight (בִּרְדוֹת for
בִּרְבוֹת), and is demanded by the parallel word 'beareth rule' in the
second line.

*a wicked man.* Some Hebr. MSS. and the Versions read 'the
wicked' (plur.); 'the righteous' in the first line is plural. With the
verse cf. xxviii. 12, 28.

**3.** *Whoso loveth.* Hebr. 'the man that loveth'; cf. x. 1, xxiii. 15,
24, xxvii. 11.

*But he that keepeth* . . . Cf. v. 9–11, vi. 26.

**4.** *by judgement.* i.e. by the exercise of justice. Cf. verse 14, xvi.
12, xxv. 5.

*he that exacteth gifts.* Lit. 'a man of exactions'. The Hebr. word
for 'exactions' (otherwise, as a rule, but not always, rendered 'heave-offering' in the R.V.), means offerings for sacred uses (*terūmōth*). In
Ezek. xlv. 13, 16 the word is used in reference to a contribution 'for
the prince in Israel'; that is the only passage which can be cited in
support of the sense of the word here, otherwise unknown in the O.T.,
though the use of it in the Ezek. passage is common in the Mishnah.
Hence some commentators propose the emendation 'a deceitful man',

s 2

5  A man that flattereth his neighbour
   Spreadeth a net for his steps.

6  In the transgression of an evil man there is a snare:
   But the righteous doth sing and rejoice.

7  The righteous taketh knowledge of the cause of the poor:
   The wicked [1]hath not understanding to know *it*.

8  Scornful men set a city in a flame:
   But wise men turn away wrath.

---

[1] Or, *understandeth not knowledge*

lit. a man of deceit (תַּרְמִית for תְּרוּמוֹת, cf. Zeph. iii. 13; Jer. viii. 5,
xiv. 14, xxiii. 26; Ps. cxix. 118; it is what the Sept. read); this gives
good sense, but upon the whole the other reading is perhaps to be
preferred. What strikes one as strange is that a 'man' should be the
parallel to 'king'; one expects 'prince' or 'ruler', cf. xxv. 6.

**5.** *that flattereth his neighbour*. Lit. that smootheth (his tongue)
against his neighbour, cf. xxvi. 28, xxviii. 23; in ii. 16, vii. 5 'words'
is used instead of 'tongue'; when used in reference to 'words' the
verb means 'to flatter'; when used with 'tongue', as here, the meaning is rather 'deceiveth'; this is borne out by the second line.

*a net.* The figurative use of the word occurs also in Babylonian
Wisdom Literature; in the poem of the *Babylonian Job* it says:

*Like a net trouble hath covered me* (Langdon, *op. cit.*, p. 44).

**6.** *In the transgression.* The text as it stands can hardly be right;
a snare does not lie in a transgression; it is laid before the transgression takes place. A difference of one point gives the 'step' or
'path' for 'transgression' (פֶּשַׁע for פֶּשַׁע, cf. 1 Sam. xx. 3; Isa. xxvii. 4);
the line should run: 'In the path of the evil man there is a snare.'

*doth sing.* Better sense is gained by adopting the emendation of
most commentators and reading 'doth run', i. e. in his path, because
no snare is there (reading יָרוּץ for יָרֹן); cf., though in a very different
connexion, Ps. xix. 5 (6 in Hebr.).

**7.** The reference in this verse is to a court of justice.

*taketh knowledge.* Or 'recognizes', in the sense of acknowledging.

*of the poor.* What is implied is: of the poor 'also'.

*hath not understanding to know it.* Hebr. 'doth not discern (or,
understand) knowledge'; in this connexion these words are somewhat pointless. Toy emends the text so as to read 'doth not plead
for the needy' (לֹא יָבִין הֵעַת for לֹא יָדִין עָנִי), following xxxi. 9, cf. Jer.
v. 28; this has much in its favour; the Sept. also gives some support.

**8.** *Scornful men.* Lit. 'men of scorn'; the same expression occurs
in Isa. xxviii. 14.

*set . . . in a flame.* The Hebr. word means to 'puff out' and in
*Proverbs* is mostly used in reference to lies, see vi. 19, xiv. 5, 25,

9 If a wise man hath a controversy with a foolish man,
  [1] Whether he be angry or laugh, there will be no rest.
10 The bloodthirsty hate him that is perfect:
  [2] And as for the upright, they seek his life.
11 A fool uttereth all his [3] anger:
  But a wise man keepeth it back and stilleth it.

[1] Or, *He rageth and laugheth, and there is no rest*
[2] Or, *But the upright care for his soul*      [3] Heb. *spirit*.

xix. 5, 9; in xii. 17 in reference to truth; in Ezek. xxi. 36 (31 in R.V.) it says: 'with the fire of my wrath will I puff (or, blow) against thee.' Here the idea is that by fanning the bad passions of men these evil-disposed people set the city in an uproar. A similar thought occurs in Ecclus. xxviii. 14, where the slanderous tongue is spoken of:

> Even strong cities hath it destroyed,
> And overturned the houses of the great.

With the verse cf. xv. 1, 18, xxii. 10.

**9.** *hath a controversy.* The Hebr. word points to a dispute at law.

*with a foolish man.* The repetition of 'man' is not in accordance with usage, and should be omitted; read, 'with a fool'.

*Whether he be* ... Read as R.V. marg., the reference is to the fool, who seeks to cover over the weakness of his case by bluster and ridicule.

**10.** *The bloodthirsty.* Lit. 'men of blood', cf. i. 11, and for the expression, Ps. v. 6 (7 in Hebr.).

*And as for the upright* ... The Hebr. has: 'And the upright seek his soul', which is, of course, out of the question. The manner of emendation must depend upon whether the two lines of the verse are to be regarded as antithetic or synonymous. If the former, we must read 'seek out' (יְבַקְּרוּ for יְבַקְּשׁוּ), as in Ezek. xxxiv. 11, 12; 'But the upright seek out his soul', i.e. seek him out, in the sense of searching for him in order to protect him. If, on the other hand, the lines were originally intended to be synonymous, then instead of 'and the upright' we must read 'and the wicked' (וּרְשָׁעִים for וִישָׁרִים); the latter seems the more probable. The former is Dyserinck's emendation.

**11.** *A fool* ... Lit. 'A fool bringeth forth all his spirit'; for 'spirit' in the sense of 'anger' see xvi. 32, xxv. 28; Eccles. vii. 9, x. 4.

*keepeth it back and stilleth it.* The Hebr has: 'And back (or, afterwards) he stilleth it', where the 'it' must grammatically refer to the fool's anger; the text is clearly corrupt. Toy adopts Bickell's emendation 'restraineth' (יְשַׁבְּחֶנָּה for יְחַשֹּׁךְ) on the basis of the Sept., and 'his wrath' for 'back' (בְּאַחוֹר for חֲרוֹנוֹ). The line, thus emended, reads: 'But the wise man restraineth his wrath', which offers a perfect antithesis.

12  If a ruler hearkeneth to falsehood,
　　All his servants are wicked.

13  The poor man and the oppressor meet together:
　　The LORD lighteneth the eyes of them both.

14  The king that faithfully judgeth the poor,
　　His throne shall be established for ever.

15  The rod and reproof give wisdom:
　　But a child left to himself causeth shame to his mother.

16  When the wicked ¹ are increased, transgression increaseth:
　　But the righteous shall look upon their fall.

¹ Or, *are in authority*

**12.** *If a ruler* . . . Hebr. 'A ruler that giveth heed to a word of falsehood'. With the verse cf. Ecclus. x. 2 (Hebr.):

> *As the ruler of a people, so are his officers,*
> *And as the head of a city, so are the inhabitants thereof.*

**13.** *the oppressor.* Lit. 'the man of oppressions'; a rare expression.
*meet together.* Although their condition and circumstances of life are so different, the oppressed and the oppressor constantly meet, e.g. in the streets or market-place, or wherever it may be. The sage, that is to say, notes the antitheses and incongruities of life, and realizes that, men being what they are, this is inevitable. But he is not for that reason a pessimist; after all, he seems to say, each possesses the inestimable treasure of life, which God has given him; let each feel gratitude for that. The similar thought occurs in xxii. 2.
*lighteneth the eyes.* Cf. Ps. xiii. 3 (4 in Hebr.); Job xxxiii. 30.

**14.** *that faithfully judgeth.* Hebr. 'that judgeth in truth'. With the verse cf. xvi. 12, xx. 28, xxv. 5. Judging spoken of as the function of a king must refer to an Israelite king; the verse points to a pre-exilic time.

**15.** *The rod and reproof.* Both methods, so it is taught, are needed before Wisdom is accepted by the young, cf. xiii. 24, xxiii. 13.
*left to himself.* Lit. 'sent off', as a careless mother would do who did not wish to be troubled by her boy.
*causeth shame to his mother.* Cf. x. 1, xvii. 21. The mother is referred to because she would be mainly responsible for a young child; the father's duties would begin a little later.

**16.** *When the wicked are increased.* See note on verse 2, where the same slight corruption of the text occurs. Read with R.V. marg. 'are in authority'.
*But the righteous* . . . Cf. Ps. xxxvii. 34; and with the verse cf. xxviii. 12. It is taken for granted that wicked rulers fall, though experience must have shown that this was not always the case. The traditional orthodox doctrine is, however, adhered to.

17 Correct thy son, and he shall give thee rest;
  Yea, he shall give delight unto thy soul.
18 Where there is no vision, the people cast off restraint:
  But he that keepeth the law, happy is he.

**17.** *Correct thy son.* Cf. xix. 18.
  *delight.* Lit. 'dainties', cf. Gen. xlix. 20, used here, of course,
figuratively; cf. x. 1.
  **18.** Frequent reference has been made to the marks of prophetic
influence upon the Wisdom writers; the first line of this verse offers
another illustration. By 'vision', the vehicle of divine revelation to
the prophets, must be understood the prophetical books in which
'vision' was to be found; this seems also to have been what the
Sept. understood by the word as it is there rendered 'guide' or
'interpreter', i.e. of Holy Writ. It is the reference to the Law (*Torah*)
in the second line which compels us to see in the word 'vision' the
prophetical books. The Law here means the Pentateuch. These two
divisions of what later became the Canon were all that so far constituted the Scriptures; the third division, the 'Writings' or Hagio-
grapha (Hebr. *Kĕthūbhīm*), was in process of formation. The meaning
of this verse, therefore, is that if the prophetical books are not read
and acted upon the people run riot morally; if, on the other hand, the
law of Moses, as contained in the Pentateuch, is followed—which
implies, of course, that the five books are studied—it will bring
happiness.
  The sage who added this saying at a time long after the collection
first began to be made, had a twofold object in doing so; first, he
wished to place on record the fact that the Wisdom writers, however
rationalistic and worldly-wise in their general attitude, did nevertheless base all their teaching on the word of God as revealed to the
writers of the holy books; and, second, his purpose was to insist upon
the need of reading the Scriptures; his exhortation was primarily to
young men who in earlier years had been taught by their fathers to be
diligent in the study of the word of God. There was a danger that,
when entering into the world and therefore necessarily free from
parental authority, these young men might be tempted to give up
the wholesome habit in which they had been brought up; it was,
therefore, necessary to show that if they ceased to regulate their lives
in accordance with the saving precepts of the Law and the prophets,
the result would be the giving way to all sorts of bad impulses. It
was with similar intent that Ben-Sira said to his pupils:

> *He that hateth the Law is not wise,*
> *And is tossed about like a ship in a storm.*
> *A man of understanding discerneth the Word,*
> *And the Law is reliable as the enquiry of Urim*
> > (Ecclus. xxxiii [xxxvi]. 2, 3).

19 A servant will not be corrected by words:
For though he understand he will not ¹give heed.
20 Seest thou a man that is hasty in his ²words?
There is more hope of a fool than of him.
21 He that delicately bringeth up his servant from a child
Shall have him become ³a son at the last.

¹ Heb. *answer*.                            ² Or, *business*
³ The meaning of the word is doubtful. The Vulgate renders it, *refractory*.

**19.** *A servant* . . . It is more pointed to begin the sentence (as in
the Hebr.) with: 'With words a servant (or, slave) will not be corrected (or, disciplined)'; the implication is that the rod must be used,
as in the case of a son (see verse 17, xix. 18).

*For though* . . . Read: 'For he understandeth, but respondeth not'
(lit. 'but there is no response').

*will not give heed.* The Sept. reads; 'will not obey'. Ben-Sira
elaborates this, and says:

> Fodder and a stick and burdens for an ass ;
> Bread and chastisement and work for a servant.
> Set thy servant to work, and thou wilt find rest,
> Leave his hands idle, and he will seek liberty.
> Yoke and a thong will subdue the neck,
> And for an evil servant there are racks and tortures

(xxxiii. 24–31 = xxx. 33–35).

**20.** This verse, which is a variation of xxvi. 12, has clearly become
misplaced; it should follow *v.* 21.

*Seest thou* . . .? There is no interrog. in the Hebr.

*in his words.* The R.V. marg. can be ignored; hasty speech is what
is referred to. With the verse cf. Ecclus. ix. 18 (Hebr.):

> Terrible in the city is the loud-tongued man,
> And hated is he that is hasty in speech.

Cf. also James i. 19.

**21.** *He that delicately bringeth up.* i.e. he that pampereth; this is
the only place in the O.T. where the word is used; but it occurs in
Ecclus. xiv. 16, though in a different connexion. The idea of a servant being brought up in this way is certainly strange (though xvii.
2 shows that it was possible for a servant to occupy a very favourable position at times); the Sept. either read a different text, or,
thinking that the saying was not in accordance with fact, altered it
slightly, and read: 'He that liveth luxuriously from childhood will
become a servant', i.e. luxurious living and refraining from work will
bring a man to such want that he will have to become a servant to
keep body and soul together.

*Shall have* . . . The Hebr. has: 'And his latter end (will be with
sorrow?).' The 'latter end' we should express by 'ultimately', or the
like. The last word in the Hebr. (מָנוֹן) is a difficulty; it never occurs

22 An angry man stirreth up strife,
   And a wrathful man aboundeth in transgression.
23 A man's pride shall bring him low:
   But he that is of a lowly spirit shall obtain honour.
24 Whoso is partner with a thief hateth his own soul:
   [1] He heareth the adjuration and uttereth nothing.
25 The fear of man bringeth a snare:
   But whoso putteth his trust in the LORD [2] shall be safe.
26 Many seek the ruler's favour:
   But a man's judgement *cometh* from the LORD.

[1] See Lev. v. 1.          [2] Heb. *shall be set on high.*

elsewhere, and its derivation is doubtful; it must be a corruption, perhaps influenced by a very similar word in the next verse. The Sept. rendering suggests 'will be with sorrow' (יִהְיֶה בְּיָגוֹן). It is quite possible that the whole verse should be read according to the Sept. rendering. The R.V. rendering of the second line is, in any case, impossible.

**22.** *An angry man* ... This line is almost identical with xv. 18ᵃ.
*a wrathful man.* The Hebr. expression denotes the general temperament of the man. With the line cf. xiv. 17, 29ᵇ, xxii. 24ᵇ.

**23.** With the verse cf. xi. 2, xv. 33, xvi. 18. The renderings 'shall bring him low' and 'lowly spirit' exactly correspond with the figurative use of the Hebr. word.

**24.** The meaning of the verse is that if a man is in any way associated with one who is a thief and keeps silence when in a court of justice the solemn adjuration is made that any one who knows anything about the matter is to speak, that man is as bad as the thief himself, and injures himself by his silence; concealing a crime, and thus hindering the course of justice, is to be partaker of the crime. The R.V. marg. rightly refers to Lev. v. 1.

**25.** *The fear of man* ... i.e. a man may easily be led to do something wrong, or to refrain from doing what is right, through being afraid of somebody.
*shall be safe.* Lit. as R.V. marg. Putting one's trust in God is to fear Him, though the fear is of a wholly different nature. The Hebr. word used here for 'fear' of man (lit. 'trembling') is a different one from that used of the 'fear of Jahweh', wherever this occurs. Cf. Ecclus. xl. 26 (Hebr.):

> In the fear of Jahweh there is no want,
> And with it there is no need to seek (other) help.

**26.** *the ruler's favour.* Lit. 'the face of the ruler'; the reference is to obtaining the influence of the highest power to intervene in judicial proceedings.
*But a man's judgement* ... i.e. what is decided in regard to man is

27 An unjust man is an abomination to the righteous:
  And he that is upright in the way is an abomination to the
    wicked.

ordained by God. The saying deprecates reliance on human power,
however exalted; this is in reality quite useless because all things are
ordered by God, and His will must override that of man in any case.

**27.** The Hebr. form of these lines is more telling, viz.:

'The abomination of the righteous (is) an unjust man;
  And the abomination of the wicked (is) he of upright way.'

# THE FIFTH COLLECTION OF PROVERBS

## XXX—XXXI

THERE is reason to believe that in this division of the book we have in reality four originally independent little collections of proverbs. In the Hebrew Bible these chapters would appear to represent only two collections, since, according to the titles, the whole of xxx includes 'the words of Agur', and the whole of xxxi includes 'the words of King Lemuel'. But with regard to the latter, the content and form of 2–9 and 10–31 are so different that they must have come from different writers. What is, however, more significant is that in the Sept. the material of which these chapters are composed is treated as forming separate sections which are independent of each other and do not follow the order of the Hebrew Bible; thus:

xxx. 1–14 of the Hebrew Bible forms xxiv. 24–37 of the Septuagint;
xxx. 15–33   ,,    ,,    ,,    ,,    xxiv. 50–68    ,,      ,,     ;
xxxi. 1–9    ,,    ,,    ,,    ,,    xxiv. 69–77    ,,      ,,     ;
xxxi. 10–31    ,,    ,,    ,,    ,,    xxix. 28–49    ,,      ,,     .

The two middle sections, it is true, run consecutively in both, but they stand in different positions in the Hebrew and Greek Bibles respectively. None of the sections have titles in the Septuagint; for xxx. 1 it reads a different text from the Hebrew. It is obvious that the Sept. represents a different recension from that of the Hebrew Bible; and probably an older one as the titles in the Hebrew Bible were added after the Greek translation had been made. We shall, therefore, be justified in following the Septuagint and regarding this division of our book as consisting of four independent collections which are very likely all excerpts from different books of proverbial sayings. Regarding the dates of these literary pieces see Introd., § III.

**XXX.** 1 The words of Agur the son of [1] Jakeh; the [2] oracle.

[1] Or, *Jakeh, of Massa* See Gen. xxv. 14.       [2] Or, *burden*

**XXX. 1–14.** This collection purports to be 'the words of Agur', and consists of four sections: title and introduction (1–4); an exhortation to trust in God, whose word is final and complete, and needs no supplementing (5, 6); a prayer to be kept from untruthfulness and poverty (7–9); miscellaneous sayings (10–14). The variety of subject-matter in these verses suggests the possibility that they may have been gathered from different sources; the haphazard way in which they are grouped makes it improbable that the writer composed them himself; it looks rather as though they were jottings, collected with a view to co-ordination later on.

**1.** Many attempts have been made to get some satisfactory sense out of this title; but the Hebrew text is so irremediably corrupt that at the best every conjectural emendation can only be tentative.

The man saith [1] unto Ithiel, unto Ithiel and Ucal:

[1] Or, as otherwise read, *I have wearied myself, O God, I have wearied myself, O God, and am consumed : for I am &c.*

*The words of Agur the son of Jakeh ; the oracle.* Neither name occurs anywhere else. Agur can mean 'collector', and Jakeh can mean 'pious'; but possibly both words are corruptions. The Sept. renders: 'Be in awe of my words, (my) son; and, receiving them, repent', which represents a text very similar to the Hebrew so far as the letters are concerned, excepting that there is nothing corresponding to the word 'repent', but see next note.

*the oracle.* The Hebr. word *Massa* can mean 'oracle' or 'burden' or 'prophecy', all of which are quite inappropriate here, as it applies to a prophetic utterance. It can also be a proper name, 'the Massaite', i.e. an inhabitant from Massa (see 1 Chron. i. 30), the locality of which is unknown, though, according to Gen. xxv. 14, Massa was an Arabian tribe. The Sept. has not got this word, but in place of it has 'repent'; and it is possible that some confusion may have arisen in the text which presumably lay before the Greek translator owing to the similarity of the Hebr. words for 'receive them' and 'repent'; in which case *Massa* may have arisen by mistake. It is impossible to see, without giving the Hebrew letters, how easily the similarities between them could give rise to mistakes, especially when the words were not divided, and there were no vowel-points, and a badly written, and possibly mutilated, manuscript was copied. The first of the two following lines gives the present Hebrew text ; the second gives the Hebrew text which the Sept. may be presumed to have read ; the words are not divided, and the vowel-points omitted :

דבריאגורבניקההמשא
דבריתגורבנוקחמסוהנחם

It has further to be remembered that the present square Hebrew characters had not yet evolved from the common Semitic source, and in certain cases some of the ancient letters were more alike than the present ones, and could therefore more easily be confused. There is, then, some justification for thinking that the Sept. represents the original Hebrew text more faithfully than the present Massoretic text.

*The man saith* . . . This line as it stands is a second title, which is quite unnatural when we have already had one. 'The man' would not be used like this unless in reference to somebody already mentioned ; but as the line is a title nobody could have been mentioned before ; probably an illegible word stood here, and a later copyist made it into 'the man', referring it to 'Agur', the corruption of the first line having already taken place. The word for 'saith' must also be a corruption ; it is the technical term for a prophet's burden, and is quite out of place here.

*unto Ithiel, unto Ithiel.* A repetition such as this is an 'insufferable

2 Surely I am more brutish than any man,
  And have not the understanding of a man:
3 And I have not learned wisdom,
  [1] Neither have I the knowledge of the Holy One.

---

[1] Or, *That I should have the knowledge &c.*

---

pleonasm' (Steuernagel), and is, on the face of it, merely an ineffective attempt to make something out of a text hopelessly corrupt. The words can, it is true, be made to mean what the R.V. marg. reads; but other manipulations of the Hebrew letters can be made to yield other meanings. Toy thinks that the second 'unto Ithiel' is an 'erroneous scribal repetition of the first, or a corruption of some other word'; that is, no doubt, so; but it is probable that the first 'unto Ithiel' is also a corruption.

*Ucal.* An entirely unknown name; a change in the vowel-points makes the meaning, 'and I pined away', which seems to be what the Sept. read.

It is clear that nothing can be made of this line; and in this case the Sept. is of but little help as the corruption was already complete in the copy which lay before the translator; one must agree with Toy that 'the text appears to be corrupt beyond possibility of restoration'.

**2.** *Surely.* The Hebr. conjunction cannot be rendered 'surely' here; it must be translated 'for', or 'because', and shows that originally a sentence preceded which was connected with what now follows. It is further evidence of the corrupt state of the text in verse 1.

*brutish.* i. e. like the brute creation in stupidity; there is no idea of anything brutal about it; in xii. 1 the same word occurs in antithesis to one who loves knowledge. It is better to render the word 'stupid' or 'dull-witted'. The sentence should run: 'For I am more stupid than men (in general).'

*And have not* . . . Lit. 'And (there is) not the understanding of man to me', i. e. 'I am lacking in human understanding'. Whether this is meant sarcastically, or whether it is an expression of humility, is a point on which commentators differ; the words in verse 4 would point to the latter, though as it is a sage who is writing, it may be a sarcasm; he does not profess to have the understanding of all things claimed by some.

**3.** *Neither have I* . . . The Sept. has no negative, and it is probable that Steuernagel is right in suggesting that this should be in the form of an interrogative: 'And have I the knowledge of . . .?' See note on verse 4.

*the Holy One.* This form, plur. in Hebr., like *Elohim*, occurs also in ix. 10, i. e. in the late portion of *Proverbs*.

4 Who hath ascended up into heaven, and descended?
  Who hath gathered the wind in his fists?
  Who hath bound the waters in his garment?
  Who hath established all the ends of the earth?
  What is his name, and what is his son's name, if thou
    knowest?

5 [1]Every word of God is [2]tried:
  He is a shield unto them that trust in him.
6 Add thou not unto his words,
  Lest he reprove thee, and thou be found a liar.

--------------------------------------------------------

[1] See Ps. xii. 6, xviii. 30.          [2] Heb. *purified*.

**4.** If verses 2, 3 are understood in an ironical sense, then this verse
must be taken in a similar sense; but if those verses are an expression
of humility, then the same will apply to this verse. The sage is contrasting his infinitesimal smallness and weakness with God's power;
'Where is the man who can do all these things? And who am I that
I should claim to be able to do them?' This is what he seems to say.
The words are the sage's reply to the question in the preceding verse;
no man has ever done these things, only God; so how can he, the
sage, have the knowledge of the Holy One?

*Who hath ascended* . . . Enoch and Elijah had ascended, but not
descended; only God could do that, e.g. Gen. xi. 7, and in the various
accounts of theophanies, Exod. xix. 11, 18, xxxiv. 5; Num. xi. 25, &c.

*Who hath gathered* . . . Cf. Am. iv. 13; Ps. cxxxv. 7.

*Who hath bound* . . . Cf. Job xxvi. 8, from which it is seen that by
'his garment' here the clouds are meant.

*Who hath established* . . . Cf. Job xxviii. 4–6; Ps. xxiv. 1, 2, cii. 25
(Hebr. 26), civ. 5. Perhaps it is better to follow the Sept. and read:
'Who hath laid hold of . . .' (הֶחֱזִיק for הֵקִים).

*if thou knowest.* Omit these words, with the Sept.; they spoil the
rhythm; probably they were added from Job xxxviii. 5, by a
glossator.

**5, 6.** It is doubtful whether these verses have any connexion with
the preceding, just as they have nothing to do with what follows.
This chapter is a collection of independent pieces.

*Every word* . . . This verse is quoted from Ps. xviii. 30 (31 in Hebr.).
The Hebr. name for God here is 'Eloah' which is never used elsewhere in this book; perhaps we ought to read 'Jahweh' as in Ps.
xviii. Cf. further Ps. xii. 6 (7 in Hebr.), cxix. 140.

**6.** *Add thou not* . . . Cf. Deut. iv. 2, xii. 32 (xiii. 1 in Hebr.). The
words of God here cannot be other than those contained in the Scriptures, and by these must be meant the threefold division of the Bible:
Law, Prophets, and Writings, since a quotation is given from this

last; though it does not, of course, follow that the third division was yet completed. The Greek Prologue to *Ecclesiasticus*, written in 132 B.C., is otherwise the earliest mention of the threefold Canon of the Hebrew Bible, but there, too, the indefiniteness wherewith the third division is referred to, 'the rest of the books', makes it quite uncertain what was included under this term. The probability is that the prohibition to 'add unto his words' did not apply to the 'books of Moses', the *Torah*, because these contained the divine words, according to the belief in those days, in a direct and literal sense; nor did they apply to the prophetical books, for these, too, contained the words of God, if not in quite the same literal sense as the *Torah*, still indirectly through the mouth of the prophets; nobody would therefore be presumptuous enough to add anything to these. But it was different with 'the rest of the books'. The third division of the Canon was at this time in process of formation; some of the books now comprised in this division were no doubt already regarded as sacred; but with regard to others differences of opinion existed. Of special interest here is *Ecclesiasticus*. Ben-Sira claims to be in the direct succession of those who wrote down the words of God; he says in xxxiii. 16–18 (xxxvi. 16ᵃ and xxx. 25–27):

> *And I, last of all, came* [so the Syr., the Greek has 'awoke'],
> *As one that gleaneth after the grape-gatherers.*
> *And by the blessing of the Lord I made progress,*
> *And, as a grape-gatherer, filled my wine-press.*
> *Consider that I laboured not for myself alone,*
> *But for all those who seek instruction.*
> *Hearken unto me, ye great ones of the people,*
> *And ye rulers of the congregation, give ear to me.*

It is hardly to be supposed that Ben-Sira intended his instruction to be for the 'great ones among the people' or for the 'rulers of the congregation'; nothing in his book suggests that. He is here making an appeal to them to be regarded as one of the 'grape-gatherers', though a humble one; in other words, he is appealing for his book to be included among the 'Writings'. He is one of those who desired to add to the words of God as contained in the Scriptures. The words in the verse before us, therefore, are an echo of the controversy, which was a long drawn-out one, regarding the question as to which books did or did not 'defile the hands', to use the technical expression of the Mishnah (i.e. which were canonical or not), but which may have been known in earlier times. *Ecclesiasticus* was one of several books about which keen discussion arose as to whether they should be regarded as Scripture; it was ultimately excluded from the Canon; but others, of inferior value, *Song of Songs, Ecclesiastes, Esther, Daniel*, were finally included, though not until Christian times.

The words of this verse are of importance also as showing that the Wisdom writers of the later period took a definite part in the formation of the third division of the Canon.

7 Two things have I asked of thee;
  Deny me *them* not before I die:
8 Remove far from me vanity and lies:
  Give me neither poverty nor riches;
  Feed me with ¹ the food that is needful for me:
9 Lest I be full, and deny *thee*, and say, Who is the LORD?
  Or lest I be poor, and steal,
  And ² use profanely the name of my God.

¹ Heb. *the bread of my portion.*        ² Heb. *handle the name.*

*and thou be found a liar.* Strong language would, no doubt, be used in controversy; but it is quite permissible to render this 'and thou become a deceiver'. In the only other instance in the O.T. of the form of the verb here used (Job xli. 1) the meaning is 'to be deceptive'.

**7-9.** A prayer to be kept from untruthfulness and from the evils which arise both from wealth and poverty.

**7.** *Two things.* Nearly all the proverbs which follow in this chapter take this 'numerical' form (verses 10, 32, 33 are exceptions); elsewhere in *Proverbs* this form is used only in vi. 16-19. The objects of its use were various; in Am. i. 3-ii. 6, where it also occurs, it is in order to express multiplicity; in Prov. vi. 16-19 and in most of the instances in this chapter it seems merely to express indefiniteness; in the case before us (and perhaps in some others elsewhere), however, it may be for the sake of emphasis. The 'numerical' form occurs also in the Elephantiné Version of the *Proverbs of Achikar* 92, 93 (Cowley).

*have I asked of thee.* Although the Sage uses the first person it must be remembered that this is merely a didactic mode; he is really speaking in the name of any one to whom his words may apply.

**8.** *vanity.* As a synonym for 'lies' the word must mean 'falsehood' or 'deceit' here, as in Ps. xii. 2 (3 in Hebr.), xli. 6 (7 in Hebr.), cxliv. 8, 11, and elsewhere.

*Feed me . . .* Render as in R.V. marg.; but this line breaks the rhythm; the sayings in this collection are couplets or quatrains, so that if this line is inserted, making three lines, it spoils the proportion. It should be omitted as a marginal gloss which was erroneously put into the text by a copyist; verse 9 follows more smoothly without it.

**9.** The second line of this quatrain is not as in the R.V., but: 'And say, who is the Lord?' The sage's experience had taught him that wealth tended to make men forget God; but that the sages in general did not think that this was necessarily the case is seen by their usual attitude towards the possession of wealth, which is regarded as a

10 Slander not a servant unto his master,
   Lest he curse thee, and thou be held guilty.

good thing if honestly gained and rightly used (cf. x. 2, xvi. 8, xxviii.
6, 20, xi. 24, 25, xxi. 26). Ben-Sira says:

> *Give and take, and indulge thy soul,*
> *For in Sheol there is no seeking of luxury;*
> *But everything that is fitting to do,*
> *Do in the sight of God* (Ecclus. xiv. 16, Hebr.).

The last two lines are regarded as a gloss, which may well be the case,
but they witness to the feeling of the Wisdom writers that wealth is
not in itself bad provided that one's duty in God's sight is not
forgotten.

*lest I be poor.* Cf. xx. 13: 'Lest I come to poverty.'

*use profanely.* See R.V. marg. note. This figurative use of the
Hebr. word is extremely rare; in Ezek. xiv. 5 it is used of 'seizing
hold' of the nation's heart, i. e. inspiring it with fear, and in Jer. ii. 8
of 'handling the Law'); otherwise it always means grasping something with the hand (in Jer. xlix. 16 of keeping hold of, i. e. occupying
a hill), cf. verse 28 of this chapter.

**10.** This is the only couplet in the chap. that stands quite unconnected with the context; if, as seems likely, it does not belong
here originally, it must have been misplaced early as the Sept. found
it where it now is.

*Slander not.* Lit. 'Use not the tongue', a very rare use of the word
in the O.T., elsewhere occurring only in Ps. ci. 5.

*Lest he curse thee.* Here the curse is effective, see note on xxvi. 2.

*thou be held guilty.* The Hebr. word can also mean 'and thou bear
the punishment'; the word is not used elsewhere in *Proverbs*; cf.
Ps. xxxiv. 21 (22 in Hebr.).

**11–14.** Four evil types of humanity are here mentioned; nothing
is said of the punishment that overtakes such; the mere statement
of each is made. In a slightly different form, but belonging to the
same literary *genre*, is Ben-Sira's enumeration in Ecclus. x. 19
(Smend's emended Hebr. text):

> *An honourable seed, what (is it)? A seed of man.*
> *An honourable seed feareth God.*
> *A contemptible seed, what (is it)? A seed of man.*
> *A contemptible seed transgresseth the commandment.*

The form of the four verses before us is not as rendered in the R.V.;
the Hebr. has: 'A generation that curseth . . .; a generation that is
pure . . .; a generation,—how lofty . . .; a generation whose teeth . . .';
i. e. the statements of fact are made, but nothing is said about them.
Such a bald enumeration can hardly have stood originally in this
derelict fashion, some introductory statement must assuredly have

T

11 There is a generation that curseth their father,
    And doth not bless their mother.

12 There is a generation that are pure in their own eyes,
    And *yet* are not washed from their filthiness.

13 There is a generation, Oh how lofty are their eyes!
    And their eyelids are lifted up.

14 There is a generation whose teeth are *as* swords, and their
    jaw teeth *as* knives,
    To devour the poor from off the earth, and the needy from
    among men.

predicted something regarding it. Ben-Sira, for example, enumerates three evil things, but he prefaces them with the couplet:

> *Of three things is my heart afraid,*
> *And concerning a fourth I am in great fear* (see also xxvi. 28).

So, too, in Prov. vi. 16. So that one is led to believe that an introductory couplet has fallen out here, or has been ousted by verse 10. Or else, it is possible that a couplet has been displaced at the end of the enumeration; Ben-Sira adds at the end of the words quoted: 'Worse than death are they all.' It will be seen (see below) that the text is out of order at the end of verse 14.

**11.** *a generation.* i.e. a certain type of man which the sage observes around him.

*that curseth* . . . Cf. xx. 20; Exod. xxi. 17.

**12.** *pure.* The Hebr. means primarily ceremonially clean; here and elsewhere in *Prov.* it refers to ethical purity (xv. 26, xxii. 11).

*washed.* Cf. Ps. xxvi. 6, lxxiii. 13; Isa. iv. 4. The kind of people referred to are such as the prophet addresses in Isa. i. 10–17. Prophetical influence shows itself here again.

**13.** *how lofty* . . . Cf. vi. 17, xxi. 4. The form of the words expresses a kind of sorrowful contempt.

*their eyelids are lifted up.* i.e. a supercilious air and disdainful look.

**14.** *jaw teeth.* Where else should the teeth be? The Hebr. word is a synonym of that used in the first line. The thought is that of a wild beast tearing its prey; and this is figuratively applied to this type of cruel men.

In the R.V. this verse is wrongly divided; the first line should end at 'swords' (so in the Hebr.). The second line in the R.V. is an added couplet which does not belong to the text as it spoils the rhythm and structure of the passage; it is a scribal interpretation.

**XXX. 15–33.** This collection consists of 'numerical' sayings, with the exception of verses 17, 20, 32, and 33. It is probable that the original form of these was: first a couplet indicating the subject to be dealt with, and then two couplets giving details. This form is not

15 The ¹horseleach hath two daughters, ²*crying*, Give, give.
There are three things that are never satisfied,
*Yea*, four that say not, Enough:

16 ³The grave;  and the barren womb;

¹ Or, *vampire*          ² Or, called          ³ Heb. *Sheol*.

kept up in the text as we now have it; but there are signs that it has
suffered from being worked over. Verses 15 (excepting the first line),
16 deal with things that are insatiable; 18, 19 with things which cannot be apprehended; 21–23 with types of people who are insufferable;
24–28 with four kinds of animals which are small, but wise; 29–31
with those who are stately in their gait. The remaining four verses,
17, 20, 32, 33, none of which are 'numerical', are shorter and different
in form; they are out of place in this collection and must have been
added by a scribe who had no eye for literary symmetry.

**15.** The first line of this verse does not belong here; it is a fragment without meaning as it stands, and is certainly corrupt. Whatever the line, more probably a couplet, contained in its original form,
it is clear enough why some scribe added it,—perhaps first as an
illustrative note in the margin,—the 'Give, give' expressed insatiability, so it was appropriate enough in connexion with what followed.

*The horseleach* . . . The Hebr. has: 'To 'Alūqah are two daughters,
give, give.' 'Aūlaq is the flesh-devouring ghoul of the Arabs, called
by them 'Alūk, a female demon (see Wellhausen, *Reste Arabischen
Heidentums*, pp. 149 ff. [1897]). She plays a part in later Jewish
Demonology; her two daughters had the names of two diseases, and
therefore their names were not pronounced. She herself became
connected with the Valley of Hinnom (Gehenna), so that the mention
of her name here, where *Sheol* figures, points to a developed belief
regarding the Hereafter, i. e. belief in a place for the wicked, opposed
to Paradise. But this applies, of course, only to the time when this
addition (the line under consideration) was made, not to the time
when the original text was written.

*Enough.* The Hebr. word (הון) is a favourite one in the Wisdom
Literature, and especially in *Proverbs*; its ordinary meaning is
'wealth'; it never has the sense of 'enough' elsewhere but in this
passage. The two lines of this verse form the introductory couplet.

**16.** Ordinarily in this collection the illustrations of the three, or
four, things mentioned in the introductory couplets occupy four
lines; here, as the text stands, we have only three; the probability,
therefore, is that 'the grave' and 'the barren womb' were each
followed by a short relative sentence; the first may have run: 'Sheol
that is never satisfied' (cf. xxvii. 20); the second: 'The barren womb
that saith, Give me children' (cf. Gen. xxx. 1). This is, of course,
merely surmise; but four lines must originally have stood here.

T 2

The earth that is not satisfied with water;
And the fire that saith not, Enough.
17 The eye that mocketh at his father,
And despiseth to obey his mother,
The ravens of [1] the valley shall pick it out,
And the [2] young eagles shall eat it.

18 There be three things which are too wonderful for me,
Yea, four which I know not:

[1] Or, *the brook*        [2] Or, *vultures*

*The earth that is not* . . . Better, 'The land'. In a climate such as that of Palestine, the soil was, excepting during the comparatively short rainy periods, very dry and parched.

**17.** This isolated quatrain is out of place here for the reason given above.

*The eye.* Although the object of the sentence, it is placed first according to the Hebr. usage of putting the subject or object as the first word of a sentence when it is desired to lay special emphasis on it; normally the predicate precedes. Through the eye these unnatural feelings towards parents were expressed, hence the special mention of this organ. The reference is, of course, to the death of the son, the penalty for his unfilial behaviour; as his dead body lies unburied the birds of prey will come and pick out his eyes.

*to obey his mother.* The Hebr. text is corrupt; following the Sept. we should read: 'the old-age of a mother' (וְקֵנַת for יִקְּהַת).

*the valley.* In the summer months this would be dry, but in the rainy season it becomes a torrent; hence the Hebr. word means both 'valley' and 'brook'.

*young eagles.* Read as R.V. marg.

In connexion with this verse the following historical episode is of interest: Gregory of Tours was once at a banquet at which Merovech, the son of Chilperic and Fredigundis, was present. The bishop had to listen to the coarse jests and sneers against the characters of his parents uttered by the king. During the banquet Merovech, 'with that strange conflict of passions and ideals which so constantly meets us in men of his time, asked the bishop for some sacred word for the edification of his soul. With all his characteristic fearlessness the bishop turned to the book of Proverbs and read the ominous lines, *Oculum qui adversus aspexerit patrem, effodiant eum corvi de convallibus*' (Dill, *Roman Society in Gaul in the Merovingian Age*, p. 455 [1926]).

**18, 19.** Wherein the wonder of these things lies seems to be as follows: the fact that a great bird like a vulture, heavy in weight, could continue its way in the air without falling to the ground; the fact that a serpent could move along without the aid of wings or feet;

19 The way of an eagle in the air;
   The way of a serpent upon a rock;
   The way of a ship in the midst of the sea;
   And the way of a man with a maid.
20 So is the way of an adulterous woman;
   She eateth, and wipeth her mouth,
   And saith, I have done no wickedness.

21 [1]For three things the earth doth tremble,
   And for four, *which* it cannot bear:

[1] Heb. *under.*

the fact that a heavy thing could sail on the water without sinking;
and the fact that connexion between a man and a woman could produce a human being. It must be acknowledged that to a thinking
man in those days, in the absence of any scientific or physical knowledge worth mentioning, all these things must have been very wonderful, and incomprehensible.

*in the air.* Lit. 'in the heavens'; in Zech. v. 9 this is expressed by
the phrase 'between the earth and the heavens'; in Hebrew there is
no real equivalent for 'in the air'.

*upon a rock.* The comparative smoothness of a rock would make
the movement of a serpent appear the more remarkable.

*in the midst of the sea.* Lit. 'in the heart of the sea', i.e. in its midst,
cf. xxiii. 34.

**20.** This is again an isolated verse. Presumably it was thought to
be an appropriate addition to the last line of the preceding verse; if
so it was, of course, a misunderstanding; in that line there is no
question of an immoral act; it is simply the fact of procreation that
is wonderful. The words 'she eateth . . . no wickedness' seem to be
the remnant of a quatrain the first two lines of which are lost; the
first line was then added to bring it into connexion with the preceding verse; but it is evident that an adulterous woman would not say,
'I have done no wickedness'; so that the first line could not originally
have anything to do with the last two. In the present connexion the
words, 'She eateth and wipeth her mouth', are meaningless. One
may conjecture that these two lines are an extract from some sage's
precepts on manners at table (such as Ben-Sira's in Ecclus. xxxi
(xxxiv). 12–24) altered to the feminine form in order to adapt it to
its new context.

**21–23.** These verses are in the normal form of two introductory
lines followed by illustrative couplets; they deal with incongruous
positions of men and women.

**21.** *For.* Read, as in R.V. marg., 'under'; it is under the weight
of the people in incongruous positions, which the sage is about to

22 For a servant when he is king;
   And a fool when he is filled with meat;
23 For an odious woman when she is married;
   And an handmaid that is heir to her mistress.
24 There be four things which are little upon the earth,
   But they are exceeding wise:
25 The ants are a people not strong,
   Yet they provide their meat in the summer;

mention, that the earth trembles, or quakes; the exaggeration is
intended to be humorous. In the Hebr. each verse begins with
'Under'.

**22.** *a servant when* . . . Cf. xix. 10; a not uncommon occurrence in
the ancient east.

*a fool when* . . . The term for 'fool' here is *nābāl*, see further Excursus XI. The incongruity lies in the fact that this type of 'fool' is
utterly unworthy of the enjoyment of any luxury; prosperity bru-
talizes him, cf. 1 Sam. xxv. 3 ff.

**23.** *an odious woman.* Lit. 'a hated woman'; the reference is to a
woman who has, for one reason or another, remained unmarried for
some time; 'disliked' would represent the thought of the Hebrew;
'hated' simply expresses the opposite of being loved, so that might
also render it 'an unloved woman', cf. Gen. xxix. 31; Deut. xxi. 15.

*that is heir to.* i.e. dispossesses her mistress of her inheritance, as in
the case of a husband who prefers his wife's maid to his own wife,
divorcing the latter and marrying the former. This was quite possible when, as among the Jews at that time, the law of divorce was
all in favour of husbands.

**24-28.** In this section the introductory couplet is followed by
four illustrations each of which has an explanatory line in addition
to the illustration, so that there are four couplets in place of two.
The thoughts are distinctly feeble; though to be sure, it must be
remembered that in an unscientific age the difference between wisdom and instinct was not clearly defined.

*exceeding wise.* Lit. 'wise, they are made wise'; a similar phrase,
to express emphasis, occurs in Ps. lviii 5 (6 in Hebr.), 'Charming
never so wisely'. The Versions have: 'wiser than the wise.'

**25.** *The ants.* Cf. vi. 6-8.

*a people.* This is only applied to animals, elsewhere, in the next
verse, in Ps. lxxiv. 14 (animal demons of the wilderness), and in Joel
ii. 2 (locusts).

*they provide* . . . i.e. they lay up for the winter during the summer.
'The Mohammedans seem to have associated the ant with Solomon;
the 27th chapter of the Koran is styled "the ant", because it mentions that Solomon, on his march, once entered "the valley of ants",

26 The [1]conies are but a feeble folk,
   Yet make they their houses in the rocks;
27 The locusts have no king,
   Yet go they forth all of them by bands;
28 The lizard [2]taketh hold with her hands,
   Yet is she in kings' palaces.

29 There be three things which are stately in their march,
   Yea, four which are stately in going:
30 The lion, which is mightiest among beasts,

---

[1] See Lev. xi. 5.          [2] Or, *thou canst seize with thy hands*

whereupon an ant said, "O ants, enter into your habitations, lest Solomon and his army tread you underfoot and perceive it not". It was a custom with the Arabs, says Bochart, to place an ant in the hand of a new-born child, with a prayer that he might grow up wise and sagacious' (*Encycl. Bibl.* i. 176).

**26.** *conies.* The cony is not a rabbit, as is shown by its habit of making its 'house' in the rocks, see also Ps. civ. 18. The Hebr. word is *shāphān*; to naturalists it is known as *Hyrax syriacus*, a species of badger. It is reckoned in Lev. xi. 5; Deut. xiv. 7 among the animals that chew the cud, a mistake which arose from the way it eats its food, the jaws move from side to side; it feeds only on vegetable matter (see further, Nowack, *Hebr. Arch.*, i. 78).

**27.** *The locusts.* Cf. Joel i. 4, ii. 1 ff.; Job xxxix. 20. Eight different kinds of locusts are mentioned in the O.T.

**28.** *The lizard.* Though the exact animal meant by the Hebr. name (*sᵉmāmīth*) cannot be stated with certainty, the probabilities point to the lizard.

*taketh hold with her hands.* It is better to read, following the Sept., 'can be taken hold of with the hands' (תִּתָּפֵשׂ for תְּתַפֵּשׂ), because the point of the saying is that the lizard is a small thing (cf. verse 24).

*in kings' palaces.* Because of its being able to climb up the walls of houses; 'kings' palaces' are mentioned merely to illustrate that this insignificant animal frequents the most august buildings.

**29-31.** There is little doubt but that in its original form this section consisted of the usual introductory couplet followed by four illustrative couplets as in verses 24-28; but the ending of the section (verse 31) has suffered corruption and cannot be even tentatively restored, although some hints are afforded by the Sept. rendering.

**29.** *which are stately in their march.* Lit. 'that do well in step'; so, too, in the next line, lit. 'that do well in going'.

**30.** *lion.* The Hebr word is not the usual one for lion, and occurs elsewhere only in Job iv. 11; Isa. xxx. 6.

*which is mightiest . . .* Lit. 'strong among the beasts'; the Hebr.

And turneth not away for any;

31 The [1]greyhound; the he-goat also;
And the king, [2]against whom there is no rising up.

32 If thou hast done foolishly in lifting up thyself,
Or if thou hast thought evil,
*Lay* thine hand upon thy mouth.

33 For the [3]churning of milk bringeth forth butter,
And the [3]wringing of the nose bringeth forth blood:
So the [3]forcing of wrath bringeth forth strife.

[1] Or, *war-horse*   Heb. *well girt* (or, *well knit*) *in the loins.*
[2] Or, *when his army is with him*        [3] Heb. *pressing.*

word applies usually only to domestic beasts, but cf. Isa. xviii. 6;
Mic. v. 7 (8 in R.V.) &c.

*And turneth not* . . . See the description in Isa. xxxi. 4.

**31.** The text of this verse is hopelessly corrupt; it appears to
consist merely of remnants. As it stands it means nothing at all;
rendered literally (though some of the words are quite uncertain) it
runs: 'He that hath his loins girded (?) or the he-goat and the king,
a band of soldiers (?) with him.' This is sufficient to show how
absolutely impossible it is to make anything out of the verse. The
Sept. has:

'The cock strutting courageously among the hens,
And the he-goat leading the flock,
And the king haranguing the people.'

This may well represent the original Hebr. text in the main, but the
mention of the king is in any case out of place among all these
animals; conceivably one might emend the Hebr. text of the last line
and read: 'And the ox ploughing the ground in his strength' (וְאֵלֶף
עֹבֵר הָאֲדָמָה בְּכֹחוֹ, cf. Prov. xiv. 4; Isa. xxx. 24); but all such emendations, and many have been proposed, must be largely a matter of
guesswork.

**32.** *If thou hast done foolishly.* If the text is correct, this is the only
place in the O.T. where the Hebr. word is used in this sense.

*Lay* thine hand . . . This is not a separate line in the Hebr., but
belongs to the preceding one; it is only two short words in Hebr.
Usually the verb (as added in the R.V.) 'lay' goes with the phrase,
e. g. Job xxi. 5; once in *Ecclus.* it is as here, simply 'hand to mouth',
i. e. be silent, in token of acknowledgement of wrong.

**33.** For 'churning', 'wringing', and 'forcing' see R.V. marg. The
first line seems out of place, as 'milk' is inappropriate in connexion
with 'blood' mentioned in the second line and implied in the third.
The Hebr. word is the same for 'nose' and 'wrath'; in the original it
is a word-play.

**XXXI.** 1 [1]The words of king Lemuel; the [2]oracle which his
mother taught him.

2 What, my son? and what, O son of my womb?
    And what, O son of my vows?
3 Give not thy strength unto women,

[1] Or, *The words of Lemuel king of Massa, which &c.* See ch. xxx. 1, margin.
[2] Or, *burden*

**XXXI. 1–9.** This little collection consists of four quatrains containing admonitions against impurity and indulgence in drink, together with an exhortation to minister true justice, purporting to
have been spoken to king Lemuel by his mother.

**1.** *The words of* ... i. e. the words addressed to ... The Hebr. has:
'The words of Lemuel, king of Massa, which his mother taught him',
or 'whose mother taught him'. In the mouth of a mother the advice
given in the verses that follow would be wholly inappropriate; by the
time that a young man had reached the age at which he would be
tempted to commit the sins indicated it would be the father, not the
mother, who would give the advice, especially such as dealt with the
evil of intercourse with women. Toy rightly suggests that the introduction of the mother into the title 'may be the result of a wrong
reading of verse 2'. The name of Lemuel is otherwise unknown; it
is not found in the Sept., and is, in all probability, the result of some
corruption in the text.

*the oracle. Massa* is the Hebr.; the rendering 'oracle' for this is
out of the question, see note on xxx. 1. The word is, as there, doubtless a textual corruption.

**2.** Here again the text cannot be in order. On the basis of the
Sept. Steuernagel emends the text so as to read:

'What, my son,—what, Lemuel,
    My first-born, shall I say to thee;
Yea what, son of my womb,
Yea what, son of my vows?'

This emendation has much in its favour; owing to the repetition of
'what' a copyist seems inadvertently to have omitted the end of the
first line ('what Lemuel') and the second line, and to have gone
straight to the third line, 'Yea what ...':

מַה־בְּרִי מָה לְמוּאֵל
בְּלִרִי אֹמַר אֵלָיִךְ
וּמַה. . .

*son of my vows.* i. e. a son granted as a result of vows, cf. 1 Sam.
i. 11. The word for 'son' in each case is Aramaic, not Hebrew.

**3.** *Give not* ... Cf. v. 8–10.

Nor thy ways to [1]that which destroyeth kings.

4 It is not for kings, O Lemuel, it is not for kings to drink wine;
    Nor for princes [2]to say, Where is strong drink?

5 Lest they drink, and forget [3]the law,
    And pervert the judgement [4]of any that is afflicted.

6 Give strong drink unto him that is ready to perish,
    And wine unto the bitter in soul:

7 Let him drink, and forget his poverty,
    And remember his misery no more.

[1] Or, as otherwise read, *them that destroy*        [2] Another reading is, *to desire*
*strong drink*.        [3] Heb. *that which is decreed*.        [4] Heb. *of all the sons of affliction*.

*Nor thy ways* . . . The Hebr. has lit.: 'And thy ways to destroy
kings', which is clearly corrupt. Steuernagel emends the text so as
to read: 'Nor thy love to women who destroy kings', which involves
only a trifling alteration of the text (וְדֹרֵךְ לַפֹּחוֹת לִמְלָכִין), i. e. so great
is their power owing to their appeal to lustful passion, that they
destroy even kings.

*kings*. The form of the plur is Aramaic.
With the verse cf. Ecclus. xviii. 30–xix. 2:

> *Go not after thy desires,*
> *And refrain thyself from thine appetites* . . .
> *Be not a squanderer and a drunkard,*
> *Else will there be nothing in thy purse* . . .
> *Wine and women make the heart lustful,*
> *And he that cleaveth to harlots will become more reckless.*

In the *Wisdom of Anii* it is said:

> *Go not after a woman lest she steal thine heart.*

In another part of the same book there are warnings against intercourse with women and against drunkenness.

**4.** *It is not for kings*. The form of the Hebr. is very unusual; there
is no verb, perhaps it has fallen out of the text; the form of the negative demands a verb.

*O Lemuel, it is not for kings*. These words should be deleted; they
overload the line; it is a case of dittography.

*to say, Where is strong drink?* Read as R.V. marg. (אַוֹּה for אִו),
'nor for princes to desire strong drink'.

**5.** *Lest they drink, and forget*. The R.V. rightly follows the Sept.,
the Hebr. has 'lest he drink, and forget'.

*the law*. Read as R.V. marg.

*judgement*. i. e. justice (for), or rights (of), 'all the sons of affliction'.
The verse warns against a ruler given to self-indulgence in sitting
over his wine instead of attending to his duties.

**6, 7.** A cynical piece of advice wholly out of harmony with the
ideals of the Wisdom writers in general.

8 Open thy mouth for the dumb,
   In the cause of all such as are [1]left desolate.
9 Open thy mouth, judge righteously,
   And minister judgement to the poor and needy.
10 A virtuous woman who can find?
   For her price is far above [2]rubies.
11 The heart of her husband trusteth in her,
   And he shall have no lack of [3]gain.
12 She doeth him good and not evil
   All the days of her life.

> [1] Or, *ready to pass away*    Heb. *the sons of passing away*.
> [2] See Job xxviii. 18.        [3] Heb. *spoil*.

**8.** *Open thy mouth.* i. e. plead the cause of.

*dumb.* This is not meant literally, the reference is to those who are unable to plead their own cause. Cf. Isa. lvi. 10, where 'dumb dogs' is used figuratively for false prophets.

*left desolate.* Cf. R.V. marg., but we should probably read 'sons of sickness', or 'suffering' (בְּנֵי־חֹלִי for בְּנֵי חֲלוֹף).

**9.** Cf. xvi. 10, xx. 8.

**XXXI. 10–31.** It is a relief, after the somewhat jejune and not always edifying sayings of the other collections in this division, to come to this poem which has much in it that is beautiful. It is an 'alphabetical' piece, each of the twenty-two verses beginning with a letter of the Hebrew alphabet in regular order from start to finish. The poem gives us a very interesting insight into the economic conditions of a wealthy Jewish householder. But more important is the fact that it presents woman in a very different light from that which is usual in the Old Testament (see further Excursus X).

**10.** *A virtuous woman* . . . The question does not mean that the writer thinks such to be a rarity (see xii. 4[a]), but as in xx. 6[b], where a similar question is asked regarding a faithful man; it is a rhetorical way of expressing admiration.

*her price.* Better, 'her worth'.

*far above.* Lit. 'distant from'.

*rubies.* See note on iii. 15.

**11.** *heart.* See Excursus IX.

*And he shall have* . . . Lit. 'And spoil will not be lacking'. The Hebr. word rendered 'gain' is otherwise used of 'spoil' in war; it is used of private gain in i. 13, xvi. 19; here the context demands some such rendering as 'gain', or that which is acquired by skilful management of the estate, and thus 'income'.

**12.** *She doeth him.* Lit. 'she rewardeth', or 'recompenseth', or 'rendereth' him, cf. iii. 30.

13 She seeketh wool and flax,
  And worketh [1] willingly with her hands.
14 She is like the merchant-ships;
  She bringeth her food from afar.
15 She riseth also while it is yet night,
  And giveth meat to her household,
  And their [2] task to her maidens.
16 She considereth a field, and buyeth it:
  With the fruit of her hands she planteth a vineyard.
17 She girdeth her loins with strength,
  And maketh strong her arms.

    [1] Or, *at the business of*        [2] Or, *portion*

**13.** *She seeketh* . . . i.e. for the weaving of garments, cf. Deut. xxii. 11; Hos. ii. 5, 9.

*willingly with her hands.* Lit. 'with the delight of her hands', i.e. she puts her hands joyfully to the work.

**14.** *like the merchant-ships.* This must refer to her procuring goods from traders from other lands; travelling merchants brought their wares to the houses of the wealthy.

**15.** *She riseth also while* . . . The method of the making of bread, says Benzinger, 'has continued in the East unchanged to the present day. The required bread is freshly baked and the grain freshly ground day by day. Before dawn in an Arab village the disagreeable sound of the hand-mills is heard in every house; the women go on grinding till the men get up' (*Hebr. Arch.*, p. 84 [1894]).

*meat.* The Hebr. word generally means 'prey'; the meaning 'food' is later usage.

*And their task* . . . For 'task' see R.V. marg., i.e. food. This third line, the only instance of such in the poem, is regarded by most commentators as a gloss on the preceding; it is not required as the preceding line has already spoken of the food being distributed.

**16.** *She considereth a field* . . . i.e. she thinks over it, or examines it with a view to buying it.

*With the fruit of her hands.* i.e. with the money she has earned.

*she planteth a vineyard.* All this verse is a rhetorical exaggeration; these things were wholly outside a woman's sphere. At the most a man might consult his wife regarding such matters, but the actual business would be strictly the husband's affair.

**17.** *She girdeth* . . . i.e. she fixes her skirt firmly round her waist so that she shall not be incommoded in her work.

*And maketh strong* . . . Presumably this means that she tucks up her sleeves which would otherwise cause grave inconvenience when using her arms; the Sept. has 'for work'.

18 She perceiveth that her merchandise is profitable:
   Her lamp goeth not out by night.
19 She layeth her hands to the distaff,
   And her ¹hands hold the spindle.
20 She spreadeth out her ²hand to the poor;
   Yea, she reacheth forth her hands to the needy.
21 She is not afraid of the snow for her household;
   For all her household are clothed with scarlet.
22 She maketh for herself ³carpets of tapestry;
   Her clothing is fine linen and purple.

                ¹ Heb. *palms.*         ² Heb. *palm.*         ³ Or, *cushions*

**18.** *perceiveth.* The primary meaning of the Hebr. word is to 'taste'; in the figurative sense of apprehending or perceiving it occurs elsewhere in the O.T. only in Ps. xxxiv. 8 (9 in Hebr.), 'O taste and see . . .', but it is common in post-Biblical Hebrew.

*merchandise.* Cf. iii. 14.

*profitable.* Lit. 'good'.

*Her lamp goeth not out . . .* Some commentators take this in the sense of prosperity not departing from her house (see xiii. 19, xx. 20; Job xviii. 6; Jer. xxv. 10), but wrongly; the entire context deals with household affairs so that the phrase cannot be understood in a figurative sense here. It refers to the custom, still prevalent among the Palestine Fellachin, of keeping a lamp alight day and night (see Nowack, *Hebr. Arch.* i. 144; *Zeitschrift des deutschen Pal.-Vereins*, iii. 115).

**19.** *distaff.* The Hebr. word occurs here only in the O.T.; its meaning is uncertain, but as parallel to 'spindle' in the next line the word probably means 'distaff'; in the Mishnah it means a 'post' or 'beam'.

*And her hands.* See R.V. marg.

**20.** Although, at first sight, the content of this verse may make it appear out of place here, it may well be that the gifts to the poor refer to garments; in which case it follows appropriately after what is said in verse 19.

**21.** *snow.* See note on xxv. 13.

*scarlet.* Cf. 2 Sam. i. 24; Isa. i. 18. The Sept. and Vulg. read 'double' (שְׁנַיִם for שָׁנִים), which is perhaps preferable, for scarlet robes were luxurious and costly (cf. Exod. xxv. 4; Jer. iv. 30; Lam. iv. 5), and would not be worn by the domestics.

**22.** *carpets of tapestry.* i.e. coverlet, cf. vii. 16; the word occurs only in *Proverbs*.

23 Her husband is known in the gates,
  When he sitteth among the elders of the land.
24 She maketh linen garments and selleth them;
  And delivereth girdles unto the [1] merchant.
25 Strength and dignity are her clothing;
  And she laugheth at the time to come.
26 She openeth her mouth with wisdom;
  And the [2] law of kindness is on her tongue.
27 She looketh well to the ways of her household,
  And eateth not the bread of idleness.
28 Her children rise up, and call her blessed;
  Her husband *also*, and he praiseth her, *saying*:
29 Many daughters have done virtuously,
  But thou excellest them all.

[1] Heb. *Canaanite*.    [2] Or, *teaching*

**23.** This verse can hardly be in its original place, coming as it does between two verses which deal with woman's clothing.
  *in the gates.* Cf. i. 21, xxiv. 7.
**24.** *linen garments.* i.e. 'linen wrappers'; the word occurs elsewhere only in Judg. xiv. 12, 13, Isa. iii. 23. 'The linen wrappers', says Moore, 'were not undergarments, but rectangular pieces of fine, thin, and therefore costly, linen stuff, which might be worn as an outer garment over the other dress, or as a night-wrapper upon the naked body' (*Judges*, p. 335).
  *merchant.* See R.V. marg ; i.e. a Phoenician trader
**25.** *. . . are her clothing.* With the thought of this figurative clothing cf. Ps. civ. 1, cxxxii. 9.
  *And she laugheth . . .* i.e. she has no anxieties for the future; the writer of xxvii. 1 was wiser.
**26.** *the law of kindness is . . .* Contrast with xxi. 19, xxv. 24, xxvii. 15; read as R.V. marg.
**27.** *looketh well.* Or 'keepeth watch over'.
**28.** *call her blessed.* Or 'happy', cf. Ps. lxxii. 17.
  *Her husband* also . . . In the Hebr. the line is so short that a word, probably 'riseth up', must have fallen out.
**29.** *Many daughters.* Toy points out that the use of the word 'daughter' as equivalent to 'woman', found elsewhere only in Song of songs ii. 2, vi. 9, 'is a survival (found only in poetry) from the time when the woman, even after marriage, remained always a member of her father's family, and was defined as his "daughter"'.

30 Favour is deceitful, and beauty is vain:
  *But* a woman that feareth the LORD, she shall be praised.
31 Give her of the fruit of her hands;
  And let her works praise her in the gates.


**30.** *Favour is deceitful.* 'Favour', the Hebr. word means 'grace' or 'comeliness'.

*vain.* Lit. 'vapour', 'breath'. Grace and beauty are transient.

*that feareth the Lord.* In a poem so entirely lacking in religious sentiment these words at the end of it read strangely, and it is probable that the Sept. has retained the original text in reading 'of intelligence' in place of 'feareth the Lord'; this latter being an alteration made by a later scribe who felt that a religious note of some kind ought to be sounded. Cf. the *Proverbs of Achikar* ii. 19:

> My son, go not after the beauty of a woman, and lust not after her in thy heart, because the beauty of a woman is her good sense, and her adornment is the word of her mouth.

**31.** *Give her of the fruit* . . . i.e. let her excellence be fully recognized.

*And let her works* . . . She is to share with her husband (cf. *v.* 23) the praise of men. The words, it is true, can hardly be meant to be taken literally,—women's domestic virtues were not the kind of things which were discussed in public assemblies; nevertheless, the exaggeration is a natural and a pardonable one.

The verse forms a fitting conclusion to what is the most remarkable exposition in the Old Testament on the position of women, exalting, sublimating, her functions in the home as wife, mother, and mistress, and showing how contentedness and happiness in the domestic circle depend upon the foresight and oversight of this queen of the hearth. The traditional beauty of Jewish home-life is both explained and illustrated by a passage like this, for we may well believe that the picture presented reflects what was a reality in many a Jewish home.

# INDEX

U

PRINTED IN GREAT BRITAIN AT THE UNIVERSITY PRESS, OXFORD
BY JOHN JOHNSON, PRINTER TO THE UNIVERSITY